P9-CDZ-803

1943-2007
*a life-long student of
worldviews, ideas,
words, and the Word*

An Introduction to the
Old Testament Historical Books

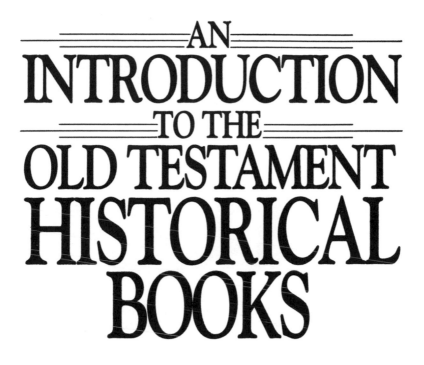

AN INTRODUCTION TO THE OLD TESTAMENT HISTORICAL BOOKS

David M. Howard Jr.

MOODY PRESS
CHICAGO

© 1993 by
DAVID M. HOWARD, JR.

ISBN: 0-8024-4127-0

5 7 9 10 8 6 4

Printed in the United States of America

To Jan

והאשה טובת-שכל ויפת תאר

ברוך יהוה אלהי ישראל אשר שלחך היום הזה לקראתי

(1 Samuel 25:3, 32)

CONTENTS

LIST OF ILLUSTRATIONS

PREFACE

The OT's historical books are at one and the same time inviting and forbidding. They are inviting because they contain many familiar characters, such as Samson and Delilah, David and Goliath, David and Bathsheba, Solomon and his wives, Queen Esther, and many others. They also are inviting because they contain many delightful and moving stories. Who does not delight at the miraculous provision of a son to Hannah, the warm friendship between David and Jonathan, or Elijah's triumph over the prophets of Baal? Who is not moved by Ruth's loyalty to Naomi, David's largesse toward Mephibosheth, or Nehemiah's deep faith?

But these books are also forbidding to many people because they contain many obscure characters and tangled plots. Who can easily remember the names of the many judges, let alone follow the details of their lives? Who can easily trace the intrigues involved in the succession to David's throne? Who can remember the names of the kings of Israel and Judah? They also repel people because they contain many strange and even repulsive events. Who does not shudder at the complete annihilation of the Canaanites in Joshua's day or at the slaughter of the Persians in Esther's day? Who is not repulsed at the graphic description of Ehud's killing of Eglon in Judges 3? Who does not puzzle about the long day in Joshua 10, the appearance of Samuel from beyond the grave in 1 Samuel 28, or Mesha's strange sacrifice of his son in 2 Kings 3?

The OT's historical books contain much more than delightful or strange stories, however. They are an important repository of God's revelation of Himself. In the details of the stories, as well as (or perhaps especially) at the higher levels of groups of stories, we see great themes unfolded—themes that tell us about God and His love for His people and the world, His holiness, His worthiness, and His unfolding plans for His people and the world. In the end, these things are much more important than the fortunes or foibles of individual characters. These larger themes bring the OT historical books into a proper focus and into harmony with the other books of the Bible.

As noted in chapter 1, this book is an invitation to read the OT historical books. For readers with little experience in reading these historical books, this book is intended to serve as a guide, elucidating their contents and messages. It also is intended to teach readers how to read the Bible, paying attention equally to microscopic details and to macroscopic structures. It is in the details, as well as in the large-scale sweeps, that we learn about the messages of the biblical books and, ultimately, about God. Such readers will probably serve their own interests best by reading the text and ignoring the footnotes.

This book also is intended to serve readers with some experience in reading these OT books. Such readers will find familiar themes elucidated in these pages and familiar historical, critical, and theological questions addressed. The hope is that new light will be shed on many questions for them and that the footnotes and bibliographies will serve to point them into both classic and recent literature, representative of the best of evangelical and nonevangelical scholarship alike.

We also note in chapter 1 that this book is not intended to serve as a substitute for reading the biblical books themselves. If readers of this book believe that it will neatly summarize for them the biblical books so that they won't have to read them themselves, then they will be disappointed and will have cheated themselves. This book pales alongside the grandeur and importance of the biblical books under consideration. *They* are the proper focus of study. The present book merely intends to whet the appetite for, and to point the way into, the biblical books.

How should someone read this book? First, the reader should have a Bible at hand. Then I suggest reading the first chapter of this book before launching into chapters on specific books. Each chapter thereafter is relatively self-contained, and they may be read in any order, although a reading from start to finish will yield the most coherent picture of the biblical books. At first, I would suggest reading the relevant chapter from this book before reading the biblical book itself, to provide a "map" of sorts. As readers see what questions and themes are important, and how to approach a biblical book, they will begin to anticipate these same questions themselves.

After some practice in reading and asking the right questions is obtained, I recommend reading the biblical book first, and then the relevant chapter in this book. There is no substitute for reading the Bible itself. If readers can become practiced at what kinds of questions to ask while reading a biblical book, and at what kinds of things to notice, then their reading will be all that much richer, and they will have the joy of self-discovery rather than depending on this or any other work to tell them what is in a biblical book.

Since this book does not provide chapter-by-chapter summaries of the biblical books (except for the book of Ruth), readers will be forced into reading the biblical texts themselves. I strongly recommend reading each biblical book in one sitting. Experienced and new readers of the OT alike constantly find that this opens up the messages of the books in ways that have never before been done for them. The biblical books are intended to be read as wholes. Students of the Bible have too often dissected, atomized, and analyzed biblical narratives until what is left is a dismembered corpse, not a living organism. When we read these books as coherent wholes, we will capture much of their vitality and their meaning. We will be able to see the contours of the forest, as well as the details of the trees.

As we read the OT historical books, we discover their revelation of God to us. We see the outworkings of His gracious plan of redemption, and we learn how to live. We cannot do so fully, however, without learning *how* to read. This book is an invitation to read the greatest Book ever written. It is intended to point to that Book and to whet readers' appetites for it and for the God revealed in its pages.

ACKNOWLEDGMENTS

It is a pleasure to acknowledge the contributions of many to this work. First, I should like to acknowledge my former teacher, and now professional colleague and friend, C. Hassell Bullock. It was he who first approached me about doing this book and who recommended my name to Moody Press. He has taught me in more ways than can be enumerated here about a love for God and about godly biblical scholarship.

Indeed, it is a privilege to join two of my teachers in this Moody series, Hassell Bullock and Herbert Wolf. I learned much from both of them in classes and was able to glean much from their books in this series as I wrote my own.

I must thank two institutions for their generous sabbatical leave programs, which enabled the writing of the bulk of this book. I was granted a two-quarter sabbatical leave from Bethel Theological Seminary in 1989, and a one-quarter leave from my present institution, Trinity Evangelical Divinity School, in 1992. I thank the boards of regents at both schools for these generous leaves. I also thank Trinity for its generous secretarial help and my secretary, Rebecca Heidenreich, who calmly, cheerfully, and competently brought my footnotes and bibliographies into some semblance of order in the face of a rapidly approaching deadline and a balky computer and who helped prepare the indexes.

Professional colleagues with whom I have discussed many of the issues in this book include Daniel I. Block of Bethel Seminary, Barry J. Beitzel and John H. Sailhamer of Trinity Divinity School, and William E. Graddy of Trinity College. I also am indebted to V. Philips Long of Covenant Theological Seminary for access to his forthcoming work, *The Art of Biblical History.* I am also indebted to students at Bethel and Trinity, whose questions and suggestions stimulated my thinking in many ways.

I thank Moody Press and its representatives for the opportunity to write this book. Dana Gould was the first to work with me on the project, and his successor, Garry Knussman, has been a gentle and gracious, but nevertheless persistent, goad toward completion of the project. Joseph O'Day has provided many good suggestions and done good work in bringing the manuscript into its final form.

My immediate family members, Jan, Christina, and Melody, deserve much credit for their forbearance during many long hours spent on this book during the last six years, especially as the project neared its completion. I was privileged to receive the news from our adoption agency of Melody's impending arrival in 1989 while I was typing part of the 1 & 2 Samuel chapter. Her middle name is Anne, partially to reflect many important things about Hannah in 1 Samuel 1–2.

It is a long-awaited privilege to dedicate this book—my first post-dissertation, academic book—to my wife Jan. She has been a loyal and steady friend, and a source of great joy and encouragement, during our fourteen years of marriage. She well exemplifies the qualities of Abigail, whose story is told in 1 Samuel 25. The verses chosen for the dedication read as follows: "Now the woman was of excellent insight and beautiful in appearance. . . . 'Blessed be the Lord, the God of Israel, who sent you this day to meet me!'" (author's translation).

In the end, it is this God of Israel who must receive the ultimate praise. He inspired the writing of these wonderful books, and it is He who makes intensive reading and study of them worthwhile. As David, the man after God's own heart, sang,

> The Lord is my rock, my fortress and my deliverer;
> my God is my rock, in whom I take refuge,
> my shield and the horn of my salvation.
> He is my stronghold, my refuge and my savior.
>   2 Samuel 22:2–3

Easter 1993

ABBREVIATIONS

Abbreviations not listed below conform to those adopted by the *Journal of Biblical Literature*.

AB   Anchor Bible
ABD   *Anchor Bible Dictionary* (1992)
ANEP   *The Ancient Near East in Pictures.* Edited by James D. Pritchard. Princeton, N.J.: Princeton Univ., 1954
ANET   *Ancient Near Eastern Texts according to the Old Testament.* 3d ed. Edited by James D. Pritchard. Princeton, N.J.: Princeton Univ., 1969
AUSS   *Andrews University Seminary Studies*
BA   *Biblical Archaeologist*
BARev   *Biblical Archaeology Review*
BASOR   *Bulletin of the American Schools of Oriental Research*
Bib Sac   *Bibliotheca Sacra*
BDB   F. Brown, S. R. Driver, and C. A. Briggs. *A Hebrew and English Lexicon of the Old Testament.* Oxford: Clarendon, 1907
BZAW   Beiheft zur die Zeitschrift für die alttestamentliche Wissenschaft
CBQ   *Catholic Biblical Quarterly*
DOTT   *Documents from Old Testament Times.* Edited by D.W. Thomas. New York: Harper & Row, 1958
EAEHL   *Encyclopedia of Archaeological Excavations in the Holy Land.* 4 vols. Edited by M. Avi-Yonah and E. Stern. Englewood Cliffs, N.J.: Prentice-Hall, 1975–78
EBC   *Expositor's Bible Commentary.* Edited by Frank Gaebelein. Grand Rapids: Zondervan, 1979–92
FOTL   The Forms of Old Testament Literature
GKC   *Gesenius' Hebrew Grammar.* Edited by E. Kautzsch, translated by A. E. Cowley. Oxford, Eng.: Oxford Univ., 1910
HSM   Harvard Semitic Monographs

IDB	*Interpreter's Dictionary of the Bible* (1962)
IDBSup	*Interpreter's Dictionary of the Bible* (1975)
IOTS	Brevard Childs. *Introduction to the Old Testament as Scripture*
ISBE	*International Standard Bible Encyclopedia*, rev. ed. (1979–88)
JANES	*Journal of the Ancient Near Eastern Society*
JBL	*Journal of Biblical Literature*
JEDP	Documentary theory acronym referring to hypothetical source documents Jahweh, Elohim, Deuteronomistic, and Priestly
JETS	*Journal of the Evangelical Theological Society*
JSOT	*Journal for the Study of the Old Testament*
JSOTSup	Journal for the Study of the Old Testament—Supplement Series
JSS	*Journal of Semitic Studies*
MT	Masoretic Text
NBD	*New Bible Dictionary*, 2d ed. (1982)
NCBC	*New Century Bible Commentary*
NICOT	New International Commentary on the Old Testament
NJPSV	New Jewish Publication Society Version (*TANAKH: A New Translation of THE HOLY SCRIPTURES According to the Traditional Hebrew Text*. Philadelphia: The Jewish Publication Society, 1985)
OTL	Old Testament Library
PEQ	*Palestine Exploration Quarterly*
POTW	*Peoples of the Old Testament World*. Edited by A.E. Hoerth, G. Mattingly, and E. M. Yamauchi. Grand Rapids: Baker, 1993
SBLDS	Society of Biblical Literature Dissertation Series
SBT	Studies in Biblical Theology
SVT	Supplements of Vetus Testamentum
TANE	*The Ancient Near East: An Anthology of Texts and Pictures*. Edited by James B. Pritchard. Princeton, N.J.: Princeton Univ., 1958
TDOT	*Theological Dictionary of the Old Testament*. Edited by G. J. Botterweck and H. Ringgren. Grand Rapids: Eerdmans, 1977–present
TOTC	Tyndale Old Testament Commentaries
TWOT	*Theological Wordbook of the Old Testament*. 2 vols. Edited by G. L. Archer, R. L. Harris, and B. K. Waltke. Chicago: Moody, 1980
VT	*Vetus Testamentum*
WBC	Word Biblical Commentary
WHJP	*World History of the Jewish People*. Vol. 3. Edited by B. Mazer. Rutgers, N.J.: Rutgers Univ., 1969
WTJ	*Westminster Theological Journal*
ZPEB	*Zondervan Pictoral Encyclopedia of the Bible* (1975)
ZAW	*Zeitschrift für die alttestamentliche Wissenschaft*

1

INTRODUCTION TO HISTORICAL NARRATIVE

As for the events of King David's reign, from beginning to end, they are written in the records of Samuel the seer, the records of Nathan the prophet and the records of Gad the seer. (1 Chron. 29:29)

The Levites . . . instructed the people in the Law while the people were standing there. They read from the Book of the Law of God, making it clear and giving the meaning so that the people could understand what was being read. (Neh. 8:7–8)

All Scripture is God-breathed and is useful for teaching, rebuking, correcting and training in righteousness, so that the man [or woman] of God may be thoroughly equipped for every good work. (2 Tim. 3:16–17)

A fabulously rich world of discovery awaits the readers of the OT's historical narratives. It is here that many of the Bible's most famous characters reside: Moses, Joshua, Deborah, Gideon, Samson, Ruth, Samuel, David, Esther. It is here that many of the Bible's most famous events are found: the arrival in the "Promised Land," the sun standing still, Samson killing the Philistines or David killing Goliath. It is here that God's gracious promises to his people are given, affirmed, and reaffirmed: God's covenant with Abraham, His promises to David, His faithfulness to His loyal remnants in Israel.

Readers with historical interests will naturally gravitate to the OT historical narratives for information about life in ancient Israel and the ancient Near East. Readers who delight in well-told tales will also enjoy these historical narratives, since they are richly endowed with complex and appealing literary characteristics.

This book is an invitation to *read* the OT historical narratives. It is intended to kindle an interest in the OT's historical books for those who have never read them seriously and to serve as a guide to their contents and messages. It also is intended to serve as a teacher of a method of reading and studying. As the contents and messages of the individual books are elucidated in the following chapters, the hope is that readers with little experience in close and careful reading of the Bible will learn to pay equal attention to microscopic details and macroscopic structures. It is in the details, as well as in the large-scale sweeps, that we learn about the messages of the biblical books and, ultimately, about God.

This book is most emphatically *not* intended to serve as a substitute for reading the historical narrative books themselves. If readers of this book believe that it will neatly summarize for them the biblical books so that they won't have to read for themselves—with a sort of "Masterplots" or "Cliffs Notes" mentality—they will be disappointed and will have cheated themselves. This book pales into nothingness alongside the grandeur and importance of the biblical books under consideration. *They* are the proper focus of study. The present book merely intends to whet the appetite for, and point the way into, the biblical books.

The biblical quotations at the beginning of this chapter point to the importance of reading, writing, and interpreting. The OT's historical books came together in many and various ways, and they stand ready for our serious scrutiny—our serious reading—as history and literature of the utmost importance. They stand ready to be read, ultimately, as life-giving and sacred *Scriptures.*

This chapter introduces the literary and historical genre of "historical narrative." It begins at the most general level, considering it as prose, then moves on to consider it first as history and then as literature.

HISTORICAL NARRATIVE AS PROSE: CONTRAST WITH POETRY

DEFINITIONS

A glance at any page of Psalms or Proverbs, followed by a perusal of almost any page in any of the historical books, will immediately reveal some differences in form: most modern English Bibles print Psalms and Proverbs as poetry, with relatively short, parallel lines whose text leaves wide margins; the historical books are printed as prose narratives, with full paragraphs whose text extends from margin to margin.

What is prose? In its broadest sense, it is any expression that is not poetry, which is defined as having a regular rhythmic pattern.[1] Historical narra-

---

1. C. Hugh Holman, *A Handbook to Literature*, s.v. "Prose"; Northrop Frye, "Verse and Prose," *Princeton Encyclopedia of Poetry and Poetics*, 885; M. H. Abrams, *A Glossary of Literary Terms*, s.v. "Prose."

tive is a type of literature written in prose, not poetry. Not all writings in prose are historical narrative, but all historical narratives are in prose form.[2]

Among prose forms the distinctive of historical narrative is that it attempts to give an account of past events.[3] In its broadest sense, historical narrative may have any number of purposes,[4] but in the Bible, it tells its story for the purposes of edification and instruction (see 2 Tim. 3:16–17).

A more careful perusal of the historical books will reveal that they are not composed entirely of historical narrative written in prose form. One finds many other literary types embedded in them, such as poems, lists of various kinds—genealogies, census lists, materials lists, and so forth—proverbs, songs, and many others. Yet, the overall structure found in the historical books reveals their intent to be *historical narratives*, that is, accounts of past events with the purpose of edification and instruction.[5] A helpful way to begin a study of historical narrative is to study it as prose in contrast to poetry. This can be done both in terms of form and of content.

FORM

Many formal features help us distinguish between poetry and prose.

Line length. Fundamental to poetry is a constriction of the length of the lines: they cannot be infinitely long, nor, in most poetry, can the line length vary radically from line to line. That is the most basic distinction between prose and poetry. Many theorists speak of the presence or absence of meter, although that is not as prominent in Hebrew poetry as it is in poetry of other languages.

In Hebrew poetry, the average line length is three to four words, each having one beat (in a metrical system), consisting of eight to nine syllables. Thus, Psalm 1:1 reads as follows (author's translation):

> Happy (is) the-man who
> does-not-walk in-the-counsel of-wicked-ones,
> and-in-the-way of-sinners does-not-stand,
> and-in-the-seat of-scoffers does-not-sit.

2. The presence of poetic "narratives," such as found in some "historical psalms"—Psalms 78, 105, 106, 135, 136—does not obviate this conclusion. The historical psalms, while telling a story of God's involvement in the past, nevertheless do so within a poetic—not a prose—framework.

3. In the field of literary study, it is one of four types of composition that are generally distinguished: argumentation, description, and exposition are the others. See Holman, *Handbook to Literature,* s.v. "Narration."

4. Holman, *Handbook to Literature,* s.v. "Narration"; Richard N. Soulen, *Handbook of Biblical Criticism,* s.v. "Narrative."

5. See also John Sailhamer, *The Pentateuch as Narrative,* 25.

The units connected by the dashes represent one metrical unit in Hebrew (in most cases, one word); thus, each line after the introductory phrase consists of three metrical units. The syllable count for these three lines in the MT is 9, 10, 9.[6]

Contrast this with the following verse from a prose text:

> At once the royal secretaries were summoned—on the twenty-third day of the third month, the month of Sivan. They wrote out all Mordecai's orders to the Jews, and to the satraps, governors and nobles of the 127 provinces stretching from India to Cush. These orders were written in the script of each province and the language of each people and also to the Jews in their own script and language. (Est. 8:9)

This verse—the longest in the Bible—is one long, extended sentence in Hebrew, which has been broken up in the NIV into three English sentences. The immediate point here is that the length of the sense units are in no way restricted in this prose passage.

Parallelism of members. A second feature of poetry—one that has long been considered the defining characteristic of Hebrew poetry—is called "parallelism of members" (i.e., equivalencies of parallel words, thoughts, or sense units). This can be seen easily in Psalm 1:1, where the second, third, and fourth lines of the verse all have a verb of bodily motion (walking, standing, sitting), a prepositional phrase with "in," and a word for God's enemies (wicked-ones, sinners, scoffers). By contrast, the prose passage in Esther 8:9 has nothing like this.

To be sure, Hebrew prose often is characterized by repetition, such as we see in Joshua 3:6: "And Joshua said unto the priests, 'Lift up the ark of the covenant and pass before the people.' So they lifted up the ark of the covenant and walked before the people.'"[7] However, in such cases—which are legion in the OT historical books—repetition is not parallelism; it is usually exact repetition of words, not the parallels of near-synonyms found in poetry. Furthermore, none of the other features of poetry is found in such prose narrative texts.

Literary devices. A third feature of Hebrew poetry is that it tends to use more literary devices than does prose. Poetry makes frequent use of such devices as alphabetic acrostics, alliteration, assonance, onomatopoeia, paranomasia, chiasms, and more.[8]

---

6. A reconstruction of the language as it was probably pronounced during the time when the text was written yields a count of 8, 9, 9.
7. Author's translation, rendered in a rather wooden fashion to bring out the repetitions between the halves of the verse better; NIV's translation obscures these exact repetitions.
8. For catalogues and explanations of poetic devices, see C. H. Bullock, *An Introduction to the Old Testament Poetic Books*, 31–38.

Psalm 1:1 features alliteration/assonance in the first three words: *'ašhrê ha'îš 'ăšer.* We also see a chiastic arrangement in the parallel elements in the second through fourth lines:

$$A - B - C$$
$$B' - C' - A'$$
$$B'' - C'' - A''$$

Again, no such patterns are discernible in the prose text of Esther 8:9. Hebrew prose does make rich use of literary and rhetorical devices, but they are of different types, and they are not usually packed as "densely" into prose narratives as they are into poetic texts.

CONTENT

Selectivity. Because of the constrictions associated with short line lengths, poets tend to be more highly selective with their words than writers of prose narratives. A glance at two parallel passages, Exodus 14 and 15, confirms this. Exodus 14 is the prose account of the Israelites' coming to and crossing the Red Sea, whereas Exodus 15 contains a hymnic reflection on the same events. Exodus 14 goes to some lengths to emphasize the fact that the Israelites crossed on dry ground (see vv. 16, 21, 22, 29). However, upon close inspection, we find that dry ground is never once mentioned in the poetic text that tells of this event. The poem in 15:1–18 is much more selective in its details—it is almost "impressionistic" in terms of the way it retells the story. The reason for this, of course, is that the poem is not concerned at all to give a coherent account of how Israel crossed the Red Sea; the details of the story are only incidental to the purpose of the poetic text, which is to glorify God for His great deliverance.[9]

Figurative language. As a generalization, figurative language finds a home more readily in poetic expression than in prose. Poetry—in any language—is more often the conveyor of deep emotions, and it breaks more easily into figurative expression. Compare the following two texts that describe situations of great distress:

> David pleaded with God for the child. He fasted and went into his house and spent the nights lying on the ground. (2 Sam. 12:16)

9. We will make the point below that narrative texts also are selective. However, when the two are compared, especially in parallel passages such as Exodus 14 and 15, or Judges 4 and 5, the point made here holds: poetry is more selective than prose.

> Save me, O God,
>   for the waters have come up to my neck.
> I sink in the miry depths,
>   where there is no foothold.
> I have come into deep waters;
>   the floods engulf me.
> > Psalm 69:1–2 [MT 2–3]

The prose passage is straightforward, telling of David's activity of mourning. The poetic text is emotive and impressionistic, conveying the psalmist's great emotion. However, we do not literally imagine the psalmist standing—or worse, treading water!—in flood waters up to his neck, pen and parchment in hand, composing this psalm. Because of the nature of poetry, we instinctively understand the language in the psalm to be figurative.

The stage. The stage on which events unfold in prose is usually limited to earthly events on an earthly stage.[10] Poetry reaches into the heavenlies more often. Compare the following two texts:

> On that day God subdued Jabin, the Canaanite king, before the Israelites. And the hand of the Israelites grew stronger and stronger against Jabin, the Canaanite king, until they destroyed him. (Judg. 4:23–24)

> "O Lord, when you went out from Seir,
>   when you marched from the land of Edom,
> the earth shook, the heavens poured,
>   the clouds poured down water.
> The mountains quaked before the Lord, the One of Sinai,
>   before the Lord, the God of Israel. . . .
> From the heavens the stars fought,
>   from their courses they fought against Sisera."
> > Judges 5:4–5, 20

The prose text is more "prosaic," i.e., more straightforward, and it tells of the Israelites' victory in a matter-of-fact manner. The poetic text reflects upon that victory and speaks of God's involvement from the heavenly perspective.

Time frame. Prose narrative is usually written from a past time perspective. Indeed, as we have noted, that is its nature: it attempts to give an account of the past for the purposes of instruction. Poetry is not so limited. It ranges from past to present to future time frames. In the books of the prophets, for example, the large majority of prophetic texts that tell of God's future intentions and activities are written in poetic, not prose, form.

---

10. A major exception is the prologue to Job (chaps. 1–2), which tells of God's and Satan's conversations about Job.

CONCLUSION

Poetry differs from prose narrative in both form and content.[11] That does not mean that poetry and prose cannot be found together, however. A number of major poems are found in the historical books: in Judges 5; 1 Samuel 2; 2 Samuel 1; 2 Samuel 22; 2 Samuel 23; 2 Kings 19; and 1 Chronicles 16. Norman Gottwald has observed that only seven OT books contain no poetry: Leviticus, Ruth, Ezra, Nehemiah, Esther, Haggai, and Malachi.[12] Conversely, only nine OT books contain no prose: Psalms,[13] Proverbs, Song of Songs, Lamentations, Obadiah, Micah, Nahum, Habakkuk, and Zephaniah. Thus, at least twenty-three OT books combine the two. Actually, one-half to two-thirds of the OT is prose, but not all prose is historical narrative. (For example, outside the historical books, we find large bodies of laws that are prose.) Nevertheless, the historical narrative component of the OT is a large and important part of that portion of Scripture.

HISTORICAL NARRATIVE AS HISTORY

The term *history* has at least three general uses in English. First, it can refer to the "facts," i.e., the events, the happenings of history. Second, it can refer to the *record* or *account* of the facts. Third, it can refer to the *study* of the facts or, more precisely, the study of the accounts of the facts. In the discussion below, we will consider all three categories, but we will focus primarily on the second category (the record of the facts), and we will consider how the Bible's historical books fit into general discussions of "history" in this sense.

DEFINITIONS

Historians have offered many and various definitions of history as they have reflected upon the historian's task. Indeed, many do not even attempt a definition, or do so with only minimal precision or clarity.[14] Following are four representative definitions that define the second meaning of history:

11. We could also attempt to distinguish the two in terms of purpose—i.e., prose narrative intends to inform as part of its task, whereas, say, hymns intend to praise and glorify God— but this is a more difficult endeavor, since, ultimately, all Scripture intends to instruct us (2 Tim. 3:16–17).
12. Norman Gottwald, "Poetry, Hebrew," *IDB* 3, 829.
13. But we do find brief prose snippets in the historical titles to fourteen psalms (e.g., at Psalms 3, 18, or 51).
14. M. Eisenberg cheerfully acknowledges this fact, and he refuses to define it himself, noting the many conflicting definitions in the process. See his section entitled "A Nondefinition," in Michael T. Eisenberg, *Puzzles of the Past: An Introduction to Thinking About History*, 3–5.

[History is] the science which first investigates and then records, in their caus-al relations and development, such past human activities as are (a) definite in time and space, (b) social in nature, and (c) socially significant.[15]

[History is] the story of experiences of men living in civilized societies.[16]

History is the intellectual form in which a civilization renders account to itself of the past.[17]

History is the undertaking of rendering an account of a particular, significant, and coherent sequence of past human events.[18]

Almost every definition here speaks of history as a societal endeavor —one that records (mainly or only) those events that are *socially significant*. In this sense not every event that ever occurred anywhere belongs in a "history" (even though they certainly did happen). A "history" records events that are significant to the author and to the group for or about which he or she is writing.

The fourth definition limits the genre significantly as well, since *any* account of the past is not "history" (such as an accounts book or a list). Rather, only that account is "history" that attempts to impose some coher-ence on the past. This limitation, though not expressed in the same way, is assumed in the first three definitions as well.

An important element in understanding "history" in the sense here is its *intent*. Written histories intend to be accurate, true accounts of the past, as well as coherent ones. As Baruch Halpern states, "Histories purport to be true, or probable, representations of events and relationships in the past."[19] Meir Sternberg makes the point even more strongly. In distinguishing be-tween history and fiction, he argues that the truth claims of the two are dif-ferent.[20] Both indeed have truth "value," but only history "claims" to be historically accurate. This does not mean that, if a single historical error is found in a work, it is then automatically relegated to "fiction" as a literary category. Many historians are proven wrong in one or more of their facts,

15. Gilbert J. Garraghan, *A Guide to Historical Method* (New York: Fordham Univ., 1946), 10. Garraghan exegetes this definition on pp. 7–10.
16. Gustaaf Johannes Renier, *History: Its Purpose and Method* (1950; Macon, Ga.: Mercer Univ., 1982), 38. He unpacks this definition on pp. 33–39.
17. Johan Huizinga, "A Definition of the Concept of History," in R. Klibansky and H. J. Paton, eds., *Philosophy and History: Essays Presented to Ernst Cassirer* (Cambridge: Cambridge Univ., 1936), 1–10 (quote from p. 9). The citation here of this oft-quoted definition comes from K. L. Younger, *Ancient Conquest Accounts*, 26.
18. Baruch Halpern, *The First Historians: The Hebrew Bible and History*, 6.
19. Ibid., 6–8; the quote is from p. 6.
20. Meir Sternberg, *The Poetics of Biblical Narrative*, 24–26.

but their works are still "histories." Rather, it means that we must treat histories on their own terms, in terms of what they claim to do, what their intent is.

At the same time, histories are selective: "Historiography cannot—and should not—be infinitely detailed. All history is at best an abridgement—better or worse—of an originally fuller reality. . . . History is always the study of one thing, or several things, and the exclusion of many others."[21]

HISTORY AS "THE FACTS"

The first use of "history" refers to the events, the happenings of history. This is "what people have done and suffered," i.e., the "historical process"[22] or "past actuality."[23]

We should remember several things about such happenings of history. First, events are always out of reach, except at the moment of occurrence. Our access to such events is through records or accounts of them. Second, evidence for such events is always limited, i.e., it is not unlimited. Absence of evidence does not prove that the event did not happen; it merely means that no record or evidence of the event is available at hand. Third, such evidence as does exist must be interpreted in order to understand it.

HISTORY AS THE RECORD OF THE FACTS

The second use of "history" refers to the writing of history, or "historiography."[24] This is sometimes called by the Greek term *historia*, which has to do with inquiry; its original use simply meant "inquiry, investigation, research," but it later came to refer to the record or narration of the results of such an inquiry.[25] Herodotus, who is called "the father of history" by the Roman statesman Cicero (and modern historians would agree), introduced his own work by this term: as an "inquiry" (*historia*).

That history writing is a record or representation of the events, not the events themselves, can be illustrated by a picture of an apple. Regardless of how realistically a picture presents the apple, it is not an apple; it cannot be eaten. Rather, it is a representation of an apple. So it is with historical events and history writing. What we study are the records of the events. In

---

21. Halpern, *The First Historians*, 7.
22. David W. Bebbington, *Patterns in History: A Christian View*, 1.
23. Garraghan, *A Guide to Historical Method*, 3.
24. "Historiography" can also refer to the third use of the term *history* (the study of the records of the facts) and thus some confusion occasionally exists. Here, we will primarily use the term to refer to the record of the facts (i.e., to the history writing itself).
25. Garraghan, *A Guide to Historical Method*, 3. H. G. Liddell and R. Scott's *Greek-English Lexicon* (s.v. *historia*) defines it as "inquiry" and a "written account of one's inquiries, narrative, history."

speaking of this type of history, we should remember that *any* record of the past is not "history." Checkbooks contain records of the past, but they are not the consciously written, coherent accounts of past, societally significant events.

We have evidence that several biblical writers wrote with a degree of historical self-consciousness. In the NT, we see this in the cases of the gospels of Luke (and the book of Acts) and John. Luke stated that

> many have undertaken to draw up an account of the things that have been fulfilled among us, just as they were handed down to us by those who from the first were eyewitnesses and servants of the word. Therefore, since I myself have carefully investigated everything from the beginning, it seemed good to me to write an orderly account for you, most excellent Theophilus, so that you may know the certainty of the things you have been taught. (Luke 1:1–4)

John acknowledged that his own record of Jesus' life was incomplete:

> Jesus did many other miraculous signs in the presence of his disciples, which are not recorded in this book. But these are written that you may believe that Jesus is the Christ, the Son of God, and that by believing you may have life in his name. (John 20:30–31)

> Jesus did many other things as well. If every one of them were written down, I suppose that even the whole world would not have room for the books that would be written. (John 21:25)

In the OT, the numerous references in the books of Kings and Chronicles to extrabiblical sources used by the authors to compose their works attest to this. Those were sources to which the public had some sort of access, since the writers asked a rhetorical question such as, "And the deeds of [king's name], are they not written in the Books of the Chronicles of the Kings of Israel?"[26] In the book of Ezra, numerous official letters and decrees are recorded in the language in which they were written (Aramaic), presumably verbatim.

Much history writing is separated by "a great gulf fixed"[27] from the people about whom it is concerned because of the historical distance between the historian and the events he writes about. That is certainly true with much of the OT's historical materials. The presumption is often that such materials will necessarily be less accurate than those produced close to the time of the events they describe. Because of this, many evangelicals have

---

26. See chapters 6 and 8 on these sources in 1 & 2 Kings and 1 & 2 Chronicles.
27. Bebbington, *Patterns in History,* 2.

been concerned to narrow the gap between their estimates of the dates of the events in particular books and the date of composition of those books.[28]

However, we should note that historical distance between events and writing does not, in and of itself, necessitate the conclusion that the writing will be less than accurate. On the one hand, records or traditions could easily have preserved earlier events for access in later times. On the other hand, the divine author of Scripture could have directly revealed to the human authors the necessary information—otherwise unknown and unrecorded—for certain portions of their works. Many who affirm Mosaic authorship of the Pentateuch have little problem with the historical distance between Moses and all the events in Genesis. By the same reasoning, there is no *necessary* compulsion to argue for early authorship of the (anonymous) works found in the historical corpus.

MODERN HISTORICAL STUDY OF BIBLICAL HISTORY

RATIONALES FOR HISTORICAL STUDY

Apologia. Strictly speaking, the modern study of biblical history is not a concern in this book, for it is not a "history" of Israel. Rather, it is an introduction to the biblical books that record that history. The focus is upon the books themselves, not upon the history (i.e., the events or happenings) behind the books. However, we devote a section here to studying the way modern historians approach biblical history for several reasons:

1. Many books called "histories" of Israel are written today, and we should be aware of how they do this and what their aims are.
2. The "historicity" of the Bible, as far as it can be ascertained by modern historians, is an important concern.
3. To some degree, understanding the way modern historians approach their task can give some insight into the way the biblical writers—especially writers of the historical narratives—executed their task. The discussions below attempt to keep separate a consideration of the work of modern historians and that of the biblical writers.

Modern historical study of the Bible. Many modern scholars consider themselves "biblical historians," or historians of Israel's history. For them, the events of Israel's history are indeed their focus. Representative works by nonevangelical scholars include the following: Martin Noth, *The History of Israel*; John Bright, *A History of Israel*; John Hayes and Maxwell Miller, *Isra-*

---

28. See, e.g., C. F. Keil, *The Book of Joshua*, 15–19; R. K. Harrison, *Introduction to the Old Testament*, 671–73.

elite and Judaean History; Miller and Hayes, *A History of Israel and Judah*; and Alberto Soggin, *A History of Ancient Israel*. Evangelical histories include Leon Wood's *A Survey of Israel's History* and Eugene Merrill's *Kingdom of Priests*. All these works, to a greater or lesser degree, use the Bible as one source among several by which to reconstruct Israel's history. Some works (such as Gösta Ahlström's *The History of Ancient Palestine*) view reconstructing Israel's history as only one component of a much larger endeavor—that of understanding the history of Palestine or the ancient Near East in a comprehensive way. In none of these is the Bible itself—in the last analysis—the focus of study; the focus is the events of Israel's history.

That is an entirely legitimate pursuit for at least two reasons. First, humans have a natural curiosity to pursue knowledge in all fields, and this is one legitimate field. The history of Israel is as legitimate a focus of study as the history of Imperial Rome or Victorian England. Second, since the study of Israel's history does indeed bring us much closer to the Scriptures than does the study of, say, Victorian England, it is legitimate to study Israel's history in order to arrive at conclusions concerning the Bible's reliability. More often than not, the study of Israel's history from this perspective points to the reliability of the Bible's accounts. Though we must admit that, in many cases, it does not do this, we must also acknowledge that the historical method does not deal with absolute certainties, only with probabilities (see below).

Many scholars would add a third reason for the study of Israel's history: namely, that it is essential to understanding the Bible itself. That is, without knowledge of extrabiblical materials that illuminate Israel's history, we cannot fully—or, in some cases, at all—understand many texts in Scripture. A certain modern arrogance sometimes creeps in here, however. It can be seen in approaches that would claim, for instance, that the writer of Genesis intentionally wrote his work against the backdrop of such extrabiblical works as the *Gilgamesh Epic* (which tells of a great flood, in many ways reminiscent of Noah's flood) or the various ancient creation epics. This would suggest that the secrets to Genesis lay unavailable to students of the Bible for centuries, only to be revealed in the modern day, when these epics were discovered.

Certainly extrabiblical discoveries have shed light on biblical texts and concepts. However, it is one thing to say this and another to say that they have uncovered secrets in the Bible previously unknown. What more properly should be said is that extrabiblical discoveries may highlight in bolder relief truths, assumptions, or patterns that already reside in the biblical texts. An example of this would be the modern discovery that portions of biblical covenants—mainly in the Pentateuch—resemble the structures of

Hittite covenant treaties of the late second millennium B.C.[29] The study of biblical covenants far antedated this modern discovery, and the relationships described within the biblical covenants already were known (i.e., covenants between equals, covenants between overlords and vassals). However, the Hittite discoveries have helped to highlight aspects of biblical covenants already present in the biblical texts.

These discoveries have also served the purpose of shedding light on matters of the Bible's reliability. That the Hittite treaties date to the late second millennium B.C. and the Pentateuchal covenants resemble them so closely suggests that the Pentateuch was written during the same time period. It would be one piece of evidence pointing to—though certainly not by itself proving—Mosaic authorship of the Pentateuch. However, knowledge of these covenants is not essential to understanding the *meaning* of the Pentateuch.

THE IMPORTANCE OF HISTORICITY

The modern focus on the events, or happenings, of history is important in the Bible's case because the Bible makes numerous claims—explicitly and implicitly—concerning the factuality of the events it records. At the most fundamental level, at the central core of Christian beliefs, is the fact that Christ did indeed die for the sins of humanity and then rose from the grave in a great victory over death. This forms the ground and basis of our faith. Paul makes that point forcefully in 1 Corinthians 15 as he discusses the resurrection (see esp. vv. 12–19).

Beyond this, in portions such as the gospels and the historical books, most of what is recorded purports to be true.[30] That is illustrated by the explicit claims from Luke and John (noted above), as well as the way in which the authors of Kings, Chronicles, and Ezra-Nehemiah used their sources. It is also illustrated by the implicit claims of the historical materials in the Bible: they present themselves as historical, and they are treated as historical elsewhere in the Scriptures.

If, in the last analysis, God is the "author" of Scripture, then He who knows all things would have "written" an accurate record of those things. Thus, what the Scriptures claim to be true is indeed true.[31] We can often discover information that will confirm to us this reliability through the study of the events of history. Our trust in the Bible's reliability can be supported via this type of study.

29. See George E. Mendenhall, "Covenant Forms in Israelite Tradition," 50–76; Meredith Kline, *The Structure of Biblical Authority*; John H. Walton, *Ancient Israelite Literature in its Cultural Context*, 95–109.
30. Exceptions include such literary forms as Jesus' parables or Jotham's fable (Judges 9).
31. See Gordon Wenham, "History and the Old Testament," 13–75, esp. pp. 22–34; V. Philips Long, *The Art of Biblical History*, chap. 3: "History and Truth: Is Historicity Important?"; and several essays in James K. Hoffmeier, ed., *Faith, Tradition, and History*.

The Bible's message is given, to a large extent, through historical writings, and not, say, abstract philosophical treatises. It is through historical writings about historical events that we learn much about God and His purposes for humans. As noted, the intent of these historical writings is to provide an accurate account of the history of God's people, and their message is undermined if their historical accuracy is compromised. Citing Will Herberg, Walter Kaiser makes this point well:

> Will Herberg says that Biblical faith is also historical, not because it *has* history, or deals *with* historical events (there's nothing particularly novel in that), but it is historical in a much more profound sense because *it is itself* history. The message that Biblical faith proclaims, the judgments it pronounces, the salvation it promises, the teaching it communicates; these are all defined historically and are understood as historical realities. This does not make it offensive to us, since it helps to humanize it, to bring it down to our level where we can understand it and where we can (as we say today) "identify" with it. To de-historicize history or to de-historicize Biblical faith is like trying to paraphrase poetry. You ruin it. You just take all that is good and meaningful out of it. It is no longer poetry.[32]

The questions of whether the Bible accurately records the events of history, on the one hand, and whether and how God revealed Himself directly through the events of history, on the other, are two separate questions. We have just argued that the answer to the first question is that the Bible does indeed accurately record the events it portrays.

The answer to the second question is that God did reveal Himself directly through events of history but that this mode of revelation was somewhat limited, even to those living through or observing these events. The introduction of the book of Hebrews may provide an insight into this: "In the past God spoke to our forefathers through the prophets at many times and in various ways, but in these last days he has spoken to us by his Son" (1:1-2). This seems to suggest that God's modes of revelation were not limited only to writings. However, it also suggests that the prophets and God's Son were necessary mediators of nonwritten revelatory modes. (The NIV's rendering ["*through* the prophets" and "*by* his Son"] somewhat obscures the parallels between the revelation via the prophets and God's Son, since the prepositions in both cases are the same: *en* ["by, through"].)

Many have argued that God's revelation was *primarily* through historical events.[33] However, this overstates the case, and it does not properly ac-

---

32. Walter C. Kaiser, Jr., *The Old Testament in Contemporary Preaching*, 73.
33. A classic statement of this position is G. Ernest Wright, *God Who Acts: Biblical Theology as Recital*.

count for the need for interpretation of such events (not to mention its de-emphasis of the Bible's claims to be the Word of God). God's revelation in historical events may be compared to His revelation in nature: both communicate something of God, but both are incomplete without written revelation. When Psalm 19:1 states, "The heavens declare the glory of God; the skies proclaim the work of his hands," we understand that these natural elements reveal something about God to us. In an analogous way, historical events also can reveal something about God. However, in both cases, the revelatory information is limited.

With reference to historical events, we can take an example such as Exodus 19, where the thunder and lightning, as well as the earth's shaking and the thick cloud that the people experienced at the foot of Mount Sinai, were clearly a communication of God's presence and power. However, these events needed to be interpreted by Moses to the people in order for them to have any clear comprehension of this revelation. Or, to take another example, the stopping up of the waters of the Jordan River in Joshua 3 was also an example of God's "speaking" through a historical event. However, it was interpreted by Joshua to the people so that its meaning was very clear, and they were to interpret it to their children in years to come (Joshua 4).

The Scriptures that record and interpret the God-directed events are not merely *testimonies* to God's revelatory activities. They themselves *are* revelation. When Paul states that "all Scripture is God-breathed" (2 Tim. 3:16), he uses the words *pasa graphe* ("all that is written [is God-breathed]"). He is stating that the written words themselves are God's revelation, not merely witnesses to some "true" (or "truer") revelation in the events of history. This is contrary to the assertions of many (e.g., G. Ernest Wright), who assert that the "Word of God" is present in Scripture but that the Scripture itself is not the "Word."

We must emphasize here that, even given that God's workings in history were revelatory in some limited way, we today only have access to these workings through the mediation of the written Scriptures.[34] This was true even in biblical times among those who experienced them first-hand: even then, these events were always interpreted. How much more is this true to-

---

34. This latter point is the thrust of John Sailhamer's important essay, "Exegesis of the Old Testament as a Text," 279-96, and his comments in *The Pentateuch as Narrative*, 15-22. He states that "given the theological priority of an inspired text (2Ti 3:16), one must see in the text of Scripture itself the locus of God's revelation today. Thus, on the question of God's revelation in history, the sense of *history* in a text-oriented approach would be that of the record of past events. . . . Even the formula 'revelation in history' then concerns the meaning of a text" (*The Pentateuch as Narrative*, 17). However, he acknowledges the theoretical possibility of nonwritten modes of revelation in the past when he says, "There is no reason to discount the fact that God has made known his will *in other ways at other times*" (*The Pentateuch as Narrative*, 17; italics added).

day. We only know of most of the events in Scripture through the Scriptures themselves. Even when we can gain independent knowledge of them, the vehicles of that knowledge are not "God-breathed"; only the Scriptures that interpret these events are God's revelation to us. Thus, the Scriptures themselves are the proper focus of our study, not the hypothetical re-creations of the events behind these Scriptures. The events themselves were never sufficient—in any time—to communicate God's revelation fully, and today they are accessible only through the written interpretations, the Scriptures.

MODERN HISTORIANS OF BIBLICAL HISTORY AND THE PROBLEM OF EVIDENCE

The fact that modern historians may have very little to work with involves the problem of evidence.[35] As we have noted with reference to the events of biblical history, the past is always mediated to us.[36] We cannot recover or repeat it in the same way mathematicians can recalculate an equation or scientists can rerun an experiment. It is mediated to us via the evidence. Often the evidence is spotty, and there are large gaps in our knowledge of the past.[37]

In reconstructing Israel's history (using the Bible along with nonbiblical sources, both written and nonwritten), the evidence must be evaluated. Mute evidence, recovered via archaeological methods, must be interpreted and evaluated. So too with written records: they can be so tendentious as to be useless, or they may even be forgeries. For example, almost no historian uses the apocryphal *Additions to Esther* (which were written much later than the events in Esther and which have different purposes from the canonical book) to reconstruct history in Esther's day or employ the *Psalms of Joshua* (which come from the late intertestamental period) to reconstruct history in Joshua's day.

Because of this, the attitude of "inquiry" in reconstructing history is important.[38] A curiosity for sources and facts, and for explicating these, is essential for a modern historian. The great historians—especially the outstanding ones in early periods, or in periods when the prevailing mood of their day was not conducive to such inquiry—are almost universally praised for having had an insatiable curiosity (e.g., Herodotus and Thucydides among the Greeks, or Augustine and Eusebius among the early Christians),

---

35. Bebbington, *Patterns in History,* 3–5.
36. This point is known by all historians. See, e.g., Garraghan, *A Guide to Historical Method,* 4–5; Edward Hallett Carr, *What is History?* (New York: Random House, 1961), 24.
37. Carr (*What is History?* 12) states, "History has been called an enormous jig-saw with a lot of missing parts."
38. Whether the extreme skepticism evidenced by many historians is altogether healthy is another question, one whose answer is usually no. (See further below.)

despite whatever flaws modern historians might otherwise point out in their methods.

In the last analysis, modern historians deal with probabilities, not absolute certainties. They must of necessity rely on sources and assume that these possess a certain reliability. Otherwise, they must sift and sort and come to their own conclusions nevertheless.

This dependence upon probabilities is important, since history cannot be repeated and even its patterns are not capable of repetition. Indeed, the historian is interested precisely in unique events, not just repetitive patterns. R. J. Shafer notes that "both historians and social scientists are interested in regularities, tendencies, or repetitive elements in social behavior, but the former are also concerned with the unique event and person for their own sakes, and the latter are more uniformly dedicated to identifying 'laws' of human conduct."[39]

Because historians do deal with the unique so often, the extreme skepticism about the possibility of any historical knowledge that has been found among so many historians should be tempered somewhat.[40] Paul Schubert, a Yale historian, notes that early in the twentieth century W. Dilthey insisted that, despite the limitations on knowledge, "one thing is still possible and necessary: true and adequate understanding of past history."[41]

MODERN HISTORIANS OF BIBLICAL HISTORY AND THE PROBLEM OF THE HISTORIAN

In modern historical study, the problems are not only of historical distance (chronologically) between events and the writing about them, nor of spotty or suspect evidence. Another problem is the modern historian him- or herself[42] because all history writing is of necessity "perspectival," even "subjective," in the sense that it owes its shape to its author's activity in selecting and communicating material. There is the inevitable picking and choosing among sources of information and a selectivity in what is reported.

That is true even when there is no historical distance between the historian and the events or people he or she is writing about or when the source material is abundant. That is certainly true today. Each of the recent presidents of the U.S. has his own presidential library, with millions of documents. Yet, those who write about Richard Nixon or Jimmy Carter, for ex-

---

39. R. J. Shafer, *A Guide to Historical Method*, 5.
40. In biblical studies, scholars such as Alberto Soggin, John Van Seters, Thomas Thompson, Keith Whitelam, Robert Coote, to name but a few, display such a skepticism, at least for some—if not almost all—periods in Israel's history.
41. Paul Schubert, "The Twentieth-Century West and the Ancient Near East," 320.
42. Bebbington, *Patterns in History*, 5–8; Shafer, *A Guide to Historical Method*, 4, 12.

ample, are inevitably selective as to what they will write, and they will inevitably take a certain slant.

Historians in the past two or three centuries have been proud to speak of history as a "science" (especially in the last century). There are established rules of evidence, research, documentation, and so on.[43] However, all historians are products of their own time and inclinations, and to pretend otherwise is merely to deny or hide one's "biases." As David Bebbington states, "Value-neutrality is impossible. The unconscious assumptions of the historian's own age are inescapable. The historian himself is part of the historical process, powerfully influenced by his time and place."[44] This is not necessarily bad, however:

> If a historian's personal attitudes do not necessarily harm his history, it is equally true that they can enhance it. Great history is commonly a consequence of a historian's pursuit of evidence to vindicate his previously formed beliefs. [Edmund] Gibbon, for instance, wrote his masterpiece, [History of] The Decline and Fall [of the Roman Empire (1776–88)], because he conceived himself to be a champion of civilization and rationalism who could point out that Rome succumbed to 'the triumph of barbarism and religion.' A pure love of scholarship is rare. Deeply held convictions are needed to drive people to major historical achievements.[45]

The modern historian should at least attempt to understand the values in the period under study, not just his or her own values. Ferdinand Lot, a French historian at the turn of the twentieth century, made a similar point. When one writes a synthesis of history, Lot stressed that

> qualities other than the erudite skills come into play. There must be sympathy with the subjects under study, for without it there can be no imaginative insight into the past. Ideally, a historian must display capacities akin to those of a poet or an artist.
>
> Such a quality was, by and large, lacking in the work of the historians of the Enlightenment, who had been unable to achieve imaginative insight into civilizations very different from their own. The greatest shortcoming of Gibbon was his temperamental inability to appreciate religion.[46]

The modern writer's purpose in writing a history, then, is important, and it is usually inseparable from his or her own background, experience, philosophies, and so on. The purpose may be reportorial, proclamative, di-

---

43. Two works that introduce the historical method in biblical studies are Edgar Krentz, *The Historical-Critical Method,* and J. Maxwell Miller, *The Old Testament and the Historian.*
44. Bebbington, *Patterns in History,* 6.
45. Ibid., 7.
46. Fryde et al., "The Study of History," 634.

dactic, nationalistic, hortatory, or polemical. Thus, in evaluating such modern histories of Israel as were mentioned above (see "Modern Historical Study of Biblical History" under the subhead "Rationales for Historical Study"), the writers' purposes and presuppositions must be evaluated as well. Their inclinations to believe or disbelieve the Scriptural accounts vary, and these inclinations must be understood by the reader.

We may apply this same insight into our evaluation of biblical writers. That is, our evaluations of them must include a sensitivity to their own purposes as expressed in their works and to their own biographies and experiences, insofar as these may be identified as essential parts of their works' purposes. Thus, in the chapters that follow, close attention will be paid to listening to these works on their own terms—their own stated (or visible) purposes, methods, and emphases.[47]

HISTORIE AND GESCHICHTE

The German terms *Historie* and *Geschichte*[48] are sometimes encountered in discussions of biblical history, and a distinction is made between the two. *Historie* is said to be "a bare account of what actually happened."[49] It is concerned with past facticity, with what is public and verifiable according to the canons of modern historical study. *Geschichte* is "an account of past events in terms of their contemporary significance."[50] It goes beyond or ignores (even denies) the element of facticity. In the case of the OT, it deals with what Israel *believed* happened, not what actually may have happened.

Bound up with this is the notion introduced by von Ranke of history *"wie es eigentlich gewesen"* (popularly understood as "as it actually was," i.e., some sort of "objective" knowledge of the past). This is related to the notion discussed above of the possibility of "objective" or nonperspectival history. However, von Ranke's phrase has been mistranslated: *eigentlich* should be understood as "essentially," referring to the "essence" of what is historical, as penetrated by the mind of the historian.[51]

---

47. See also in this regard, Halpern, *The First Historians,* 6–13; Sailhamer, "Exegesis of the Old Testament as a Text," 279–96; and the remarks below on "Implied Reader."
48. For brief introductions to these concepts, see R. T. France, "The Authenticity of the Sayings of Jesus," 103; Alan Richardson, *History Sacred and Profane,* 154–56; also Will Herberg, in his *Faith Enacted as History,* 133–34. In more detail, see W. L. Craig, "The Nature of History," 139–47 (dealing with NT scholars' development of the terms). Martin Kahler introduced the distinctions in biblical studies: Kahler, *The So-Called Historical Jesus,* 63.
49. France, "The Authenticity of the Sayings of Jesus," 103.
50. Ibid. However, Gilbert Garraghan (*A Guide to Historical Method,* 3) points out that, etymologically, *Geschichte* comes from *geschehen* ("to happen") and that it originally meant "'things that have happened': history as past actuality." Thus, etymologically, at least, this distinction is not valid.
51. See Younger, *Ancient Conquest Accounts,* 32–33 (esp. n. 35); Carr, *What is History?,* 5–7, 26; Bebbington, *Patterns in History,* 107–8.

Alan Richardson helpfully points out that *Historie* ("the merely historical," or "mere facts") cannot stand on its own. As noted, there is no abstract, "objective," or uninterpreted history. "In the last resort . . . , nothing
can be *historisch* without being in some way *geschichtlich*; no 'facts' can be
'mere facts', and every 'fact' that can be discovered is worth discovering because all history is somehow significant."[52] Seen in this light, then, the radical distinction often made between the two in biblical studies, and the
disparagement of *Geschichte* that often comes with it, is not well taken.
And, as already noted, the absence of evidence for an event—or the impos-
sibility of repeating it—does not prove that it did not occur.

HISTORICAL METHOD: THE STUDY OF THE FACTS

The sources for history writing: written sources. Written materials usually form the most important source for historians as they construct their
histories. These come in two categories: (1) casual (or official) history, and
(2) deliberative (or literary) history.

Casual history consists of the "raw material" of history, of the records
produced at all levels of society, from the individual to the international. Today, this consists of many types of records: checkbooks; appointment cal-
endars; business receipts; courthouse records of births, marriages, and
deaths; governmental rules, regulations, and laws; international treaties;
and so forth. They consist of information presented in statement form, im-
personal, with minimal analysis (usually none).

In the ancient Near East, the raw materials include gravestone inscriptions, administrative and economic documents of the great empires, petty
receipts, letters, and more. Modern biblical scholars use these alongside
the Bible in attempting to reconstruct Israel's history.

We can also identify the raw materials of history writing in the Bible
itself. These include songs, poems, genealogies, census lists, lists of clean
and unclean animals, king lists, and many more. Often, the Bible's sources
are named explicitly, such as "The Book of the Wars of the Lord" (Num.
21:14).[53]

Deliberative history represents true historiography: it is analytical, interpretive, written history. It is the product of selection by an author, with
specific purposes in mind, creatively arranging the final product. (In the Bible's case, we would affirm that it is by inspiration, as well as by "creativi-
ty.") Deliberative history is built upon casual history. It uses the raw data as
building blocks for its construct, which is the final written history.

52. Alan Richardson, *History: Sacred and Profane,* 155; see also n. 1 there.
53. See chapters 6 and 8 for extended discussion of the many sources behind the books of 1 &
    2 Kings and 1 & 2 Chronicles.

In the Bible, we see much of this type of history writing. In the OT it includes most of the Pentateuch and all of the books covered in the present work. In the NT it certainly includes Luke-Acts, and also the other three gospels.

The sources for history writing: material remains. Material remains are the objects and artifacts left behind by people and societies. These represent mute evidence and usually come into play after written sources are analyzed. For modern historians of Israelite history, the material remains are recovered archaeologically. These have included pottery, building remains, bones and tomb remains, tools and weapons, and jewelry. Archaeology is becoming increasingly sophisticated, and now such things as pollen, teeth, and even feces are studied for information about ancient diets; on Egyptian mummies, DNA studies are carried out, and even "autopsies" performed.[54]

There is no clear evidence that the biblical historians engaged in study of material remains while writing their histories. The erection of memorial stones may, however, be an example of this (e.g., Gen. 31:45–53; Joshua 4).

The sources for history writing: tradition. Many things are passed down orally or as customs in a society. The former are such things as genealogies, nursery rhymes, place names, folk tales, and so on. The latter are the rituals and customs of a society.

In modern times, historians and anthropologists can study these firsthand in many societies. However, for societies such as ancient Israel, which are long-since dead, the only way to recover these is if they have been committed to writing at some point; if so, the materials in this category would be studied as the "casual" history mentioned above. One way around this problem is taken up by emerging sociological and anthropological approaches to studies of ancient societies, and these are increasingly common in biblical studies.[55] These include the assumption that traditions and customs are long-lived at the grass-roots level, and thus, by studying modern-day peasant or nomadic life in the lands of the Bible, we can get a fairly good picture of what life was like in biblical times. There is some justification for this, but it must be done with caution.

In the Bible, tradition and customs undoubtedly were part of the biblical writers' building blocks. Many were written down (casual history) and many undoubtedly came to them as oral tradition, as customs, or even by direct revelation from God. Many etiologies, for example, could very well have been oral tradition passed down. However, today, we only have access to these via the final written compositions now existing as the Scriptures. (See chapter 3 for an explanation of etiology.)

---

54. See H. Darrell Lance, *The Old Testament and the Archaeologist.*
55. See Robert R. Wilson, *Sociological Approaches to the Old Testament*; Norman K. Gottwald, *ABD* 6, s.v. "Sociology (Ancient Israel)."

HISTORICAL NARRATIVE AS LITERATURE

HISTORICAL NARRATIVE AS STORY

As already mentioned, historical narrative attempts to give an account of past events, and it is selective in doing so. In this sense, it tells a *story.* It is literature. Here are two popular definitions of *story*:

> The telling of a happening or connected series of happenings, whether true or fictitious; account; narration.[56]

> Any account, written, oral or in the mind, true or imaginary, of actions in a time sequence.[57]

Note that the idea of "fiction" or "fictitiousness" or, more specifically, the idea that a story speaks of something that did not happen is *not* an integral part of either definition. Leland Ryken states that "taken as a whole, the Bible tells a story that has a beginning, a middle, and an end. The Bible is above all a series of events, with interspersed passages that explain the meaning of those events."[58]

These definitions of *story* are close to Halpern's definition of *history.*[59] Both assume some coherence and some ordering. Indeed, both English words—"story" and "history"—come from Greek and Latin *historia.* However, "history" is more limited than "story" in that it does assume some correspondence with facts or events. "Story" *might* have such a connection; "history" *must* have such a connection (or at least that must be its intent).

CHARACTERISTICS OF HISTORICAL NARRATIVE

We can characterize historical narrative in any number of ways. Tremper Longman identifies six "functions" of biblical literature in general—and these would all apply to historical narratives more narrowly: it is historical, theological, doxological, didactic, aesthetic, entertainment.[60] Leland Ryken characterizes biblical literature with a long list: it "images" reality (preferring the concrete to the abstract); it is artistic, unified, experiential, interpretational, universal or comprehensive (i.e., it uses "master images" or "archetypes"); it is anthological, religious, revelatory, values-laden, real-

---

56. *Webster's New World Dictionary,* s.v. "story" (New York: Simon & Schuster, 1980).
57. Holman, *A Handbook to Literature,* s.v. "Story."
58. Leland Ryken, *Words of Delight,* 31.
59. "History is the undertaking of rendering an account of a particular, significant, and coherent sequence of past human events" (Halpern, *The First Historians,* 6).
60. Tremper Longman, *Literary Approaches to Biblical Interpretation,* 68–71.

istic, romantic, response-evoking, and concise (selective).[61] Here we will highlight some of the most important of these.

Historical. A primary characteristic of historical narrative is its historical nature, i.e., its intent is to tell of past events. We have discussed this at some length already.

Artistic. Historical narrative is a work of art, with careful attention paid to how it is crafted. A writer not only asks, *"What* do I want to say?" but also, *"How* do I want to say it?" "What kind of artifact do I wish to make?"[62] The sections in the historical books that pay the most attention to the artistic forms of communication include the books of Ruth and Esther, as well as large portions of the stories about David and Elijah and Elisha.

The presence of artistic touches does not mean, of necessity, that a text is historically inaccurate. The assumption that literary artistry and historical accuracy are mutually exclusive has led Robert Alter, for example, to classify biblical narrative as "prose fiction."[63] Alter understands prose fiction as "a mode of writing we understand to be the arbitrary invention of the writer, whatever the correspondences such a work may exhibit with quotidian or even historical reality."[64] Despite his stated agnosticism with regard to the historical accuracy of this "prose fiction," Alter more often than not assumes that the events recounted did not occur as they are stated to have occurred. Furthermore, his assumption that this "prose fiction" is an "arbitrary invention" of a writer is unnecessarily pessimistic. His position at this point has been legitimately criticized by several scholars.[65]

Entertaining. Closely related to the artistic nature of historical narrative is its value as entertainment. The Bible's stories have captivated audiences for centuries, and they have entertained children and adults alike with their stories of heroism, love, treachery, deceit, miraculous intervention, and so on. Who reads the book of Ruth and does not come away with a deeply satisfied feeling? Or who reads the story of Ehud in Judges 3 and does not come away laughing (and perhaps somewhat revolted) at the characterizations of King Eglon?

Anthological. The Bible—including its historical narratives—is a vast, diversified collection of works from many different authors. As such, we en-

---

61. This list is culled from Ryken's introductory essay in *The Literature of the Bible,* 13–30, and the introductory and first chapters of *Words of Delight,* esp. pp. 14–43. The latter work is a thorough revision and expansion of the former, but the former includes some items of value omitted in the latter.
62. Ryken, *Literature of the Bible,* 13.
63. Alter, *The Art of Biblical Narrative,* 23–26.
64. Ibid., 23.
65. E.g., Meir Sternberg, *The Poetics of Biblical Narrative,* 23–35; V. Philips Long, *The Art of Biblical History* (chap. 2, "History and Fiction: What Is History?").

counter a wide range of styles, and a wide teaching. This last point is particularly important to remember. In general, almost no given text will contain the Bible's entire range of teaching on the topic it addresses. Scripture must be checked with Scripture. In the case of historical narrative especially, since its teaching is usually done indirectly, we must check the teachings of individual narratives with teachings elsewhere. Thus, the harsh measures taken in Ezra and Nehemiah against foreigners must be placed against the implicit teachings of Ruth, in which a foreigner is a central character, or Jonah, in which foreigners are called to repent. Furthermore, *implicit* teachings in narratives must be measured against *explicit* teachings in expository sections of Scripture. Ryken states that "the paradoxes of human life are held in tension in what can be called the most balanced book ever written."[66]

Selective. The Bible's historical narrative, like all literature and all history writing, is of necessity selective. That point was made in connection with history writing (p. 31). Furthermore, the Bible's selectivity is relatively sparse. In spite of the length of many of its narratives, these narratives have an economy of expression such that the smallest details become significant. Note in the next chapter, for example, the subtle interplay between Joshua's being called "Moses' aide" when he becomes Israel's leader (Josh. 1:1)—in contrast to Moses' being called "the servant of the Lord"—and Joshua's being called "the servant of the Lord" at the end of his ministry (Josh. 24:29). This makes a subtle point about Joshua's having "grown into the job" that God had for him and his having achieved, in some measure at least, a stature as a "second Moses."

Unified. Despite its diversity and selectivity, the Bible possesses a remarkable degree of unity. It has a unity of purpose (to teach, rebuke, correct, and train us: 2 Tim. 3:16) and a unity of subject matter: God. Historical narratives are unified as well. Despite the complexities of the underlying sources of, say, Judges, 1 & 2 Chronicles, or Ezra-Nehemiah, each of these works speaks with a remarkable singleness of vision as it presents its message. And, when the historical books are brought together, they ultimately speak of God Himself and of His kingdom.

Realistic. The Bible's stories are nothing if not realistic. There are certainly elements of some stories that allow them to be identified as "type scenes" in which certain "types" that display fixed conventions are recognizable.[67] One such type scene is the encounter with a future betrothed at a well; we meet Rebekah (Isaac's future wife) in Genesis 24, Rachel (Jacob's future wife) in Genesis 29, and Zipporah (Moses' future wife) in Exodus 2.

---

66. Ryken, *Words of Delight*, 29.
67. See Alter, *The Art of Biblical Narrative*, 47–62; p. 51 lists the most common type scenes.

In the historical books, a type scene encountered at least twice is the annunciation of a birth of a son to a barren woman, a son who will become a hero (see Samson's parents in Judges 13 and Hannah, Samuel's mother, in 1 Samuel 1).

However, in treating such patterned texts, we must be sensitive to the details of the patterns and how they may diverge from the norm. Usually, there is enough realistic detail to enable us to read the texts as realistic portrayals of events and not merely as schematic representations of them. Furthermore, many texts are extremely detailed, and they are unique; they do not fit patterns. Certainly the passage telling of Ehud's killing of Eglon is realistic: "And Ehud stretched out his left hand, took the sword from his right thigh and thrust it into [Eglon's] belly. The handle also went in after the blade, and the fat closed over the blade, for he did not draw the sword out of his belly; and the refuse came out" (Judg. 3:21–22 NASB).

Thus, we can see that the historical narratives attempt to mirror the reality of the world in accurate ways. This has been called a "representational" approach to the world,[68] and it is the thrust of Erich Auerbach's influential work *Mimesis.* Auerbach attempts to show how literature "mimes," or "mimics," reality, how it reflects reality like a mirror.[69]

Romantic. Ryken points out that, in addition to being realistic, the Bible's stories are "literary romances," that is, stories that highlight and delight in the extraordinary and the miraculous.[70] They are full of mysteries, God and the gods, heroes and villains, surprises and happy endings. Who can read the book of Ruth and not be moved by the beauty of the story, with its dramatic and satisfying plot and its appealing characters? Or who can read the Elijah stories and not be impressed with his virtue, Ahab's and Jezebel's wickedness, and God's providential interventions in the affairs of humans?

Revelatory. The Bible is not just human words about God; it is God's words to humans. The biblical authors consistently show themselves to be conscious of analyzing history or human nature from God's perspective and even to be "the agents by which supernatural truth is communicated to [humans]."[71] This is less obvious in the historical narratives than in many other portions and genres of Scripture. Even here, however, the human authors consistently evaluate historical events from God's perspective. The repetitive evaluations of each king's reign in the books of Kings and Chronicles, for example, show these books' authors reflecting God's perspectives on

68. Robert Scholes and Robert Kellogg, *The Nature of Narrative*, 82–105.
69. Erich Auerbach, *Mimesis: The Representation of Reality in Western Literature*.
70. Ryken, *Words of Delight*, 37–39.
71. Ryken, *Literature of the Bible*, 18.

this. People were judged for not doing things God's way. Accordingly, Erich Auerbach's statement is appropriate: "The Bible's claim to truth is not only far more urgent than Homer's, it is tyrannical—it excludes all other claims."[72]

Response-Evoking. The Bible in its entirety—including its historical narratives—is not something that is morally neutral; it cannot be taken or left, according to one's whims. It demands a response. On the literary level, it calls for both naive and sophisticated responses.[73] Children can delight in the stories of David killing Goliath or of Elijah being fed by birds. Literate adults will be much more attuned to larger themes in these stories, how the stories are told, and how they fit into the larger schemes of the authors of the books.

The Bible also demands a spiritual response. It demands commitment, and it changes lives. It is not enough merely to appreciate it on a literary level, although that can be done legitimately and with much profit. It lays a claim upon people and forces them to respond. In this sense, it is "rhetorical," that is, it attempts to convince and persuade.[74] The historical narratives do that more indirectly than, say, epistolary works, but, nevertheless, the authors of the historical narratives clearly had certain purposes in mind that were to encourage, warn, and persuade people of their right and wrong attitudes and courses of action. What Amos Wilder aptly says of the gospels applies equally to the historical narratives of the OT: "It is as though God says to men one by one: 'Look me in the eye.'"[75]

Theological. Above all, we must remember that the Bible is a "theological" work, i.e., it deals with God. In the end, God is the subject and the hero of the Bible.[76] Even in works that emphasize human individuals, such as 1 & 2 Samuel, which highlight David, these individuals are important only as they are instruments in God's plan. We will note in several chapters to follow that David is much more important as a theological symbol—as one whom God chose and blessed and as one who was attuned to God— than he ever was as a "historical" figure—one who was, say, a great military leader, administrator, and musician.

In the end, God's dealings with humans in the historical narratives reveal to us much about Himself. We are more than entertained; we are taught. C. S. Lewis once said that the Bible is "not merely a sacred book but

---

72. Auerbach, *Mimesis,* 14.
73. Ryken, *Words of Delight,* 39–41.
74. George A. Kennedy, *New Testament Interpretation Through Rhetorical Criticism,* 6–7.
75. Amos Wilder, *Early Christian Rhetoric,* 54, quoted in Ryken, *Literature of the Bible,* 21.
76. See Gerhard Hasel, "The problem of the Center in the OT Debate," 65–82; C. Hassell Bullock, "An Old Testament Center: A Re-evaluation and Proposition."

a book so remorselessly and continuously sacred that it does not invite, it excludes or repels, the merely aesthetic approach."[77]

The three primary elements of narratives and stories that are usually discussed are plot, character, and setting. We will call these *internal elements* (elements within the story). However, in understanding these, we must also consider the presence of a story-teller (author) and an audience (reader), and the story's being told from a particular point of view. We will call these *external elements* (elements that are not as readily visible in the story).[78] We will deal with the latter first.

External elements: author. To the uninitiated reader, this concept is simple enough: the author is the person who wrote the story. However, literary critics speak of an author, an implied author, and a narrator in a text.

The *author* is the person who actually wrote the story. The *implied author* is the textual manifestation of that (living and breathing) author. That is, the author may have much more to say about any given topic than he or she expresses in a given text. However, for the purposes of reading the text, we are limited to what was written. This limited portion of an author's total sum of knowledge, that which is expressed in the text at hand, is the implied author.

This distinction is helpful in clarifying what the focus of interpretation should be. Interpretation is not an exercise in mind-reading, getting behind the words and into the mind of the author and guessing what he or she *might* say on a certain topic. Rather, it is an exercise in interpreting a given, written text, and what an author actually says in that text.

The *narrator* is the one who tells the story.[79] In the Bible, the narrator almost always is the same as the implied author. Elsewhere, however, authors often create narrators to tell the story, such as Herman Melville's Ishmael in *Moby Dick* or Mark Twain's Huck Finn in *The Adventures of Huckleberry Finn.*

---

77. C. S. Lewis, *The Literary Impact of the Authorized Version* (Philadelphia: Fortress, 1963), 33, quoted in Ryken, *Words of Delight*, 30.
78. Brief introductions to these by biblical scholars may be found in Longman, *Literary Approaches to Biblical Interpretation*, 83–100; Grant Osborne, *The Hermeneutical Spiral*, 154–64. In more depth, see Jacob Licht, *Storytelling in the Bible*; Alter, *The Art of Biblical Narrative*; Adele Berlin, *Poetics and Interpretation of Biblical Narrative*; Sternberg, *Poetics of Biblical Narrative*; Shimon Bar-Efrat, *Narrative Art in the Bible.* Among literary critics at large, the following are good introductions: Wayne Booth, *The Rhetoric of Fiction*; Scholes and Kellogg, *The Nature of Narrative*; René Wellek and Austin Warren, *Theory of Literature*; Seymour Chatman, *Story and Discourse*; S. Rimmon-Kenan, *Narrative Fiction.*
79. Scholes and Kellogg (*The Nature of Narrative*, 4) assert that fundamental to a definition of narrative is not only the presence of a story but also of a story-teller (i.e., narrator). A drama is an example of a story without a story-teller, in which the characters themselves act out the story's "imitations" of life.

Narrators can tell their story in third-person narratives or in first-person narratives. If narratives are cast in the first-person ("I"/"we"), the perspective of the narrator is usually more limited. For example, in the book of Nehemiah, the implied author and the narrator are Nehemiah, and the character tells of the events from his own perspective. As such, his knowledge is sometimes limited. He has to wait to be told of problems, for example, rather than knowing about them independently (e.g., Neh. 5:6–8).

A third-person narrator is more detached, and therefore usually is omniscient and omnipresent. In this regard, we cannot see any distinction between the narrator and God in biblical narratives; the human and divine viewpoints are fused.[80] Most historical narratives in the Bible have this type of narrator, who can tell us what characters are thinking. An example of this is when we are told that Agag, the Amalekite king, came to Samuel "confidently, thinking, 'Surely the bitterness of death is past'" (1 Sam. 15:32), whereupon Samuel fell upon him and killed him. Also, this omniscient and omnipresent narrator can tell us of the details of conversation when no one was present except for the protagonists. Examples of this are found everywhere in historical narratives; one is when Elijah fled from Ahab and Jezebel—his private conversations with the angel of the Lord are recorded verbatim (1 Kings 19).

External elements: reader. The reader can be distinguished in three ways as well. There is a reader, an implied reader, and a narratee.[81]

The *reader* is the actual person who reads the work. With reference to the Bible, we can speak of contemporary readers (ourselves) and ancient readers (the original readers).

The *implied reader* is the reader addressed by the author of the work. This is the reader the author has in mind when he or she is writing the work (whether this person actually read the work or not). In the modern day, it is helpful to keep alive the distinction between the reader (we ourselves) and the implied reader, since the biblical texts were not addressed in the first instance to us. Our task is to place ourselves into the world and the minds of the implied readers as much as possible.[82] The implied reader is usually assumed by the author to be engaged and intelligent, and so the competent author anticipates questions that the reader might have and supplies all necessary

---

80. Sternberg, *Poetics of Biblical Narrative*, 84–128; Osborne, *The Hermeneutical Spiral*, 155–57.
81. We are not here speaking of the questions—very popular in literary-critical and biblical circles today—surrounding a "reader-response" theory of interpretation, in which the reader participates in determining the meaning of a text. For recent discussion and evaluation, see Osborne, *The Hermeneutical Spiral*, 377–80; John Goldingay, "How far do readers make sense? Interpreting biblical narrative," 5–10.
82. Scholes and Kellogg, *The Nature of Narrative*, 83; Osborne, *Hermeneutical Spiral*, 162–63; John Goldingay, "How far do readers make sense?" 5.

information.[83] Information may also be withheld, but the author's assumption is that the reader will elicit the meaning even from this.[84]

The *narratee* is the person or group addressed specifically by the narrator.[85] Often, the narratee is not identified or is the same person as the implied reader. However, occasionally in the Bible we see them separated. For example, Theophilus is the narratee of Luke's gospel, whereas the implied reader is anyone who is searching for truth about Jesus. In the OT Solomon's son is the narratee of Proverbs 1–9, whereas the implied reader is anyone of the faithful in Israel. However, in OT narratives we do not find any meaningful distinctions between implied reader and narratee.

External elements: point of view. The place the narrator chooses to stand from which to tell the story is important and can contribute to our understanding and appreciation of it. Five different points of view have been identified in narratives.[86]

First, from a *psychological* perspective, an "omniscient narrator"[87] can tell us of the internal thoughts and feelings of the characters. We have mentioned above the example of the narrator's insight into King Agag's thought processes (1 Sam. 15:32). Similar is the account of Samson's thoughts when he awoke with his head shaven: "He awoke from his sleep and thought, 'I'll go out as before and shake myself free'" (Judg. 16:20a–b). The narrator shows us his omniscience even more with his next comment: "But [Samson] did not know that the Lord had left him" (16:20c). Here we see clearly that the narrator's perspective is different from Samson's and that his knowledge is far greater.

Second, from an *evaluative* or *ideological* perspective, narrators will occasionally insert themselves into the text itself with a direct comment on the action or situation. Examples of this include the repeated comment woven into the narratives at the end of the book of Judges, "In those days there was no king in Israel" (Judg. 17:6; 18:1; 19:1; 21:25 NASB); in the first and last references, a further comment is added: "Every man did what was right in his own eyes." Another example is the evaluative aside about David and his son Adonijah: "[David] had never interfered with him by asking, 'Why do you behave as you do?'" (1 Kings 1:6). We should note, however,

---

83. Sailhamer, *The Pentateuch as Narrative*, 10–11.
84. See Alter, *The Art of Biblical Narrative*, 114–30; Sternberg, *Poetics of Biblical Narrative*, 186–229.
85. Longman, *Literary Approaches to Biblical Interpretation*, 86–87.
86. See briefly, Longman, *Literary Approaches to Biblical Interpretation*, 87–88; Osborne, *The Hermeneutical Spiral*, 156–57; in more depth, see Berlin, *Poetics and Interpretation of Biblical Narrative*, 43–83.
87. See, among many others, Shimon Bar-Efrat, *Narrative Art in the Bible*, 17–23; Sternberg, *Poetics of Biblical Narrative*, 58–185, and "Biblical Poetics and Sexual Politics: From Reading to Counter-Reading," 463–88.

that this viewpoint is one that is taken relatively rarely by biblical narrators.[88] More commonly, their evaluative viewpoint comes out in the ways they portray their characters, how selective they are with information they convey or withhold, and so on.

Third, from a *spatial* perspective, biblical narrators can be anywhere. In the story of David and Bathsheba, for example, the narrator is present with the army at Rabbah ("They destroyed the Ammonites and besieged Rabbah," 2 Sam. 11:1), with David on the rooftop ("From the roof he saw a woman bathing," 11:2), and with Bathsheba cleansing herself ("She had purified herself from her uncleanness," 11:4). In the book of Esther, the narrator moves freely back and forth—and in quick succession—between private conversations between Esther and Mordecai, Haman and his wife and friends, the king and his attendants (Esther 2–6).

Fourth, from a *temporal* perspective, narrators can tell the story in strict chronological order with a limited temporal perspective, or they can tell of events from a less time-bound perspective. We have already noted the limitations in perspective inherent in such first-person narratives as the book of Nehemiah. The book of Esther unfolds in a very sequential fashion as well, which adds to its suspense. On the other hand, the book of Judges (2:6–10) opens with a flashback in time (see chapter 3 for more on this), and the story of Rahab and the two Israelite spies includes a temporal flashback in its unfolding (Josh. 2:16–21). An example of where the narrator inserts a future-oriented reference is in the comment in Judges 14:4 concerning Samson's parents: "His parents did not know that this was from the Lord, who was seeking an occasion to confront the Philistines; for at that time they were ruling over Israel."

Fifth, from a *phraseological* perspective, the narrator can use linguistic symbols to indicate whose point of view is being taken at any one time.[89] An example of this is the narrator's switching briefly from his own viewpoint to Eli's in his account of Hannah's presence at the sanctuary at Shiloh: "Eli thought she was drunk" (1 Sam. 1:13). Another example shows the quick shift from the narrator's omniscient, omnipresent stance to the characters' more limited viewpoint in 19:16: "When the messengers entered [David's bedroom], behold, the household idol was on the bed with the quilt of goat's hair at its head" (NASB). The word "behold" signals a shift in perspective from the narrator's omniscient viewpoint to the characters' more limited perspective: this "behold" captures some of their surprise at what they noticed when they entered the room.

Internal elements: plot. Within the confines of narrative itself, plot, character, and setting are important. Loosely speaking, plot is equivalent to

88. Ryken, *Words of Delight*, 84–85.
89. See especially Berlin, *Poetics and Interpretation*, 59–73.

action unfolding in a sequence. Robert Scholes and Robert Kellogg state that plot is "the dynamic, sequential element in narrative literature. Insofar as character, or any other element in narrative, becomes dynamic, it is a part of the plot."[90]

All plots depend on conflict and resolution of conflict. Stories will build toward a climax where the conflict is resolved. On the highest level in the Bible, there is a continuing conflict between good and evil, obedience and disobedience, God and the forces of evil. On the lowest levels are also conflicts between human characters, between value systems, between nations, between humans and God. Very often, the plot layers conflict upon conflict. At one level, the story of David's rise in 1 Samuel 16–31 is a conflict between Saul and David as individuals. However, it is far more than that. For one thing, it is a conflict between Saul and God. It is also a conflict between David's natural human impulses and his "sanctified" self: the natural human reaction would be for him to kill Saul, yet he does not, knowing God's greater purposes. It is also a conflict over models of kingship: What form was the monarchy going to take? It can even be read for its implications regarding a conflict between the tribe of Judah (David's) and the tribe of Benjamin (Saul's): several hints at the end of the book of Judges prepare us for this. (See chapter 5 under "The Place of 1 & 2 Samuel in the Canon.")

Internal elements: character. Characters are what give life to a plot. A story's action cannot proceed without characters. A widely recognized feature of the Bible's characters is its realistic portrayal of them. They are interesting and multidimensional, not "flat, static, and quite opaque," as is the case in most "primitive" stories.[91] A unique feature of the Bible's narrative portrayals of its characters is its transparency. Not only are many of its characters interesting and multidimensional, but they are portrayed with all their flaws as well. No major character in the OT is shown only in a positive light—not Abraham, Sarah, Jacob, Moses, Aaron, Samson, Samuel, David, nor a host of others. The OT narratives present them all as complex, full-bodied, and fully human characters.

We can even go so far as to say that only in narrative (as opposed to other literary genres) can we truly see into the inward lives of characters. As Scholes and Kellogg point out, "The most essential element in characterization is this inward life. The less of it we have, the more other narrative elements such as plot, commentary, description, allusion, and rhetoric must contribute to the work."[92] It is a distinctive of biblical narratives that this window into the inner life of characters is expressed to a large degree

90. Scholes and Kellogg, *The Nature of Narrative,* 207.
91. Ibid., 164.
92. Ibid., 171.

through dialogue.[93] That is, the words of the characters that the authors choose to pass on to us, and the way in which they are said, reveal much about the inner beings of the narratives' characters.

Adele Berlin speaks of three types of characters: (1) full-fledged (what other scholars call "round"), (2) types (what other scholars call "flat"), and (3) agents. Full-fledged characters are the main protagonists in any given story; they are portrayed in their many dimensions. Types are revealed in terms of a single trait or quality. Agents serve merely as props to move a story along; they have no inherent qualities as characters.

Examples of these three varieties of characters can be found everywhere in the OT narratives. In the narratives of David and his wives, Bathsheba functions as a "full-fledged character" in the story of David's old age and the succession to his throne (1 Kings 1–2). She is very much involved in the action, she speaks and reveals her feelings, and she makes her influence felt. In the story of David's adultery, however (2 Samuel 11–12), Bathsheba is much more a "prop" for the telling of David's sins, and thus Berlin characterizes her here as an "agent."[94] In the story of another one of David's wives, Abigail, we only see her positive qualities as a model of a godly woman and wife. As such, the author is portraying her as a "type."

The biblical writers' artful characterizations in no way compel the conclusion that these characters did not exist, that they are merely literary creations.[95] The writers merely chose those things about each character that they wanted to highlight for the purposes of their stories. This can especially be seen in the characterization of Bathsheba just noted: in one episode she is portrayed as an agent and in another as a full-fledged character. Most assuredly, Abigail was more complex than she is shown in 1 Samuel 25—she certainly sinned at some points in her life (as Paul affirms in Romans 3:23!). But the author's interest in that chapter is only in her many positive qualities as they were displayed in her encounter with David.

Internal elements: setting. The setting of a story is the stage upon which the events unfold or the backdrop against which they occur. It is an essential part of a narrative, but it often is neglected in favor of study of plot and character. Settings can be of different types; among the most important are geographical, temporal, social, and historical settings.[96]

Geographical setting is perhaps the most obvious. Events in the OT's historical narratives take place in any number of places, including the desert, mountaintops, fields, cities, palaces, houses, caves. The OT writers did not have as much leeway as modern writers of fiction to create their set-

---

93. See especially Alter, *The Art of Biblical Narrative,* 63–87.
94. Berlin, *Poetics and Interpretation,* 25–27.
95. See also Longman, *Literary Approaches to Biblical Interpretation,* 88–89.
96. Ryken, *Words of Delight,* 54–62; Osborne, *The Hermeneutical Spiral,* 160–61.

tings—after all, they were writing "history"—but it is interesting to note the role that certain settings play in certain narratives. For example, the encounter with God on a mountaintop is an important setting: Moses met with God on Mount Sinai (Exodus 19, 32–34), and Elijah also met God at the very same site (1 Kings 19). In both episodes, God's appearance was accompanied by thunder, fire, and earthquake. It is interesting to note that it was precisely these two OT characters who appeared with Jesus on another mountain, the "mountain of transfiguration," accompanied by a flash of light and a cloud (Luke 9 and parallels).

Temporal settings are significant. The same three characters—Moses, Elijah, and Jesus—each spent forty days in wilderness settings alone. Dates also are significant. When Ezra read the law, it was done on the first day of the seventh month (Neh. 8:2). This was a month in which several significant festivals took place, including the Day of Atonement and the Feast of Tabernacles, and in which several other significant events took place throughout Israel's history. (See chapter 9 under "Importance of Scripture" for details.)

Social settings can reveal significant information about characters or plot development. King David's taking in of the crippled and outcast Mephibosheth—Saul's son—said much about David's largesse of spirit (2 Samuel 9). Queen Esther's rise in fortunes from an obscure Jew to the queen of an empire with unrestricted access to the king reveals much of God's providential care in that story.

Historical settings also are important, both in terms of background to the events in the biblical books and in terms of background to the composition of these books. The events in the books of Ezra and Nehemiah, for example, reveal the relatively benign nature of Persian rule—a fact that is known from extrabiblical sources as well. The freedom given to God's people in both books would have been inconceivable against the backdrop of the harsh Assyrian rule or even the relatively more lenient Babylonian rule. On the other hand, the historical backdrop of the postexilic era for the composition of 1 & 2 Chronicles gives us an interpretive handle for understanding the Chronicler's purpose, method, and message.

THE STYLISTICS OF HISTORICAL NARRATIVE

There is a host of stylistic (or "literary") devices used by the authors of the biblical narratives to unfold their plots, build their characters, and lay out their settings. More often we read catalogues of the poetic devices used in Hebrew poetry,[97] but Hebrew narratives do not lack for such devices, either. Prominent among these devices are repetition, dialogue, omission, irony,

---

97. Several of these were noted near the beginning of the chapter under "Form."

and many others, including stylistics on the linguistic levels of words, sounds, and rhythms.[98]

Repetition. Repetition is perhaps the most widespread and widely recognized stylistic feature of biblical narratives. We find seemingly endless catalogues of repeated actions, in which characters state that they or others intend to (or should) do something and then the narrator states that they did indeed do it. We noted above the example from Joshua 3:6: "And Joshua said unto the priests, 'Lift up the ark of the covenant and pass before the people.' So they lifted up the ark of the covenant and walked before the people." This is far from mindless repetition, however. The narrator's reports that certain actions were performed—reports that echo the statements of intention word for word—function as assurances to the reader that the actions were indeed accomplished. Meir Sternberg notes another function of repetition: "In repetition, one of the members invariably comes from the omniscient narrator himself, so as to establish an objective reference point for making sense of the characters' fallible versions."[99]

Repetition can be of statements, as just noted, or of entire scenes—type scenes, such as the encounter with God in the wilderness or on a mountain[100]—or of key words.[101] One function of key-word repetitions is to link texts together. For example, the Hebrew root *NKR* ("to recognize") performs such a linking function in Genesis 37 and 38 (two texts usually seen as very disparate). In Genesis 37:32–33 Joseph's brothers tell their father to "recognize" Joseph's bloody cloak that they had brought back, and he indeed "recognized" it. In the next chapter, Judah's daughter-in-law Tamar entrapped him into doing his duty to her by commanding him to "recognize" the seal, cord, and staff she had taken from him, and he too "recognized" them (38:25–26).[102] Another function of key-word repetitions is to emphasize or highlight certain features of characters, plot, setting, theology, and so on. For example, in 1 Kings 4, the twelvefold repetition of the small word "all" reinforces the point in that chapter about Solomon's universal appeal and his all-encompassing sovereignty in Israel.

Dialogue. Hebrew narratives depend heavily upon dialogue to reveal things about the characters and even to advance the action in the plot.[103] For example, we learn much about Samson's self-absorbed personality in

98. See Bar-Efrat, *Narrative Art in the Bible,* 200–218; Longman, *Literary Approaches to Biblical Interpretation,* 95–100.
99. Sternberg, "Biblical Poetics and Sexual Politics," 464.
100. See Alter, *The Art of Biblical Narrative,* 47–62.
101. Ibid., 88–113; Bar-Efrat, *Narrative Art in the Bible,* 212–15.
102. See Alter's masterful development of the many connections between Genesis 37 and 38 in *The Art of Biblical Narrative,* 3–11.
103. Alter, *The Art of Biblical Narrative,* 63–87; Berlin, *Poetics and Interpretation,* 64–72.

Judges 14–16, not by means of the narrator's explicit comments, but rather from his own words—in his conversations with his parents, his wife, his wedding guests, the men of Judah, and his Philistine lover Delilah. Dialogue highlights contrasts between characters. Alter notes "Esau's inarticulate outbursts over against Jacob's calculating legalisms in the selling of the birthright" in Genesis 25 or "Joseph's long-winded statement of morally aghast refusal over against the two-word sexual bluntness of Potiphar's wife" in Genesis 39.[104]

Omission. Often the information a narrator does not give us is as significant as what he does. Omissions or gaps function in several ways, one of which is to pique our interest.[105] For example, chapter 10 mentions the importance of the absence of any reference to God in the book of Esther as having a crucial role in communicating that book's theology.

Irony. Irony is a literary device that expresses contrasts for literary effect or impact. It usually involves surprise or the unexpected. The OT's narratives are full of ironic twists and reversals.[106] For example, the book of Genesis is replete with ironic reversals, with younger sons being favored over older ones (Jacob over Esau, Ephraim over Manasseh, Judah and Joseph over their older brothers) or Jacob's unloved wife Leah being rewarded over his beloved Rachel (by becoming the mother of Levi and Judah, ancestors of the two most favored tribes in later times). The ironic reversal-of-fortunes motif is also obvious in the book of Esther. For example, Haman is hung on the gallows he had erected for Mordecai, and—previous to this—he is forced to honor Mordecai in ways he had expected Mordecai to honor him. Also, the Jews strike down their enemies on the very day their enemies had expected to strike them down.

CONCLUSION: READING HISTORICAL NARRATIVE

We have noted the wonderful varieties of historical narratives in the OT, and we have considered them as prose, as history, and as literature. It is helpful here to keep in mind the concept of "genre fluidity" spoken of by many scholars.[107] Any given narrative text will fit into several genres and can be studied from that perspective.[108] Take, for example, the account of Deborah's and Barak's victory over the Canaanites in Judges 4. On the most general level, it is a prose text; more specifically, it is a historical account of events in the life of Israel; even more specifically, it is an account of a mili-

---

104. Alter, *The Art of Biblical Narrative,* 72.
105. Ibid., 114–30; Sternberg, *Poetics of Biblical Narrative,* 186–229.
106. See the full-length treatment of irony by Edwin Good in *Irony in the Old Testament.*
107. Longman, *Literary Approaches in Biblical Interpretation,* 78–80.
108. Ryken (*Words of Delight,* 14, 16) also notes the fact that literary categories are not "watertight," with no overlapping.

tary victory. It shares many characteristics with prose texts of all types, as well as many characteristics with historical accounts. It also shares many characteristics with literary stories, even fictional stories (plot and character development, point of view, selectivity).

In conclusion, we would echo the chapter's opening invitation that the OT's historical narratives be *read*. Biblical scholarship has too often dissected, atomized, and analyzed biblical narratives until what is left is a dismembered corpse, not a living organism. The painstaking work of analyzing texts at the lowest levels of analysis—morphemes, words, phrases, clauses, sentences—is essential to proper interpretation. Also crucial, for different reasons, is analysis of various critical questions associated with these texts. However, the interpretive task is not complete until narrative texts—or any texts, for that matter—are analyzed as coherent wholes at the higher levels of sentences, paragraphs, episodes, books, and beyond. When these higher levels are analyzed—when the texts are *read* and not just "studied" or "dissected"—then we will capture much of their vitality and their meaning. We will be able to see the contours of the forest as well as details of the trees.

In the chapters that follow, attention is paid to most of the standard critical questions that readers expect to find in an introduction. As noted in the discussion about the importance of historicity, many such critical questions are of the utmost importance in the endeavor of affirming and defending the coherence and reliability of the Scriptures. Many standard critical questions, especially ones concerning historical and cultural contexts that range beyond the pages of the Bible, are also of immense interest to modern students of the Bible. As such, these are addressed below.

However, attention in the following chapters also is consistently paid to the messages of the books, to their themes and theologies, to their purposes.[109] These are elucidated from careful attention to the books as "texts," and attention is paid to them at all levels, from the lowest to the highest. We cannot build a theology of anything biblical unless it is rooted in the words and sentences—as well as the structures and patterns—of actual texts.

Ultimately, that is the best reason for reading the Bible: to discover its revelation of God to us, to learn of His gracious plan of redemption, and to discern how to live. We cannot do so fully, however, without learning *how* to read. This book is intended to point to *the* Book and to whet readers' appetites for that Book. And, in the end, that Book itself is merely a guide and pointer to someone infinitely more important: the God revealed in its pages.

---

109. We should proclaim in advance a certain diffidence in attempting to ascertain the purposes of the biblical authors, especially when trying to boil them down to statements of one or a few main purposes. The statements of books' purposes in the chapters to follow are built upon analyses of the books' messages and circumstances, but in many cases certain alternative statements of purpose could undoubtedly have equal or greater validity.

2

JOSHUA

Be strong and very courageous. Be careful to obey all the law my servant Moses gave you; do not turn from it to the right or to the left, that you may be successful wherever you go. Do not let this Book of the Law depart from your mouth; meditate on it day and night, so that you may be careful to do everything written in it. Then you will be prosperous and successful. (Josh. 1:7–8)

If serving the Lord seems undesirable to you, then choose for yourselves this day whom you will serve, whether the gods your forefathers served beyond the River, or the gods of the Amorites, in whose land you are now living. But as for me and my household we will serve the Lord. (Josh. 24:15)

The book of Joshua is one of the most action- and adventure-filled books in the OT. One can almost hear the battle-cries and sounds of conflict. The first half of the book describes resounding military victories for Israel at Jericho, Ai, Gibeon, Hazor, and numerous other cities. It contains intrigue in the Israelite spies' infiltration of Jericho, in the ambush of Ai, in the Gibeonite deceit. It shows dramatic miracles from God in the stopping of the Jordan's waters, in the destruction of Jericho's walls, in the hailstones and the long day at the battle of Gibeon. It might be argued that a certain bloodthirstiness resides in the book's pages, as well, in the utter destruction of Canaanites and their cities.

In the second half of the book, a more sedentary mood prevails. The land has been secured, the people have obeyed (in the main), Joshua is getting old, and the land is parceled out. God's blessing abides with the people. He has fulfilled His promises to the patriarchs—with respect to descendants, blessing, relationship, and now land—and the book ends quietly, with the people and the land at rest.

JOSHUA: TITLE AND MAN

The book of Joshua received its title from its major character—Moses' successor and Israel's leader. Some have supposed that the title has indicated authorship (see below), but that does not necessarily follow.

Joshua means "the Lord saves," or "may the Lord save." Originally, his name was Hoshea, but Moses changed it to Joshua (Num. 13:8, 16). The Old Greek versions (Septuagint) render the name as *Iēsous* (which is the same as the NT name for Jesus, *Iēsous*), and the Latin Vulgate renders it as *Iosue.*

Joshua the man is typically called "the son of Nun," but nothing is known of his father. As presented in the book, he is a worthy successor to Moses, Israel's great leader and law-giver. He had proven his worth earlier by being one of two spies (out of twelve) who counseled entering the land of Canaan despite seemingly prohibitive odds (Numbers 13–14). Now—despite clear differences between the two men, both in terms of personality and office—he was called by God to function as Moses' successor (1:1–9). The book is clear that God was with him and that he enjoyed the same stature that Moses did (1:9, 16–18; 3:7; 4:14; 6:27; 10:14; 11:15, 23). The entire nation vowed to obey him at the beginning of his ministry (1:16–18),[1] and they obeyed his challenge at the end of his life as well, in vowing with him to follow the Lord (24:16–18).

Joshua appears throughout the book speaking and acting with authority, and he is as eloquent as Moses in his farewell speeches (Joshua 22–24). He is referred to at the beginning of the book merely as "Moses' aide" (1:1), but he appears in the end as the "servant of the Lord" (24:29), just as Moses was (1:1). This indicates that he was indeed a worthy successor to Moses (cf. also Deut. 34:9). He is mentioned in the NT twice: in Acts 7:45 and Heb. 4:8.

AUTHORSHIP AND DATE OF COMPOSITION

The book is anonymous. The Talmud and some rabbis (Rashi, David Kimchi) attributed it to Joshua, but some saw parts of the book as written by later hands (e.g., the account of Joshua's death or other fragments). Avravanel attributed it to Samuel, due especially to the phrase "to this day" (4:9; 5:9; 6:25; 7:26; etc.).[2] Modern scholars generally attribute the book to the Deuteronomistic writer(s), ca. seventh and sixth centuries B.C. (see below). Joshua undoubtedly wrote portions of the book: 24:26 states that "Joshua recorded

---

1. For a defense of this statement, see David M. Howard, Jr., "All Israel's Response to Joshua: A Note on the Narrative Framework in Joshua 1."
2. Marten H. Woudstra, *The Book of Joshua*, 5.

these things in the Book of the Law of God," referring to the covenant that the people had made at Shechem. But there are no further indications here or elsewhere in the Bible concerning the book's authorship.

The formula "until this day"[3] can be instructive in indicating a date for the book, or at least parts of it. Brevard Childs has noted that the use of the formula in 15:63 and 16:10 points to a period not later than the tenth century B.C.[4] That is because 15:63 mentions Judahites living in Jerusalem alongside Jebusites, whom they could not drive out. Since David captured Jerusalem from the Jebusites in ca. 1003 B.C. (2 Sam. 5:6–10), by the end of the next century, at least, Jebusites presumably would not have lived there in any significant numbers. Furthermore, 16:10 mentions Canaanite inhabitants of Gezer among the Ephraimites. Since an Egyptian pharaoh—probably Siamun (ca. 978–959 B.C.)[5]—destroyed the Canaanites at Gezer and gave the town to Solomon as a dowry (1 Kings 3:1; 9:16), the reference to Canaanites in Gezer would have come from a period prior to that. The reference in 6:25, however, about Rahab still being alive "to this day," argues for a date much earlier. Thus, portions of the book, if not the entire book, date to the time closely following the events in the book, unless the reference to Rahab refers to her descendents, as the reference to David in Hosea 3:5 does to his.

PURPOSE

In general, Joshua was written—as were most of the biblical books covered in the present work—to provide an interpretive history of one slice of Israel's life as a people. More specifically, it interprets the period in which Israel entered and settled in the land promised to Abraham and his descendants. Again and again it shows God to be in control of the events of history, not only in the dramatic miracles mentioned in the introductory comments above but also in the consistent way He is given credit for *all* of Israel's victories (chaps. 10 and 11). God's activity in all of this is for the purpose of giving the land to Israel. That it is a gift from God is repeatedly emphasized.[6] That it is a fulfillment of the land promise to Israel's ancestors is also emphasized (11:23; 21:43–45). In this way, God emerges as a trustworthy Sovereign, as one who keeps His promises. This also is emphasized in Joshua's farewell speeches (chaps. 22–24).

This message of a powerful, yet trustworthy, God who keeps covenant commitments would have been relevant in any period of Israel's history— as, indeed, it is still relevant today. Undoubtedly it was particularly cherished by the Israelites in Babylonian exile, when the land had been lost.

---

3. See 4:9; 5:9; 6:25; 7:26 (twice); 8:28, 29; 9:27; 13:13; 14:14; 15:63; 16:10.
4. Brevard S. Childs, "A Study of the Formula, 'Until This Day,'" 292.
5. Kenneth A. Kitchen, *The Bible in Its World*, 100–101, 105–6.
6. The idea of God's "giving" the land to Israel is found more than fifty times in the book.

God's trustworthiness with respect to the land in Joshua's day—after a period of hundreds of years when Abraham's family had been absent from it—certainly would have offered hope to those in this "second exile."

HISTORICAL AND CULTURAL CONTEXT FOR THE BOOK OF JOSHUA

DATE OF THE EVENTS

There are no firm synchronisms in the book of Joshua to enable a precise dating of its events. The problem of the date of these events is bound up with that of the date of the Exodus from Egypt, which is one of the knottiest and most-discussed issues in OT chronology.[7] The biblical evidence is not entirely clear, and the archaeological evidence has been interpreted variously. In general, the biblical evidence has tended to support an early date for the Exodus, whereas the archaeological evidence has been seen as supporting a late date.

Early dating of the Exodus. On the face of it, the problem is simple enough, since two biblical data are unambiguous and point to an early date. (1) In 1 Kings 6:1, we are told that Solomon began building the Temple in the 480th year after the Exodus, which was the fourth year of his reign. This year was 966 B.C., using Thiele's chronology.[8] Thus, the Exodus would have occurred in 1446 B.C. (2) In Judges 11:26, Jephthah the judge, in speaking with his Ammonite adversaries, mentions that, for the 300 years since Israel had first settled in Transjordan, the Ammonites had not disputed Israel's claims to that territory. Jephthah came relatively late in the period of the judges, perhaps ca. 1100 B.C.; thus, this number would indicate a settlement in Transjordan ca. 1400 B.C.[9] However, other biblical data are not so clear, and the archaeological evidence has tended to point in other directions.

7. Entrée into the discussion may be obtained via the following: W. F. Albright, "Archaeology and the Date of the Hebrew Conquest of Palestine," 10–18, and "The Israelite Conquest of Canaan in the Light of Archaeology," 11–23; H. H. Rowley, *From Joseph to Joshua*; Kenneth A. Kitchen, *Ancient Orient and Old Testament*, 57–75; J. Maxwell Miller, "The Israelite Occupation of Canaan," 213–84; Charles F. Aling, *Egypt and Bible History*, 77–96; John J. Bimson, *Redating the Exodus and Conquest*; John J. Bimson and David Livingston, "Saving the Biblical Chronology," 40–53, 66–68; William H. Shea, ISBE 2, s.v. "Exodus, Date of the"; Eugene H. Merrill, *Kingdom of Priests*, 66–75; Herbert Wolf, *An Introduction to the Old Testament Pentateuch*, 141–48.

8. Edwin R. Thiele, *The Mysterious Numbers of the Hebrew Kings*, 79–81 and passim. The alternative would be ca. 956 B.C., found in D. N. Freedman and E. F. Campbell, "Chronology of Israel and the Ancient Near East," but Thiele's appears to have stood the test of new evidence better. In either case, however, 480 years prior to this time places the Exodus in the fifteenth century B.C.

9. An early date for the Exodus is defended by Bimson, Aling, Shea, and Merrill, among those in n. 7.

Late dating of the Exodus. The prime impetus for a late dating of the Exodus has come from archaeology. A fairly consistent and widespread layer of destructions has been discovered in Palestine dating to the late thirteenth and early twelfth centuries B.C., and 1200 B.C. is used as the date of convenience for the end of the Late Bronze Age and the beginning of the Early Iron Age. These destructions have been attributed to the entering Israelites, and the Exodus has been placed forty years previous to that.[10]

A *terminus a quo* for the Exodus would be ca. 1279 B.C., the beginning of the reign of the pharaoh Rameses II (ca. 1279–1213 B.C.).[11] That is because Exodus 1:11 mentions the Israelites building two store-cities for the Egyptians—Pithom and Rameses. The latter city logically would have been named for this long-lived pharaoh known for his building projects.[12]

A *terminus ad quem* for Israel's presence in the land is usually seen to have been ca. 1213 B.C., since a stele of the Egyptian pharaoh Mer-ne-Ptah from his fifth year mentions Israel as a people whom he encountered and subdued in a campaign into Canaan.[13]

In this understanding, the above biblical data are seen to have been glosses, mistakes, or round or symbolic numbers. The number 480 in 1 Kings 6:1, for example, perhaps can be seen as a symbolic number, consisting of twelve generations of forty years. If the actual life-span at that time was closer to twenty-five years, then the time span mentioned in 1 Kings 6:1 would be closer to 300 years, placing the Exodus early in the thirteenth (rather than in the fifteenth) century B.C.

Other biblical data seem to be incompatible with the number 480 (and with Jephthah's number of 300). Adding up the total of dates in Joshua, Judges, and, Samuel, for example, gives more than 470 years.[14] Added to forty wilderness years, forty years for David, and the first years of Solomon, this yields a minimum total of 553 years (plus three unknown amounts) for the 480-year period referred to in 1 Kings 6:1 (see also chapter 3 under "Date of the Events").[15] Thus, these numbers, and especially those in the book of

---

10. See the works of Albright, Rowley, and Kitchen in n. 7 for defense of this late-date view. Kitchen, for example, dates the Exodus to 1290/1260 B.C. (p. 61).
11. The Egyptian dates used here are the "low" dates laid out by K. A. Kitchen in "The Basics of Egyptian Chronology in Relation to the Bronze Age," 37–55. There is near unanimity now among Egyptologists concerning a low dating scheme, particularly after the accession of Rameses II (1279 B.C.). Previously, the date of Rameses was given as 1290–1224 B.C. (e.g., John Bright, *A History of Israel*, 468).
12. Rameses I, the founder of the Nineteenth Egyptian Dynasty (the first Ramesside dynasty), reigned less than two years (ca. 1295–1294 B.C.) and is not reckoned by scholars to have commissioned any such projects.
13. *ANET*, 376–78; *TANE*, 231; *DOTT*, 137–41. The fact that Israel is the only name in his list designated as belonging to a people, rather than to a land, is seen to suggest that Israel was not yet completely settled but was a relatively recent entrant into the land.
14. Kitchen, *NBD*, s.v. "Chronology of the Old Testament."
15. Kitchen, *Ancient Orient*, 72–73; Rowley, *From Joseph to Joshua*, 87–88.

Judges, are seen to be round or symbolic as well. Also, the chronologies in the book of Judges may have been overlapping, rather than consecutive, and thus the period easily could be telescoped into a much shorter time span.[16] (Slightly less overlapping would also allow for an early date. See below.)

Evaluation. There are good arguments for both dating schemes, as well as weaknesses in both. In general, mainstream critical scholarship has tended to favor late dating schemes, while evangelical scholars have tended to favor the early one.[17]

The view in this work favors an early date for the Exodus. This is largely because the late dating schemes have tended to arise out of interpretations of the archaeological data: since archaeology tended to show large-scale destructions at a late date, the biblical data then were adjusted to accommodate it. However, the recent defenses of an early date plausibly show how the archaeological and historical data from the fifteenth century B.C. easily fit the biblical data.[18] The two most direct pieces of evidence in the Bible concerning date—1 Kings 6:1 and Judges 11:26—both point to an early Exodus. The numbers in Judges, in this scheme, still need to be considered to have overlapped somewhat, but not nearly so drastically as under a late dating scheme.

It should be noted that scholars favoring an early date for the Exodus differ among themselves as to the exact date for it. Most accept 1446 B.C.,[19] but Bimson's important work places it earlier, ca. 1470 B.C. Thus, he accepts the number in 1 Kings 6:1 as approximately accurate, although not exactly so.[20] These differences do not materially undermine the arguments for the early date, however.[21]

Several facts concerning the archaeological data were overlooked in the early attempts at correlating them with the biblical evidence. For one, the widespread destructions in Canaan dating to ca. 1200 B.C. and the period immediately following actually represent a far greater destruction than the Bible indicates the Israelites inflicted on the land. According to the Bible, only three cities actually were burned by the Israelites: Jericho, Ai, and

16. Kitchen, *Ancient Orient,* 73–75.
17. However, evangelicals such as Kenneth Kitchen (see n. 7) and R. K. Harrison (*Introduction to the Old Testament,* 174–77 and passim) have favored the late date.
18. Especially Bimson's and Shea's but also the others, and works cited therein (see n. 9).
19. E.g., Aling, Shea (ca. 1450 B.C.), Merrill (see n. 9).
20. Bimson, *Redating the Exodus and Conquest,* 74–79.
21. Hans Goedicke has proposed an even earlier date, 1477 B.C., based on completely independent evidence—i.e., postulating that a tidal wave of that year caused by the volcanic eruption that destroyed the Minoan civilization was the cause of the Egyptian army's drowning in the Red Sea (Hershel Shanks, "The Exodus and the Crossing of the Red Sea, According to Hans Goedicke," 42–50). This proposal has not met with any general acceptance, however.

Hazor. Earlier, God had indicated that he would give Israel "large, flourishing cities you did not build, houses filled with all kinds of good things you did not provide, wells you did not dig, and vineyards and olive groves you did not plant" (Deut. 6:10–11). That would indicate that they were not to destroy the cities and towns at all but, rather, that they would be receiving these relatively unharmed.[22] Indeed, the reports in Joshua 10 and 11 about the conquest of most of the land consistently mention the annihilation of people but not of property; the account of the destruction of Hazor goes so far as to point out that Joshua did not burn the other cities on their tells (Josh. 11:13).

Second, the destructions in Canaan that once were thought to have been due to the Israelite invasion actually are now known to have been part of a far-ranging pattern of upheaval that covered much of the eastern Mediterranean area, not just Canaan.[23] Evidence for this can be seen, for example, in the migrations throughout the eastern Mediterranean seaboard of the Land and Sea Peoples.[24] Thus, there is no special compulsion for seeing Israel involved in any exceptional way in these upheavals.

Third, with a conquest of Canaan dated to ca. 1200 B.C., this leaves merely 150 years before the rise of King Saul. Granted that there may have been some flexibility and overlap in the Judges accounts and chronologies, it nevertheless appears to be too short a period to accommodate everything in that book. This is particularly so when one considers a scheme such as Mendenhall's, who places the "Yahwistic revolution" that he postulates (see below) as having occurred no earlier than 1150 B.C.[25] This leaves no more than a century for the events in Judges.

Therefore, we need not see the destructions of ca. 1200 B.C. as due to Israelite invasion; thus the primary impulse for dating the Exodus and Conquest late is removed. Also, the narrowing time frame for the period of the Judges to accommodate a late date appears too short. Thus, the early dating for the Exodus and Conquest appears more plausible than it has for quite a number of years.

22. This point is made by Bruce K. Waltke ("Palestinian Artifactual Evidence Supporting the Early Date for the Exodus," 33–47) and Eugene H. Merrill ("Palestinian Archaeology and the Date of the Conquest: Do Tells Tell Tales?" 107–21).
23. For a bibliography, see David M. Howard, Jr., "The Philistines," n. 9; see also V. R. d'A. Desborough, "The End of Mycenaean Civilization and the Dark Age," 658–77; George E. Mendenhall, "Ancient Israel's Hyphenated History," 91–103.
24. See Mendenhall, "The 'Sea Peoples' in Palestine," in *The Tenth Generation*, 142–73; R. D. Barnett, "The Sea Peoples," 359–78; N. K. Sandars, *The Sea Peoples,* 105–15, 198–201.
25. Mendenhall, "Ancient Israel's Hyphenated History," 100. Several other scholars, on various grounds, also argue for placing the conquest in the twelfth century B.C. rather than the thirteenth. (See Bright, *A History of Israel,* 133 and n. 68; Gary Rendsburg, "The Date of the Exodus and the Conquest/Settlement: The Case for the 1100s," 510–27; Howard, "The Philistines," n. 31.)

NATURE OF THE EVENTS

Three major models now exist to explain the nature of Israel's entrance into Canaan. The first sees it in terms of a traditional conquest: a large-scale, hostile Israelite invasion, resulting in major destructions of Canaanite cities and towns. The second sees it in terms of a peaceful, sedentary infiltration into the land, with the Israelites settling down among the Canaanites. The third sees it in terms of an internal upheaval, a "peasant revolt," perhaps precipitated by the entrance of a small group of outsiders (who formed the core of "Israel").[26]

1. *The conquest model.* On their face, the biblical accounts speak plainly enough of a forced conquest of the land of Canaan by the Israelites. They spied out the land, then entered it, conquered a gateway city in central Canaan (Jericho), and then proceeded to defeat several other cities in this area. They then embarked on a southern campaign and a northern campaign and effectively took control of the land.[27]

This is the traditional viewpoint, and it was not seriously questioned until the twentieth century. The archaeological evidence of destructions ca. 1200 B.C. would seem to have confirmed that these destructions did take place, and many scholarly treatments incorporated this evidence into the biblical accounts.[28]

2. *The settlement model.* In this century, an alternative model was proposed by Albrecht Alt, whereby the Israelites are seen to have been a loosely connected group of pastoral nomads from independent tribes who gradually infiltrated Canaan from the desert and settled there in a largely peaceful enterprise. Any conflicts with Canaanites were certainly not military in nature but, rather, natural, to-be-expected ones between settled farmers and incoming nomads.[29] Once in the land, for various reasons these tribes banded together into a loose federation that eventually came to be called "Israel."

26. The literature on all of these is vast. See the overviews by Norman K. Gottwald, *The Tribes of Yahweh,* 189–233; George W. Ramsey, *The Quest for the Historical Israel,* 65–98; Marvin Chaney, "Ancient Palestinian Peasant Movements and the Formation of Premonarchic Israel," 39–90.
27. A survey such as Leon Wood's (*A Survey of Israel's History,* 137–53) essentially summarizes the biblical account in this way.
28. E.g., W. F. Albright (see n. 7); John Bright, in his first edition (1959) of *A History of Israel,* 110–27; G. E. Wright, *Biblical Archaeology,* 69–85; Paul W. Lapp, "The Conquest of Palestine in the Light of Archaeology," 283–300.
29. Though first proposed by Albrecht Alt ("The Settlement of the Israelites in Palestine," 173–221), it was then accepted by many scholars, such as Martin Noth (*The History of Israel,* 53–109), Manfred Weippert (*The Settlement of the Israelite Tribes in Palestine,* and "The Israelite 'Conquest' and the Evidence from Transjordan," 15–34), and Volkmar Fritz ("Conquest or Settlement?" 84–100).

The Conquest of Canaan

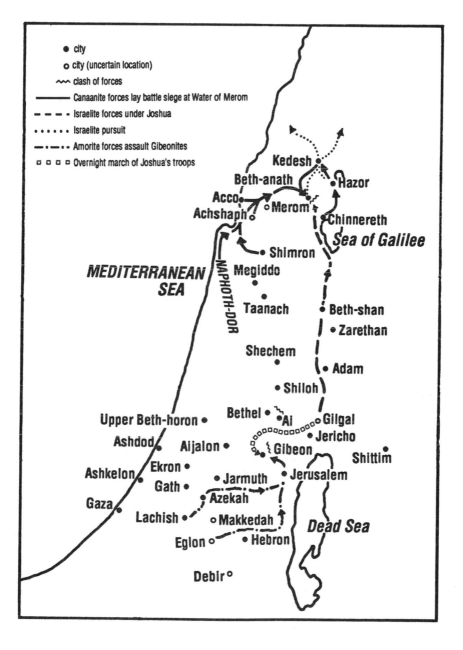

This model was based on a traditio-historical approach that exhibited a thoroughgoing skepticism concerning the accuracy of both the biblical and archaeological records. It was never accepted by those with confidence in either or both of these records, and it has been severely criticized from both directions.[30] A recent, important defense of Alt's position has been mounted by Israel Finkelstein, based upon archaeological research, but it too has its problems.[31]

3. *The revolt model.* In 1962, a third alternative was proposed by George E. Mendenhall,[32] and it has since gained significant acceptance in the field, with varying modifications. It is argued that the turmoil in Canaan visible in both the biblical and archaeological records was not due to any significant external force entering the land but, rather, to an internal peasants' revolt that toppled existing Canaanite power structures, located primarily in the large urban centers. This may very well have been precipitated by the entry into the land of a small band of worshipers of Yahweh, perhaps an escaped band of slaves from Egypt (thus is the Exodus accounted for), who provided the religious (or political-ideological) glue that melded the diverse groups in the revolt together, forming a Yahwistic tribal confederation. These groups were not descended from a common ancestor, as the Bible pictures it, but came together around this common ideology.

This model is based on various sociological approaches. Whereas it incorporates the archaeological evidence into its considerations, it dismisses much of the biblical record that does not fit the theory.[33] It self-consciously uses modern sociological and anthropological models and fits the biblical data into them.[34] Criticisms of this model have come from many directions as well.[35]

4. *Excursus: Recent sociological approaches.* In the past decade, sociological and anthropological approaches to the study of Israel's history in all

30. E.g., Chaney, "Ancient Palestinian Peasant Movements"; Merrill, *Kingdom of Priests*, 122–26.
31. Israel Finkelstein, *The Archaeology of the Israelite Settlement.* See the reviews by P. R. S. Moorey, in the *Journal of Jewish Studies* 40 (1989), 238–40; Douglas L. Esse, *BARev* 14.5 (Sept.-Oct. 1988), 6–12; J. R. Bartlett, *Biblica* 70 (1989), 290–95; M. M. Schaub, *CBQ* 52 (1990), 114–15.
32. George E. Mendenhall, "The Hebrew Conquest of Palestine," 100–120. Modifications are found in Gottwald, *The Tribes of Yahweh.* See also Mendenhall, *The Tenth Generation*; the essays in the special theme issue of *JSOT* 7 (1978); and Chaney, "Ancient Palestinian Peasant Movements."
33. Several have attempted to integrate the traditional conquest model and this revolt model. See John Bright, *A History of Israel*, 133–43; Robert G. Boling, *Joshua*, 128–32 and passim.
34. This especially is Gottwald's approach. Note that Mendenhall strenuously objects to being classified with Gottwald ("Ancient Israel's Hyphenated History," 91–103), but their two approaches are similar enough to be grouped in the same discussion, despite their differences.
35. See, e.g., the debate in several essays in *JSOT* 7 (1978), 2–52, and *JSOT* 8 (1978), 46–49; Barry J. Beitzel, "Review of Norman Gottwald, *The Tribes of Yahweh*," 237–43.

periods, but especially of the period of Israel's emergence in the land of Canaan, have burgeoned, building upon the methods adopted by those proposing the revolt model.[36] These have self-consciously adopted many different sociological and anthropological models. Most have used the biblical data alongside these models,[37] but the most radical have discarded the biblical data altogether in reconstructing Israel's early history.[38] Characteristic of all is a use of "holistic" analyses, whereby research data from widely divergent fields is gathered together into a comprehensive picture, or model, of what the historical situation was like. These fields include widespread specialties that have come under the umbrella of archaeology: comparative ethnography; physical and cultural anthropology; paleoethnobotany and zoology; sociology; agriculture; geology; hydrology; climatology; soil science; land utilization and irrigation studies; paleontology; technology; even economics; alongside biblical studies.[39] Many scholars have accepted these sociological approaches, and many speak cautiously about a "consensus" emerging.[40]

Evaluation. Both sets of alternative models to the traditional biblical model—especially the revolt model and its offshoots—have contributed to our understanding of the biblical materials in places. For example, such passages as Exodus 12:38 and Numbers 11:4—which mention a "mixed multitude" and the "rabble" that were part of Israel's company—show that the group that entered Canaan was indeed not an undifferentiated ethnic unity. Rather, it seems to have been composed of at least some marginal, lower-class groups. Here and there throughout the biblical texts can be seen traces of what could be seen as evidence that "Israel" was an outcast,

36. On sociological approaches in general, see the following: Walter Brueggemann, "Trajectories in Old Testament Literature and the Sociology of Ancient Israel," 161–85; Bruce Malina, "The Social Sciences and Biblical Interpretation," 229–42; Burke O. Long, "The Social World of Ancient Israel," 243–55; Robert R. Wilson, *Sociological Approaches to the Old Testament*; the theme issue of *Semeia* 37 (1986) entitled "Social Scientific Criticism of the Hebrew Bible and Its Social World: The Israelite Monarchy"; and Norman K. Gottwald, *ABD* 6, s.v. "Sociology of Ancient Israel."
37. E.g., Frank S. Frick, *The Formation of the State of Ancient Israel*; David Hopkins, *The Highlands of Canaan*.
38. Robert B. Coote and Keith W. Whitelam (*The Emergence of Early Israel in Historical Perspective*) explicitly reject any reliance on the biblical data, although they undercut their argument by referring to biblical characters or institutions, and even by citing the OT on occasion, in support of their reconstructions. See the review by J. M. Miller, "Is it Possible to Write a History of Israel without Relying on the Hebrew Bible?"
39. An example of this method applied to the period of the early monarchy is the extensive and important work by James Flanagan, *David's Social Drama: A Hologram of Israel's Early Iron Age*. See also the issue of *Semeia* 37 (1986).
40. See the essays in Diana Edelman, ed., "Toward a Consensus on the Emergence of Israel in Canaan," 1–116; William G. Dever, *ABD* 3, s.v. "Israel, History of (Archaeology and the 'Conquest')."

lower-class entity.[41] It certainly cannot be denied, even using the traditional model, that the Israelites would have been poorer and less well-equipped than the Canaanites, in the cosmopolitan Canaanite societies of the Late Bronze Age.[42]

However, both alternative models (and their offshoots) are, at root, profoundly skeptical of the biblical records as they now stand, and they essentially are alien models imposed on the biblical data.[43] They do not adequately account for important biblical data, and thus they ultimately fall short. We must conclude that, even given the schematic approach and selectivity of narration of the data that we find in the book of Joshua, the conquest model is the one that best understands and represents the biblical material.

That is not to say that the stereotypical model of an all-consuming Israelite army descending upon Canaan is to be accepted uncritically. The biblical data, when carefully considered, will not allow for this. Nowhere in Joshua does Israel win a battle on the basis of superior force in an all-out, frontal offensive attack. Rather, it used various means (ambush, diversionary tactics), along with God's direct help at times, to defeat its enemies.[44] Also, as noted above, it appears that Israel actually annihilated very few cities in its conquest of Canaan. Furthermore, the evidence in Judges 1 suggests that Israel's victories over Canaanite peoples was also somewhat incomplete.

Despite this, the biblical picture of an "Israel" descended from Abraham entering Canaan from without, and engaging and defeating various Canaanite forces, is eminently reasonable and defensible, and that is the model assumed here.[45]

HISTORICAL SETTING OF THE CONQUEST

Assuming a rough date ca. 1400 B.C. for the Israelite entrance into Ca-

---

41. See especially Gottwald, *The Tribes of Yahweh.*
42. The biblical text even suggests this in Numbers 13:27–29, where the Israelite spies were awed by the wealth they encountered there. See also J. A. Thompson (*The Bible and Archaeology,* 89–92, 96–98) on the disparity between Canaanite and Israelite cultures and standards of living.
43. An even more radical proposal concerning Israel's origins comes from Thomas Thompson (*Early History of the Israelite People*), who believes that there never was an entity called the "children of Israel," and that the biblical pictures concerning the Israelites arose during the Persian period (539–330 B.C.). For criticism and evaluation, see the review of Thompson by Barry Beitzel in *Trinity Journal* (forthcoming).
44. See Yigael Yadin, *The Art of Warfare in Biblical Lands,* 1:1–31, 76–114, 182–245; Abraham Malamat, "Israelite Conduct of War in the Conquest of Canaan," 35–55.
45. See also the following surveys by evangelicar scholars: Merrill, *Kingdom of Priests,* 93–128; John Bimson, "The Origins of Israel in Canaan," 4–15; Bruce Waltke, "The Date of the Conquest," 181–200.

naan would place it in the Late Bronze Age (ca. 1550–1200 B.C.).[46] The Middle Bronze Age II period (ca. 1750–1550 B.C.) was probably the peak of civilization throughout the entire ancient Near East.[47] The greatest myths and epics originated in this period,[48] pottery was at its technical peak, and the great law code of Hammurabi had just been codified.[49] Economically, this was a time of great prosperity for Canaan, which was on the trade routes between Africa and Asia.

On the international scene, there were three great power centers during the Middle Bronze Age: in Mesopotamia (under the Babylonians), in Asia Minor (under the Hittites), and in Africa (under the Egyptians). These groups constantly struggled for supremacy with each other, and the small states and regions between them were under their economic and military domination. Canaan in this period was relatively unstable, undoubtedly under the influence of the Hyksos groups that can be seen in Egypt at this time. Most of the Hyksos were Semites who came into Egypt from the north and who dominated its institutions until they were expelled ca. 1550 B.C.[50]

The Egyptian expulsion of the Hyksos usually is seen as marking the transition to the Late Bronze Age (although this is disputed by some[51]). Other than this political change, the differences between the Middle and Late Bronze Ages are relatively minor, compared, say, to those between the Bronze and Iron Ages. The Late Bronze Age continued as a period of prosperity, although it declined as the period progressed. In Canaan, the system of relatively small, independent city-states under loose foreign domination gave way to one of large empires (e.g., Egyptian, Hittite) that maintained tighter control over these city-states. The land that Israel occupied was dominated in the coastal areas and low-lying hills by Egypt and by its vassals in

46. Under Bimson's scheme, the Middle Bronze Age came to an end more than a century later than is commonly accepted—ca. 1430–1400 B.C. (see his convenient chart on p. 222)—and the Conquest would have been roughly during this time. Despite the basic sympathy here for Bimson's scheme, the descriptions below will proceed along the generally accepted dating for the periods, since it is not yet clear how the history should be understood if his scheme indeed is accurate.
47. The most thorough summary of the period may be found in the essays of *The Middle East and the Aegean Region* c. 1800–1380 B.C., vol. 2, pt. 1 of *Cambridge Ancient History.* A convenient short summary of the period immediately preceding and following Israel's entry into the land may be found in Merrill, *Kingdom of Priests,* 94–108.
48. Convenient translations of the great Ugaritic myths about Baal and the other gods may be found in *ANET,* 129–55; *TANE,* 92–132; *DOTT,* 118–33; G. R. Driver, *Canaanite Myths and Legends*; Cyrus H. Gordon, "Poetic Legends and Myths From Ugarit," 5–133; and Michael David Coogan, *Stories From Ancient Canaan.*
49. Ca. 1792–1750 B.C., using the "middle chronology" proposed by several scholars (see Harrison, *Introduction to the Old Testament,* 159–66). See the translation of this law code in *ANET,* 163–80; *TANE,* 138–67; *DOTT,* 27–37.
50. See W. W. Hallo and W. K. Simpson, *ANEH,* 250–60; William C. Hayes, "Egypt: From the Death of Ammenemes III to Seqenenre II," 54–73.
51. Bimson, *Redating the Exodus and the Conquest,* 124–32 and passim.

the hill country. The interdependence throughout the region is illustrated by the fact that at Ugarit, in the far north, there have been at least five different writing systems and eight different languages found among the texts discovered there.[52]

At the time of Israel's entry into Canaan, the two kingdoms to the north—the Hittite empire, under Shuppiluliumash, and the smaller Mitannian empire, under Tushratta—were engaged in struggles for control of the north.[53] The Hittites prevailed, but they did not push their territorial claims southward into Egyptian territory; rather, a fragile but peaceful balance of power prevailed. Egypt, under Amenophis III (ca. 1390–1352 [or 1382–1344] B.C.) and his son, the reformer king Amenophis IV (Akhenaten, ca. 1352–1336 B.C.), was not much interested in military affairs.[54] Thus, a relative power vacuum existed in southern Canaan[55] that Israel was able to exploit.

Ugarit. The ancient city of Ugarit, on the northeast Mediterranean coast, was just entering its golden age when Israel entered Canaan far to the south. It was a city-state that had existed for centuries but whose existence climaxed in the period from 1400–1200 B.C. It sat astride significant trade routes, and its commercial influence was widespread. Its special significance for biblical studies lies in the ca. 1400 (Late Bronze Age) texts that have been unearthed at its site (modern Ras Shamra) since its discovery in 1929. These tablets give a vivid picture of life in the land that Israel entered under Joshua and lived in during the period of the judges. We can see a flourishing internationalism, and we are given thorough insights into Canaanite religion and culture. The long mythological texts about the Canaanite gods have shed light on the challenge that faced Israel in keeping its worship pure (see "Purity of Worship [Holiness]" below); they have also shed much light on our understanding of the Hebrew language and its poetry.[56] The city's and its texts' direct relevance to the book of Joshua are relatively minor, however.[57]

The Amarna Letters. Israel entered Canaan just before a period of considerable social and political unrest there, which is attested by a series of

52. Peter C. Craigie, *Ugarit and the Old Testament,* 22.
53. A. Goetze, "The Struggle for the Domination of Syria (1400–1300 B.C.)," 1–20.
54. William C. Hayes, "Egypt: Internal Affairs From Thutmosis I to the Death of Amenophis III," 338–46; Cyril Aldred, "Egypt: The Amarna Period and the End of the Eighteenth Dynasty," 49–63.
55. Kathleen M. Kenyon, "Palestine in the Time of the Eighteenth Dynasty," 526–56.
56. Entrée into the vast literature on Ugarit may be had via Adrian Curtis, *Ugarit (Ras Shamra)*; Margaret S. Drower, "Ugarit," 130–60; Craigie, *Ugarit and the Old Testament*; M. Liverani, *ISBE* 4, s.v. "Ugarit, Ugaritic." Translations of the texts are mentioned in n. 48 above.
57. But see n. 98 on Canaanite religion. See also chapter 3 for more on Canaanite religion and culture in the Late Bronze Age. The Ugaritic texts shed much light on the religion that confronted Israel during that and subsequent periods.

more than 350 documents (mostly letters) uncovered at Tell el-Amarna in middle Egypt beginning in 1887 and by a few discovered in Palestine.[58] These letters are now dated to the middle of the fourteenth century B.C. They are primarily correspondence from the petty kinglets in Canaan appealing (in a rather shrill manner) to their Egyptian overlords—Amenophis III and IV—for assistance against rivals and threats from the general populace, and they portray fairly chaotic conditions throughout Canaan.

The Hapiru. In the Amarna letters, groups of persons called "Hapiru"[59] are mentioned regularly as a source of trouble for the kinglets. Because of the similarities between this word and the biblical word "Hebrew" (*'ibrî*), and because of the close correspondence in dates between the biblical chronology and the Amarna letters, the Hapiru were initially assumed to be the invading Hebrews of the biblical accounts.

However, it has been shown that the Hapiru in Canaan were not an external, invading ethnic force but, rather, a disparate band of internal groups linked by political and social realities, not ethnic ties. They were a marginal group, consisting of disenfranchised persons who became disaffected with the power systems in Canaan; "outlaw" is an English word that approximates their status. They withdrew from everyday life in Canaan and eventually turned against the power structures, causing the turmoil seen in the Amarna letters. People and towns could *become* Hapiru; the term was used pejoratively in almost all its references. Furthermore, references to these groups have been found in far-ranging areas, outside Canaan, and from late in the third millennium B.C., not just the Amarna period.[60]

Study of the Hapiru has been a major element in the formulation of the "revolt" model of the "conquest" discussed above. The assumption has been that the biblical Hebrews (and thus the biblical Israelites) and Amarna Hapiru were the same people, and the biblical picture thus has been radically revised to fit the Amarna data. The "invasion" by an external, ethnically related force is seen instead as an internal revolt by marginalized groups who eventually created a fictional ancestry (i.e., that which is found in the Bible) to link them together.

58. See Edward F. Campbell, Jr., "The Amarna Letters and the Amarna Period," 54–75; Margaret S. Drower, "The Amarna Age," 483–93; William F. Albright, "The Amarna Letters From Palestine," 98–116; Ronald F. Youngblood, *ISBE* 1, s.v. "Amarna Tablets"; Nadab Na'aman, *ABD* 1, s.v. "Amarna Letters."
59. These people are also known as *'apiru* and *Habiru.* See the works in n. 60 for these and other terms used to refer to these peoples.
60. See Moshe Greenberg, *The Hab/piru*; and "Hab/piru and Hebrews," 188–200; Mendenhall, "The Hebrew Conquest of Palestine"; and *The Tenth Generation,* 122–41; H. Cazelles, "The Hebrews," 1–28; Gottwald, *The Tribes of Yahweh,* 401–9 and passim; B. J. Beitzel, *ISBE* 2, s.v. "Habiru."

However, this equation has been challenged on two grounds. First, there is serious question as to whether the two terms (*'apiru* and *'ibrî*) truly are related to each other etymologically.[61] It would appear that this equation was made originally at least partly because the date of the Amarna Hapiru fit the prevailing late date of the Israelite Conquest, and it has survived among those who question the early dating. However, those making the equation do not focus as much attention on the Hapiru outside Canaan in other periods as they do on the Amarna Hapiru.

A second challenge is independent of the etymological argument: that one cannot equate the biblical terms "Hebrew" and "Israelite" in too facile a manner. It should be noted, for example, that in the Bible the term "Hebrew" is mainly found on the lips of foreigners.[62] Thus, it is entirely conceivable that non-Israelites used the term in describing the Israelites but that the Israelites did not normally call themselves that.[63] Certainly an equation between the terms "Hebrew" and "Hapiru" could have been made in some people's minds (i.e., as a popular etymology), even if linguistically there was no actual etymological connection.

We should note, further, that acceptance of the equation of Hapiru = Hebrew and a redefinition of the biblical Hebrews as marginal "outlaws," seeing them as related only socially, legally, or religiously, discounts the clear and unanimous biblical picture of them as also—if not primarily—related ethnically to each other.[64]

It does not seem appropriate, then, to equate the Amarna Hapiru with the biblical Israelites in too firm a way. It certainly is conceivable that some among the Israelite tribes became "Hapiru" after they encountered them in Canaan[65] or that they were perceived as such by the Canaanites,[66] but to see the Israelites (or even Hebrews) merely as identical with the Hapiru stretches the evidence too far.

The significance of the above, however, indicates that Israel entered a Canaan that was beginning to destabilize due to the Hapiru problem. This destabilization led to a gradual decline in Late Bronze Age culture and institutions until they collapsed ca. 1200 B.C.

---

61. Greenberg, *The Hab/piru,* 90–96; Manfred Weippert, *The Settlement of the Israelite Tribes in Palestine,* 63–102; Beitzel, *ISBE* 2, s.vv. "Habiru" and "Hebrew (People)."
62. E.g., in Genesis 39:14, 17; Exodus 2:6; 1 Samuel 4:6, 9. See, briefly, Cazelles, "The Hebrews," 1–3.
63. This may have been due to its pejorative associations in the popular mind, but it certainly need not have been; it could have been because the terms were indeed understood differently (see Beitzel, *ISBE* 2, s.v. "Hebrew [People]").
64. See Beitzel, "Hapiru," *ISBE* 2, 589–90, and "Hebrew (People)," for these and other objections to equating the Amarna Hapiru and the biblical Hebrews.
65. See, e.g., Bimson, *Redating the Exodus and the Conquest,* 224–30, esp. pp. 228–29.
66. Merrill, *Kingdom of Priests,* 100–108.

THE PLACE OF JOSHUA IN THE CANON

JOSHUA AND THE PENTATEUCH

The book of Joshua forms the logical conclusion of much that is found in the Pentateuch. In particular, it has much in common with the book of Deuteronomy. They each chronicle events at a pivotal time in Israel's history, they each focus on a great leader's words and actions, and they are logically connected with each other. The one anticipates the other, and the other picks up where the first left off. To understand the book of Joshua, then, one must know something about Deuteronomy.

The book of Deuteronomy claims to be the words Moses spoke at the end of his life to the generation of Israel that was poised to enter the Promised Land. As such, it is the last of the "Books of Moses." Several times Moses' speaking to the people is mentioned: 1:1, 5; 4:44–45; 5:1; 27:1; 29:2 [MT 1]; 31:1, 30; 33:1. He is also depicted as writing: 31:9, 22, 24.[67]

The book looks back to the Sinai and wilderness experiences, and it uses these as the basis for exhortation about the future. It looks ahead to life in the Promised Land and speaks of centralization of worship (chap. 12) and many other concerns. It is in a real sense a "second law" (which is what its title means), since much of it is devoted to recapitulating and expanding upon the law that had been given earlier (chaps. 12–26).

Mainstream critical views of Deuteronomy. Critical scholarship, in the last two centuries, has taken a very different view of the book's provenance and purpose. To generalize, it is seen as a product of the seventh century B.C., dating from—or just prior to—the time of Josiah (2 Kings 22–23). It was the "Book of the Law" that was discovered in the Temple during the repairs commissioned by Josiah, and it formed the basis for the further reforms he instituted. It is usually seen as a "pious fraud" ascribed to Moses by its seventh-century author(s) in order to give it the maximum authority. It was written, then, in order to stimulate religious reform in the wake of the apostasy of the time of Manasseh and Amon (2 Kings 21).[68]

This view of Deuteronomy is part and parcel of what has come to be known as the "documentary hypothesis" of the sources of the books of Genesis–Deuteronomy. In brief, four major, independent literary sources for the present Pentateuch are postulated, sources that came together over time,

---

67. Other Pentateuchal references to Moses' writing include Exodus 17:14; 24:4; 34:27–28; Numbers 33:2.

68. See the reviews of work on Deuteronomy in Otto Eissfeldt, *The Old Testament: An Introduction*, 171–76, 219–33; Harrison, *Introduction to the Old Testament*, 637–53; Brevard S. Childs, *IOTS*, 204–10; Moshe Weinfeld, *ABD* 2, s.v. "Deuteronomy, Book of."

woven together as strands that make up the present narrative.[69] Most of Deuteronomy is seen as a discrete unit, coming from the time of Josiah.

Deuteronomy, Joshua, and the "Hexateuch." Because of the obvious continuities in thought, subject matter, and style between Joshua and Deuteronomy, Joshua has been seen as the logical conclusion of the Pentateuch, and the idea of a "Hexateuch" (i.e., a literary unit composed of six books: Genesis–Joshua) has been given credence.[70] At root was the thought that the Pentateuch was incomplete, that it "remains a torso,"[71] without the fulfillment of the land promises that is found in Joshua. Fundamental to this idea is the assumption that the documentary strands found in the Pentateuch can also be found in the book of Joshua. Accordingly, many scholars indebted to this hypothesis have focused on identifying these strands in Joshua.[72]

An obvious strength of this idea is that it is based on an undisputed fact: the Pentateuch does end somewhat inconclusively. David Clines speaks of the "partial fulfillment—which implies also the partial non-fulfillment—of the promise to or blessing of the patriarchs."[73] It is obvious to the reader at the end of Deuteronomy that there is more to come.

On the other hand, there are several problems with the hypothesis of a "Hexateuch." First, despite the fact that Deuteronomy does not end with the patriarchal promises fulfilled, it does end at a very logical place, namely, at the death of Moses, the major character of four of the five books of the Pentateuch. Taken on its own terms, it represents Moses' last words, given to a people poised to enter the land. Life in the land begins in the next book and continues in that land through the rest of Israel's history.

A second problem with the "Hexateuch" hypothesis lies in its severing of the many obvious ties that Joshua (and Deuteronomy) has with the material following it (see "Joshua and the Present Canon" below). The book of Judges is a strange place for another large, independent work to have begun.[74]

A third problem concerns the documentary hypothesis itself. On the one level, there is little agreement about the various "sources" themselves,

---

69. See Eissfeldt, *The Old Testament: An Introduction,* 158–212. Evangelical analyses include Harrison, *Introduction to the Old Testament,* 495–541; E. E. Carpenter, *ISBE* 3, s.v. "Pentateuch"; Herbert M. Wolf, *An Introduction to the Old Testament Pentateuch,* 62–71; Duane Garrett, *Rethinking Genesis,* 13–33.
70. See the classical formulations of this in S. R. Driver, *Introduction to the Literature of the Old Testament,* 1–159; Gerhard von Rad, "The Form-Critical Problem of the Hexateuch," 1–78.
71. Childs, *IOTS,* 231.
72. E.g., W. H. Bennett, *Joshua: A New English Translation*; Eissfeldt, *The Old Testament,* 241–48, 250–57; Georg Fohrer, *Introduction to the Old Testament,* 192–205.
73. D. J. A. Clines, *The Theme of the Pentateuch,* 29.
74. See also David Noel Freedman, *IDB* 2, s.v. "Hexateuch"; Childs, *IOTS,* 231.

both within the Pentateuch itself or within Joshua. On a more fundamental level, there is not even agreement about the existence of *any* such "sources," ones that are intertwined strands of material. Conservative Christian scholars have questioned this hypothesis from the beginning,[75] and they have been joined over the years by others.[76] Currently, the entire hypothesis is being radically reworked among mainstream critical scholars, and even widely rejected or ignored.[77]

JOSHUA AND THE "DEUTERONOMISTIC HISTORY"[78]

An alternative hypothesis that has implications for the book of Joshua (and the books following it) was given its classical formulation in 1943 by Martin Noth.[79] Noth saw a literary unity beginning with Deuteronomy and stretching through 2 Kings that he called the "Deuteronomistic History." Noth contended that this was the work of a single theologian, the "Deuteronomist," who wrote after the fall of Jerusalem and who sought to explain the events of 723/22 and 586 B.C. (the falls of Samaria and Jerusalem). He saw this work as attempting to demonstrate that these events were the direct consequence of Israel's unrepentant following after other gods and her failure to obey God. As such, it had an essentially negative purpose.[80]

Basic themes in the "Deuteronomistic History" are (1) the graciousness of Yahweh's covenant, (2) the evils of idolatry and a decentralized cult, and (3) the inevitability of reward and punishment, according to obedience or disobedience.[81] A primary emphasis here is in the keeping of the Mosaic Covenant (although the Abrahamic and Davidic covenants do figure as well).[82]

---

75. See, e.g., William Henry Green, *The Unity of the Book of Genesis*; and *The Higher Criticism of the Pentateuch*; Oswald T. Allis, *The Five Books of Moses*; Harrison, *Introduction to the Old Testament*; Gleason F. Archer, Jr., *A Survey of Old Testament Introduction.*
76. See Cyrus H. Gordon, "Higher Critics and Forbidden Fruit," 131–34; U. Cassuto, *The Documentary Hypothesis*; M. H. Segal, *The Pentateuch—Its Composition and Authorship—and Other Biblical Studies.*
77. See, e.g., Robert Alter, *The Art of Biblical Narrative*; Isaac M. Kikawada and Arthur Quinn, *Before Abraham Was: The Unity of Genesis 1–11*; Y. T. Radday and H. Shore, *Genesis: An Authorship Study*; Gary A. Rendsburg, "Two Book Reviews," 554–57.
78. For fuller discussion of the "Deuteronomistic History," see chapter 6.
79. M. Noth, *The Deuteronomistic History.*
80. Recent reviews of work on the Deuteronomistic History may be found in Gerald Gerbrandt, *Kingship According to the Deuteronomistic History*, 1–18; Steven L. McKenzie, *The Trouble With Kings: The Composition of the Book of Kings in the Deuteronomistic History*, 1–19; and *ABD* 2, s.v. "Deuteronomistic History."
81. The first and third points here conflict somewhat; both patterns can be seen, however. See Polzin, *Moses and the Deuteronomist*, 144–45 and passim on this.
82. See David M. Howard, Jr. ("The Case for Kingship in Deuteronomy and the Former Prophets," 113–14), on the merging of these divergent covenants in the "Deuteronomistic History."

There are some obvious strengths to this approach. First, there *is* a strong "Deuteronomistic" influence found throughout Joshua–2 Kings, one that is not nearly so visible in Genesis–Numbers.[83] Second, the theory of consecutive, discrete blocks of literary materials joined together at various "seams" (as Noth envisioned in the case of the Deuteronomistic History) is easier to countenance than the "documentary" theory of various intertwined strands coming together. Third, on the whole, there is more of a unity, both in content and in outlook, to Deuteronomy–2 Kings than there is to Genesis– Joshua.

However, there are some deficiencies as well. First, this approach does not take seriously the biblical witnesses to Deuteronomy's provenance at a far earlier period in Israel's history than the time of Josiah or the Exile.[84] Second, the removal of Deuteronomy from Genesis–Numbers leaves that corpus as a torso; the resulting "Tetrateuch" is most unsatisfactory as a literary unit. Third, Noth's essentially negative understanding of the Deuteronomist's purpose has not been generally accepted: "It is hard to imagine a negative cause as sufficient reason to compose and preserve the tradition."[85]

JOSHUA AND THE PRESENT CANON

The present order of books from Genesis to Esther in the Protestant canon, and from Genesis to 2 Kings in the Hebrew canon, is basically chronological with reference to the events in them. In the former, the first five books generally are known as the "books of Moses," the "Pentateuch," or the "Law." In the Jewish traditions, the five Mosaic books form the "Torah," and the narrative books from Joshua to 2 Kings are part of a larger corpus entitled the "Prophets." Within this division are the "Former Prophets" (Joshua to 2 Kings) and the "Latter Prophets" (Isaiah, Jeremiah, Ezekiel, and the "Twelve"). References to the "Prophets" as a canonical division are found very early, in the Prologue to the book of Ecclesiasticus (Sirach; ca. 180 B.C.), Josephus, and the NT.[86] The Bible itself refers to the "former

---

83. Thus, there can be some value in speaking of a "Deuteronomistic" philosophy of history (i.e., one in which there is a strong—and almost always immediate—correlation between obedience and reward, disobedience and punishment) or a "Deuteronomistic" history (i.e., a corpus of books that reflects the same viewpoints that are found in Deuteronomy). The term thus can be used adjectivally, with no conclusions concerning authorship or date of Deuteronomy implicit in its use. This is the understanding of the term when it is employed in the present work.

84. See Gordon Wenham, "The Date of Deuteronomy," Part One: 15–20; Part Two: 15–18.

85. Childs, *IOTS,* 237. See further the discussion in chapter 6.

86. Josephus, *Against Apion* 1.7–8. Matthew 5:17; 7:12; 11:13; 22:40; Luke 16:16, 29, 31; 24:27; 24:44; John 1:45; Acts 13:15; 24:14; 26:22; 28:23; Romans 3:21. Each of these cases refers to two of the three canonical divisions: "the Law and the Prophets" or to "Moses and the Prophets"; Luke 24:44 refers to all three divisions: "the Law of Moses, the Prophets and the Psalms."

prophets" (Zech. 1:4; 7:7), but these would seem to be references to the classical prophets in the tradition of Elijah, Amos, or Jeremiah, and not to a canonical corpus. The earliest extant reference to the "Former Prophets" as a canonical division comes from the Middle Ages.[87]

In many ways, both Deuteronomy and Joshua act as fulcrums between the material preceding and following. With reference to Deuteronomy, the first part of the book (chaps. 1–11) is Moses' personalized review of the past, along with his exhortations and warnings about the future. The core of the book (chaps. 12–26) is a restatement—with many additions—of the law given earlier; the changes and additions reflect a concern for life in the land, which Israel is about to begin. Childs has noted the importance in this connection of von Rad's idea of "actualization" in Deuteronomy, whereby each generation appropriates and enters into the covenant for itself.[88] The best examples of this are in Deuteronomy 5:2–3 and especially 29:14–15 [MT 13–14], but it occurs throughout the book. That is, the book is more than merely a historical review for one generation; it applies the Sinai experiences and law to all succeeding generations as well (cf., e.g., Deut. 4:25–31; 6:7, 20–25).

Similarly, Joshua builds upon the Pentateuch, most notably with respect to the fulfillment of the land promises, but also with respect to the continued story line involving people such as Joshua himself, who earlier had been introduced. At the end of the book, Joshua and the people renew the covenant. This has a backward- as well as a forward-looking component to it. Also, the book as a whole looks ahead to settled life in the land.

Despite all of this, the testimony throughout both Protestant and Hebrew canons is unanimous and unambiguous in seeing a major canonical break between Deuteronomy and Joshua.[89] Both of the above theories—of a "Hexateuch" and a "Deuteronomistic History"—have cogently made valid observations about the flow of thought across the boundary between Deuteronomy and Joshua. However, they are modern critical constructs, and they both cut across the present canonical division, thus ignoring some important features that are clearly present in the biblical text.

One such feature is Joshua's position at the head of the prophets, which must be taken seriously. The prophets carried God's words to the people. Whereas the "Former Prophets" are "historical" books in the main, they are "prophetic" in that they are God's words, and they "bear testi-

---

87. Childs, *IOTS*, 230.
88. Ibid., 214–15, 222.
89. In the Syriac version, Job is placed between Deuteronomy and Joshua, on the theory that Job was written by Moses, and in some early Christian traditions mention is made of a "Heptateuch" and even an "Octateuch" (Harrison, *Introduction to the Old Testament*, 665). However, these did not survive as mainstream traditions, and they never were part of the Jewish traditions.

mony to the working out of the prophetic word in the life of the nation."[90] It is interesting to note the wholesale incorporation of historical material in the books of the prophets, which softens the distinction between the two types of material (cf., e.g., Isaiah 36–39 // 2 Kings 18–20; Jer. 40:7–9 // 2 Kings 25:23–26; Jer. 50:31–34 // 2 Kings 25:27–30; Jer. 52:1–27, 31–34 // 2 Kings 24:18–25:21, 27–30).[91]

A second feature is Joshua's position at the head of the books whose history is played out in the Promised Land. In Joshua the capture of the land is recounted, and in 2 Kings the loss of the land is related. All the history in between takes place in this land that God gave to Israel. The book of Joshua, then, plays an important role in introducing us to this land.

Third, Joshua the man is very different from Moses. Joshua is Moses' successor as leader of the nation (Joshua 1), yet he does not occupy the same office as Moses. He is not called a prophet as Moses is (Deut. 34:10). Moses is the "servant of the Lord," whereas Joshua is merely "Moses' aide" (Josh. 1:1). Joshua is not the recipient of the law as Moses was, but rather only its guardian; Moses was the great law-giver, whose role is not duplicated in Israel's history.

Fourth, Joshua is the first in the line of leadership that received its full expression in the kings of Israel and Judah. Joshua was not a king, yet several facts about him show that elements of his leadership were forerunners to the leadership the kings were to exercise. For example, the emphasis in Joshua 1:1–9 on his keeping the law, the fact that he was responsible for Israel's entering and keeping the land, and the very fact that there is a narrative devoted to his entering his office,[92] all place him in this line of leadership, since all of these are characteristic of the kings.[93]

Finally, despite its own status as a prophetic word, indeed, the very Word of God, the book of Joshua also recognizes the existence of an earlier, authoritative, written Word of God: the Book of the Law (e.g., Josh. 1:8; 4:10; 8:31, 32, 35). The words of God that Moses wrote down and deposited in the ark (Deut. 31:24) have an authoritative function as written Scripture in Joshua. This idea certainly is not as visible with respect to what Joshua himself said. The Pentateuch as a whole forms an authoritative basis for the book of Joshua; indeed, it does so throughout the rest of the OT.[94]

90. Childs, *IOTS*, 236.
91. Ibid.
92. In contrast to the absence of such in the accounts of the pre-kingship charismatic judges.
93. See Gerald Gerbrandt, *Kingship According to the Deuteronomistic History*, 116–23.
94. See Childs (*IOTS*, 223–24, 233) for more on this point.

SPECIAL ISSUES IN THE BOOK OF JOSHUA

THE DESTRUCTION OF THE CANAANITES[95]

One problem many people have with the book of Joshua is the apparent bloodthirstiness displayed by the Israelites and the God who demanded these annihilations. (See especially 6:21; 8:22; 10:26, 28, 30, 32, 33, 35, 37, 39, 40; 11:8, 10–14.) God had informed Moses that Israel was to carry out this complete destruction in Canaan (Deut. 7:2; 20:16–17; Josh. 11:15, 20), and Moses had so instructed Joshua (11:12, 15; cf. 10:40). God spoke to Joshua directly about this as well (6:17, with reference to Jericho). Thus, the question arises concerning God's basic justice: How can a holy, just, and loving God command such barbarities? The Bible gives two reasons for this destruction.

The first is the requirement of purity of Israel's worship (discussed below under "Purity of Worship [Holiness]"). The second is that it was due to the Canaanites' sin. Concerning sin, we should first note that, from God's perspective, *all* peoples have sinned and fallen short of His standards (Rom. 3:23) and thus are deserving of the severest punishment (Rom. 6:23). On this level, the Canaanites only received what all peoples deserved, and any peoples who were spared were so spared only by God's grace.

Though this is completely true, and thus it could legitimately stand as the complete answer to the question, it is somewhat incomplete, since it is clear that God did not choose to annihilate other peoples in biblical times (or since) who also were sinful. What was distinctive about the Canaanite situation that triggered the unprecedented injunctions to destroy everyone and everything?

A preview of the Canaanites' sin is presented to Abraham, where he is told that the fulfillment of the promise to him would be delayed, in part because "the sin of the Amorites is not yet complete" (Gen. 15:16). That is, the return of Abraham's descendants finally to inherit the land would have as part of its mission the punishing of the Canaanites[96] for their sin. For many years, the Canaanites' sins apparently would not justify the annihilation that would come when the Israelites took the land. However, that time *would* arrive, and we see that it did arrive by the time of Joshua.

The sins of the Canaanites appear in several places. In Leviticus 18:24–30, Israel is solemnly warned to abstain from the many abominations that the Canaanites had practiced (see also v. 3). The context suggests that

---

95. Other treatments of this problem may be found in William Brenton Green, "The Ethics of the Old Testament," 206–35, esp. pp. 213–16; and Kaiser, *Toward Old Testament Ethics*, 67–72, 266–69.
96. The term "Amorite" in Genesis 15:16 is synonymous with "Canaanite" here.

the entire list of sins in 18:6–23 falls under the sins the Canaanites practiced. These include engaging in incest, adultery, child sacrifice, homosexuality, and bestiality. Furthermore, in Deuteronomy 9:4–5, "the wickedness of the nations [in the land of Canaan]" is given as a major reason why the Lord would drive them out before Israel. Also, the promise to Abraham included the provision that God would curse anyone who cursed Israel (Gen. 12:3), and we specifically see the Canaanites seeking to destroy Israel on at least two occasions (Josh. 9:1–2; 11:1–5).[97]

By most cultures' standards, these sins are particularly heinous. The evidence outside the Bible confirms the biblical picture of an extremely wicked society. Archaeological excavation has shown that the practice of child sacrifice was especially the province of the Canaanites and their descendants who migrated westward to Carthage. Furthermore, texts and artifacts of the cults of the Baals, spoken of frequently in the Bible, have been discovered in the soil of Syria, Lebanon, and Israel. Among the common cultic practices was ritual prostitution.[98]

The instructions to Israel to annihilate the Canaanites were specific in time, intent, and geography. That is, it was not a blanket permission to do the same to any peoples they encountered, at any time or in any place. It was limited to the crucial time when Israel was just establishing itself as a theocracy under God, to protect Israel's worship as well as to punish these specific peoples. Thus, harsh as it may seem to our sensibilities, we should remember that it was for very clearly stated reasons, and it was very carefully circumscribed.[99]

RAHAB'S LIE

Another problem that some people raise concerning morality in the book of Joshua deals with the lie that Rahab told the men pursuing the Israelite spies (Josh. 2:4–5). Some would not call it such, arguing that this is a permissible act of deception in warfare.[100] Some would argue that "truth" in

---

97. We should be very clear that Israel was not inheriting Canaan because of any inherent merit. Deuteronomy 9:5 states, "It is not because of your righteousness or your integrity that you are going in to take possession of their land; but on account of the wickedness of these nations."
98. Good introductions to the religion of the Canaanites may be found in Donald Harden, *The Phoenicians*, 82–114; John Gray, *The Canaanites*, 119–38; and *The Legacy of Canaan*; William F. Albright, *Yahweh and the Gods of Canaan*, 110–52; Sabatino Moscati, *The World of the Phoenicians*, 30–41, 136–44; Helmer Ringgren, *Religions of the Ancient Near East*, 127–54.
99. We also see that God commanded Saul to annihilate the Amalekites (an order he did not carry out—1 Samuel 15) and Ahab to do the same to Ben-hadad (1 Kings 20:42), but these again were circumscribed and limited orders. (See W. C. Kaiser, Jr. [*Hard Sayings of the Old Testament*, 106–9], on the Amalekite situation.)
100. See, e.g., Louis B. Smedes, *Mere Morality*, 232–33.

Israel meant something different from "agreement with fact"; rather, it meant "loyalty toward the neighbor and the Lord," and thus Rahab did not truly lie.[101]

Others stress that the text does not comment one way or the other on the morality here and that the seriousness of the sin of lying (Lev. 19:11; Prov. 12:22; cf. Eph. 4:25) still stands.[102] The ends do not justify the means. (See, e.g., Rom. 3:8, where Paul condemns the attitude: "Let us not do evil that good may result.") NT commendations of Rahab are for her *faith*, as expressed in her help for the spies, not for her lying per se:

> By faith the prostitute Rahab, because she welcomed the spies, was not killed with those who were disobedient. (Heb. 11:31)

> Was not even Rahab the prostitute considered righteous for what she did when she gave lodging to the spies and sent them off in a different direction? (James 2:25)

In particular, the James passage seems fairly explicit. It mentions two actions: (1) giving lodging, and (2) sending the spies out by a safer route. It does not mention her lying, or even her "protection" of the men accomplished by the lie. It very well may be that the deception was omitted in James deliberately (to avoid the appearance of condoning it), since the passage is fairly explicit otherwise. (But this is an argument from silence and cannot be pressed too far.)

The judgment here is that the prohibitions against lying are paramount and that Rahab ultimately cannot be excused for her deception. (One prohibition in effect when she lived is found in Lev. 19:11.) However, she cannot be judged too harshly either, because her motivations certainly were right. For one, she did exhibit a true and active faith in Israel's God. Second, apparently she did not have the full revelation of the Mosaic Law that the Israelites had. Third, it is much easier to judge an action in the cool light of hindsight than to make a crisis decision in the heat of the moment. The biblical judgment is that her faith and related actions were more important ultimately than this one ethical lapse.

101. For example, Woudstra (*The Book of Joshua*, 71 n. 14) mentions B. Holwerda in this regard.
102. E.g., C. F. Keil, *The Book of Joshua*, 34–35 and n. 1; W. C. Kaiser, Jr., *Toward Old Testament Ethics*, 271–73 and references there; Archer, *Encyclopedia of Bible Difficulties*, 155–56; C. J. Goslinga, *Joshua, Judges, Ruth*, 44–45. Various scenarios are proposed as to what might have happened had she not lied but instead told the truth or remained silent. (Some are more plausible than others.)

ETIOLOGY IN JOSHUA

In Joshua, we see several occasions in which the name of a place is explained in terms of events that transpired there. For example, the place where the Israelites were circumcised was called Gibeath-haaraloth, which means "Hill of Foreskins" (Josh. 5:3). It was also called "Gilgal" (5:9), a wordplay on the reproach of Egypt's being rolled away (since Hebrew *gālal* means "to roll").

Such explanations of place names belong to a class of stories called "etiologies." This term is derived from the Greek word *aitiologia* (consisting of *aitia* ["cause"] + *logia* ["description"]), and it means the assignment of a cause, origin, or reason for something; it is used in biblical studies to describe those stories that explain how an existing name, custom, or institution came into being. The pages of Joshua contain several such examples.[103]

Many scholars have seen any sign of an etiology in the Bible as a signal that this explanation is fanciful, that the need to explain a place name gave rise to various stories that would do this. The assumption is that the explanations given are historically false but that they reveal the folk traditions that gave rise to them.

This skepticism about the historicity behind etiologies has drawn much criticism, and recent work is much more moderate in understanding them.[104] There is no inherent reason why such stories could not, in fact, be true. Thus, many scholars recognize that certain stories were not invented to give an etiological explanation, and it is even conceded by some that the biblical text may indeed preserve the actual reasons for certain names or customs. That is the assumption in the present work. In some cases, the etiology may be mentioned because it highlights a play on words that is relevant or illustrative; that is certainly the case with the name "Gilgal" in Joshua 5.

JERICHO AND THE ARCHAEOLOGICAL RECORD

Archaeologically, Jericho is known very well; it was one of the oldest cities in the world, having been occupied since the eighth millennium B.C.[105] However, it does not appear to have been occupied during the latter part of

---

103. See, e.g., the stories explaining the heap of stones near the Jordan River (chap. 4); the name "Achor" (7:26); the name "Ai" (which means "ruin"; 8:28); and the social status of the Gibeonites (chap. 9).
104. See John Bright, *Ancient Israel in Recent History Writing*, 91–110; Burke O. Long, *The Problem of Etiological Narrative in the Old Testament*; B. S. Childs, "The Etiological Tale Re-examined," 385–97; J. F. Priest, *IDBSup*, s.v. "Etiology"; Trent Butler, *Joshua*, xxx–xxxiii.
105. See R. A. Coughenour, *ISBE* 2, s.v. "Jericho"; John R. Bartlett, *Cities of the Ancient World: Jericho*; T. A. Holland and E. Netzer, *ABD* 3, s.v. "Jericho."

the Late Bronze Age (ca. 1400–1200), and this has raised problems for understanding the biblical accounts.

Jericho's early excavator, John Garstang, found a large wall that was destroyed, and dated it to 1400 B.C., attributing its fall to the Israelite takeover.[106] However, it is now known that this wall dates almost 1,000 years earlier, to the Early Bronze Age. Garstang also had dated the end of his "City IV" to 1400 B.C., but Jericho's later excavator, Kathleen Kenyon, raised this date to 1550 B.C. Furthermore, she dated its period of nonoccupation from 1550 until ca. 1100 B.C., except for a brief period just prior to 1300 B.C.[107] This caused difficulties for those holding to a late date for the Exodus, as well as those holding to an early date.[108]

Proponents of an early date have pointed to evidence uncovered by Kenyon that nonetheless supports an occupation ca. 1400 B.C.[109] More significant, however, has been the recent reaffirmation of Garstang's dating of City IV's demise to ca. 1400 B.C. by Bryant Wood, calling into question Kenyon's dating.[110] Wood presents convincing evidence that Kenyon's methodology in dating was flawed, using as it did imported pottery types from tombs for its typology, rather than the much more common local, domestic wares found much more widely throughout the Jericho mound.[111] He presents several lines of evidence that Garstang's dating of the demise of City IV and its walls (a set of walls different from the Early Bronze wall mentioned above) was indeed correct, ca. 1400 B.C.[112] If he is correct (as seems likely), then the archaeological evidence from Jericho fits the biblical picture very well.

AI AND THE ARCHAEOLOGICAL RECORD

As with Jericho there are archaeological problems in confirming the destruction of the city, so also with Ai. Here, however, the problem is different, since the location of the site is by no means certain. It traditionally has been identified with et-Tell, a mound two miles east of Beitin (assumed to

---

106. See his popular presentation of the city's excavations in John Garstang and J. B. E. Garstang, *The Story of Jericho.* He did not live to produce a final excavation report.
107. See Kenyon, "Jericho," 264–75. A popular presentation by Kenyon is her *Digging Up Jericho*; see also her *Archaeology of the Holy Land.*
108. See the reviews of the problem for the late dating and suggestions for solution of these in Kitchen, *Ancient Orient*, 62–64; and *NBD*, s.v. "Jericho."
109. See especially Waltke, "Palestinian Artifactual Evidence," and Merrill, "Palestinian Archaeology and the Date of the Conquest."
110. Bryant G. Wood, "Did the Israelites Conquer Jericho?" 44–58.
111. Piotr Bienkowski's thorough review of the evidence (*Jericho in the Late Bronze Age*) would appear to suffer from the same methodological problem that Kenyon's does, since it relies on her dating schemes.
112. Bimson (*Redating the Exodus and Conquest*, 106–36) comes to similar conclusions, but following somewhat different lines of evidence.

be biblical Bethel).[113] The problem with this site identification is that et-Tell was unoccupied from ca. 2400–1220 B.C. (and inhabited from 1220–1050), causing problems for both early or late dating of the Conquest, but especially for the former. This site identification has been challenged, however, on several grounds.[114] Despite a vigorous rejoinder, it would seem that a good case can be made for an alternate site proposal.[115] If so, the archaeology of et-Tell poses no problem for the biblical account, and the true site of Ai remains yet to be identified.

JOSHUA'S LONG DAY

In Joshua 10, we find an account of a battle between Israel and an Amorite coalition of five kings in which part of the account mentions the sun's standing still for an entire day. This has raised many questions as to the nature of the event and the text that describes it. The account of the battle proper is told in 10:6–15, and it falls into two parallel sections: vv. 6–11 and 12–15. The first section (vv. 6–11) begins with the Gibeonites appealing to Joshua for protection from the Amorite coalition, doing so under terms of the treaty they had just concluded with Israel (Joshua 9), and with Joshua responding (vv. 6–7). God threw the coalition into a panic, and there was a great slaughter (v. 10). Then, in the retreat, more were killed by the hailstorm than had died in the encounter (v. 11). A midsummer hailstorm would have been a rarity, functioning as a miraculous intervention here.[116] The picture is of a great and complete victory in this battle.

The second section (vv. 12–15) is introduced with the disjunctive particle "then" (*'az*), introducing important action that took place at the same time as—not subsequent to—that of verses 6–11.[117] That is, somehow, the hailstorm of verse 11 and the phenomena of verses 12–13 either describe the same things or (more probably) they happened at the same time, as part of the same miracle. Verses 12–14 read as follows:

> [12]On the day the Lord gave the Amorites over to Israel, Joshua said to the
> Lord in the presence of Israel:

113. See Joseph A. Callaway, *EAEHL* 1, s.v. "Ai"; and "Ai (et-Tell): Problem Site for Biblical Archaeologists," 87–99.
114. See especially J. M. Grintz, "Ai which is beside Beth-Aven," 201–16; David Livingstone, "Location of Biblical Bethel and Ai Reconsidered," 20–44; and "Traditional Site of Bethel Questioned," 39–50.
115. Anson F. Rainey, "Bethel Is Still Beitîn," 175–88. Compare Bimson (*Redating the Exodus and Conquest*, 201–11), who reviews the debate and cautiously adds several arguments of his own in favor of another site identification.
116. There are only five to eight days of hail per year in the coastal plain, mostly in midwinter (E. Orni and E. Ephrat, *Geography of Israel*, 15; cited by Robert Boling, *Joshua*, 282).
117. Boling, *Joshua*, 282; Woudstra, *Joshua*, 172–73.

"O sun, stand still over Gibeon,
      O moon, over the Valley of Aijalon."
[13]So the sun stood still,
      and the moon stopped,
      till the nation avenged itself on its enemies,
as it is written in the Book of Jashar.
      The sun stopped in the middle of the sky and delayed going down
about a full day. [14]There has never been a day like it before or since, a
day when the Lord listened to a man. Surely the Lord was fighting for
Israel!

Several difficult issues present themselves in this section.[118] However,
before considering these, we should carefully note the emphasis in the section. The author marvels not so much at the miracle of verse 13, but rather
at the fact that the Lord heard and responded to the voice of a man (v. 14)
interceding miraculously for Israel because of Joshua's petition (v. 12)! The
two previous miracles on Israel's behalf had been at God's initiative: the
stopping of the Jordan's waters, and the defeat of Jericho. This time, it was
in response to one man's petition. This again highlights Joshua's importance in the book, and it also underscores God's faithfulness to His people.
      The first difficulty in this section is the question of what exactly consti-
tutes the quote from the Book of Jashar. Many see it beginning with "O Sun"
in verse 12b and ending just before "as it is written" in verse 13a, thus including the five lines of poetry indicated in the NIV (quoted above). Others
think it begins a few words earlier in verse 12, with "Joshua said to the Lord
in the presence of Israel," or even at the beginning of verse 12. The fourth
view sees the quote extending from verse 12b through the end of verse 14,
or even to verse 15 (italicized portion quoted below).

      [12]On the day the Lord gave the Amorites over to Israel, Joshua said to
      the Lord in the presence of Israel:
         "O sun, stand still over Gibeon,
            O moon, over the Valley of Aijalon."
      [13]*So the sun stood still,*
            and the moon stopped,
            till the nation avenged itself on its enemies,
      as it is written in the Book of Jashar.

118. For good discussions of all the questions below, see Goslinga, *Joshua, Judges, Ruth*,
      98–101, 189–93; Boling, *Judges*, 282–85. For discussions of the "scientific" questions, see
      also E. W. Maunder, *ISBE* 1 (1927 ed.), s.v. "Beth-Horon, The Battle of"; and "A Misinter-
      preted Miracle," 359–72; Robert Dick Wilson, "Understanding 'The Sun Stood Still'"; Ber-
      nard Ramm, *The Christian View of Science and Scripture*, 107–10; John S. Holladay, Jr.,
      "The Day(s) the *Moon* Stood Still," 166–78; Kaiser, *More Hard Sayings of the Old Testa-
      ment*, 123–26.

> *The sun stopped in the middle of the sky and delayed going down about a full day. [14]There has never been a day like it before or since, a day when the Lord listened to a man. Surely the Lord was fighting for Israel!*

It would seem possible, too, that the quote might have been only verse 13b, which follows the reference to the Book of Jashar—namely, "The sun stopped in the middle of the sky and delayed going down about a full day." This gives a succinct summary of the key events here, and it is certainly plausible enough, since quotations are more often *introduced* by a narrative tag line such as found here ("as it is written in the Book of Jashar"), rather than followed by one.[119]

A second question that arises here is, Who is speaking "in the presence of Israel" (v. 12)? Most understand this to be Joshua, but some argue that it could be God. Verse 12, then, would read as follows: "Then Joshua spoke [or appealed] to the Lord on the day the Lord gave the Amorites into the power of the Israelites, and [the Lord] said in the sight of Israel" (author's translation). In this construct, God is the subject of the second verb of speaking.[120] Thus, the words in verses 12b and 13 are God's, not Joshua's. That is made more plausible when it is remembered that God is a more appropriate subject than Joshua to have addressed the sun and moon directly: He created them and was their sovereign.[121]

A third question concerns the status of verse 15, which is out of place chronologically and which is identical to verse 43. Those who see the Book of Jashar quote as including verse 15 have little problem here, and they see it functioning proleptically, anticipating the end that comes in verse 43. Others usually see it as a scribal duplication, since the ends of verses 14 and 42 are very similar. This may very well be the correct solution here.[122]

A fourth question—and it is the one most often asked of this passage—concerns what actually happened to the sun and moon (vv. 12–13). Two extremes can be seen here. The first sees the passage as purely mythological, completely nonhistorical, describing no actual events. The other speaks of a miracle of colossal magnitude, whereby the earth's rotation ac-

---

119. In the only other reference to the Book of Jashar in the Hebrew versions of the OT (2 Sam. 1:18), the quotation follows the reference to this book. (In the Greek versions of 1 Kings 8:13, the quotation precedes it.)
120. This suggestion comes from Boling, *Joshua*, 282.
121. The Greek adds "Joshua" as the subject of "he said," whereas in the Hebrew the subject is ambiguous. The Greek translation has influenced later translations and understandings of the verse (see, e.g., NIV esp.).
122. The Greek versions entirely omit the verse in both places. The narrative reads smoothly enough without it in either place.

tually stopped for an entire day. Others have sought to explain the event in mediating ways, via various natural phenomena, such as refraction of light in the earth's atmosphere (such that the sun remained visible for a lengthy period of time) or a solar eclipse.[123] It also is argued that the verb translated "stand still"[124] in verses 12–13 is more plausibly translated "cease, stop" (i.e., from shining). The request is then for relief from the heat of the sun, which comes via the hailstorm of verse 11[125] or via a solar eclipse.[126] It also has been argued that the passage is similar to ancient Near Eastern incantations involving the sun and the moon and that it is nothing more than a request that God look favorably upon Israel on that day and not Israel's enemies. The proof of this favor would be the alignment of the sun over Gibeon, to the east, and the moon over the Aijalon valley, to the west.[127] The hailstorm, then, would have nothing to do with these sources of light specifically, but it would be seen as the means of destruction of Israel's enemies.

Explaining what actually took place is a matter of considerable debate. The opinion here is that one of three possibilities is the most probable in understanding the phenomena of that day. First, they indeed could have involved a large-scale miracle of stopping of the earth's rotation for a day.[128] Second, the hailstorm indeed could have been the cause of the "stopping" of the sun's and the moon's light. Third, verses 12b–13a may indeed have recalled an incantation.[129] There are difficulties with each of these interpretations, however, and we must remain cautious about any conclusions drawn.

THEOLOGY OF THE BOOK OF JOSHUA

At least four important themes can be discerned as central to the theology of the book of Joshua: (1) the land, (2) rest, (3) the covenant, and (4) purity of worship. Of these, the first three could be subsumed under the ru-

---

123. See Ramm (*The Christian View of Science and Scripture*, 107–10) for a good summary of naturalizing explanations.
124. The root is *DWM* or *DMM*.
125. So Maunder, *ISBE* I (1927 ed.), s.v. "Beth-Horon, The Battle of"; and "A Misinterpreted Miracle," 359–72.
126. So Wilson, "Understanding 'The Sun Stood Still.'" Wilson does not deal with verse 11, however, nor does he address the issue of the Canaanites being refreshed by the sudden darkness.
127. Holladay, "The Day(s) the *Moon* Stood Still," 166–78.
128. Although nothing is known of this astronomically (see Ramm, *The Christian View*, 109), and it would appear to be out of character—proportionately—with other miracles recorded in the Bible. Furthermore, the extended shining of the sun that resulted seems to be at odds with the hailstorm of verse 11, especially when it is remembered that the events in verses 12–15 should be understood concomitantly to those in verses 6–11.
129. A difficulty here is that the Bible specifically rejects ancient Near Eastern magical practices. However, if the words in verses 12b–13a were God's, He could have been "co-opting" the pagans' own words, using a practice common among pagans to remind them (and Israel) of His control over even these practices.

bric of "A Promise-Keeping God."[130] Joshua 21:45 states that "not one of all the Lord's good promises to the house of Israel failed; every one was fulfilled," and 23:14 adds, "You know . . . that not one of all the good promises the Lord your God gave you has failed. Every one has been fulfilled; not one has failed."[131] God had for centuries promised Israel that it would have a land, and rest in that land, in accordance with the covenant He made with the patriarchs. God promised that Israel's continued existence in that land would be dependent on its obedience to the covenant He made with them under Moses, at Sinai.

THE LAND

The major theme in the book is the possession of the Promised Land, which had been promised to Abraham (Gen. 12:7; 13:14–15, 17; 15:18–21; 17:8; 22:17) and repeated to Isaac (26:3–4), to Jacob (28:4, 13; 35:12), and to succeeding generations (see 48:4ff; 50:24).

The land is a central goal toward which the action and thought in the Pentateuch move. Moses was called to bring God's people to "a good and broad land, a land flowing with milk and honey" (Ex. 3:8, 17; cf. also 6:4, 8). The book of Exodus shows the beginning of the move toward that land, and Numbers shows the continuation of the journey. Indeed, it has been noted that twelve "journeying" texts in these two books form their framework[132] in the same way that the "generations" formulas form the framework of Genesis (in 2:4; 5:2; 6:9; 10:1; 11:10; 11:27; 25:12; 25:19; 36:1; 36:9; 37:2). Beyond this, several chapters in Numbers are concerned with tribal and individual land inheritances (chaps. 27; 32; 34–36).

The land is seen as God's gift to Israel over and over again, especially in Deuteronomy. In Joshua, the concept occurs more than fifty times.[133] As a gift of God, it never belongs absolutely to Israel: it belongs to God (Lev. 25:23; Deut. 9:4–5). The dividing of the land by lot further indicates that it was at God's disposal (Num. 26:55–56; Josh. 14:2; 18:1–10), as does the demand for the land's first-fruits to be given to God (Deut. 14:22–29; 26:9–15).[134]

130. See Robert Polzin, *Moses and the Deuteronomist*, 74–80, 144–45.
131. This idea of fulfillment of God's promises is similar to the motif of fulfillment of prophecies in 1 & 2 Kings (see chapter 6).
132. Frank Moore Cross, *Canaanite Myth and Hebrew Epic*, 308–17. The twelve texts are Exodus 12:37a; 13:20; 14:1–2; 15:22a; 16:1; 17:1a; 19:2; Numbers 10:12; 20:1a; 20:22; 21:10–11; 22:1. Note also the "journeying" chapter at the end of Numbers (chap. 33).
133. See, e.g., Exodus 6:4, 8; Deuteronomy 1:6–8; 4:38, 40; 5:31; 7:13; 8:1–10; 9:4–6; 11:8–12, 17; 26:1, 9; 32:49, 52; 34:4. The following are typical references in Joshua: 1:2–3, 6, 11, 13, 15; 13:8; 22:7; 23:13, 15–16.
134. See also Patrick D. Miller, Jr., "The Gift of God: The Deuteronomic Theology of the Land," 451–65; Gerhard von Rad, "The Promised Land and Yahweh's Land in the Hexateuch," 79–93; B. L. Bandstra, *ISBE* 3, s.v. "Land."

Tribal Allotments in Canaan

The fact that a major portion of the book of Joshua is devoted to detailing the specific inheritances of individuals and tribes (chaps. 13–21) is very important in this regard. Though these chapters do not make for very easy (or interesting) reading, their importance lies in showing that the land promises were now indeed being fulfilled—in tangible ways. It is as if the author of the book were saying, "If you don't believe it, here is the 'map' and here are the details; you can check them out for yourself."

An important concept, especially in Deuteronomy and carried over into Joshua, is that possession and retention of the land is tied to obedience to the law (e.g., Deut. 4:1, 25–27, 40; 6:17–18; 8:1; 11:8; 30:15–20; 32:46–47). In Joshua, the complete possession of the land and extermination of its inhabitants is seen as a result of Joshua's obedience to God's command (10:40; 11:20, 23; 23:9–13). Israel's continued possession of it also is tied to obedience (23:9–13, 15–16).[135]

REST

The idea of the possession of the land as the accomplishment of God's "rest" is important as we consider the book of Joshua.[136] The "rest" is a gift, part of the inheritance. The inheritance is of two parts: (1) the land, and (2) "rest" from conflict with enemies.[137] That was promised from the beginning. To the Transjordan tribes, Joshua said, "Remember the command that Moses the servant of the Lord gave you: 'The Lord your God is giving you rest and has granted you this land'" (Josh. 1:13). This refers back to promises given in Numbers 32:20–22 and repeated in Deuteronomy 3:18–20. The idea of rest for the entire nation from their enemies is found in such passages as Deuteronomy 12:10 and 25:19, and it is echoed in the summarizing passages in Joshua 21:44 and 23:1. In two places, we read that the land itself had rest from war (11:23; 14:15; cf. Deut. 12:9–10; 25:19; 2 Sam. 7:1, 11; 1 Kings 8:56). That anticipates the same idea repeated several times in Judges: "And the land had rest ____ years" (3:11; 3:30; 5:31; 8:28).

Typologically, the NT equates the OT concept of rest with entering into Christ's "rest." Hebrews 3 and 4 develops this in greatest detail, and speaks of God resting on the seventh day of creation. Hebrews 4 quotes several times from Psalm 95, mentioning the rebellious wilderness generation,

---

135. The importance of the land motif in the OT is highlighted also by Walter Brueggemann, *The Land: Place as Gift, Promise, and Challenge in Biblical Faith.* See also W. Janzen, *ABD* 4, s.v. "Land."

136. Gerhard von Rad, "There Remains Still a Rest for the People of God: An Investigation of a Biblical Conception," 94–102.

137. The passages in Joshua about Israel or the land having rest are the following: 1:13, 15; 11:23; 14:15; 21:44; 22:4; 23:1.

whose disobedience prevented them from entering the Lord's rest (building upon Heb. 3:7–11, quoting all of Ps. 95:7d–11). The offer of rest to that generation was rejected, but, in the "today" of Psalm 95:7d and Hebrews 3:7, 15; 4:7, the offer is repeated. Hebrews 4:8 mentions Joshua, under whom the rebellious generation was *not* allowed to enter the land; it was rather a new generation to whom the offer of rest was made. It was an offer that was to be appropriated in each generation.

THE COVENANT

Another prominent theme in Joshua is the covenant, or, better, *the keeping of the covenant.* There is the Deuteronomistic stress upon obedience to the law (the covenant) and the cause-and-effect relationship of obedience and blessing, disobedience and punishment. Obedience to the law and the covenant is urged upon Joshua in 1:7–8, upon the Transjordan tribes in 22:5, upon the people in 23:6, 16; 24:15.

Covenant renewal ceremonies. Two covenant renewal ceremonies are recorded in the book. The first took place on Mount Ebal, when Joshua built an altar to the Lord and offered sacrifices (8:30–35). There, "Joshua copied on stones the law of Moses, which he had written" (v. 32). Then he read the entire law to the people (vv. 34–35). In doing so, Joshua was fulfilling the requirements that a king was supposed to keep (Deut. 17:18–19).

The covenant renewal ceremony at Shechem in Joshua 24 is also very significant. See especially verses 25–27, where Joshua wrote the words of their covenant renewal in "the Book of the Law of God" and erected a large stone as a witness and a memorial for them. The people committed themselves to keeping the law as well (24:16–18, 21–22, 24, 27).

The ark of the covenant. In chapter 3, the ark of the covenant occupies an important place. The priests were responsible for carrying it, in accordance with the Mosaic legislation.[138] The ark was the symbol of God's very presence, and a healthy distance was to be maintained between it and the people (3:4). The ark is referred to in various ways in this chapter, the most common phrase being "the ark of the covenant." However, we should note that several references elevate it to even more prominent status when the Hebrew is read carefully:[139] (1) verse 11, "the ark of the covenant, the Lord of all the earth";[140] (2) verse 14: "the ark, the covenant"; (3) verse 17: "the ark,

---

138. Deuteronomy 10:8; cf. 31:9. The ark was to be carried with poles and not touched: Exodus 25:12–13; 37:3–5; Numbers 4:4–15.

139. No major English version or commentator (except Woudstra, *Joshua*, 85–86 [but only at v. 11]) takes these minor differences into account. Rather they all smooth them over, understanding scribal errors to have crept in here. The texts as they stand, however, must be read as noted.

140. The phrase is parallel to that in verse 13: "the ark of the Lord—the Lord of all the earth."

the covenant of the Lord." These references suggest such a close relationship between the ark and the covenant it represents that it is almost as if the ark *is* the covenant. God, who is associated with the ark, is closely associated with the covenant as well, and these ways of referring to the ark highlight this fact.

PURITY OF WORSHIP (HOLINESS)

The idea of Israel's separate identity in Canaan—especially religiously—pervades the book of Joshua. That is the essence of holiness in the OT: the Hebrew word *qādôš* ("holy") has at its base the idea of separateness—away from the everyday and the mundane, from evil, and set apart for the sacred, the good.

An important passage in Joshua that speaks of holiness is chapter 5. Here we find recorded several ceremonies, all of which show the importance of ritual purity. First is a circumcision ceremony (5:2–9) in which those who had not been circumcised in the wilderness were now circumcised. Second, the Passover is kept (5:10–12), after which the manna stopped appearing and the Israelites ate from the fruit of the land. Third, Joshua met the commander of the Lord's army (5:13–15). In this little episode, the key to the encounter lies in Joshua's falling face down to the ground and in the commander's indications that Joshua was standing on holy ground and that he should remove his sandals (vv. 14–15). This obviously echoes Moses' encounter with God at the burning bush (Ex. 3:5–6). It is interesting that the Lord's commander did not answer Joshua's military-type question: "Are you for us or for our enemies?" Rather, he answered by pointing out the holiness of the spot.

Thus, we can see that all three episodes concern holiness in one way or another.[141] That such spiritual preparations preceded the actual "conquest" of the land illustrates the biblical priorities, which are spiritual (see, e.g., Matt. 6:33). Thus, the real "action" of the book is delayed by several important—even essential—preliminaries: memorializing God's miraculous help (Joshua 4) and sanctifying the people (Joshua 5). The tasks ahead were far too important to enter into lightly or unprepared in any way.

Another passage that speaks of purity of worship is found in Joshua 22. Here, when the Transjordan tribes built an altar of commemoration, the other tribes were greatly concerned that this was a rival and illegitimate altar that would compromise the purity of the one true altar of the Lord.

Holiness is rooted in God's very nature. Leviticus 19, a crucial chapter in a book on holiness, shows that the commands to be holy are rooted in

---

141. The word *holy* (or any of its forms) only occurs once in the chapter, but the common idea behind each event is precisely that of holiness and ritual cleanness.

God's own character, since He himself is holy: "Be holy, because I, the Lord your God, am holy" (v. 2). This command was behind Israel's self-understanding in the land of Canaan.

An important insight into holiness is given us in Numbers 16. This chapter concerns the rebellion of various individuals against the authority God had given Moses and Aaron. In 16:38 [MT 17:3], the censers of the sons of Korah are seen as holy because they had been offered to the Lord (see vv. 17–18).

Thus, we see that *dedication to the Lord* is an important part of the concept of holiness. Such dedication had the effect of separating the individual who was dedicated out and away from the ordinary or the profane (i.e., the common). That is the thrust of the rituals in Joshua 5. Circumcision marked the dedication of the individual to the Lord, to the covenant He had established with Abraham and his descendants. The Passover observance marked the individuals' dedication to Him as well and commemorated the separating out of the Israelites from the Egyptians years earlier.

The ḥērem. Related to this is the idea of the *ḥērem*, the placing of things "under the ban" or "devoting them to the Lord."[142] As such, these things were forbidden to common use but, rather, were to be an "offering" to the Lord. The concept especially was related to warfare: things would be offered to the Lord by being utterly destroyed. This could happen with respect to material wealth (e.g., Josh. 6:18–19; 7:1, 11), people (e.g., 10:28, 35, 39, 40, 41; 11:11, 20), or even entire cities (e.g., 6:21; 8:26; 10:1, 37; 11:12, 21).

This practice, though referred to extensively in the OT, is not commonly seen in surrounding cultures. That is somewhat remarkable, given the bellicose nature of so many of these cultures and also given their developed religious systems. There is only one clear occurrence of the root *HRM* in cognate Semitic literature.[143] Second Kings 19:11 mentions the Assyrian kings "utterly destroying" lands they conquered, but it is not in the context of religious destruction.

The special emphasis at the time of Joshua was that Israel was to keep itself undefiled, and the land itself was to be undefiled. In the particular circumstances of the Israelites entering the long-promised land as a newly constituted nation, it was vitally important that they do so uncontaminated by pagan worship. Already they had yielded to temptation and the Baal of Peor in the wilderness (Numbers 25; 31:1–4). In Deuteronomy, the Lord had made His desires clear: "You shall utterly destroy them . . . *precisely so that*

---

142. See N. Lohfink, *TDOT* 5, s.v. "hāram, hērem."
143. In the Moabite Stone, where Mesha, king of Moab, states that he had devoted Nebo and its inhabitants for destruction to Ashtar-Chemosh (*ANET*, 320).

they might not teach you to do according to all their abominations which they have done on behalf of their gods" (20:17–18; author's translation).

When Israel did not obey the command to utterly destroy things, this did indeed contaminate its religion. This is most visible in the story of Achan's and Israel's "breaking faith" concerning things placed under the ban (Joshua 7). When Israel was defeated at Ai because of this, Joshua and the elders of the people went into mourning (7:7–9).

God's response was couched in terms of holiness (vv. 10–15). Israel (not just Achan) had sinned, and He would not tolerate it. This passage shows that God is not open to the charge of a double standard with regard to His treatment of Israel and the Canaanites. He had ordered Israel to exterminate the Canaanites because of their sin, but here He allows all Israel as well to be affected by the sin of one man. The overriding concern in *all* such episodes is God's demand for holiness and obedience and the concern for purity of worship. Thus, 7:11 underlines the seriousness of the offense attributed to the nation: Israel had (1) "sinned," (2) "violated" the Lord's covenant, (3) "taken some of the devoted things," (4) "stolen," (5) "lied," and (6) put the things among their own possessions. The quick, staccato accumulation of these verbs in verse 11 accentuates the severity of the action, since it was essentially one act, but it is described in these various ways. Verse 12 shows that the people of Israel themselves now are, literally, "a thing for destruction" (as Jericho had been). God would no longer be with Israel until the sin was removed from the camp. Verse 13 again emphasizes the importance of holiness in God's eyes: the people were to sanctify themselves, since they had been defiled by the presence of the banned things.

Achan was found out, and he and his family were stoned and burned (vv. 16–26). Because he had violated God's command concerning the booty from Jericho, Achan found himself in the position of the inhabitants of Jericho: he himself was placed under the ban. He in effect had become a Canaanite by his actions.

Another illustration of the effects of not completely destroying pagan influences comes in the book of Judges. Despite the indications in Joshua 10–11 that Israel completely carried out the requirements of the complete annihilation, Judges 1 indicates that the various tribes did not fully obey (see esp. vv. 19, 21, 28, 29, 30, 31, 32, 33, 34). We then see in Judges 2—and indeed throughout the rest of the book of Judges—the effects this had on Israel's life: the people turned to the Baals, the gods of the Canaanites who were living among them, and forsook the Lord. Israel's worship did not remain pure.

OUTLINE OF THE BOOK OF JOSHUA

The Conquest of the Land (Joshua 1–12)
  Preparations for Entering the Land (chap. 1)
    The Charge to Joshua (1:1–9)
    First Instructions (1:10–11)
    The Charge to the Transjordan Tribes (1:12–15)
    All Israel's Response (1:16–18)
  Two Spies in Jericho (chap. 2)
    Entry, Discovery, and Hiding (2:1–7)
    The Oath of Protection (2:8–14)
    Departure and Sign of the Scarlet Cord (2:15–24)
  Crossing of the Jordan (3:1–5:1)
    Preparations for Crossing (3:1–6)
    The Crossing (3:7–17)
    The Twelve Memorial Stones (4:1–10a)
    The Crossing Completed (4:10b–5:1)
  Ritual Preparations (5:2–15)
    Circumcision (5:2–9)
    The Passover Kept (5:10–12)
    The Commander of the Lord's Army (5:13–15)
  Conquest of Jericho (chap. 6)
  Covenant Disobedience and the Conquest of Ai (7:1–8:29)
    The Sin (7:1)
    The Defeat (7:2–5)
    The Aftermath (7:6–26)
    The Victory (8:1–29)
  Covenant Affirmations (8:30–35)
  The Gibeonite Treaty (chap. 9)
    Introduction (9:1–2)
    The Gibeonites' Deceit (9:3–15)
    The Gibeonites' Lot (9:16–27)
  The Southern and Northern Campaigns (chaps. 10–11)
    Victory over Southern Coalition (10:1–27)
      The Coalition Gathers (10:1–5)
      The Battle Proper (10:6–15)
      The Task Finished (10:16–27)
    The Southern Campaign Completed (10:28–43)
    Victory Over Northern Coalition (11:1–15)
      The Coalition Gathers (11:1–5)
      The Battle Proper (11:6–9)
      The Task Finished (11:10–15)
    The Northern Campaign Completed (11:16–23)

The List of Conquered Kings and Land (chap. 12)
The Kings and Land of Transjordan (12:1–6)
The Kings and Land of Cisjordan (12:7–24)

The Division of the Land (Joshua 13–21)
The Command to Distribute the Land (13:1–7)
The Transjordan Distribution Recalled (13:8–33)
The Cisjordan Distribution (chaps. 14–19)
Introduction (14:1–5)
Caleb's Inheritance (14:6–15)
Judah's Inheritance (15:1–63)
Joseph's Inheritance (chaps. 16–17)
The Other Tribes' Inheritance (chaps. 18–19)
The Cities of Refuge and the Levitical Cities (chaps. 20–21)
The Cities of Refuge (20:1–9)
The Levitical Cities (21:1–42)
Conclusion (21:43–45)

Farewells (Joshua 22–24)
Joshua's Farewell to the Transjordan Tribes (chap. 22)
The Parting (22:1–9)
Crisis of Unity (22:10–34)
Joshua's First Farewell to All Israel (chap. 23)
Joshua's Second Farewell to All Israel (24:1–28)
Introduction and Review of the Past (24:1–13)
Covenant Affirmations (24:14–28)
Conclusion: Burial Notices (24:29–33)

3

JUDGES

Then the Lord raised up judges, who saved them out of the hands of these raiders. Yet they would not listen to their judges but prostituted themselves to other gods and worshiped them. (Judg. 2:16–17)

In those days there was no king in Israel; everyone did what was right in his own eyes. (Judg. 21:25 NASB)

The book of Judges is one of sharp contrasts with the book of Joshua. It consists of a series of independent episodes, all joined by a common motif of Israel's apostasy and God's faithfulness; the overall impression is one of near chaos in Israel's political and spiritual life, salvaged only by God's repeated intervention and provision.

The book of Joshua had presented things as having gone well, and it ended on a peaceful note, with every family settling down on the land it had inherited (see Josh. 21:45; 22:4, 6; 23:14; 24:13, 28). Joshua, who early on was merely Moses' aide (Josh. 1:1), was now the servant of the Lord (24:29). The land was now Israel's, in fulfillment of the long string of promises from Abraham's day on, and this fulfillment had been tied to Israel's obedience.

Now, however, the hints in Joshua that the conquest had been incomplete and that Israel's obedience had been something less than total become full-blown realities in the book of Judges. We see that the warnings repeatedly sounded against foreign religious entanglements were well spoken, since Israel repeatedly turned away from the Lord to follow after the Canaanite gods. The period begins with Israel fighting the enemies it should have annihilated, continues with Israel fighting various other foreign enemies as a result of its apostasy, and concludes with Israelites fighting among themselves in the aftermath of a sordid breach of covenant. The only positive notes in the book are God's constancy and the hints that things should get better under a new order.

TITLE

English versions derive their title for the book from the Hebrew title, *šōpĕṭîm*. This word usually is translated "judges"; it is the term given the twelve leaders of Israel during the period between Joshua and Samuel. The Old Greek versions (Septuagint) title it *Kritai*, and the Vulgate terms it *Judicum*, both of which mean the same thing ("judges").

AUTHORSHIP AND DATE OF COMPOSITION

Like the book of Joshua, Judges is anonymous. It is a collection of various blocks of material about different judges, but these blocks are not attributed to any particular source. Mainstream scholarship dates its final form in the seventh or sixth centuries B.C., since it sees 2:6–16:31 as "Deuteronomistic."[1] Harrison dates it to the early monarchy, i.e., in the eleventh or tenth centuries B.C.[2] Certainly it was written after the last events recorded in it (ca. 1050 B.C.). The reference in 18:30 to "the day of the captivity of the land" refers to the Exile (in the sixth century B.C.), suggesting that at least the final "edition" of the book came from the Exile or afterwards. Otherwise, there are no clear indicators of its date of composition in the book or elsewhere in the canon.[3]

UNITY

As the outline at the end of the chapter indicates, the book of Judges is divided into several distinct sections. It begins with a prologue indicating that the Conquest described in Joshua was incomplete (1:1–2:5). It then proceeds with an introduction that summarizes the cycle of events that recur over and over again in the book (2:6–3:6; esp. 2:10–23). Then the core of the book tells the stories of the individual judges (3:7–16:31). Finally, the book ends with two appendixes that portray the period as almost completely debased (17:1–21:25).

Mainstream critical scholarship[4] has made much of these divisions, understanding the stories in the core to have circulated independently (on the oral level) and to have been concerned with local tribal heroes. Later,

---

1. See chapter 2 under the "Joshua and the Deuteronomistic History." See also the next section on "Unity" for more on dating and composition.
2. R. K. Harrison, *Introduction to the Old Testament*, 690.
3. The reference to Jebusites living in Jerusalem "to this day" (1:21) could point to composition of that portion of the book at least prior to David's capture of the city (ca. 1003 B.C.) on the presumption that Jebusites would not have lived there afterward. On the other hand, evidence does suggest that they persisted in the city to some degree (e.g., 2 Sam. 24:16).
4. Representative are J. Alberto Soggin, *Judges: A Commentary*, 4–6; John Gray, *Joshua, Judges, Ruth*, 194–232.

they would have been incorporated into one of the early "Deuteronomistic" editions (seventh century B.C.), in which the "Deuteronomistic" introduction was added (2:6–3:6), followed by the incorporation of the prologue (1:1–2:5) and appendixes (chaps. 17–21) sometime in the sixth century B.C.

A priori, there need be no objection to any of this type of formulation, at least for the book of Judges. No questions of authorship or date are at stake here the way they are for the books in the Pentateuch. Thus, theoretically, we can easily agree with these mainstream formulations about the structure and the process of compilation.[5]

However, the key to understanding the message of the book comes in focusing on the unity of its final form. Here, the material can be seen to have been brought together to form an intelligible, coherent final product with a clear authorial purpose.[6]

PURPOSE

The book was written to show the consequences of disobedience to God and to point the way to a king, who, if he were righteous, would lead the people to God. In contrast to the serene way in which the book of Joshua ends, as a consequence of all Israel obeying (for the most part) God's commands, the book of Judges shows that, in fact, Israel began to disobey God even in the time of Joshua and that this disobedience grew more serious— and more debased—throughout the period. Judges 2:16–23 points out the cyclical, or repetitive, nature of history during this period. However, the book makes clear that the repetitions were not merely of the same degree each time; rather, each cycle took Israel further downward in its relationship with God and in its own religious malpractice. By the end of the book, it is clear that Israel had violated its covenant with God in almost every way imaginable.

A number of scholars have pointed out that chapters 19–21 are out of place chronologically, that, despite their placement at the end of the book, the events themselves would have taken place early in the period of the judges. This is for several reasons.[7] (1) Phinehas, Aaron's grandson, is still alive in 20:28 (cf. Num. 25:1–15; 31:6; Josh. 22:9–34). (2) The tribal league —whatever its exact nature—is still functioning and able to take combined action (chap. 20), as it had under Phinehas and others in Joshua's day

---

5. Arthur E. Cundall (*Judges*, 18–28) is an evangelical commentator who incorporates these questions into his analysis of the book.
6. Representative of this approach are Robert G. Boling (*Judges*, 29–38), Cundall (*Judges*, 26–28), and especially the following: J. P. U. Lilley, "A Literary Appreciation of the Book of Judges," 94–102; D. W. Gooding, "The Composition of the Book of Judges," 70*–79*; and Barry G. Webb, *The Book of Judges: An Integrated Reading.* On the understanding here of "author," see the discussion in chapter 6 (on authorship of 1 & 2 Kings).
7. Cundall, *Judges*, 193; Gray, *Joshua, Judges, Ruth*, 357; Boling, *Judges*, 286–87. Cundall lists all four reasons given here.

(Josh. 22:9–34). (3) The Philistines are not mentioned as a military threat; the action described in chapters 20–21 would have been well-nigh impossible in later times, when the Philistines dominated the areas in question. (4) Bethel or Mizpah appear as the major sanctuary (20:1, 18; 21:1), rather than Shiloh, which was more prominent in the Philistine period.[8]

This chronological displacement would reinforce the point that, during the period of the judges, things were "going downhill" spiritually. The sordid events in these last chapters, while they may have occurred early in the period, are related at the end as a fitting capstone to a degenerate period.

As a corollary to Israel's apostasy, God emerges as the true "hero" in the book. There is a certain irony in this, since the book focuses on a succession of heroes who delivered Israel. It was God who raised up the various heroic judges to deliver Israel from its crises, and it was He who remained faithful to the covenant. Israel failed because it did what was right in its own eyes, rather than what was right in God's eyes. (Also see "Theology of the Book of Judges" below.)

THE PLACE OF JUDGES IN THE CANON

The book of Judges is part of the "Former Prophets" in the Hebrew canon and of the "Deuteronomistic History" identified by modern scholars. It logically and chronologically follows Joshua, developing themes from that book and showing the contrast with the idealized picture presented there. It naturally points ahead to the books of Samuel (which follow it in the Hebrew canon), in which the monarchy was established and began to flourish. The events of the book of Ruth (which follows it in the Christian canon) took place during the period of the judges.

HISTORICAL AND CULTURAL CONTEXT FOR THE BOOK OF JUDGES

DATE OF THE EVENTS

The book of Judges covers a lengthy period, beginning after the death of Joshua (some time in the early fourteenth century B.C.) and ending prior to the rise of Samuel to prominence and the coronation of Saul (ca. 1050 B.C. or shortly thereafter). As such, it covers some 300–350 years.[9]

---

8. See 1 Samuel 1:3, 9; 3:21; 4:4–5; although cf. Judges 21:19, where Shiloh does appear as a religious center.
9. See chapter 2 under "Date of the Events" for a discussion of the early dating of the Exodus, upon which this understanding of the extent of the period depends. See also Sean M. Warner ("The Dating of the Period of the Judges," 455–63), who proposes that the period probably began ca. 1373 B.C. and not 1200 B.C. (although his confidence in the evidence—biblical and extrabiblical—is very slight, and he suggests that the Conquest could have come after the period of the judges).

The book has numerous references to lengths of time, mostly to periods when Israel was oppressed or to periods of rest between the oppressions.[10] If these are added up, the total for the period comes to at least 410 years.[11] Added to the known lengths of Eli's, Samuel's, Saul's, and part of David's tenure as leaders (at least 100 years), plus the time in the wilderness and the Conquest (at least 40 years), we have a period of at least 550 years between the Exodus and the time that Solomon took office in 970 B.C. That is clear conflict with the statement in 1 Kings 6:1 about there being 480 years between the Exodus and the laying of the foundation of the Temple in Solomon's fourth year.

The generally agreed-upon solution sees many of the episodes in Judges as happening concurrently, in different parts of the land. For example, in 3:12–14, Eglon, king of Moab, along with Ammonites and Amalekites, oppressed Israel, but they only took possession of "the city of palms" (Jericho: cf. Deut. 34:3; 2 Chron. 28:15). Ehud's actions (3:15–30) may have been localized in the territory of Ephraim and Benjamin. Gideon's encounter with the Midianites was with the help only of Manasseh, his own tribe (6:15), and Asher, Zebulun, and Naphtali (6:35; 7:23), and later Ephraim (7:24).[12] Thus, we cannot simply add up the numbers to arrive at the length of the period. That is true whether an early or a late date for the Exodus and Conquest is preferred; only the *degree* of overlapping differs.[13]

Toward the end of the period, dating becomes somewhat easier, assuming the accuracy of Jephthah's statement about the three-hundred-year period in 11:26 and the early dating of the Exodus. Given an Exodus ca. 1446 B.C. and a defeat of Sihon ca. 1406 B.C., then Jephthah's statement would have come ca. 1106 B.C., eighteen years after the Ammonite and Philistine oppressions (10:7–8) began, ca. 1124 B.C. The Philistine oppression lasted forty years (13:1), until it was finally broken by Samuel at Mizpah (1 Sam. 7:11, 13), ca. 1084 B.C. Samson's exploits would have overlapped Samuel's somewhat; his death likely came toward the end of the period of Philistine oppression.[14]

10. Judges 3:8, 11, 14, 30; 4:3; 5:31; 6:1; 8:28; 9:22; 10:2, 3, 8; 12:7, 9, 11, 14; 13:1; 16:31; cf. 2:7; 3:31.
11. See the convenient discussions of the entire issue, with readable charts, in Cundall, *Judges*, 28–33; John N. Oswalt, *ISBE* 1, s.v. "Chronology of the Old Testament." See, at greater length, John J. Bimson, *Redating the Exodus and the Conquest*, 79–103.
12. See Cundall (*Judges*, 31–32) for further examples.
13. On the question of overlapping, in addition to the works cited in n. 11, see Eugene Merrill, "Paul's Use of 'About 450 Years' in Acts 13:20," 246–57; Kenneth A. Kitchen, *Ancient Orient and Old Testament*, 72–75. Kitchen gives instructive examples of the same phenomenon from Egypt.
14. See further, Merrill, *Kingdom of Priests*, 148–51, 176; Bimson (*Redating*, 84–94) presents a similar analysis, but his dates differ from Merrill's by twenty years.

HISTORICAL SETTING OF THE EVENTS

This 300 to 350 year period of the judges spanned a major transition in the ancient Near East, when the Late Bronze Age gave way to the early Iron Age shortly after 1200 B.C. The Late Bronze Age (ca. 1550–1200 B.C.) was a period of prosperity (noted in chapter 2). In Palestine, the system of relatively small, independent city-states gave way to one of large empires (e.g., Egyptian, Hittite). Israelites and Canaanites were able to live there relatively undisturbed, however—the former in the hill country and the latter in the lowlands and coastal areas.[15]

At the end of the Late Bronze Age, a major discontinuity appears in the archaeological record (ca. 1200 B.C. and shortly thereafter), signaling the beginning of the Iron Age.[16] Widespread destructions are evident all across the Mediterranean basin. In Canaan, the evidence shows a radical drop in population in the major population centers and an increase in one-period sites in outlying areas—in the hill country and desert fringe areas. Imported pottery abruptly ceases to show up. Local (Philistine) pottery is distinctive and rougher than Cypriot and especially the beautiful Mycenean pottery so prevalent in Canaan and throughout the Mediterranean basin that had been the norm in the Late Bronze Age.[17]

The large, visible signs of society collapsed: empires, extensive international trade, dense population centers, fine crafts and trades. However, there was a continuity of culture at the grass-roots level. Rough as it was, pottery did continue to be made. The same type of dislocation that occurred at the Early Bronze Age–Middle Bronze Age transition—i.e., depopulation of urban centers, with the rise of one-period sites in the hills and the desert fringes—also can be seen at the Late Bronze Age–Iron Age transition.

The causes of these widespread destructions are not clearly known, but they coincide with the migrations of the "Land and Sea Peoples" known from Egyptian texts.[18] These peoples clashed with Egypt at the end of the thirteenth century B.C., and they are seen involved in other disturbances in the eastern Mediterranean as well.

Thus, the early Iron Age (ca. 1200–1000 B.C., known as Iron I) was a "dark age" of sorts.[19] The judgment made above (on other grounds) about

15. For more on the Late Bronze Age, see chapter 2 under "Historical Setting of the Conquest." On the Early Iron Age, see the text below and n. 19.
16. See chapter 2 under "Nature of the Events" for further discussion and bibliography.
17. See Ruth Amiran, *Ancient Pottery of the Holy Land,* 172–90, 266–68.
18. See chapter 2 under "Date of the Events" and accompanying n. 24.
19. For convenient surveys of the history and archaeology of the period, see William F. Albright, *The Archaeology of Palestine,* 110–28; "Syria, the Philistines, and Phoenicia," 507–36; Yohanan Aharoni, *The Archaeology of the Land of Israel,* 153–91; James A. Thompson, *The Bible and Archaeology,* 80–98; Eugene H. Merrill, *Kingdom of Priests: A History of Old Testament Israel,* 151–58.

most of the biblical judges' activities being localized in relatively small geographical areas easily accords with the picture here. It was not until ca. 1000 B.C. that a true internationalism reasserted itself throughout the eastern Mediterranean, and houses and cities began to rival those of the Late Bronze Age again.

There were two technological advances worthy of note in the early Iron Age. The first was the development of iron tools and weapons. This allowed for more sophisticated agricultural and military techniques. The second was the development of plastered cisterns for water storage. These are seen for the first time in Iron I, all over Palestine. They freed settlements from being completely dependent on wells, springs, or bodies of water.

Now, for the first time, Philistines[20] appear as a major, identifiable grouping on the southwest coast of Canaan.[21] They settled in, manufacturing their own crude but distinctive pottery, carrying on a limited sea-based trade, and eventually achieving a monopoly in the use of iron weapons, which they used to their advantage against Israel (Judg. 1:19; 1 Sam. 13:19-21). During the judges period, Samson was the major Israelite foe of the Philistines; later, Samuel, Saul, and David led Israel against them, and it was David who finally broke their hold on Israel.

The Israelites eventually did gain access to iron weapons (1 Sam. 13:21). It is interesting to note that by the tenth century B.C. the technological tide seems to have turned: Samuel, Saul, and David were successful in subduing the Philistines. Archaeologically, this picture is illustrated dramatically: blacksmiths from northern Palestine were producing carburized iron (steel), while Philistine sites show no corresponding technological advances.[22] This corresponds with the biblical picture in which, by this time, a political structure was in place capable of supporting such specialized technology (namely, the monarchy).

The Bible pictures the Philistines as a coarse people who were uncircumcised (e.g., Judg. 14:3; 15:18). Their major god was Dagon (known from Mesopotamian and Syrian sources as "Dagan"). They were organized into a federation under five "lords," chiefs of their five major cities: Gaza, Ashkelon, Ashdod, Ekron, and Gath. A distinctive "Philistine" pottery has been unearthed at Philistine sites, beginning shortly after 1200 B.C., which imitates (rather poorly) the Mycenean pottery of the Late Bronze Age. No true Philistine texts have been discovered to date.

---

20. Recent introductions to the Philistines include Neal Bierling, *Giving Goliath His Due*; Trude Dothan and Moshe Dothan, *People of the Sea: The Search for the Philistines*; David M. Howard, Jr., "The Philistines."
21. The use of the term *Philistine* in the Pentateuch does not refer to this specific people but to earlier groups of Aegean peoples. See Howard, "The Philistines."
22. T. Stech-Wheeler et al., "Iron at Taanach and Early Iron Metallurgy in the Eastern Mediterranean," 245.

CANAANITE RELIGION AND CULTURE

The major problem for Israel during the period of the judges was its penchant for turning away from the Lord and toward the gods of the Canaanites. What was it about Canaanite religion and culture that proved to be such an irresistible attraction?

Why it attracted the Israelites. The land of Canaan was awe inspiring to the Israelites, as evidenced in the story of the spies who came back with a report on its wealth and strength (Numbers 13). We already have noted the cosmopolitanism of the Late Bronze Age: the large urban centers, with their wealth and development. To a recently-freed slave people, accustomed to the hardships of life in the wilderness, this could not have failed to impress. The Canaanites were clearly superior to the Israelites on many levels: art, literature, architecture, trade, political organization, and more. It is not difficult at all to see how the Israelites would have been tempted by the elaborate Canaanite religious system, which ostensibly supported—even provided—all of this.[23]

The religion of Canaan posed the greatest threat to Israel during this period; indeed, we see pictures of it throughout the Bible. In the book of Judges, Israel repeatedly follows after the Canaanite Baals, Ashtaroth, and other gods (Judg. 2:11–13, 17, 19; 3:7; 8:33; 10:6; etc.).

The first concern of any primitive culture was food. Thus, fertility motifs were central in almost every such culture, and Canaanite religion was no different. Because of this, it had drawing power because of its association with agricultural fertility.

An additional attraction undoubtedly was in the system of sacred prostitutes—"priestesses" of Baal. A follower of Baal could go in to a priestess and, by means of lovemaking with Baal's representative in a human "fertility" rite, persuade Baal to grant fertility to the worshiper's fields. This mixture of sex with religion undoubtedly was a positive factor in many Israelite minds (cf. the story of the Israelites and the Moabite women in Numbers 25).[24]

Another of the Canaanites' attractions was the wealth evident among them. The Canaanite cities of the Late Bronze Age were vastly superior to Israelite towns in the hill country. The lure of materialism was as powerful then as it is today.

---

23. See Thompson, *The Bible and Archaeology,* 89–92, 96–98.
24. For more on Canaanite religion and culture, see the works cited in chapter 2, n. 98. For the Canaanite religious texts, see the works in chapter 2, n. 48. For illustrations of many of the Canaanite religious figurines, see Ora Negbi, *Canaanite Gods in Metal; ANEP,* pls. 464–501; *TANE,* pls. 28, 30, 128–35.

The Canaanite Pantheon. The Canaanite system included numerous gods, five of which were most prominent: El, Asherah, Baal, Astarte, and Anath.

El was the head of the Canaanite pantheon, father of the gods and of mortals. Although the head of the gods, he appears as relatively weak and enfeebled, at least when compared to Baal.

Asherah was El's wife, the mother of the gods, goddess of the sea ("Lady Asherah-of-the-Sea").[25] She appears in the Bible (1 Kings 15:13; 18:19; 2 Kings 21:7; 23:4; 2 Chron. 15:16), and the wooden "Asherah poles" associated with her cult are also in evidence (e.g., Deut. 16:21; Judg. 6:25, 28, 30; 2 Kings 23:6). She appears in a striking example (from a later period) in a drawing and inscription found at Kuntillet Ajrud in southern Israel. A bull and cow are pictured, with the inscription, "For Yahweh . . . and his Asherah," suggesting that some of those worshiping there felt he needed a "wife," just as El had had one (see chapter 7).

Baal was the storm-god; he ended up as the most powerful god in the pantheon, probably because of his connections with fertility. The storm represents power but also life-giving rain, rain that makes the land fertile.[26] In the Baal cycle of texts from Ugarit, he is shown dying and rising, in keeping with his role as fertility god, reflecting the annual cycle of the seasons. He is mentioned often in the Bible; the climax of his influence in Israel came under the permissive reign of Ahab (1 Kings 16:29–22:40).

Astarte/Ashtoreth was a female fertility goddess and a goddess of love and war, closely associated with Baal. She also appears to have had some astral connections. She is not mentioned very often in the Ugaritic texts but corresponds to Ishtar in Mesopotamian texts, and she appears in Egyptian representations of Canaanite religion. The "Ashtaroth" (i.e., the Ashtoreths) are mentioned in the Bible, along with the Baals (e.g., Judg. 10:6; 1 Sam. 7:4; 12:10).

Anath was Baal's sister and wife, and also a goddess of love and war. She often appears in winged form. In the Baal cycle, she appears as rather bloodthirsty. She does not appear in the Bible, except perhaps in connection with Shamgar's name: Shamgar's father was named "Anath" (Judg. 3:31).

25. Two recent studies of Asherah, mostly reflecting scholarly consensus, are John Day, "Asherah in the Hebrew Bible and Northwest Semitic Literature," 385–408; Walter A. Maier III, *'AŠERAH: Extrabiblical Evidence.*
26. This adds a new dimension to the drought that Elijah predicted would come (1 Kings 17:1; 18:41–46); it shows the Lord striking directly at the heart of the Canaanite religious system.

SPECIAL ISSUES IN THE BOOK OF JUDGES

ISRAEL'S ORGANIZATIONAL STRUCTURE

At the end Joshua's life, he gathered the Israelites for his final addresses and a final covenant renewal ceremony (Joshua 23–24). Representing each tribe were the "elders, heads, judges, and officers" of Israel (23:2; 24:1). Throughout the book of Judges, judges are raised up to deliver Israel from its enemies. In the case of Deborah and Barak, the victory was a triumph on behalf of the entire nation. At the end of the book, we see the tribes banding together to confront the tribe of Benjamin.

Considerations such as these (and many others) have given rise to speculation about the precise nature of Israel's organizational structure during the period of the judges. A proposal by Martin Noth made in 1930 has defined the discussion ever since.[27] Studying evidence from Greece in the first millennium B.C., he concluded that Israel's twelve-tribe system was formed on the analogy of the Greek "amphictyony," the classic example of which comes from Delphi in central Greece, dating to ca. 600 B.C. This was a religious association of twelve members revolving around a shrine at Delphi, pledged to a peaceful coexistence and a common defense against outside aggression; it met yearly for religious assemblies and affirmations of the ties that bound it together. In the years since Noth's proposal, many other tribal leagues of various types have been explored, many much closer to Canaan than Greece.

The twelve-tribe Israelite system—revolving around the place God would choose (Deut. 12:5, 11, 14, 18, 21, 26), which originally was Shechem and then was moved to Shiloh after Shechem's destruction by Abimelech (Judges 9)—seemed naturally to fit this model. It met occasionally to affirm the covenant, and a system of common defense seems to have been in place. This is a logical enough proposal in many ways, and the hypothesis has had many adherents ever since.

The amphictyonic model has been widely criticized, however, especially recently.[28] Among the most telling criticisms has been that the primary characteristic of Greek amphictyonies was a central shrine, whereas the specific number of its members was secondary—it was not always twelve. Noth, on the other hand, elevated the number "twelve" to primary status, since the biblical evidence is very unclear about the precise status of the

27. Martin Noth, *Das System der zwölf Stämme Israels*; *The History of Israel*, 85–109.
28. For representative reviews, although somewhat lengthy, see A. D. H. Mayes, *Israel in the Period of the Judges*; C. H. J. de Geus, *The Tribes of Israel*; Norman K. Gottwald, *The Tribes of Yahweh*, 345–86. For briefer overviews, see Mayes, "The Period of the Judges and the Rise of the Monarchy," 299–308; M. C. Astour, *IDBSup*, s.v. "Amphictyony"; Mayes, *ABD* 1, s.v. "Amphictyony."

Israelite shrines at Shechem, Shiloh, or elsewhere during this period. Also, despite much circumstantial evidence that Noth and others gathered, the fact remains that nowhere in Joshua, Judges, or Samuel is such an organization mentioned at all. Indeed, the emphasis (especially in Judges) is precisely that there was *no* centralized authority, political or religious. Many of the alternative proposals follow in the general direction charted by Noth but propose different bases for the organization, modeled after examples closer to Israel in time and geography.[29]

What should be clear is that the biblical writers were not so interested in political or religious structures per se, and it would be a mistake to read the book of Judges with the question of organization as the primary concern. The book's main theme is Israel's relationship to God and God's character in responding to His people. The period clearly is a transitional one, showing Israel between its status as a landless people entering a new land, newly released from captivity (as found in the book of Joshua), and its status as an established political entity, with national boundaries and a king (as found in 2 Samuel). Its political and religious organization in all three periods, however, is not nearly as important as the relationship it fostered with the Lord, under whatever system.

THE OFFICE OF "JUDGE"

The "judges" (*šōpĕṭîm*) of the book of Judges do not fit the modern conception of a "judge." That is, they did not normally hold court, listen to complaints, or make legal decisions. (Deborah is the exception in 4:4–5.) Rather, they were primarily leaders of Israel, delivering the nation from foreign threat or oppression. A key to understanding them is provided in the book itself: "And the Lord raised up judges, who *saved* (or delivered) them from the hand of those who plundered them" (2:16; author's translation).

No individual is called a "judge" in the book; the only time the term is used in that way it refers to God (11:27).[30] This is a significant part of the book's message: It is the Lord who is the true judge of His people, and He controls their fortunes, both for blessing and for punishment.

Many scholars have seen a distinction in the roles or offices of judge. The "major" judges (Othniel, Ehud, Deborah, Gideon, Jephthah, Samson; cf. Shamgar) are seen as charismatic military leaders whose primary function was to deliver Israel, and the "minor" judges (Tola, Jair, Ibzan, Elon, Abdon) are seen mainly as juridical leaders, whose major function was to dis-

---

29. To the works in n. 28, add Henry E. Chambers, "Ancient Amphictyonies, Sic et Non," 39–59; George E. Mendenhall, *The Tenth Generation*, 174–97; "Social Organization in Early Israel," 132–51; John Bright, *A History of Israel*, 162–73.

30. The noun *judge* is used six times in 2:16–19 to refer to the judges to come in the book, but none is named there.

pense justice.[31] Noth spoke of a particular office for the latter, who were part of the amphictyony and only later became combined with the charismatic heroes.

The case is not as clear as Noth and others would suggest, however. For one thing, his formulation depends heavily on his hypothesis of an "amphictyony" as the organizational structure binding Israel together in this period, and this hypothesis has been severely criticized (see above). Second, there are good indications that there was not such a radical distinction between the major and minor judges. For example, the account of Jephthah occurs in the midst of the accounts of the minor judges, carrying many features of these short accounts, yet he is clearly a "major" judge by virtue of his activity. Also, both Othniel (3:9–10) and Tola (10:1–2) not only "judged" but also "delivered" Israel.[32]

Thus, we conclude that all of the judges had some sort of a military function in delivering God's people. Even though several of the minor judges are not said specifically to have "delivered" Israel, we need not conclude that they did not do so in some way. The book certainly appears to be selective about the information related, even about the judges it includes.[33] Some (or all) may have had juridical functions as well, but this was only secondary.[34] The terms "major" and "minor" are useful only in describing the length and style of the narratives that inform us about each judge.[35]

THE PLACEMENT AND FUNCTION OF JUDGES 1:1–2:5

The first section of the book of Judges (1:1–2:5) introduces us to the states of affairs during the period immediately after the death of Joshua, and it forms the basis for the summaries of the book's message found in 2:11–23. Two issues arise concerning its relationship and context: (1) the relationship of this passage to the book of Joshua; and (2) its relationship to Judges 2:6–10.

Judges 1:1–2:5 and the book of Joshua. The prologue to the book sets the stage and the tone for all that follows. Initially, it shows some continu-

---

31. Albrecht Alt first made this distinction in "The Origins of Israelite Law," 101–71, esp. pp. 130–32. The idea was developed more fully by Martin Noth, "Das Amt des 'Richters Israels,'" 404–17. See also Georg Fohrer, *Introduction to the Old Testament*, 206–8.
32. See, in more detail, Alan J. Hauser, "The 'Minor Judges'—A Re-Evaluation," 190–200; E. Theodore Mullen, Jr., "The 'Minor Judges': Some Literary and Historical Considerations," 185–201.
33. That its listing of judges is incomplete is indicated by Samuel's reference to "Bedan" (1 Sam. 12:11, assuming that the MT reading is correct here).
34. Mullen ("The 'Minor Judges,'" 201) suggests that they may have been called judges only for theological reasons: to remind Israel of its covenant unfaithfulness and as a testimony to God's mercy.
35. Hauser, "The 'Minor Judges,'" 200.

Major and Minor Judges

MAJOR	MINOR	TRIBE
Othniel* (3:7–11)		Judah
Ehud (3:12–30)		Benjamin
	Shamgar (3:31)**	?
Deborah (4:1–5:31)		Ephraim?
Gideon (6:1–8:32)		Manasseh
	(ABIMELECH [8:33–9:57])***	
	Tola* (10:1–2)	Issachar
	Jair* (10:3–5)	?
Jephthah* (10:6–12:7)		?
	Ibzan* (12:8–10)	Judah or Zebulun
	Elon* (12:11–12)	Zebulun
	Abdon* (12:13–15)	Ephraim
Samson* (13:1–16:31)		Dan

* These eight are said specifically to have "judged" Israel (see also Deborah in 4:4). In addition, Eli (1 Sam. 4:18) and Samuel (7:15–17) are considered to be judges in the tradition of the above.

** Shamgar is a "minor" judge because he is mentioned in only one verse, but he delivered Israel like the "major" judges.

*** Abimelech was not a judge at all in the sense that the others were. He arrogated kingship to himself and was a leader of sorts in Israel for three years before he was killed (Judges 9).

ing military activity (1:1–26), which indicates that all military conquests had not been completed during Joshua's day. Then it makes explicit the incomplete conquests of several of the tribes (1:27–36). That Israel had disobeyed in the matter of the Conquest is confirmed in 2:1–5, when the angel of the Lord makes this accusation clear.

According to Brevard Childs, the notice in 1:1 about all of this happening after Joshua's death shows that a new period in Israel's history has begun.[36] In sharp contrast to the peaceful and unified picture we have of Israel at the end of the book of Joshua, Judges introduces a less optimistic picture. The breakdown in Israelite society detailed in 1:1–2:5 forms the keynote for the book, one that is made more explicit in the balance of chapter 2, which presents the cycles of sin, slavery, and salvation.

The book begins exactly as Joshua did: "And it happened, after the death of [Moses/Joshua], that . . ." (1:1; author's translation). This indicates clearly the start of a new era; the old leader is gone. We see a contrast here, however, in that no new leader is commissioned to lead Israel; rather, the tribe of Judah is designated to lead in the fight against the Canaanites

36. Childs, *IOTS*, 258–59.

(1:1–4). On the one hand, this foreshadows the rather chaotic conditions that would prevail in this period because there was no identifiable leader. On the other hand, the choice of Judah hints at the leadership position predicted for it long ago (Gen. 49:8–12), which would come to fruition with the establishment of the monarchy under David and his descendants (who were from the tribe of Judah).

One issue that arises regarding the relationship between Judges 1 and Joshua is the incomplete nature of the conquests presented in Judges contrasted with the complete pictures of the Conquest in Joshua, especially Joshua 10. In Judges 1:21, 27–36, we have detailed accounts of land that various tribes had left unsubdued. This contrasts with the emphasis in Joshua 10, which is one of complete and swift annihilation of people throughout the entire region. For example, according to Joshua 10:40, "Joshua subdued the whole region, including the hill country, the Negev, the western foothills and the mountain slopes, together with their kings. He left no survivors. He totally destroyed all who breathed" (see also v. 42a).

The contrast, however, is not merely between Joshua 10 and Judges 1. Even in the book of Joshua, we have indications that the Conquest was not complete. This is especially evident in 11:22; 13:2–6; 15:63; 16:10; 17:12–13, all of which speak of people in the land who survived, who were not driven out. Also, in contrast to the picture conveyed in Joshua 10 about a quick sweep, Joshua 11:18 states that "Joshua waged war against all these kings for a long time."

Because even the book of Joshua gives this more realistic picture, we must understand the statements in Joshua 10 as a sort of stylized summary, or a "provisional conclusion."[37] Some support for this idea can be adduced when it is noted that exactly seven cities, along with their kings and people, are listed as having been destroyed in the summaries (10:29–39). The number seven may be symbolic, rather than comprehensive.[38]

Judges 1:1–2:5 and Judges 2:6–10. A question of chronology arises in these two passages, since both of them mention the death of Joshua (1:1 and 2:6–10). The second passage presents his death as having occurred after the events of chapter 1, but the events in chapter 1 supposedly *followed* his death (v. 1).

Many scholars see this duplication as due to the convergence of independent traditions.[39] At least one scholar treats verse 1a—"After the death of

37. Marten Woudstra, *Joshua,* 184.
38. See also G. Ernest Wright, "The Literary and Historical Problem of Joshua 10 and Judges 1," 105–14; Walter R. Roehrs, "The Conquest of Canaan According to Joshua and Judges," 746–60; Webb, *The Book of Judges,* 116, 208, and passim.
39. E.g., Boling, *Judges,* 36, 72; Soggin, *Judges,* 20, 40–42.

Joshua"—as a title to the entire book, and sees the events in chapter 1 as all taking place *before* Joshua died. Thus, in this understanding, the account of his death in 2:6–10 is correctly placed chronologically.[40] This suggestion is attractive, since it resolves the problem of 1:11–15, which essentially duplicates Joshua 15:15–19. However, the grammatical construction in verse 1 is a common one, demanding that the reference to Joshua's death be read in conjunction with the words immediately following, not detached from them.

Thus, the judgment here is that 1:1 is correctly placed and most of the events in chapter 1 followed Joshua's death. Thus, the reference in 2:6–10 about Joshua's death is out of place chronologically. It is a "flashback" inserted at the beginning of the second section of the book (2:6–3:6). It duplicates Joshua 24:28–31 almost word for word, and its purpose is to tie closely the material that follows to the book of Joshua. Indeed, Cassell has well shown the function of 2:6–10 by aptly titling the passage "an extract from the Book of Joshua showing when and through what occasion the religious apostasy of Israel began."[41]

Thus, we see that the book opens with two parallel introductions (1:1–2:5 and 2:6–3:6), both of which refer to Joshua's death and point us in various ways to the book of Joshua. Both introduce materials that clearly show the contrasts between the period of the judges and Joshua's day.

THE ANGEL OF THE LORD IN JUDGES

The term "angel of the Lord" occurs some fifty-nine times in the OT. One-third of these occurrences (eighteen) is found in Judges:

(1) Judges 2:1, 4
(2) Judges 5:23
(3) Judges 6:11, 12, 20, 21, 22, 22
(4) Judges 13:3, 13, 15, 16, 16, 18, 20, 21, 21

In addition, the term "angel of God" appears nine times in the OT, at least three times in Judges: 6:20 and 13:6, 9. In all these cases, the two appellations seem to be synonymous. Thus, there are four true loci in Judges for these terms. Though they do not occur in Joshua (but cf. 5:13–15), they do appear several times in Samuel. (See esp. 1 Sam. 29:9; 2 Sam. 24:16.)

---

40. Cundall, *Judges*, 19, 51.
41. P. Cassell, *Lange's Commentary*, 54. In this understanding, Judges 1:11–15, which duplicates material already written in Joshua 15:15–19, represents another "flashback." Both passages have their roots in Joshua 10:36–39, which mentions the taking of Hebron and Debir. The insertion about Caleb at this point in Judges 1 is due to the similarity of this later campaign to the earlier one in Joshua 10: both mention Hebron, followed by Debir.

The appearances of the Angel of the Lord. In each of the four cases in Judges, the angel makes a sudden appearance, and he appears as the representative of the Lord.

1. Judges 2:1–5: The angel of the Lord had been at Gilgal and went up to Bochim. He spoke to the people about their covenant disobedience.
2. Judges 5:23: The angel of the Lord uttered the curse on Meroz.
3. Judges 6:11–24: The angel of the Lord came to Ophrah and appeared to Gideon to speak with him. He also performed a sign for Gideon, then vanished.
4. Judges 13:1–25: The angel of the Lord appeared to Manoah's wife and to him, performed a sign, then vanished.

In the last two cases, when the angel vanished, the humans' responses were similar: Gideon "saw [*rā'āh*] that it was the angel of the Lord" (6:22), and he feared for his life (6:22–23); Manoah "knew [*yādā'*] that it was the angel of the Lord" (13:21), and he too feared for his, and his wife's, life (13:22). Such a reaction of fear appears to have been rooted in the Pentateuchal stricture against humans seeing God: in Exodus 33:20, God, speaking to Moses, says, "You cannot see my face; for man shall not see me and live."[42]

The appearance of the angel was a supernatural one, and it is described in Judges 13 as awesome (v. 6). Manoah's wife did recognize him as "a man of God" (v. 6). However, his essential character, as revealed in his name, was not to be revealed to them (vv. 6, 17–18). This could mean that it was the Lord Himself (cf. Ex. 3:14–15) or that it was the Lord's close representative.

The point here is that, in all these cases, the Lord and the angel of the Lord seem to be closely identified with each other. This is confirmed in Judges 6, where the individual who visits Gideon is referred to alternately as the "angel of the Lord" and the "Lord" Himself. (Compare especially 6:12 with 6:14 and 16.) Note also Manoah's judgment that, in seeing the angel of God/the Lord, he and his wife had seen God Himself (13:22). And in 2:1–3, the angel speaks as God, in the first person.

The identity of the Angel of the Lord. Because of the close association of the angel of the Lord and the Lord Himself, many students have won-

---

42. The context of Exodus 33:18–23 suggests that it was the full range of God's glory that Moses could not see; however, Moses did speak with God and know Him "face to face" (Ex. 33:11; Deut. 34:10) and "mouth to mouth" (Num. 12:8); he even "beheld" the form of God Himself (Num. 12:8).

dered about the precise identity of this angel.[43] Essentially, there are three options:[44] (1) he is a true angel with a special commission; (2) he may be a momentary descent of God Himself into visibility; (3) he may be the Logos Himself (i.e., Christ) "a kind of temporary preincarnation of the second person of the trinity."[45] Because of the close relationship—even alternation—of the angel of the Lord and the Lord Himself, it would seem that the first option is not adequate (unless the merging or alternating of the two is only in the language used and not in the actual reality). The angel represents God Himself in very real ways.

Exodus 23:20–23 is a key text in this regard, since it shows how this angel carries the Lord's character and authority. Exodus 23:21 shows that the angel has the authority to forgive sins and that the Lord's name is "in him," and verses 21–22 both specify the angel's authority to speak for God. On the other hand, in Exodus 32:34–33:17, we see more of a distinction between the Lord and His angel: the Lord pledges to send His angel before Israel, despite their sin (32:24; 33:2), but He Himself will not go with them (33:3). This seems to distinguish this "angel" from God Himself. When the passage speaks in 33:14 of God's presence with Israel, it does not refer to His "angel" but, rather, His "face" (*pānay*: lit., "my face") that goes with them.

Some evangelical interpreters take these manifestations of the angel of the Lord to be pre-NT revelations of Christ.[46] In support, the descriptions of an angelic-type being (though the term angel is not used) in Daniel 10:6 and Ezekiel 1:26–28 are compared with John's descriptions of Jesus (Rev. 1:14, 16). Also, it is noted that the angel of the Lord is not mentioned in the NT when Jesus is on earth. Furthermore, the fact that Jesus was "sent" to do His Father's work (John 8:18) is compared to the angel's also being sent by God. Thus, G. B. Funderburk concludes, "Only the Logos, or some other manifest personification of God, would be able to [speak with authority as if he were God Himself]."[47]

However, we should note that the NT, which certainly is not loath to identify Jesus Christ with OT figures (as King and Messiah, as Priest, as the "Word" of God incarnate) never makes this identification explicitly. Obviously, Jesus was the self-expression of God in the NT, but nothing in the Scriptures requires our understanding God's self-expressions prior to Jesus' birth to have been this selfsame Person. Thomas McComiskey's conclusion

---

43. Two critical scholars who deal with the issue are Walther Eichrodt, *Theology of the Old Testament*, 2:23–29; and Gerhard von Rad, *Old Testament Theology*, 1:285–89. Several evangelical treatments are represented in the following notes.
44. J. M. Wilson, *ISBE* 1, s.v. "Angel," 125.
45. Ibid.
46. E.g., J. B. Payne, *The Theology of the Older Testament*, 167–70; G. B. Funderburk, *ZPEB* 1, s.v. "Angel," 162–63; Walter Kaiser, *Hard Sayings of the Old Testament*, 98–100.
47. Funderburk, *ZPEB* 1, s.v. "Angel," 163.

is a judicious one: "It is best to see the angel as a self-manifestation of Yahweh in a form that would communicate his immanence and direct concern to those to whom he ministered."[48] This self-revelation of God certainly anticipated Christ in a typological way, even if it was not Christ Himself. This may be analogous to the way in which "wisdom"—as it is described and personified in Job 28 and Proverb 8—displays remarkable affinities with the incarnate Word.[49]

JEPHTHAH'S VOW

The eighth judge in the book of Judges is Jephthah (10:6–12:7). The Spirit of the Lord came upon him, and he delivered Israel from the Ammonite threat (11:29). Prior to the battle, Jephthah gave an impressive speech, telling the Ammonites that it was the Lord Himself, not the Israelites, who had taken the land (11:14–27). The Lord Himself was to judge the dispute between Ammon and Israel (11:27), which He did in a decisive way by giving Israel the victory (11:32–33).

The story of Jephthah is not merely about a military victory, however. The story reaches its climax with the grotesque episode of Jephthah's ill-advised vow and sacrifice of his own daughter (11:30–31, 34–40). In an attempt to curry favor with the Lord, he promised to sacrifice "whomever" (or "whatever") came out of his house to meet him upon his victorious return (vv. 30–31).

The first question that arises here is, What exactly did Jephthah intend to vow? The issue revolves around whether he intended to offer a human sacrifice, whether he expected to offer an animal sacrifice, or whether he was being intentionally ambiguous, intending to offer *whatever* came out, either a human or an animal. The Hebrew in verse 31 literally states "the one going out, who(ever) goes out of the doors of my house." Some versions and commentators understand the form here impersonally and translate it as "whatever,"[50] while others render it personally, as "whoever."[51] In theory, either case is permissible grammatically. However, in the context, the strong probability points to the personal reference. If an animal were intended, the gender of the form in question should be feminine,[52] whereas in

---

48. Thomas E. McComiskey, *Evangelical Dictionary of Theology,* s.v. "Angel," 48. See also Millard Erickson (*Christian Theology,* 443), who draws a similar conclusion.
49. See Hartmut Gese, "Wisdom, Son of Man, and the Origins of Christology: The Consistent Development of Biblical Theology," 23–57.
50. E.g., NIV, NASB, NJPSV; Boling, *Judges,* 208.
51. E.g., RSV, NRSV; Goslinga, *Joshua, Judges, Ruth,* 388.
52. That is because things with no specified gender—abstracts or neuters—are expressed in Hebrew by the feminine (GKC, § 122q and n. 2). "Whatever" is an inclusive form that would fall into this category.

actuality it is masculine. Furthermore, the phrase "to meet me" refers more appropriately to a human than to an animal.[53] Thus, it is most likely that Jephthah intended to offer a human sacrifice to the Lord.

It might be argued that Jephthah's grief reaction in verse 35 when he learned that he would have to sacrifice his daughter indicates that he expected to offer an animal. However, that is not a necessary conclusion. Equally plausible is the suggestion that he expected a servant—who presumably would be more expendable than his daughter—to meet him.

A second question that arises is whether or not Jephthah actually carried out his vow. This arises because the text does not explicitly say that he killed his daughter, only that "he did to her as he had vowed" (v. 39). When the verse goes on to say that "she was a virgin," some assume this meant that she had merely been "sacrificed" (i.e., dedicated) to a life of perpetual virginity (v. 39), which was "to the Lord" (v. 30), i.e., dedicated to the Lord in a manner similar to Hannah's dedication of Samuel.

However, the plain meaning of the words is that Jephthah did exactly what he had vowed to do, namely, he offered his daughter as a burnt offering. The verb in verse 39 can easily be understood as a "past perfect": "and she had been a virgin" (i.e., before she died).[54] Afterward, the commemoration of Jephthah's daughter certainly was not a celebration of this awful event but rather a mourning (vv. 37–40).

How could a judge such as Jephthah—who had God's Spirit upon him and who is commended in 1 Samuel 12:11 and Hebrews 11:32—do such a thing? Human sacrifice in Israel was expressly prohibited in the law and condemned in the prophets (Lev. 18:21; 20:2; Jer. 19:5; Ezek. 20:30–31; 23:37, 39). Jephthah certainly was familiar with Israel's history, which included such prohibitions (11:15–27). The answer simply is that he was rash, foolish, and he sinned in doing this. If the Scriptures were to withhold commendation of people because of some sinful aspects to their lives, no commendations would ever have been issued, except in the case of Jesus. Jephthah's vow reflects a misguided application of the principle of offering to God the best of one's treasure. It also demonstrated a certain lack of faith, since earlier he had indicated that he believed the Lord would intervene on his behalf (vv. 9, 27), and especially since the Spirit of the Lord already had descended on him (v. 29) before he made his vow.

Did Jephthah have to follow through on his vow? Essentially, the answer is yes. Vows were made only to God, and they were solemn affairs that did indeed have to be kept. People were not forced to take them, but, if they did, they must be kept (Deut. 23:21–23; Ps. 15:4; Eccles. 5:4–5).

---

53. Webb, *Judges*, 64.
54. See RSV, NRSV, NJPSV; Kaiser, *Hard Sayings of the Old Testament*, 105.

In the end, although he was used by God and he knew of God Himself, Jephthah is one more example of the deterioration of morality and of the "Canaanization"[55] of life that is depicted in the book of Judges.[56]

THEOLOGY OF THE BOOK OF JUDGES

THE LAND

A major theme of the book of Joshua is Israel's inheritance of the land in fulfillment of God's promises. In the book of Judges, concern for the land remains in focus, but with a difference. Now the issue is why Israel had not been able to possess the land completely (see above). The answer comes clearly that Israel's disobedience—in not completely annihilating the Canaanites, and especially in turning to their gods—was to blame (2:1–3, 20–22).

Thus, we see the concern for the land in Judges being tied to another major theme of Joshua as well—that of the purity of Israel's worship. The warnings sounded in Joshua were not heeded, and the book of Judges records the consequences. The gift of the land, such a prominent motif in Joshua, is seen in Judges as compromised by Israel's apostasy. The note in 18:30 about "the day of the captivity of the land" sounds an ominous warning that, eventually, even this gift would be withdrawn for a time.

ISRAEL'S APOSTASY

Israel's apostasy is the cause of the threats to the land. The text explicitly states that in 2:1–3, 20–22. Repeatedly we see the Israelites breaking the covenant, turning to the Canaanite gods, and generally "doing evil,"[57] and repeatedly we see them suffering the consequences. The oppressions, chaos, and generally negative picture in the book are due to the repeated sin.

GOD'S FAITHFULNESS

God's faithfulness forms the counterpoint in the book to Israel's apostasy. Despite Israel's repeated falling away, He repeatedly provided for deliv-

---

55. See Daniel I. Block, "The Period of the Judges: Religious Disintegration under Tribal Rule," 39–57.
56. Three thorough treatments of all the questions involved with Jephthah's vow are Goslinga, *Joshua, Judges, Ruth,* 388–96; Kaiser, *Hard Sayings of the Old Testament,* 101–5; and especially Patricia A. Halverson, "The Influences Upon and the Motivation for the Making of Jephthah's Vow," 104–29. All three agree that Jephthah intended a human sacrifice, and Kaiser and Halverson agree that he carried it out on his daughter. Goslinga shrinks from the latter conclusion; his motivation, however, is primarily theological, not rooted in the text of Judges 11.
57. See 2:3, 11–13, 17, 19; 3:6, 7, 12; 4:1; 6:1, 10; 8:24–27, 33; 10:6; 13:1; 17:6; 21:25.

erance. He did not do this unthinkingly or mechanically, manipulated by Israel's cries for help (see 3:9, 15; 4:3; 6:6; 10:10), and He did not spare Israel from the consequences of its actions. (Indeed, He angrily delivered the nation into various foreign hands.) Rather, He delivered Israel because of His promises about the land; He remained faithful to these promises. We should emphasize that the immediate cause of God's deliverance was not because of any merits on Israel's part, nor even because of Israel's repeated "repentance," but rather because of God's compassion and His pity (2:16, 18).

After a careful reading, one cannot escape the impression that God emerges as the "hero" of the book,[58] that He acted on Israel's behalf in spite of its faithless character, and that even the judges themselves did not contribute greatly to improvement of spiritual conditions in the land. The judges certainly acted as God's agents of deliverance from foreign oppressions, but most of them exhibited personal qualities and behavior that were rather coarse, even sinful. Note, for example, the coarse but vivid details of Ehud's killing of Eglon (3:21–22, 24), the apostasy into which Gideon led Israel (8:24–27), the poor light in which Abimelech is cast (chap. 9), the rashness of Jephthah's vow (11:30–31, 34–40), and the erratic behavior of Samson (chaps. 13–16).

Two of the most famous judges were anything but paragons of virtue. After an auspicious beginning, Gideon displayed a decided lack of faith in badgering God for a confirmatory sign (6:36–40), and later he made an ephod that became an object of worship and a snare for him, his family, and all Israel (8:24–27). Samson violated all the main provisions of the Nazirite vow imposed upon him (Judg. 13:7; cf. Numbers 6): he drank wine at his wedding feast (Judg. 14:10);[59] he had much contact with the dead (e.g., 14:8–9, 19; 15:15); and he allowed his hair to be cut (16:17–19). Furthermore, he married an unbelieving Philistine (14:1–20), and he had intimate relations with at least two other Philistine women (16:1, 4).

In general, the judges did not lead Israel in true repentance and in putting away foreign gods, certainly not in the way the reforming kings did later in the kingdom of Judah. The one judge who did the most along this line—Gideon (6:25–23)—did so at the beginning of his ministry; by the end, he was leading the people in exactly the opposite direction (8:24–27).

58. Cundall (*Judges*, 45–47), in his section on the permanent religious value of the book, lists attributes of God as three of his four subheadings: God's righteousness, sovereignty, and graciousness and long-suffering. These all legitimately are important concerns in the book, and they reinforce our judgment that God is the true hero of the book.

59. The word for "feast" here is *mišteh*, which more properly is understood as a "drinking feast."

We should note that the NT has a more positive view of Gideon, Samson, and others than we find in the book of Judges: Hebrews 11:32 lists Gideon, Barak, Samson, and Jephthah (along with David, Samuel, and the prophets) as examples of those "who through faith conquered kingdoms, administered justice, and gained what was promised; who shut the mouths of lions" (v. 33). (Hebrews' positive view here is similar to the one found in Sirach 46:11.) However, two things should be noted. First, not every one of these "heroes of faith" did all of these things, as the phrase about lions' mouths shows. These are representative examples of what they did through their faith. Second, and more significantly, to say that these heroes had faith (in some measure, at some point in their lives) is not to say that they were consistent models of faith and virtue (throughout their lives). Undoubtedly they demonstrated faith (at times) that allowed God to "conquer kingdoms" through them. But, just as surely, the book of Judges focuses more upon other aspects of their character to point out the widespread apostasy during the period.

THE CASE FOR KINGSHIP

The book of Judges argues that Israel needed a king. It presents its case that kingship was something positive in three major ways.

First, it does so via its general outline and structure. Far from presenting us with a series of repetitive cycles leading nowhere, the book of Judges more precisely shows these cycles as part of a downward spiral, leading to a virtual bankruptcy of any positive virtues in the land.[60] This downward spiral applies to Israel's fortunes themselves—the enemies at the outset are external, whereas at the end of the book they are internal (a civil war has just ended)—and to religious conditions. The latter judges (especially Jephthah and Samson) seem worse than the earlier ones, and chapters 17–21 reveal a tangled web of covenant violations as the final stories unfold.

However, the book does not end on a completely hopeless note. For one thing, some good came out of the civil war in chapters 20–21: the tribes acted in a unified fashion in confronting Benjamin, and they were even concerned about the continuity of that tribe (21:6–7).

A second note of hope points toward a resolution of Israel's problems, and this is found in the editorial comment repeated four times in the last chapters of the book: "In those days there was no king in Israel" (17:6; 18:1; 19:1; 21:25 NASB). To this comment is added the phrase "every man did what was right in his own eyes" in two of the references (17:6; cf. 21:25 NASB).

These comments do much more than convey information about Israel's political organization; indeed, the reader already is well aware of this.

---

60. This point is made forcefully by Block in "The Period of the Judges: Religious Disintegration under Tribal Rule," 39–57.

Rather, the comments make the clear point that things would be better under a king.[61] The biblical norm was that people should do what was right *in the Lord's eyes*, not their own.[62]

The standard for Israel was that a king was to lead the nation in true worship and truly trust in the Lord to fight Israel's battles (see esp. Deut. 17:14–20).[63] Under such a king, people would no longer do what was right in their own eyes but what was right in the Lord's.

A second way in which the book of Judges speaks to the issue of kingship is in the episode where the men of Israel asked Gideon to rule over them (Judg. 8:22–23). In this passage, Gideon refuses the offer by saying that it is the Lord (and no other) who is to rule over them. This passage is usually seen as one of the clearest statements in the OT against kingship. However, the message here is not that kingship per se is the problem. Rather, the problem is the motivation for the request; it is because "you have saved us out of the hand of Midian" (v. 22). That is in direct contradiction to Deuteronomy 17:16 about the Israelites' not building up the number of horses they owned (i.e., their military power: horse-drawn chariots were the ancient equivalent of modern tanks). It is also in direct contradiction to the entire point of the story in Judges 7:1–8 about the paring down of the numbers of Gideon's army from 32,000 to 300 men! The point there was that Israel should not boast "that her own strength has saved her" (7:2). Yet the men of Israel asked Gideon to rule over them. Because of this (and perhaps also because it was not God calling him to rule over Israel, but rather the people),[64] Gideon had no responsible choice but to refuse. The refusal is not a statement about the illegitimacy of the institution of kingship but, rather, a more limited comment about the circumstances under which Gideon was asked to rule.

A third way the book of Judges speaks to the issue of kingship is its perspectives on Abimelech's abortive kingship in chapter 9. Here, Gideon's son Abimelech made himself king by means of a bloodbath. In reaction, Jotham told a fable about the trees of the forest, in which only the lowly thornbush consented to become king (9:7–15). The point is obviously to compare Abimelech with the thornbush, and many scholars have concluded that the larger point is that kingship itself was illegitimate. However, Gerald Gerbrandt correctly observes that the purpose of the chapter in its present form

---

61. This is pointed out by Gerald E. Gerbrandt in his *Kingship According to the Deuteronomistic History*, 123–40; see also Howard, "The Case for Kingship in Deuteronomy and the Former Prophets," 106–11. Against those scholars who argue that the book of Judges presents a positive view of the states of affairs then in existence, see pp. 109–11 in the Howard article.

62. Howard, "The Case for Kingship," 110 and esp. n. 27.

63. See Gerbrandt, *Kingship*, 103–16; Howard, "The Case for Kingship," 106–7.

64. Deuteronomy 17:15 makes clear that God was to do the choosing of a king.

is *not* to condemn the institution of kingship per se but, rather, "to indict Abimelech and the citizens of Shechem."[65] Nowhere is Abimelech condemned for becoming king. Rather, his crime is in killing his brothers (vv. 24, 56), and he is cursed for this. The larger passage emphasizes the curse motif: the curse of fire that is to devour the bramble in the fable (v. 15) is reiterated by Jotham concerning Abimelech and the others (v. 20), and the conclusion to the passage explicitly points to its fulfillment (vv. 56–57). The point of the passage, then, is "not that kingship is a crime, but that when kingship is based on crime and the abuse of force, . . . then the inevitable outcome of such a kingship will be destruction."[66]

Nothing in the book of Judges suggests that the final author was anti-kingship. Rather, he was clearly arguing that things would have gone better under a king. In this sense, then, the book functions as an introduction to— and a justification of—the monarchy. The end of the book serves as an appropriate preface to the next stage of the larger story related in 1 Samuel, the introduction of the monarchy.

OUTLINE OF THE BOOK OF JUDGES

Prologue: Incomplete Conquest of Canaan (Judges 1:1–2:5)
Southern Conquests: Fulfillment and Nonfulfillment (1:1–21)
Northern Conquests: Fulfillment and Nonfulfillment (1:22–36)
The Angel of the Lord and the Broken Covenant (2:1–5)

Israel in the Period of the Judges (Judges 2:6–16:31)
Introduction to the Period (2:6–3:6)
Othniel vs. Cushan-rishathaim, King of Aram (3:7–11)
Ehud vs. Eglon, King of Moab (3:12–30)
Shamgar vs. the Philistines (3:31)
Deborah vs. Jabin, King of Canaan (4:1–5:31)
    Victory over the Canaanites (4:1–24)
    Victory Song of Deborah (5:1–31)
Gideon vs. the Midianites (6:1–8:32)
    Continuing Apostasy (6:1–10)
    Gideon's Call (6:11–40)
    Gideon's First Military Encounter (7:1–8:3)
    Gideon's Second Military Encounter (8:4–28)
    Gideon, Father of Abimelech (8:29–32)

---

65. Gerbrandt, *Kingship*, 131.
66. Ibid., 132.

4

RUTH

Where you go I will go, and where you stay I will stay. Your people will be my people and your God my God. (Ruth 1:16)

The women living there said, "Naomi has a son." And they named him Obed. He was the father of Jesse, the father of David. (Ruth 4:17)

The book of Ruth contains one of the most delightful stories in the Bible. In it we see things "working out right" for all the main characters, and the reader finishes the story with the satisfied feeling that all is well. Things really do "work together for good to those who love God," as Paul was to write many years later (Rom. 8:28 NASB).

The book of Ruth tells us that the period of the judges was not characterized totally by chaos, that God was still in control, that human virtues such as kindness and loyalty still had a place in Israel, and that an exemplary king was about to be raised up. The book provides a refreshing contrast to the incessantly negative message about conditions in Israel during the time of the judges. It tells a simple, yet profound and carefully constructed story about one family's fortunes during a difficult time, and of God's low-key—but sure and steady—involvement in blessing their lives.

RUTH: TITLE AND WOMAN

The book's title comes from its main character, Ruth, a Moabite woman who was a godly, loyal daughter-in-law to Naomi, a woman from Judah who lost her husband and two sons while living in Moab. Ruth is a good example of a foreigner who came to embrace Israel's God through contact with Israelites. She indeed blessed Abraham's descendants, and she was blessed through them (see Gen. 12:2–3). She was an ancestor of David, and one of four women—all foreigners—in Matthew's genealogy of Jesus (Matthew 1).

Her name is not known elsewhere in the OT, and its meaning and national origin are uncertain. It appears to mean "refreshment, satiation, comfort,"[1] which certainly would fit her character and the character of the book. However, the book does not make a point of this.

AUTHORSHIP AND DATE OF COMPOSITION

The book's author is unknown. The suggestion has been made by several that the author was a woman, since the two main characters were women and they are presented as acting assertively throughout.[2] The author was a consummate crafter of stories: the story is rightly lauded far and wide as a literary masterpiece (see below).

The Talmud attributed the book to Samuel (*Baba Bathra* 14b), but scholars today date it later.[3] Discussions of the book's date often hinge on what the book's purpose was (see below). For example, those who have seen it as a polemic against Nehemiah's marriage reforms and who have seen substantial Aramaic influence in the book's language suggest a postexilic date in the fifth or fourth centuries B.C. For those who have seen in it some form of legitimization of the Davidic monarchy, a date sometime during the monarchy is postulated, but exactly when is uncertain. The gloss in 4:7 explaining the practice of redemption that took place between Boaz and the "kinsman-redeemer" as having been done "in earlier times" suggests a significant time lapse between the events and the writing, time enough for a general forgetting of such earlier customs, but even this may not be so.[4] Several have noted that the theology and the narrative style of the story accord best with other early Israelite stories, such as many of those in Genesis, Judges, and the "Court History of David" in 2 Samuel.[5] A reasonable consensus exists today that the book was written sometime during the early monarchy, perhaps during the reign of Solomon or earlier (in David's reign).

LITERARY NATURE

The book is short (eighty-five verses), but it is a masterful composition. Hermann Gunkel did the first extensive analysis of the book from a literary standpoint, and he termed it a "novella," by which he meant a short, well-constructed story, with carefully developed plot and characters, extensive use of dialogue, which moves to a climax and denouement, put togeth-

---

1. E. F. Campbell, Jr., *Ruth,* 56; Robert L. Hubbard, *Ruth,* 94 and n. 15.
2. Hubbard, *Ruth,* 24 and n. 6.
3. See the detailed discussions in Leon Morris, *Ruth,* 229–39; Campbell, *Ruth,* 23–28; Hubbard, *Ruth,* 23–35.
4. See Hubbard, *Ruth,* 33–34, 247–49; Campbell, *Ruth,* 27–28, 147–48.
5. Campbell, *Ruth,* 24–25; Hubbard, *Ruth,* 31–34; Ronald Hals, *Theology of the Book of Ruth,* 20–53.

er by one author.[6] Gunkel saw this as coming together from earlier popular sagas in several stages. The assumption was that the major thrust of the story was fictitious. Many have followed Gunkel in searching for literary antecedents to the present story that might be identified.[7]

Many who have accepted Gunkel's form-critical categorization nonetheless do not accept the notion of partial or complete fictitiousness implied in the term. Campbell calls it "a Hebrew historical short story," and he is followed in this by Hubbard.[8] As such, it possesses a distinctive literary style, manifests an interest in ordinary people, carries a combination of purposes, and is meant to entertain.[9] A rich bibliography of studies devoted to Ruth's literary qualities (as opposed to those devoted to identifying and classifying its literary genres) has arisen as well.[10]

There can be no disputing that the book is a masterful composition, whatever the modern literary label it is given. At the same time, it need not have been fiction either (see chapter 1). For purposes here, Campbell's term is certainly acceptable: "a Hebrew historical short story." (See "Exposition of the Book of Ruth" below for further development of the literary nature and artistry of the book.)

UNITY

In the search for literary antecedents, much has been written about earlier, shorter forms of the present story.[11] However, almost all agree that the present story—at least through 4:17—exhibits a remarkable unity and literary "polish."

Much wider disagreement is visible, however, when the extended genealogy of David in 4:18–22 is considered, which is usually seen as a later, secondary addition to the already-finished story.[12] There are several reasons for this. First, this genealogy duplicates information already found in the short genealogy in 4:17b. Second, such a pedestrian list as a genealogy

6. See Brevard S. Childs, *IOTS,* 562; Hubbard, *Ruth,* 8–9, 47.
7. See Hubbard's helpful review of the literature (*Ruth,* 8–11).
8. E.g., Oswald Loretz, "The Theme of the Ruth Story," 396; Campbell, *Ruth,* 3–4, 9–10; Childs, *IOTS,* 562; Hubbard, *Ruth,* 47–48.
9. Campbell, *Ruth,* 5–6.
10. See, e.g., D. F. Rauber, "Literary Values in the Bible: The Book of Ruth," 27–37; Campbell, *Ruth,* 10–18; Phyllis Trible, *God and the Rhetoric of Sexuality,* 166–99; Barbara Green, "The Plot of the Biblical Story of Ruth," 55–68; Adele Berlin, *Poetics and Interpretation of Biblical Narrative,* 83–110; Murray F. Gow, "The Significance of Literary Structure for the Translation of the Book of Ruth," 309–20, and the bibliography in n. 4 (p. 309). A "deconstructive" literary reading of Ruth is Danna Nolan Fewell and David Miller Gunn, *Compromising Redemption.*
11. See Hubbard, *Ruth,* 8–11.
12. See the surveys of the discussion in Campbell, *Ruth,* 172–73; Jack Sasson, *Ruth,* 179–83; Hubbard, *Ruth,* 15–21.

scarcely seems to fit with the careful artistry of the rest of the book. Third, this is the only case in the OT of a genealogy following (rather than introducing) the narrative to which it is connected. Fourth, this genealogy clearly is intended to focus on David, whereas little in the book to this point has seemed to indicate such an interest.

Recently, much more emphasis has been placed on the connections of 4:18–22 with the rest of the book.[13] First, it balances the narrative "family history" of the introduction (1:1–5). Second, it serves to link the short genealogy of 4:17b with the mention of Perez in 4:12, and it confirms the blessings uttered in 4:11b–12.[14] Third, it shows the story's characters receiving their just rewards, in being part of the long, blessed line of King David. Fourth, it honors Boaz, not only by including him, but by placing him in the seventh position.[15] Hubbard argues for an *original* unity with the rest of the book, whereas most of the others argue for a later, redactional (i.e., editorial) unity. The resolution of this question is not as important as showing what connections do exist, however, since, in the final analysis, the genealogy *is* part of the inspired Scripture that we have.

PURPOSE

While the book clearly is satisfying to read, the primary reason for its having been written is not clearly stated, and this has led to many proposals concerning its purpose.[16]

A popular proposal has been that Ruth was written at the time of Ezra and Nehemiah, who prohibited Jews to intermarry with foreigners, as a polemic against their "nationalistic" marriage reforms. The book of Ruth, with its Moabite heroine, would have made an effective counterpoint to this. However, it is doubtful that this was the book's primary purpose: first, undoubtedly the book dates from an earlier period, and thus does not speak directly to such postexilic concerns (see above); second, if it is indeed a polemic, it is a most curious one, since the book's tone is so pleasant and the polemical "point" is easily missed.

13. See, e.g., Stephen Bertman, "Symmetrical Design in the Book of Ruth," 165–68; Campbell, *Ruth,* 14–18, 172–73; Childs, *IOTS,* 566; Sasson, *Ruth,* 179–83; Gow, "Significance of Literary Structure," 318–20; Hubbard, *Ruth,* 15–23; and many of the works cited in n. 10.
14. For more on the connections between David and Perez (and, more importantly, Judah) in Ruth, see David M. Howard, Jr., "The Case for Kingship in the Old Testament Narrative Books and the Psalms," 25–26; and Eugene H. Merrill, *Kingdom of Priests,* 182–87.
15. See Hubbard, *Ruth,* 20, and the works in his n. 58. (This note contains several errors; the first half of line 1 should read as follows: "Sasson, 181–84 [referring to Sasson's 1979 edition]; idem, *IDBS,* 354–56.")
16. See Morris (*Ruth,* 239–42), Childs (*IOTS,* 563–64), and Hubbard (*Ruth,* 35–42) for good reviews of these.

Some maintain that the book intends to show various social customs in action, such as levirate marriage or redemption (see below). However, strictly speaking, there is no levirate marriage in the book (again see below), and, in any case, these customs do not play a role central enough to justify seeing them as the book's primary purpose.

Others emphasize a more prosaic purpose: simply to entertain or to tell a pleasing story about friendship. However, on the latter point, we should note that the story emphasizes family relationships more than it does friendship; on the former point, while affirming its aesthetic value, most would go beyond that as a primary purpose for the book.

Perhaps the best rubric under which to see the book's purpose has to do with God's activity, with God as the controlling agent behind the events of the book.[17] This fits well with various statements within the book (e.g., 2:12, 20; 3:10, 13; 4:14), and it allows for the inclusion of (and accounting for) the Davidic genealogy, since by God's providence Ruth and Boaz are included into the "royal" line that He had been providentially overseeing since the days of the patriarchs.

THE PLACE OF RUTH IN THE CANON[18]

In the present Hebrew Bible, the book appears as the fourth in the Writings (after Psalms, Job, Proverbs), and the first of five *megillot* ("scrolls"): Ruth, Song of Songs, Ecclesiastes, Lamentations, Esther. The five *megillot* were used liturgically—they were read at the major festivals. The Song of Songs was read at Passover, Ruth at the Feast of Weeks (Pentecost), Ecclesiastes at the Festival of Tabernacles, Lamentations on the Ninth of Ab (an extrabiblical fast), and Esther at Purim. The order of the books follows the order of the festivals, except that Ruth and Song of Songs have been transposed, since Passover comes before the Feast of Weeks. This transposition has placed Ruth immediately after Proverbs, and it might have been for reasons of subject matter. Campbell has noted, "Proverbs concludes with an acrostic poem [Prov. 31:10–31] celebrating a 'worthy woman,' in Hebrew *'ēšet ḥayil*, and Ruth then goes on to describe just such a woman, calling her an *'ēšet ḥayil* in 3:11."[19] We can also note that the book of Proverbs as a whole has an interesting focus on women. "Dame Wisdom" is prominent in chapters 1–9, especially chapters 8–9, and she is contrasted with the "foolish woman" (*'ēšet kĕsîlût*), the harlot (*zônāh*), and the "loose

---

17. See this position, expressed in various ways, in Hals, *Theology of the Book of Ruth*, 3–19; Morris, *Ruth*, 242; Childs, *IOTS*, 563–64; Hubbard, *Ruth*, 39–42.
18. The most extensive treatment of this question is L. B. Wolfenson, "Implications of the Place of the Book of Ruth in Editions, Manuscripts, and Canon of the Old Testament," 151–78; see also Campbell, *Ruth*, 32–36; Childs, *IOTS*, 564–68; Hubbard, *Ruth*, 5–7.
19. Campbell, *Ruth*, 34.

woman" (*'iššāh zārāh*). Ruth provides a salutary contrast to these latter women as well.

One early Hebrew tradition, probably the earliest, places Ruth before Psalms.[20] This is eminently understandable, since the book would thus function as an introduction to the Psalter or as a memoir of its "author," David.[21] Since the major purpose of the book has to do with showing God's hand in the lives of people who were David's ancestors and with introducing David himself (see above), this placement has much to commend it.[22]

The same Hebrew tradition treated Ruth as a part of the book of Judges, which reflects the Septuagintal traditions that are followed in our Protestant English Bibles today. In the latter, the book appears among the Former Prophets, between Judges and 1 Samuel. This placement, too, has a clear logic to it. The first factor in this is chronological, since the book opens with the line "In the days when the judges ruled [lit., 'judged']." There also are several links between Judges 19–21 and Ruth. On one level, the events in Ruth provide a healthy, positive contrast to the rather sordid events at the end of Judges. On another level, several terms function as keywords linking the two books.[23] Perhaps the most prominent is the term *ḥayil* (usually translated as "valor" or "worth"), which is used in Judges 20:44, 46 to describe the men of Benjamin (NIV: "valiant fighters") and in Ruth 2:1 to describe Boaz (NIV: "a man of standing") and in Ruth 3:11 to describe Ruth (NIV: "a woman of noble character"). Also of note is the mention in Judges 19:16 that the only one who would offer the Levite and his concubine hospitality at Gibeah was a "sojourner" (RSV; NASB marg. n.); Ruth was a "sojourner" as well.[24] Finally, we should note that Elimelech, Naomi's husband, was from "Bethlehem in Judah" (Ruth 1:1, 3). This recalls the final two episodes in Judges, where characters from "Bethlehem in Judah" also figured: first, in chapters 17–18, where the Levite who went to work for Micah and then the Danites was from Bethlehem (17:7), and second, in chapters 19–21, where another Levite took the concubine, who later was killed, from Bethlehem (19:1).

The book introduces 1 Samuel very appropriately as well. The book of Ruth is concerned with the Davidic line, and 1 Samuel introduces the monarchy and David's selection as God's choice for the position.

---

20. The Babylonian Talmud, Tractate *Baba Bathra* 14b (reference from Hubbard, *Ruth*, 6–7).
21. Wolfenson, "Implications," 167–68.
22. Another early tradition begins with the following order: Genesis, Exodus, Leviticus, Joshua, Deuteronomy, Numbers, Ruth, Job, Judges. This considers Ruth as a "historical" book, not among the Writings, although the entire ordering is somewhat curious. (See Morris, *Ruth*, 231 and nn. 2, 3.)
23. Boling, *Judges*, 276; Campbell, *Ruth*, 35.
24. The term is not found in Ruth, except in 1:1, with reference to Elimelech's family's "sojourning" in Moab. But a sojourner is clearly what Ruth was when she came to Israel. She identified herself as a "foreigner" in 2:10.

Historically, the book's placement preceding Psalms was probably the earliest, with its placement following Proverbs next; both of these locations were in Jewish traditions and included the book among the "Writings."

HISTORICAL AND CULTURAL CONTEXT FOR THE BOOK OF RUTH

There is no real question concerning the dating of the events in the book of Ruth: they occurred during the period of the judges (Ruth 1:1). Exactly when within that period is more uncertain. It may have been relatively late in the period, as Boaz is presented as David's grandfather; however, the genealogy may have been somewhat flexible, and Boaz may have been somewhat further removed from David than the genealogy implies (see below).

Questions of historical background for the book, then, are essentially the same as those for the book of Judges (see chapter 3). What follows is brief consideration of the Moabites (since Ruth was a Moabite) and of the customs of "levirate" marriage and redemption found in the book.

THE MOABITES

The land occupied by Moabites[25] was on the plateau directly east of the Dead Sea, primarily its southern half. It was characterized by nomadic pastoralists and small agrarian settlements, with no large cities. It sat astride the "King's Highway," which was an important north-south trade route. It was settled in almost every period covered by the OT.

Moab was the son of Lot, via his incestuous relationship with his oldest daughter (Gen. 19:37); thus the Moabites and Israelites were distantly related. The Bible frequently mentions contacts between the two peoples. After the Exodus from Egypt, Israel clashed with Sihon, king of the Amorites, who had seized control of Moab (Numbers 21). Eglon was a Moabite kinglet (Judges 3). During the period pictured in Ruth, relations between these peoples seem to have been stable. Later, conflict again ensued at various times. A dramatic picture of that is seen in an inscription from a Moabite king, Mesha, who spoke of conflict with the Israelite kings Omri and Ahab in the ninth century B.C.; Ahab's son's (Joram's) conflict with Mesha is recorded in 2 Kings 3.

The religion of the Moabites was similar to that of the Canaanites in its major practices. Its major god was Chemosh, but it also worshiped his wife, Ashtar, and Baal, among others. Many of Chemosh's attributes, described by Mesha, are very close to Yahweh's in the OT, indicating similar religious sensibilities in some respects. In other respects, however, they were very

25. For more details on the Moabites, as well as bibliography, see chapter 7.

different, such as in the matters of polytheism and human sacrifice (see 2 Kings 3:27). If the embrace of a God foreign to her was at all a problem for Ruth, these similarities might have eased the transition somewhat.

LAWS OF "LEVIRATE" MARRIAGE AND REDEMPTION

Numerous laws and customs lie behind events in the book of Ruth, and in many cases the author assumes that the reader knows them first-hand, not bothering to explain them.[26] Of these, the most often discussed is the institution of "levirate" marriage and the related laws of redemption.[27]

The law of levirate marriage is found in Deuteronomy 25:5–10, where a widow's brother-in-law is obligated to marry her and father a son for her, in order for his dead brother's name to continue.[28] In Ruth, the transactions bringing together Ruth and Boaz (and the potential one between Ruth and the "near kinsman" in chapter 4) are seen to have been of this type.

We should note, however, that these are not, strictly speaking, levirate marriages as discussed in Deuteronomy. For one thing, the relevant root in Deuteronomy, *YBM* ("to perform the duty of a brother-in-law"[29]), is not found in Ruth in this sense.[30] In Ruth, the institution appears to be broader: the word used is *G'L* ("to redeem, to act as a kinsman").[31] Second, in Ruth there is no case of a brother actually marrying a widow (and there are three cases of widows portrayed in Ruth, so this certainly could have happened). The closest reference to a true levirate marriage is in Ruth 1:11, when Naomi bemoaned her lack of sons to marry Ruth and Orpah. The use of the term "levirate" marriage in connection with Ruth represents the extension of the concept beyond what the law stated.

More properly, the relevant Pentateuchal legislation involves the laws of redemption found in Leviticus 25; there the root is *G'L*,[32] as in Ruth. There,

---

26. See Hubbard (*Ruth*, 48–63) for a review of these.
27. The most extensive discussion of these is in Donald A. Leggett, *The Levirate and Goel Institutions in the Old Testament, With Special Attention to the Book of Ruth.* See, more briefly, H. Ringgren, *TDOT* 2, s.v. "*ga'al*"; J. Murray, *ISBE* 4, s.v. "Redeemer; Redemption"; R. K. Bower and G. L. Knapp, *ISBE* 3, s.v. "Marriage."
28. The term *levirate* comes from the Latin word for brother-in-law: *levir.*
29. The term is found elsewhere in the OT only in Genesis 38:8, referring to Onan's duty to his brother's wife, Tamar.
30. In Ruth 1:15, the feminine noun occurs twice: "sister-in-law," referring to Orpah.
31. The root occurs twenty-two times: as a verb in 3:13 (4 times); 4:4 (4 times); 4:6 (3 times); as a noun (*gō'ēl*) in 2:20; 3:9, 12 (twice); 4:1, 3, 6, 8, 14; a cognate noun occurs in 4:6, 7.
32. There is another related Hebrew term: *PDH* ("to ransom, rescue, deliver"). It basically means "to achieve the transfer of ownership from one to another through payment of a price or an equivalent substitute" (W. B. Coker, "*pādâ*," *TWOT,* 716). The two terms are close to being synonymous and are used in parallel in places. However, there might be a shade of difference in that *G'L* refers more to the family situation. That is, both terms involve payment of a ransom to "redeem" something or someone, but *G'L* is the term used to refer to redemption by a kinsman.

people or property that had been lost through indenture could be recovered by payment of a fee, usually by a relative or an owner. For example, the redemption of a slave is mentioned in Leviticus 25:47–54 and of property in 25:24–34. This redemption of land seems to be behind the reference in Ruth 4:3–4.

However, marriage was not specifically a part of the Levitical law of redemption, whereas it seems clearly to have been assumed by Ruth and Boaz (in chapters 3 and 4). Furthermore, the provision that Boaz mentioned in 4:5, whereby the near kinsman, in buying a field belonging to Elimelech, also was obligated to marry Ruth, is not found in the Pentateuch. These, too, are examples of extensions of the law that may, in fact, have been practiced but of which we have no direct knowledge.[33]

THEOLOGY OF THE BOOK OF RUTH

GOD'S SOVEREIGNTY AND STEADFASTNESS

There are numerous ways in which God's sovereignty and steadfast nature can be seen in the book. First, there is a special focus on God Himself in the book, particularly by the characters. Of its eighty-five verses, twenty-three mention God; of these, only two are the narrator's comments (1:6 and 4:13 bracket the book); the rest are from the mouths of the protagonists.[34] The characters themselves are conscious that God sovereignly orders events, and they depend on Him to do so.

This focus on God emphasizes a second (related) point, namely, that He is seen as acting continually throughout the book. The well-ordered direction and pace of the story assure us that things will indeed work out for the family of Elimelech that is threatened with extinction, and God does provide for them in the end.

God's steadfastness also can be seen in His loyalty to His people, in His refusal to abandon them, and in His rewarding their faithfulness to Him. These qualities are mirrored in remarkable ways in many examples of steadfast loyalty among the human characters in the book, particularly Ruth and Boaz. The most relevant Hebrew term here is *ḥesed*, which is usually translated as "steadfast love," "kindness," or "mercy." In Ruth, the term occurs three times, translated as "kindly" or "kindness,"[35] but we should note that loyalty and commitment are integral components of *ḥesed*. In God's case, these involve commitment to His covenant with His people.[36]

33. See Hubbard (*Ruth*, 48–63) on this idea of extension of the law, esp. pp. 49–52.
34. Hals, *Theology of the Book of Ruth*, 3–19, esp. p. 3.
35. Ruth 1:8; 2:20; 3:10; so translated by NASB, NIV, and RSV. NJPSV and NRSV have "loyalty" in 3:10.
36. Nelson Glueck, *Hesed in the Bible*; Katherine D. Sakenfeld, *The Meaning of Hesed in the Hebrew Bible: A New Inquiry*. For more on *ḥesed* in Ruth, see Campbell, *Ruth*, 29–30; Hubbard, *Ruth*, 72–74.

GOD'S HIDDENNESS

Paradoxically, in a book in which the characters express such confidence in God, and in which we see events always working out for their good, we also can note that God's presence and guiding hand are more hidden than in many other biblical books. It is not that God is at all absent from the book but that His role is a steady, quiet one; as noted above, the narrator seems deliberately to show restraint in referring to God, doing so only twice. Again and again, crucial turns in the story, which easily could have been attributed to God, instead are attributed to human action or even chance. See, for example, the comments about happenstance at 2:3—"As it turned out, she found herself working in a field belonging to Boaz"—and at 3:18—"Then Naomi said, 'Wait, my daughter, until you find out what happens.'"[37] Also, no special miracles are referred to outside of the two passing references at the book's beginning and end (1:6; 4:13). Even the genealogy is missing any comment about God's giving David to Israel.[38]

The lesson communicated by this is that God's hand is to be searched for in the everyday affairs of life, in the turns of fortune of God's faithful people. The story's characters certainly were aware of this. His presence is a continuous, faithful one, not merely of the dramatic, "hit-and-run" type.

INCLUSIVENESS

The book of Ruth communicates powerfully that God's purposes are not limited to Israelites. Ruth stands with a proud group of other foreigners in the OT, such as Melchizedek,[39] Rahab, Naaman, and the Ninevites of Jonah's day, who knew or embraced Israel's God. She was one of four women—along with Tamar, Rahab, and Bathsheba, all foreigners—included in the line of Jesus in Matthew 1. She illustrates the principle laid out in Genesis 12:2–3, that people would be blessed through their contact with Abraham's descendants and their God.

THEOLOGY OF THE MONARCHY

The last word in the book is "David." As noted above, the genealogical concern with David (both in 4:17b and 4:18–22) shows the book's interest in this great king and, by extension, in the institution of the monarchy itself. A major concern is the threat of eradication of Elimelech's name (i.e., line-

---

37. See Hals, *Theology of the Book of Ruth*, 11–19; Campbell, *Ruth*, 28–29; Hubbard, *Ruth*, 68–71.
38. Hubbard, *Ruth*, 69.
39. He was a priest of "God Most High" (*'ēl 'elyôn*), before Israel was constituted as a nation. (On this title for God, see G. Lloyd Carr, "*'elyôn*," *TWOT*, 668–69.)

age). Not only does the book show how his name was preserved, it goes on to show how his name became part of that great lineage so important in later centuries.[40] Conversely, the book also functions to show that God's choice of David had its roots much earlier than David's own time. As Loretz has asserted, "His choice is not made in a moment; it has a long prehistory, and took place before the chosen one was formed in the womb of his mother (cf. Jer. 1:5). . . . The mysterious workings of God in behalf of David began during the lives of his ancestors."[41]

This emphasis on the (Davidic) monarchy is reinforced by the prominent place Judah occupies in the book as well.[42] Several patriarchal wives, related to Judah in one way or another, are mentioned in Ruth 4:11–12, as is his son, Perez, in 4:12, 17, and even Judah himself (4:12). Judah was the tribe from which the true monarchy was to come (Gen. 49:8–12). We can even note that the book goes beyond Judah per se and emphasizes all the patriarchs via many allusions and customs.[43] In this way, Ruth and Boaz, and ultimately David, are seen as standing in continuity with all of these, to whom God had promised, among other things, kings from their line (17:6, 16; 35:11).

EXPOSITION OF THE BOOK OF RUTH

As noted above, the consummate literary nature of the book of Ruth is often commented on. Here we present a very brief exposition of the book that especially focuses upon its literary qualities: the flow of thought, the overall coherence, the thematic and plot developments, and the characterizations. This is done here (and nowhere else in this volume) for two reasons. First, the book of Ruth lends itself well to this type of analysis, better than most of the historical narrative books. Second, its short length allows for this to be accomplished within the scope of this volume.

INTRODUCTION:
A GODLY FAMILY EMPTIED (RUTH 1)

A tragic family history (1:1–5). The story begins with a rapid overview of the family that Ruth married into. Theirs was a tragic history to date: they were driven out of Bethlehem by the land's "emptiness" (famine)[44] to a neighboring country, Moab, one that usually was hostile to Israel. In rapid

---

40. See especially Loretz, "Theme of the Ruth Story," 391–99.
41. Ibid., 398.
42. See Howard, "The Case for Kingship," 25–26; Merrill, *Kingdom of Priests,* 182–87.
43. See especially Hubbard, *Ruth,* 39–42.
44. The pattern of emptiness-fullness in Ruth has been perceptively traced by Rauber ("Literary Values in the Bible: The Book of Ruth").

succession, the family patriarch, Elimelech, died, his two sons married Moabite women, Orpah and Ruth, and then these sons died,[45] leaving the wife and mother, Naomi, bereft of any true family ties or anyone to support her.

The return home (1:6–22). Naomi purposed to return home, drawn partly by reports of food there (v. 6). Her daughters-in-law would not let her go alone; Ruth persisted in "clinging" to her even when her sister-in-law did not (v. 14), and she promised her loyalty to Naomi in a beautiful speech (vv. 16–17). Despite this encouragement, the chapter ends with Naomi disconsolate over her fate: she wanted to be called "Mara," which means "bitter," rather than "Naomi," which means "pleasant." She was acutely aware that God had emptied her life of its fullness (v. 21). A telling comment at the end sets the stage for hope and fullness to come: it was the beginning of the barley harvest (v. 22). Food was now available again, and it was through events associated with this harvest that Naomi's family was to be saved.

DEVELOPMENT (A):
RUTH AND BOAZ MEET (RUTH 2)

Chapter 2 begins at the outset of the barley harvest and ends at its and the wheat harvest's conclusion. Ruth set out to glean in the fields of whomever would grant her favor (v. 2). By "chance"[46] she came to Boaz's field and found favor there (vv. 3–16). The narrator had mentioned him in verse 1 as being related to Naomi through Elimelech, but Ruth and Naomi did not know where she would end up. This "coincidence" is typical of the many signs in the book of God's unseen hand directing things. The meeting between Boaz and Ruth unfolds in three stages.

First (vv. 3–7), she went out to the field, and he noticed her when he arrived and inquired as to who she was. The foreman identified her for Boaz, stating that she had requested permission to glean among the sheaves and that she had been waiting (lit., "standing") most of the day (for permission).[47] Her request was somewhat bold. Previously (v. 2), she had intended merely to glean among the standing ears of grain, but now her request was to do so among the piles or bundles of already-harvested grain, a

---

45. They actually died ten years later (v. 4), but the story's telling does not emphasize the time interval at all; the impression left is one in which Naomi is left battered by the relentless onslaught of events.
46. Verse 3; see NASB marg. n.: "her chance chanced upon."
47. The text of verse 7 is extraordinarily difficult, as a comparison of translations and commentaries will reveal immediately. The understanding presented here (of one of several problems) follows Hubbard (*Ruth,* 142, 147–52), who sees the statement about Ruth's going forth and gleaning in verse 3a as an introductory summary and that she did not actually begin gleaning until Boaz granted permission.

much more assertive request.[48] Nevertheless, Boaz was to grant even this (v. 15).

Second, the actual meeting occurs (vv. 8–13). A key verse in this section is verse 10, which includes Ruth's words as she bowed at Boaz's feet. Structurally, it occurs almost exactly at the chapter's midpoint, and Ruth's comment about her being a "foreigner" and yet Boaz's taking her in, evokes many images about the Israelites' having been aliens and foreigners in Egypt, yet under God's care.[49] Boaz's response was a most gracious one, indicating an awareness of what Ruth had done already for her mother-in-law.

In the third stage of the meeting (vv. 14–16), Boaz's words provided for her by inviting her in for a generous meal and by instructing his workers to be generous in allowing her to reap.

The chapter closes (vv. 17–23) with Ruth's report to Naomi. Naomi saw God's hand in Ruth's meeting of Boaz. Her confidence helps to set the stage for the important developments in chapter 3.

DEVELOPMENT (B):
RUTH AND BOAZ ENGAGE (RUTH 3)

The next scene (chapter 3) begins and ends with references to "rest."[50] It opens with Naomi making plans for Ruth with regard to Boaz (vv. 1–5). Whether Ruth's suggestion of marriage in verse 9 went beyond what Naomi had instructed her is not clear. Nevertheless, Ruth did ask for Boaz's "protection" in a scene that hints of the sexual union that is to come later (vv. 6–13).[51] She justified her request by appealing to Boaz's status as her "close relative" (her *gō'ēl*),[52] representing some sort of an extension of the laws of the *gō'ēl*.[53] We should note that her request for Boaz's protection recalls an earlier scene: the phrase "spread the corner of your garment" (3:9) is literally "spread your wings" in Hebrew, which recalls Boaz's words about God's protection (2:12): "under whose wings you have come to seek refuge." Thus, we see that God's protection of Ruth was to be accomplished through Boaz.

48. Two sets of Pentateuchal laws are somewhat similar to the situation here, although they do not exactly correspond to her request: (1) Leviticus 19:9–10; 23:22; and (2) Deuteronomy 24:19.
49. Rauber, "Literary Values in the Bible: The Book of Ruth," 31–32.
50. 3:1; 3:18. The Hebrew word is *mānôaḥ* ("rest") in verse 1 (see NIV and NASB marg. nn.), and *ŠQṬ* "to have peace" in verse 18 (NIV: "rest").
51. There is no reason to assume any sexual consummation on that night, but certainly the scene is suggestive of sexuality (esp. vv. 4, 7, 9–10, 14). See also Hubbard, *Ruth,* 203 and references there.
52. See n. 31 and the discussion under "Laws of 'Levirate' Marriage and Redemption."
53. See n. 33. However, it is very possible that this was only custom and not binding; if legally binding, Naomi's elaborate preparations (vv. 1–5) would have been unnecessary. (See Green, "The Plot of the Biblical Story of Ruth," 61–63.)

Boaz's response (vv. 10–13 and 14–15) was a pleased (and pleasing) one, and Ruth and Naomi were assured that he would do all he could for her. The only complicating factor was the presence of a relative nearer than he, who thus should have prior claim to acting as her "redeemer" (gō'ēl). Thus, the stage was set for the story's climax, and the scene ends with Naomi anticipating precisely that.

CLIMAX AND RESOLUTION:
A GODLY FAMILY FILLED (RUTH 4)

A new home established (4:1–10). The tension concerning whether Boaz will be able to marry Ruth is extended in the opening verses of the final scene as the legal groundwork is covered, establishing the legality of whatever was to ensue (4:1–4). The near relative was informed of a field Naomi had for sale and offered an opportunity to buy it under the laws of redemption. He readily agreed. However, when he was informed that marriage to Ruth was part of the obligation (again referring to an understood Israelite law or custom otherwise unknown in the Bible), he demurred, citing the risk to his own inheritance.

At least two issues worthy of comment present themselves here.[54] First, why did Naomi appear so destitute early in the book if she, in fact, had owned property such as this? Neither the book nor any known Israelite law or practice presents any answer. The property may have been taken over by someone when the family moved to Moab, depriving her of any benefits from it when the famine was over. Second, what occasioned the near relative's initial acceptance and subsequent change of mind in verses 4–6? Here, too, there is no established law or custom to provide a clear answer. However, assuming that he did not know about Ruth initially, undoubtedly he saw an opportunity for an improvement in his own wealth; even if he were obligated to care for Naomi, she was old and the field would have been his when she died, presumably in the not-too-distant future. However, Ruth's presence suggested that she (or the son born to her by this man) would retain (or regain) rights to the land after Naomi's death. Thus, he would have endangered his own wealth by assuming the care and keeping of Ruth and any of her children, along with Naomi. So his answer was, in essence, "I do not have the resources to do this!"[55]

The near relative's refusal to redeem the land and marry Ruth marks the climactic turning point in the story. The rest of the section flows from

54. Many questions, in fact, arise in this chapter, most of them undoubtedly due to our lack of knowledge of Israelite customs. See Campbell (*Ruth*, 157–61) and Hubbard (*Ruth*, 52–63) for reviews of these.
55. See Hubbard, *Ruth*, 245–47.

this refusal, emphasizing it further (vv. 7–10). The next section also emphasizes it, since it shows the resolution of the issue of Elimelech's and Naomi's lineage via the son that was born to Ruth (vv. 11–22). Legally, Ruth and Boaz's son Obed perpetuated the line of Elimelech and Naomi and Ruth's deceased husband, Mahlon (vv. 9–10, 14–17a). However, it also is clear that Boaz is reckoned as legally part of the lineage in question (vv. 12, 17b–22). Evidently both assumptions were accurate, and so understood at the time.[56]

A new family history (4:11–22). The last sections of the chapter reveal that the satisfying resolution to the crises introduced earlier went beyond merely showing God's hand in the life of one family, for its own sake. The townspeople's blessing in verses 11b–12 and the genealogies in verses 17b and 18–22 make clear that these events were part of the great family and great scheme of things that had begun in patriarchal days and stretched into the establishment of the Davidic monarchy. As such, the book forms an important prelude to the monarchy, and its canonical place following the book of Judges—which also points to the monarchy—is most appropriate. Its focus in the end upon David points the way to the books of 1 & 2 Samuel, in which David is the dominant figure, both historically and theologically.[57] The book reminds us that God's care extended at the same time to one family and to the entire nation and that nothing happens to people without His eye upon them and His wings over them.

OUTLINE OF THE BOOK OF RUTH

Introduction: A Godly Family Emptied (Ruth 1)
A Tragic Family History (1:1–5)
The Return Home (1:6–22)

Development (A): Ruth and Boaz Meet (Ruth 2)

Development (B): Ruth and Boaz Engage (Ruth 3)

Climax and Resolution: A Godly Family Filled (Ruth 4)
A New Home Established (4:1–10)
A New Family History (4:11–22)

---

56. Campbell, *Ruth,* 160–61; Hubbard, *Ruth,* 62–63.
57. See discussion under "Unity" and "Theology of the Monarchy" for more on this.

5

1 & 2 SAMUEL

Those who oppose the Lord will be shattered. He will thunder against them from heaven; the Lord will judge the ends of the earth. He will give strength to his king and exalt the horn of his anointed. (1 Sam. 2:10)

He gives his king great victories; he shows unfailing kindness to his anointed, to David and his descendants forever. (2 Sam. 22:51)

The books of Samuel deal with the establishment of kingship in Israel and its theological significance. The books begin with Israel still under the decentralized system of the judges period and end with the Israelite monarchy firmly in place. They begin with the last of the judges (Samuel) and end with the first—and the greatest—king of the line of Judah (David).

The questions of *whether* and *how* the monarchy should be established dominate the first portions of 1 Samuel. These are followed by the question of *who* should be the king of Israel. When it becomes clear that the first king, Saul, had forfeited his crown and that David would acquire it, the question becomes whether David would survive Saul's attempts to kill him. Saul's death—and David's survival—at the end of the book effectively answer all these questions.

Second Samuel is devoted entirely to David's kingship. It opens with consolidation of his rule, and then details God's great promise of a perpetual dynasty to David. Soon thereafter David falls into great sin, and the second half of the book depicts David in decline, absorbed with internal problems in the kingdom, mostly revolving around his children. Nevertheless, the royal line of David and the attendant promises concerning it are well established at the end of the book.

The two books unfold against the backdrop of a persistent Philistine menace to Israel. First Samuel, then Saul, and finally David engaged them in battle, and they were not subdued as a threat to Israel until David's time. Indeed, David's reputation was built in part on his victories over Philistines and Ammonites.

These two books revolve around their major characters: Samuel, Saul, and David. There are basically four stories: Samuel (1 Samuel 1–7), Samuel and Saul (1 Samuel 8–15), Saul and David (1 Samuel 16–31), and David (2 Samuel 1–24). Through (and often despite) these figures, God's essential purposes were accomplished in the life of Israel.

TITLE AND DIVISION OF THE BOOKS

The books of Samuel are titled in the Hebrew Bible after the first major character in them. The early chapters focus on Samuel, but after 1 Samuel 15, he no longer figures in the action. However, by this point, he had been instrumental in anointing the other two major characters of the books, Saul and David, and thus his influence extended far beyond his own lifetime.

Originally, these books were one, and they were treated as such in all the Hebrew traditions until the fifteenth century A.D.[1] Long before that (ca. 200 B.C.) they were divided in two when the Hebrew Bible was translated into Greek, since the Greek text (with its vowels) required more space than the Hebrew (written without vowels). The Greek translators titled the books "1 and 2 Reigns," and what we now know as 1 and 2 Kings were known as "3 and 4 Reigns." The Vulgate shortened these to "Kings."[2] Following the example of such books as Genesis, Deuteronomy, and Joshua, 1 Samuel ends with the death of a great figure in Israel (Saul).

AUTHORSHIP, UNITY, AND DATE OF COMPOSITION

AUTHORSHIP

The books of Samuel were anonymously written. The Talmud (T.B. *Baba Bathra* 14b) attributed authorship of the book (singular) of Samuel, along with the book of Judges, to Samuel himself. However, his death is recorded in 1 Samuel 25:1, and few today seriously accepts this attribution. Samuel did apparently write about David's life in a work known as "the records of Samuel the seer" (1 Chron. 29:29), but to what extent this work coincided with the canonical books of Samuel is impossible to know.[3] Samuel also wrote about the kingship (1 Sam. 10:25).

More so than most of the previous books in the Bible, the books of Samuel, especially 2 Samuel, demonstrate close literary attention to detail.

1. P. Kyle McCarter, *I Samuel*, 3–4.
2. R. K. Harrison, *Introduction to the Old Testament*, 695
3. The same is true of the "records of Nathan the prophet" and the "records of Gad the seer" (1 Chron. 29:29), which also told of David's life.

Long, verbatim dialogues are included, and details of characters and events are meticulously recorded. Because of this, many scholars have argued that the books were written by a participant in (or an eyewitness of) the events themselves; many proposals concerning the books' author(s) have been advanced, including Nathan, Seraiah, Ahimaaz, or Abiathar.[4] The fact remains, however, that we do not know who wrote 1 & 2 Samuel.

UNITY OF COMPOSITION

The question of the unity of composition of the books of Samuel has interested critics at least since the days of Wellhausen. In the core sections of 1 Samuel concerning the transition to the monarchy, Wellhausen identified two "sources"—an anti-kingship one (1 Sam. 7:2–8:22; 10:17–27; and chaps. 12, 15) and a pro-kingship one (1 Sam. 9:1–10:16; and chaps. 11, 13–14). His work has dominated subsequent scholarship for a full century.[5]

He and others have expanded upon this work to cover the entire scope of 1 & 2 Samuel; some searched for traces of the Pentateuchal "documents" · (J and E), but the most influential treatments have focused on Noth's "Deuteronomistic History" (see the discussion in chapters 2 and 6). The pro-kingship source, for example, was seen as early, and the anti-kingship one was supposedly late (and Deuteronomistic). Other sections of the books were seen as having been composed of large, discrete blocks of material placed together in an end-to-end fashion. Three of the blocks, for example, were the ark narratives (1 Samuel 4–6; 2 Samuel 6), the "History of David's Rise" (1 Samuel 16–2 Samuel 5) and the "Court History of David" or "Succession Narrative" (2 Samuel 9–20, along with 1 Kings 1–2).[6]

In theory, there is no problem with postulating underlying sources for the books of Samuel; indeed, the Bible itself indicates that various sources existed for the periods covered by these books (e.g., 2 Sam. 1:18; 1 Chron. 29:29). However, searches for Pentateuchal-type "documents" in 1 & 2 Samuel founder for the same reasons they did in the Pentateuch (see the discussion in chapter 2), and Wellhausen's pro- and anti-kingship dichotomy is somewhat overdrawn.[7] More productive is the identification of various "sources" laid end-to-end, connected by editorial commentary. However, even here, these remain hypothetical; scholars, in dealing with them, have

---

4. See Harrison (*Introduction to the Old Testament*, 699–700) on these proposals.
5. Julius Wellhausen, *Der Text der Bücher Samuelis untersucht*; and *Prolegomena to the History of Ancient Israel*, 245–72.
6. For reviews of approaches to composition, see Otto Eissfeldt, *The Old Testament: An Introduction*, 242–48, 268–81; Harrison, *Introduction*, 696–708; McCarter, *I Samuel*, 12–30; Gerald E. Gerbrandt, *Kingship According to the Deuteronomistic History*, 18–38, 140–45; David M. Howard, Jr., *ABD* 2, s.v. "David" (esp. p. 47).
7. See Gerbrandt, *Kingship*, 23–36; J. Robert Vannoy, *Covenant Renewal at Gilgal: A Study of I Samuel 11:14–12:25*, 228 n. 96.

tended to ignore the final shape of the text. For example, the so-called Ark Narrative is divided into two sections, the second widely displaced from the first; likewise, the "Succession Narrative" is interrupted by the "Appendix" to 2 Samuel (chaps. 21–24). Focus on such units ignores the presence and functions of the intervening materials. Alternatively, scholars have asked questions—political, historical, sociological—that are not the primary concerns of the text.[8] Recently, there has been much more of a focus on unitary readings of the books of Samuel or their sections, readings that take better account of the whole or attempt better to hear the text's primary concerns.[9]

A large factor in the identification of "sources" has been the presence of supposed "doublets" (i.e., duplicate accounts of the same events that have survived in the text's final form) in 1 & 2 Samuel. A prime example is the pro- and anti-kingship accounts (see above), in which different reasons appear to be presented for Saul's accession (at God's command or at the people's request). Saul is twice rejected from being king (1 Sam. 13:13–14; 15:10–31). David appears to meet Saul twice (1 Samuel 16, 17). He attached himself to the Philistines twice (1 Sam. 21:10–15 [MT 11–16]; 27:1–4). He spared Saul's life twice (1 Samuel 24, 26). Goliath appears to have been killed twice, by two different people (1 Samuel 17; 2 Sam. 21:19).

Behind such reasoning, however, lie assumptions that events could never be repeated in similar fashion or that ignore the real differences between accounts that are similar on the surface or that do not fully allow for textual corruption. All of these may be accounted for adequately, either by apologetic, harmonizing approaches,[10] or by literary readings of various types.[11]

DATE OF COMPOSITION

Portions of the books of Samuel may have been written by a close observer of the events therein (ca. 1050–970 B.C.), as noted above. However, there are indications—e.g., the reference in 1 Samuel 27:6 to the kings of Judah—that the final form of the books was not compiled at least until some time after division of the kingdom (ca. 930 B.C.), perhaps even centu-

---

8. This can be seen in much of McCarter's analysis in his two commentaries on 1 & 2 Samuel.
9. See, e.g., Richard G. Bowman, *The Fortune of King David*; Lyle M. Eslinger, *Kingship of God in Crisis*; J. P. Fokkelman, *Narrative Art and Poetry in the Books of Samuel*; David M. Gunn, *The Story of King David*; *The Fate of King Saul*; Robert Polzin, *Samuel and the Deuteronomist*; V. Philips Long, *The Reign and Rejection of King Saul*.
10. E.g., as found in Harrison, *Introduction*, 696–708; or Gleason L. Archer, Jr., *A Survey of Old Testament Introduction*, 285–87; *Encyclopedia of Bible Difficulties*, 169–90. See Craig A. Blomberg ("The Legitimacy and Limits of Harmonization," 135–74) for a defense of a reasoned, harmonizing approach.
11. See n. 9.

ries later. There is no mention of the fall of Samaria, leading some to date the books' composition between 930 and 723/22 B.C.[12]

Others see the final edition as "Deuteronomistic," coming from the Exile or later. It must be admitted that a strong case exists for seeing 1 & 2 Samuel as closely connected to 1 & 2 Kings in approach and outlook, as championed by those who argue for the existence of the "Deuteronomistic History" (see the discussions in chapters 2 and 6). There are many more ties between these two pairs of books than, say, between 1 & 2 Samuel and Joshua or Judges. All four books focus on the fortunes of Israel's (and Judah's) monarchy, and all four see that institution as under God's care, responsible for loyalty and obedience to Him.

Ultimately, the question of the books' date is unanswerable. We should note, in any case, that no direct theological issue is at stake in the answer to this question. It appears reasonable enough to assume composition of their major portions in the days of David and Solomon themselves and to postulate final compilation and editing some time near or during the Exile.

THE TEXT OF 1 & 2 SAMUEL

The present Masoretic Hebrew text of the books of Samuel has suffered greatly in transmission, more so than almost any other OT book. Many passages are almost unintelligible on their own. As a result, the Greek (Septuagintal) and (to a lesser extent) Latin traditions have no small value as aids in recovering the original text. In many places they appear to have been based upon earlier, and purer, Hebrew texts than the present Masoretic texts are. Many of these corrections may be found in the marginal notes of the major English Bible versions, including the NASB, NIV, and NRSV.

Further light has been shed on the text of 1 & 2 Samuel by the discovery of several significant texts or text fragments of these books among the other manuscript finds at Qumran, near the Dead Sea, beginning in 1952. These have not received their final (or official) publication yet, but several preliminary studies have been made.[13] In many cases where the Greek traditions diverge from the MT, the Qumran readings side with the Greek, confirming judgments about the reliability of the latter in those instances. At other times, the Qumran readings are independent of both the Greek traditions and the MT. In general, the Qumran manuscripts, being the earliest, are closest to the originals, but judgments ultimately must be made on a case-by-case basis.

---

12. E.g., Harrison, *Introduction*, 709; Archer, *Survey*, 283–84.
13. See, e.g., Eugene C. Ulrich, Jr., *The Qumran Text of Samuel and Josephus*, and further bibliography in McCarter, *I Samuel*, 6–11.

All major English Bible versions at present use the MT as a base, correcting or supplementing it on the basis of other manuscript evidence as seen fit. A truly eclectic text—produced by choosing the best readings from among many manuscripts at any given point—such as has been produced for the NT has not been completed for the OT as yet. However, several important works have attempted this for the books of Samuel,[14] and such a project is now being undertaken for the entire OT.[15]

PURPOSE

Interest in the Israelite monarchy dominates the books of Samuel, as noted above. They were written to detail its establishment, including

- the initial request for it
- the actual establishment
- the tragic reign of the first king, Saul
- the consolidation of power by its second king, David
- God's great promises to David
- and David's decline in his later years.

We see both the benefits and pitfalls of kingship. Saul is depicted as a tragic hero, and David, prominent a character as he is, is presented with many flaws unhidden. The climax in the two books surely is found at 2 Samuel 7, where David is promised an everlasting dynasty.

In light of the importance of the Davidic monarchy in these and subsequent books of the OT, we can only conclude that the books of Samuel were written to show and to legitimate its establishment. In 1 Samuel, David shines by comparison with Saul, and he presents a heroic figure early in 2 Samuel as well. Nevertheless, we also clearly see David's shortcomings (in 2 Samuel 11–12 and in subsequent chapters). Far from undermining the legitimacy of the Davidic monarchy, however, these realistic portrayals of David serve to show that the dynastic promise was dependent on God's faithfulness, not David's or any other individual's (see esp. 2 Sam. 7:11b–16).

---

14. The most important of these are Wellhausen, *Der Text der Bücher Samuelis untersucht*; S. R. Driver, *Notes on the Hebrew Text and the Topography of the Books of Samuel*. These are both based on the Greek and Latin versions alongside the MT. Recently, McCarter (*I and II Samuel*) has incorporated the Qumran material as well in producing an eclectic text.
15. See D. Barthélemy et al., eds., *Historical Books*. Vol. 2 of *Preliminary and Interim Report on the Hebrew Old Testament Text Project*. See also the Hebrew University Bible Project and its occasional publication, *Textus*, vols. 1–16 (1960–1991), which is in process of producing an exhaustive critical edition based upon the earliest complete Hebrew manuscript, the *Aleppo Codex*.

The emphasis upon kingship by no means signals that kings were given a free hand in God's eyes, however. Whereas the author certainly highlights the monarchy, he also presents it in a prophetic perspective. The prophets Samuel and Nathan played prominent roles in dealing with Saul and David, both in encouraging and in condemning them. The exercise of true kingship in Israel was not to be done apart from loyalty to the Lord and obedience to His covenant.[16] By emphasizing the prophetic perspectives in a work devoted mainly to chronicling the establishment of kingship, the author "showed that the kings were obligated to be sensitive to the prophets, who interpreted the covenant for the nation."[17]

HISTORICAL AND CULTURAL CONTEXT FOR 1 & 2 SAMUEL

DATE OF THE EVENTS

The events in the books of 1 & 2 Samuel spanned a relatively short time period, roughly one and a half centuries from Samuel's birth, at the end of the twelfth century B.C., to the end of David's reign, ca. 970 B.C. First Samuel ends with the death of Saul, ca. 1010 B.C., which is the date of David's accession to the throne of Israel.

1 Samuel. Though the end date of 1 Samuel is well established (ca. 1010 B.C.), earlier dates, such as Samuel's birth or Saul's accession, are uncertain. We know little about Samuel's dates, except that his tenure as judge covered at least twenty years (7:2); more likely, it was much longer, since he appears to have been very young when Eli died and he began his judgeship (2:18–22; 3:1–2) but was "old and gray" when Saul became king (8:1, 5; 12:2). On the basis of information from the book of Judges and early chapters in 1 Samuel, we can tentatively place Samuel's birth at ca. 1120 B.C.[18]

The most difficult chronological problem in 1 Samuel concerns the length of Saul's reign and his age at accession to the throne. The present MT of 1 Samuel 13:1 reads (in a literal translation) "a son of a year [i.e., one year old] was Saul when he began to reign, and he reigned two years over Israel." These data clearly are incorrect, and many solutions have been advanced as corrections.[19] The most plausible suggest that two numbers have

16. See Gerbrandt (*Kingship*, 156–58) on the prophetic perspective. See also chapter 6 in this volume.
17. William Sanford LaSor, David A. Hubbard, and Frederic L. Bush, *Old Testament Survey*, 229.
18. See chapter 3; Eugene H. Merrill, *Kingdom of Priests*, 149–50, 177–78, 192–94. See also John J. Bimson (*Redating the Exodus and the Conquest*, 91–92), who does not specify a date but presents similar data and reasoning.
19. For reviews of this problem, see McCarter, *I Samuel*, 222–23; Bimson, *Redating the Exodus and the Conquest*, 89–91; Merrill, *Kingdom of Priests*, 192–94; Joyce Baldwin, *1 & 2 Samuel*, 102–3 and n. 1.

dropped out of an early text and that he became king somewhere between ages twenty and forty, and reigned between twenty and forty years. Acts 13:21 states that the length of his reign was forty years, a round number that is behind the NIV's reading of "forty-two years" in the Samuel passage.[20] This figure is fairly accurate, since Saul's son Ish-bosheth, who was forty years old when he succeeded Saul (as the short-lived king of a portion of Israel: 2 Sam. 2:10), appears not to have been born when Saul became king (cf. 1 Sam. 14:47–51 with 1 Chron. 8:33; 9:39). If this is so, Saul's reign would have begun ca. 1050 B.C.

2 Samuel. In 2 Samuel (and in later historical books), the dates are not nearly the problem they are for the earlier books of Joshua, Judges, or 1 Samuel. That book covers the forty-year period (2 Sam. 5:5) of David's reign, ca. 1010–970 B.C. The ease of dating here is due to the firm synchronisms that are available between the Bible and Assyrian and Babylonian records. (See chapter 6 for an extensive discussion of chronological matters.) Often the Bible will refer to an event with the formula "in the Nth year of the reign of a biblical king," an event that can be correlated with Assyrian or Babylonian chronologies. After ca. 1000 B.C., the margin for error in these records is only ten years, and after ca. 900 B.C., the margin for error shrinks to no more than a year in most cases. In later times, especially after 620 B.C., the margin for error is almost nil.

That is because of the careful records maintained by the kings of Assyria and Babylon, recording events in each year of their reign, and occasionally recording some datable astronomical event that can be recovered by modern science, such as a solar eclipse. Egyptian records also were carefully kept, but they are more relevant to the earlier periods of Israel's history. Unfortunately for biblical chronologies, the Bible does not have exact synchronic references in these earlier periods, and thus we see wider margins for error in dating such events as the Exodus.

HISTORICAL SETTING OF THE EVENTS

1 Samuel. The book of 1 Samuel unfolds against the backdrop of the end of the early Iron Age (Iron I, ca. 1200–1000 B.C.). This period was a relatively quiet one, both in Canaan and internationally. Architecture was very modest; large building projects were not undertaken in Israel until the days of David and Solomon. The context for 1 Samuel is much the same as that of the period of the judges, which did not end until Saul's accession.

---

20. In 1 Samuel 13:1, the NIV reads, "Saul was thirty years old when he became king, and he reigned over Israel forty-two years." Contrast NASB: "Saul was *forty* years old when he began to reign, and he reigned *thirty*-two years over Israel."

The major external problem for Israel in the period of Samuel, Saul, and David was the Philistine threat.[21] The Philistines oppressed Israel for forty years early in the period (Judg. 13:1; cf. 10:7–8), ca. 1124–1084 B.C. (On these dates, see chapter 3 under "Date of the Events.") Samson, although he had had several impressive successes against the Philistines, had not succeeded in breaking their hold over Israelite territory; that task fell to Samuel. Israel suffered a major defeat at Philistine hands at Aphek, ca. 1104 B.C., in which the ark was lost to the enemy (1 Sam. 4:1–11). It was soon recovered, but a hiatus of twenty years passed before the Philistines were engaged again and this time defeated under Samuel's leadership (7:2–14), such that "throughout Samuel's lifetime the hand of the Lord was against the Philistines" (v. 13).

Despite this success, Philistines fought Israel intermittently throughout Saul's reign (chaps. 13–14; 17; 23:1–5, 27–28; 27–29, 31). Saul (and Jonathan) had some limited success against them, but it was not until David had become king and consolidated power that Israel was able to defeat them so decisively that they did not disturb Israel again (2 Sam. 5:17–25; 8:1, 12).

Saul's home town was Gibeah, about three miles north of Jerusalem in Benjaminite territory (1 Sam. 10:26), and he apparently maintained it as his capital city while king (see 15:34; 22:6; 23:19). This town has been excavated, and a small fortress has been unearthed from this period, which very possibly served as Saul's headquarters.[22]

2 Samuel. The context for 2 Samuel was somewhat different, at least within Israel itself. Internationally, things still were quiet as far as the great powers in Egypt, Mesopotamia, and Asia Minor were concerned. Assyria was experiencing the beginning of a resurgence that was to reach a climax under Shalmaneser III, more than a century after David, but at the beginning of the tenth century B.C. that kingdom was not concerned with territories to the west. In Egypt, the Twenty-first Dynasty (ca. 1070–930 B.C.) was in decline, now that the glory years of the New Kingdom had just ended.[23] In Asia Minor, the great Hittite empire of the Middle and Late Bronze Ages had collapsed; it survived in several Neo-Hittite city-states in northern Syria that had

---

21. See chapter 3 for an introduction to the Philistines; on Saul's struggle with them, see A. D. H. Mayes, "The Reign of Saul," in *Israelite and Judaean History*, 322–31.
22. See Lawrence A. Sinclair, *EAEHL* 2, s.v. "Gibeah"; William S. LaSor, *ISBE* 2, s.v. "Gibeah."
23. See *ANEH*, 123–25, 286–87, for brief overviews of this quiet period in Assyria and Egypt; in more depth, see D. J. Wiseman, "Assyria and Babylonia c. 1200–1000 B.C.," 443–81; J. Černy, "Egypt: From the Death of Rameses III to the End of the Twenty-First Dynasty," 606–57. The dates listed here follow the "low" dating scheme mentioned in chapter 2, n. 11. William Kelly Simpson gives the date as 1085–945 B.C. (*ANEH*, 286).

little interest in conquests to the south; indeed, David and Solomon had several peaceful contacts with them (2 Sam. 8:9–11; 1 Kings 10:28–29; 11:1).[24]

That left a relative power vacuum in the eastern Mediterranean that allowed numerous small states to exist in relative independence. These included Aramean, Philistine, Ammonite, Moabite, Edomite, Amalekite, Phoenician, and Israelite states. Under David, Israel was able to assert itself as dominant among these in its region. He bequeathed a large territory to his son Solomon, whose direct or indirect influence reached from "Lebo-Hamath" (NIV) in the northeast, even as far as the Euphrates River itself (1 Kings 4:24), to the "brook of Egypt" in the southwest (8:65).[25]

Within Israel itself, the accession of David marked the beginning of a new era, one marked by numerous building projects, by consolidation and centralization of power, and by the beginning of international relations and trade. These came to full bloom under Solomon, during whose time Israel remained at peace.

David's Jerusalem. David captured Jerusalem ca. 1010 B.C. from the Jebusites who lived there (2 Sam. 5:6–9). It was a walled city, well fortified and supplied with water from a spring nearby, and had developed a fairly large bureaucracy over the years. His capture of Jerusalem was especially significant in unifying the northern and southern portions of the land; already in his day there appear to have been north-south rivalries.[26] Jerusalem was in territory not strongly identified with any tribe: it had been included in the tribal allotment of Benjamin (Josh. 18:28), but it also appears in the description of the borders of the tribe of Judah (15:8) and is included in the list of cities the Judahites did not conquer (15:63). Thus, it could play the role of a "neutral" capital well.

David began to rebuild portions of Jerusalem after its capture.[27] Second Samuel 5:9 states that he "built up the area around [the City of David] from the supporting terraces inward." These terraces were likely the terraced "fill" that has been excavated in recent years, which undoubtedly

---

24. For general introductions to the Hittites, see O. R. Gurney, *The Hittites*; Harry A. Hoffner, "The Hittites and Hurrians," in *Peoples of Old Testament Times*, 197–228; and "The Hittites," in *POTW*.
25. See Barry J. Beitzel, *The Moody Atlas of Bible Lands*, 121–25; Carl G. Rasmussen, *NIV Atlas of the Bible*, 116–23.
26. The two kingdoms were not yet divided, and yet "Israel" and "all Israel" are several times referred to early in 2 Samuel in contrast to "Judah" (e.g., 2 Sam. 2:9, 17; 3:10, 17, 19, 37; 4:1).
27. Convenient introductions to the Jerusalem of David's and Solomon's day may be found in Hershel Shanks, *The City of David*; Yigal Shiloh, *Excavations at the City of David, I (1978–1982)*; and "The City of David After Five Years of Digging," 22–38; Donald Ariel et al., *Excavations at the City of David 1978–1985*, vol. 2; W. Harold Mare, *The Archaeology of the Jerusalem Area*, 59–88; David Tarler and Jane M. Cahill, *ABD* 2, s.v. "David, City of."

The Kingdom of Israel Under David and Solomon

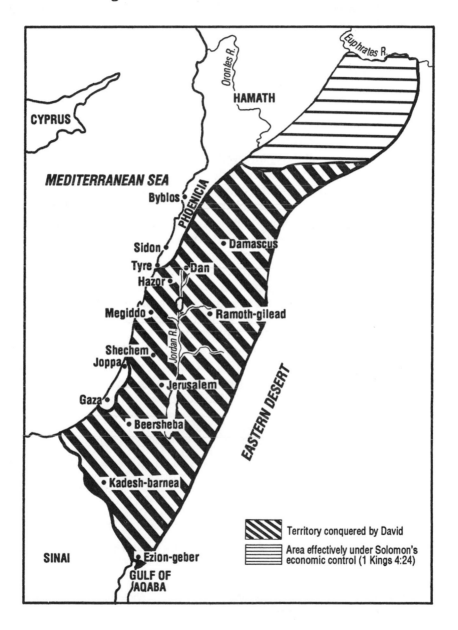

CYPRUS

Oronles R.

Euphrales R.

HAMATH

MEDITERRANEAN SEA

Byblos

PHOENICIA

Sidon • Damascus

Tyre • Dan

Hazor •

Megiddo • • Ramoth-gilead

Jordan R.

Shechem
Joppa

• Jerusalem

Gaza

• Beersheba

EASTERN DESERT

• Kadesh-barnea

SINAI

• Ezion-geber

GULF OF
AQABA

Territory conquered by David

Area effectively under Solomon's
economic control (1 Kings 4:24)

supported a large building of some sort.[28] He also had a house built for himself (5:11).

David also laid the foundations for Solomon's great building projects by purchasing the site north of his city for the Temple (24:18–25) and by providing abundantly for its supplies.[29] His contacts with Hiram, king of Tyre, enabled Solomon to build the Temple with Phoenician materials and workmanship (5:11; 1 Kings 5:1–12 [MT 15–26]; 7:13–47). (See chapter 7 for more on Israel and the Phoenicians.)

David's administration. The development of a state administration under David required much organization and manpower. It is likely that he utilized some of the Jebusite administrative machinery already in place, assuming of course that those involved sympathized at least somewhat with his religious convictions. However, despite assertions that David merely took over a Canaanite bureaucracy (he himself representing a secular, Canaanized political ideology in establishing his state),[30] we should note that there are numerous indications that he skillfully blended the various tribal elements within Israel and incorporated non-Israelite elements under a truly Yahwistic banner. His "mighty men," for example, included all of these elements (2 Sam. 23:8–38; cf. 1 Chron. 11:10–46). His arrangements for the Temple service gave prominence to the Levites, who functioned as a cohesive element within Israel (see 1 Chron. 23–26; esp. 26:30, 32).

He also organized military and civil officials into efficient administrative units (see 1 Chronicles 27).[31] He instituted a system of forced labor to accomplish many of the large building tasks (2 Sam. 20:24), a system that was greatly expanded under Solomon (1 Kings 4:6; 9:15–22).[32] The "elders" of Israel appear to have had special advisory status during several periods in Israel's history, including the united monarchy.[33]

28. Shiloh, "The City of David After Five Years," 27–29.
29. The latter is not a concern in 1 or 2 Samuel, but it is mentioned in 1 Chronicles 22:2–5 and 29:1–9.
30. E.g., George E. Mendenhall, "The Monarchy," 155–70; Gary A. Herion and Andrew F. Hill, "Functional Yahwism and Social Control in the Early Israelite Monarchy," 277–84.
31. On aspects of David's political organization, see B. Mazar, "The Era of David and Solomon," in *The Age of the Monarchies: Political History,* 76–99; S. Yeivin, "Administration," in *The Age of the Monarchies: Culture and Society,* 147–71. On Saul's taxation, see M. Tsevat, "The Emergence of the Israelite Monarchy: Eli, Samuel, and Saul," in *The Age of the Monarchies: Political History,* 70–71.
32. On this, see J. Alberto Soggin, "Compulsory Labor under David and Solomon," in T. Ishida, ed., *Studies in the Period of David and Solomon and Other Essays,* 259–67, and references there.
33. See Hayim Tadmor, "Traditional Institutions and the Monarchy: Social and Political Tensions in the Time of David and Solomon," in ibid., 239–57; Abraham Malamat, "Organs of Statecraft in the Israelite Monarchy," 163–98. On the societal changes in general at the time of the establishment of the monarchy, see H. Reviv, "The Structure of Society," 125–46.

SPECIAL ISSUES IN 1 & 2 SAMUEL

PROPHECY IN 1 & 2 SAMUEL[34]

Samuel is the first prophet to be identified by name in 1 & 2 Samuel. In 1 Samuel 3:20 he is called a "prophet" (a *nābî'*). He is also called a "seer," in 9:19 (a *rō'eh*). A third word for a prophet is *ḥōzeh*, also translated as "seer" and used in 2 Samuel 24:11 to refer to "the prophet Gad, David's seer."

The normal word for a prophet is *nābî'*, and it has to do with the speaking of a word from God. Note, for example, that the narrative of Samuel's call introduces Samuel as a prophet by emphasizing his words (1 Sam. 3:19; 4:1a) and the Lord's words (3:21), after a time in which the Lord's words had been rare (3:1). During this time, there also had been no frequent "vision" (3:1); the term here is *ḥāzôn*, which is related to *ḥozeh* ("seer"). A *ḥōzeh* was one who "saw" messages from God via visions. The other term for a "seer" (*rō'eh*) is related to the normal word for seeing (*rā'āh*), and it connotes one who "sees" or perceives things from God that others do not. That such a seer's functions were essentially identical to those of a "prophet" is indicated by the comment in 1 Samuel 9:9, where "prophet" is shown to be the later term for what earlier had been known as a "seer."

Prophecy is a phenomenon known throughout the ancient Near East during the biblical periods. Many similarities can be seen, as well as many differences. In the Bible, true prophets from God spoke His word fearlessly and with a strong ethical and moral content; the classical prophets, whose words are recorded in the biblical books bearing their names, are good examples of this. In 2 Samuel, Nathan stands out as a fine example of one fearlessly confronting the king, despite the risk to his life if the king should have so decided (2 Samuel 12).

In 1 Samuel, the activity of prophesying was also being manifested in actions resembling ecstatic behavior, whereby prophets "prophesied" accompanied by music and dancing (1 Sam. 10:5–13). This type of activity often was associated with "bands" or "schools" of prophets, who appear to have lived and prophesied together (see, e.g., 19:18–24; 2 Kings 2:3, 5, 7, 15; 4:1, 38, 42–43; 6:1; 9:1), often under the influence of the Lord's Spirit (1 Sam. 10:10; 19:20, 23).

---

34. For a fuller discussion of prophecy in Israel, with bibliography, see chapter 6 under "Prophets and Prophecy in 1 & 2 Kings."

The Spirit of the Lord.[35] The terms "Spirit of the Lord" or "Spirit of God" occur fifteen times in 1 & 2 Samuel. Seven times we read of an "evil spirit" of/from the Lord/God (1 Sam. 16:14, 15, 16, 23, 23; 18:10; 19:9) and eight times of the true Spirit of the Lord/God. Of these eight references, five of them have to do with the Spirit's association with speaking or prophesying (10:6; 10:10; 20:20, 23; 2 Sam. 23:2). One refers to His association with military might (of Saul: 1 Sam. 11:6), one to His coming mightily upon David (16:13), and one to His leaving Saul (16:14).[36]

In the OT as a whole, we find thirty-nine references to the Spirit of "the Lord" or "God," as well as numerous other indirect references to this Spirit, such as "his Spirit" or "your Spirit" or "the Spirit."

A common activity of the Spirit of the Lord was that He came mightily upon various judges, and they were empowered to accomplish various military feats. Four references are to Samson and some very impressive feats of strength. The same language is used with reference to Saul in 1 Samuel 11:6, when he was empowered for the task of defeating the Ammonites. In this and several other respects, we see Saul, the first king, functioning as a "judge"; indeed, the Israelites' request had been for a king to "judge" them like the nations (8:5, 6, 20; see NIV marg. n.).

The Spirit of the Lord often is also associated with speaking. Four times in the OT, He is specifically associated with prophesying, and eight times generally with speaking God's word(s):

PROPHESYING: In Samuel, three times the Spirit of God comes on individuals, and they prophesy (10:10; 19:20, 23); once the Spirit of the Lord does so with the same result (10:6).

SPEAKING: God's Spirit empowers individuals to speak and gives them the words to say: Genesis 41:38 (God, of Joseph); Numbers 24:2 (God, of Balaam); 2 Samuel 23:2 (the Lord, of David); 1 Kings 22:24 // 2 Chronicles 18:23 (the Lord, of Zedekiah and Micaiah); 2 Chronicles 15:1 (God, of Azariah); 2 Chronicles 20:14 (the Lord, of Jahaziel); 2 Chronicles 24:20 (God, of Zechariah).

35. Two works dealing specifically with God's Spirit in the OT are Lloyd Neve, *The Spirit of God in the Old Testament,* and Leon J. Wood, *The Holy Spirit in the Old Testament.* See also Walther Eichrodt, *Theology of the Old Testament,* 2:46–68; William Dyrness, *Themes in Old Testament Theology,* 201–9; J. Barton Payne, *The Theology of the Older Testament,* 172–76; Michael Green, *I Believe in the Holy Spirit,* 18–31; George T. Montague, *The Holy Spirit: Growth of a Biblical Tradition,* 1–124.
36. On the interplay between the Spirit of the Lord's coming on David and leaving Saul, as well as the evil spirit's coming upon Saul, see David M. Howard, Jr., "The Transfer of Power from Saul to David in 1 Sam 16:13–14," 473–83.

It is also instructive to note that the "Spirit of God" is mentioned in Genesis 1:2, a chapter that heavily emphasizes creation by word (1:3, 6, 9, 11, 14, 20, 24, 26).

We might generalize, then, by saying that, in the OT, the Spirit of the Lord/God "comes upon" individuals for specific purposes (mainly military- or prophecy related). He is not mentioned as leaving any of them but one: Saul, in 1 Samuel 16:14 (cf. 18:12; note also that "the Lord" left Samson when his hair was cut [Judg. 16:20]). Bezalel was "filled" with God's Spirit. The Spirit of the Lord came mightily upon David "from that day forward" (1 Sam. 16:13) as well.

It appears that in some way the Spirit's presence was an ongoing one, however. The reference in 1 Samuel 16:14, for instance, states that the Spirit's presence with David was an ongoing one, which is confirmed by David's reference in Psalm 51:11 [MT 13]: "Do not cast me from your presence or take your Holy Spirit from me." Several references to God's Spirit in the prophets also suggest that the Spirit's presence with His people was an ongoing one. See, for example, the reference in Haggai 2:5: "This is what I covenanted with you when you came out of Egypt. And my Spirit remains among you. Do not fear." (Also see Isa. 30:1; 59:21; Zech. 4:6.) An analogy here might be with the Spirit's presence in the NT: He indwells all believers, yet "fills" them in special ways.

The evil spirit from the Lord. As noted, on eight occasions an "evil spirit" emanated from, or belonged to, the Lord (or God). The term occurs once with reference to Abimelech (Judg. 9:23) and seven times with reference to Saul (1 Sam. 16:14, 15, 16, 23a, 23b; 18:10; 19:9).

It is noteworthy that the only occasions where God sent an evil spirit on individuals involve (technically) Israel's first two "kings," both of whom proved to be unworthy candidates for the office. Undoubtedly this was a reflection of how God felt about the way the monarchy was established in these two cases and about these two individuals. Abimelech was "king" over at least a portion of Israel for three years. However, he seized the kingship illegitimately, he was a very poor candidate for the office, and he exercised authority wrongly when he did have power.[37] Saul, too, came to power out of ill-conceived and illegitimate motives on the part of those asking for a king, and he, too, quickly demonstrated his unsuitability for the office, despite his initially having been chosen and anointed by God for the kingship.

It is the next king—David—who is the standard throughout the rest of Israel's history. He is the first "king" who did not disqualify himself from the office, and he was favored by the ongoing presence of the Lord's Spirit, from

---

37. See Gerbrandt (*Kingship*, 129–34) for a review of Abimelech's defects and sins, and reference to the larger literature on him.

the day of his anointing onward (1 Sam. 16:13). This reinforces the points noted above about God's positive attitude toward the idea of Israelite kingship in general and toward David in particular.

Concerning the "morality" of God's sending such a spirit upon individuals, the answer, in brief, is that it happened in response to their sin.[38] For example, with reference to Abimelech, the evil spirit was "between" (bên) him and the Shechemites, and it was the cause of discord between them. Both parties had sinned (Judg. 9:1–9), and they deserved each other. In Saul's case, the evil spirit terrorized him after his offenses, which led to his forfeiting the throne of Israel (1 Samuel 13, 15; see esp. 15:23b).

Concerning the nature of this spirit, it must be seen as more than a mere mental imbalance in Saul's case.[39] It certainly introduced the effects of mental disturbance, but, coming immediately after the departure of the Lord's Spirit, it must be seen as an active, external power. Some suggest a demon here, i.e., an agent of moral evil.[40] However, it may have been more in the nature of a spirit that brought calamity or distress upon Saul, one that boded ill for him, producing harmful results.[41]

THE "REPENTANCE" OF GOD

First Samuel 15 presents a curious picture of God, because twice we see Him "repenting" that he had made Saul king (vv. 11 and 35).[42] On the face of it, that would seem to indicate a somewhat capricious God; after all, He Himself had chosen Saul to begin with (10:1). As an added complication, this chapter explicitly states that God does *not* "repent" (v. 29).[43]

Several things may be said to clarify the issue. First, the Hebrew term here (NHM) has two primary meanings: (1) "to comfort" or "to be comforted," and (2) "to repent, regret, change one's mind." It is the second of these that is in view here. However, NHM is not the term normally used to speak of human repentance (which is ŠWB, "to turn"); rather, it is used most often of God's "repentance." When that is the case, the sense is more properly one of "changing His mind," with no overtones of moral deficiency on God's

---

38. For brief attempts to deal with this theological dimension of the problem, see Gleason L. Archer, *Encyclopedia of Bible Difficulties*, 179–80; C. F. Keil, *The First Book of Samuel*, 170, 195; Walter C. Kaiser, Jr., *More Hard Sayings of the Old Testament*, 151–53.
39. So also, e.g., H. W. Hertzberg, *I & II Samuel*, 140–41; P. Kyle McCarter, *I Samuel*, 280–81.
40. E.g., Keil, *The First Book of Samuel*, 170; Wood, *Holy Spirit in the Old Testament*, 127–29.
41. BDB, for example, lists the 1 Samuel references under the heading of "bad, unpleasant, giving pain, unhappiness, misery," and the Judges reference under the heading of "*bad, unkind*, vicious in disposition or temper" (BDB, 948). The root *R'* often carries connotations of unpleasantness or misery, free of moral or ethical dimensions.
42. So RSV; NIV has "grieved"; NASB has "regretted." The Hebrew root is NHM.
43. Again, so RSV; NIV, NASB both have "change his mind." The root is the same as in verses 11 and 35: NHM.

part. Indeed, in Jeremiah 18:7–10, God proudly declared that He would gladly "change his mind" (*NHM*) concerning the good or evil that He had promised to bring upon people, depending on their response to His warnings or promises. The "unchangeableness" of God concerns fidelity to His own character, which is steadfast and cannot tolerate evil. However, this character desires human obedience and loyalty; God is willing to alter almost any of His promised judgments when humans use them as catalysts for their own repentance.

With respect to the internal consistency of the texts in 1 Samuel 15 concerning God's repentance (vv. 11, 29, 35), the context of Samuel's statement about God's not "changing his mind" (v. 29) is a statement of universal truth, and its application here has to do with His not reversing the judgment He had just made upon Saul (to take away the kingdom). Saul had had enough opportunity to do things right, but he had finally forfeited his claim permanently, and God would not change His mind in regard to this. The narrator's comments in verses 11 and 35 make clear that God did indeed "change His mind" regarding His initial actions concerning Saul because of Saul's sins.

The language here is often said to be "anthropomorphic" (i.e., describing God using human forms), or "anthropopathic" (describing God using human emotions), whereas that in verse 29 is said to be "theomorphic" (describing God in "real" terms). Theologically, given His omniscience, this must be so. However, to attempt to solve this problem solely with reference to these concepts obscures the important truth about the conditionality inherent in almost every one of God's promises of punishment or reward.[44]

THE PLACE OF 1 & 2 SAMUEL IN THE CANON

In the Hebrew Bible, the books of Samuel are part of the "Former Prophets," immediately following the book of Judges. This placement is logical, and it is chronologically based. The books of Samuel present the next period in Israel's history (after the period of the judges), when the united monarchy was established, and how it developed under Saul and David. The books of Kings pick up the story where 2 Samuel leaves off, with the accession of David's son Solomon and the history of the two monarchies after that. Essentially, therefore, the entire corpus of the Former Prophets is chronologically laid out.

In the Greek traditions, and in today's Protestant Bibles, 1 Samuel immediately follows the book of Ruth. That is because of the chronological

---

44. On this entire issue, see Marvin R. Wilson, *"nāham," TWOT,* 570–71; Kaiser, *Toward Old Testament Ethics,* 249–51; and *Hard Sayings of the Old Testament,* 113–15. (See also, more broadly, Kaiser, *Back Toward the Future,* 61–68.)

placement of that book's events during the time of the judges. Ruth also forms a fitting prelude to 1 & 2 Samuel, since it shows God's workings in the life of a family that was part of the great line extending from Judah to David and ends with a genealogy that focuses upon the latter (see chapter 4 under "The Place of Ruth in the Canon"). It functions as a fitting introduction to two books in which David is introduced as God's chosen king and his line is established as the one upon which God would show favor in perpetuity.

Literarily (as well as historically), 1 Samuel echoes the ending of Judges in the references to the "hill country of Ephraim."[45] This is the area in which the story of Micah and his Levitical priest takes place (Judges 17–18), and it is the area from which the Levite in Judges 19 hailed and in which he found hospitality. In 1 Samuel 1, it is the area Samuel's family was from.

The final story in Judges also serves to anticipate material early in 1 Samuel. That story involves an outrage perpetrated by inhabitants at Gibeah, a town in Benjamin, the subsequent civil war between Benjamin and the rest of the tribes, and the eventual provision for the survival of the Benjaminites as a tribe. First Samuel presents the story of Saul, who was a Benjaminite from Gibeah. As noted in chapter 3, the final two stories in Judges are not in their correct chronological place (they occurred early in the period). Thus, their placement at the book's end—in addition to its internal function in Judges—serves to introduce Saul in 1 Samuel. The Benjaminites do not appear in an entirely favorable light at the end of Judges; the Benjaminite Saul, of course, likewise appears as a tragic figure, one who forfeited his kingship.

THEOLOGY OF 1 & 2 SAMUEL

JUSTIFICATION FOR THE DAVIDIC MONARCHY

The promises about kingship given to the patriarchs (Gen. 17:6, 16; 35:11; 49:8–12) and the unmistakable notes anticipating the monarchy found in Judges and Ruth now find their fulfillment in the books of Samuel. The book of 1 Samuel serves to show the (somewhat rocky) transition from the tribal confederation to the Davidic monarchy. More important, it, along with the significant material in 2 Samuel 7, serves to provide a theological justification for this transition, since the Israelites' request for a king was seen to have been sinful (1 Samuel 8).[46]

Israel's request for a king. Early in 1 Samuel, the elders of Israel came together to ask Samuel to appoint a king over Israel (1 Samuel 8). The prob-

---

45. The phrase occurs in the Judges "appendix" as follows: 17:1, 8; 18:2, 13; 19:1, 16, 18. It occurs in 1 Samuel in 1:1; 9:4; 14:22.
46. See Gerbrandt *(Kingship)* for an extended exposition of the positive rationale for Israelite kingship. See also David M. Howard, Jr., "The Case for Kingship in Deuteronomy and the Former Prophets," 101–15.

lem with this request was *not* that God was against the kingship per se. The opposite was actually the case: God was for it. He had promised kings to Abraham from the beginning (Gen. 17:6, 16; 35:11), and He had spoken of kings as His blessings upon the people several times since (see esp. Gen. 49:8–12; Num. 24:7, 17). Kingship was to be carefully established and monitored, and kings were to keep faithfulness to God and his Word as their top priority (Deut. 17:14–20).

The problem with the request for kingship in 1 Samuel 8 was the motivations behind it. The people wanted a king to rule over them "like all the nations" (1 Sam. 8:5, 20). First Samuel 8:20 goes beyond this and reveals the Israelites' true agenda in asking for this king: "Then we will be like all the other nations, with a king to lead us and *to go out before us and fight our battles*" (italics added). This desire flew in the face of the injunctions in Deuteronomy 17:14–20 (esp. v. 14 in its prohibition against hoarding horses, the symbol of military might), and it was couched in terms of the common ancient Near Eastern conception of a king as one who would fight the nation's battles and receive the glory for it.

This reasoning already had been encountered in Israel in the request that Gideon rule over them because "you have saved us out of the hand of Midian" (Judg. 8:22), and it is behind Abimelech's grab for power in Judges 9. In effect, this desire served to "depose" the Lord as Israel's king, for He had been the one who had delivered Israel time and time again. The king's major responsibilities were to lead Israel in being faithful to the Lord in keeping His covenant (Deut. 17:15–20, esp. vv. 18–20).

The point about the Lord's being Israel's warrior and the king's duty to be faithful to Him is reinforced when we consider how David is presented in 1 & 2 Samuel and in the rest of the Deuteronomistic History.[47] It is significant to note that, whereas David certainly was an important military figure *historically*, his military leadership and exploits are downplayed in the Deuteronomistic History. After his death, these are scarcely mentioned, whereas such things as David as a model king, the Davidic Covenant, and the linking of the promise of a dynasty with keeping of the law are frequently mentioned. Furthermore, even in the accounts of David's military activities, God—not David—is prominent as Israel's ultimate warrior. This can be seen, for example, in the language of 2 Samuel 5:19: "Go up, for I will indeed hand the Philistines over to you." It is also evident in the contrast between 2 Samuel 5:24, where the Lord promises that He "has gone out in front of you to strike the Philistine army," and 1 Samuel 8:20, where Israel asked for a king who would "go out before us and fight our battles." Note also that 2 Samuel 7:1 and 11 speak of God's giving rest to the land under

---

47. See Gerbrandt, *Kingship,* 170–73.

David. This is significant in that this true rest from God did not come under the judges but only after the rise of kingship and the first king who did right in the Lord eyes.[48]

Thus, the problem with Israel's request for a king was not that God did not ever want Israel to have a human king.[49] Indeed, kingship was part of His plan from the beginning. However, a proper kingship, in which God retained His supreme place over Israel as its God and its warrior, was not what Israel actually asked for when it requested a king, and that was the reason for the verdicts about its sinfulness.

The Davidic Covenant.[50] After God had given David rest from his enemies, he made a series of promises to him that stand, in one scholar's words, as "the theological highlight of the Books of Samuel . . . if not of the Deuteronomistic History as a whole"[51] because of its significant content and its importance in later texts. It is found in 2 Samuel 7, especially verses 11–16.

Walter Kaiser notes that this "Davidic Covenant" consisted of four elements: (1) a house for David; (2) a seed for David; (3) a kingdom for David; (4) a Son of God from David.[52] This covenant was of the unconditional, "royal grant" type of covenant, whereby the sovereign bestows benefits upon the underling.[53] Furthermore, it was a covenant "forever." That is stated six times in the chapter (2 Sam. 7:13, 16, 24, 25, 26, 29), and it is affirmed as such later (23:5). When God stated a condition to this covenant in 2 Samuel 7:14—"When [your son] commits iniquity, I will chasten him with the rod of men, with the stripes of the sons of men"—He was stating no more than that individual descendants of David would surely fall away from the Lord and that God would just as surely punish them. Some would even cut themselves out of any blessings of the covenant at all. God was not saying, however, that the promises to David were thereby invalidated.

48. Ibid., 171 n. 186.
49. This is against the position of evangelicals such as Leon J. Wood, who has seen the monarchy as a "second-best" concession by God to Israel's wickedness in his *Distressing Days of the Judges,* 23–33, 54–65; or *Israel's United Monarchy,* 21–31; and against the position of many critical scholars, who have seen the anti-monarchical tendencies in the book of 1 Samuel to have been the earliest and the most "legitimate" (see Gerbrandt, *Kingship;* Howard, "The Case for Kingship").
50. For the extensive discussion and bibliography of the Davidic Covenant, see Dennis J. McCarthy, "II Samuel 7 and the Structure of the Deuteronomistic History," 131–38; Frank M. Cross, *Canaanite Myth and Hebrew Epic,* 249–60; Walter C. Kaiser, Jr., "The Blessing of David: The Charter of Humanity," 298–318; and *Toward an Old Testament Theology,* 149–55; Gerbrandt, *Kingship,* 160–69.
51. A. A. Anderson, *2 Samuel,* 112.
52. Kaiser, *Toward an Old Testament Theology,* 149–52.
53. Moshe Weinfeld, "The Covenant of Grant in the Old Testament and in the Ancient Near East," 184–203; Michael D. Guinan, *ABD* 2, s.v. "Davidic Covenant."

In many ways, the Davidic Covenant stands in a direct line with the Abrahamic Covenant, another unconditional covenant. In it, God promised to provide Abraham with descendants like the stars in the heavens and the sands of the sea and to provide for the blessing of all the nations of the earth through his seed. It was through Abraham's line—specifically the Judahite-Davidic strand—that this blessing was accomplished.

David was truly blessed by God and was "a man after God's own heart" (1 Sam. 13:14; Acts 13:22). Indeed, he was important in many respects—as a great leader, administrator, warrior, musician, and so on. However, he is remembered in the Scriptures for his faithful heart and especially for his status as God's chosen one, God's anointed, to whom God gave the great promises about an eternal dynasty.[54]

Thus, the Davidic Covenant forms the basis for much theological reflection in the Scriptures. God did not completely tear away the kingdom from David's son Solomon because of His commitment to David and this covenant (1 Kings 11:34–36). The books of Chronicles focus to a large extent on David and God's promises to him (see chapter 7 under "Theology of 1 & 2 Chronicles"). Several important royal psalms mention this promise.[55] David and the promises to him certainly figure in many of the great eschatological passages in the prophets.[56] And, of course, Jesus' descent from David is of great importance for our understanding of who He is. Note that Matthew's genealogy begins thus: "A record of the genealogy of Jesus Christ the son of David, the son of Abraham" (1:1). From the beginning, Jesus is placed in His proper perspective as the fulfillment of the great promises of blessing for the world that were given to and through Abraham and David.

The Davidic monarchy and the canonical shaping of 1 & 2 Samuel. The first reference in 1 & 2 Samuel to kingship occurs early in 1 Samuel—in the Song of Hannah. Hannah's song is a hymn of praise to the Lord, a prayer of thanksgiving for the birth of her son, Samuel (1 Sam. 2:1–10). At the end of that psalm, we find a reference to God's king and anointed one: "[the Lord] will give strength to his king and exalt the horn of his anointed" (2:10).

We should emphasize here the point made in chapter 1 about the selectivity and viewpoint of a writer. In any number of cases, the Scriptures record that people prayed, without specifying the content of their prayer. Here, however, the author of 1 & 2 Samuel includes the entire contents of Hannah's prayer. Careful scrutiny of the prayer and its context reveals at least two things.

---

54. On David as a historical personage and as a theological symbol, see David M. Howard, Jr., *ABD* 2, s.v. "David."
55. E.g., Psalms 21:6–7 [MT 7–8]; 89:3–4, 19–37 [MT 4–5, 20–38]; 132:11–12.
56. E.g., Isaiah 7:13–25; 9:1–7; 11:1–16; Jeremiah 23:5–6; 33:14–17; Ezekiel 34:20–24; Amos 9:11–15; Zechariah 3:8–9; 6:12–13.

First, it intrudes upon the narrative. That is, the narrative flows smoothly around 1 Samuel 2:1–10 with no discernible break. The inclusion of the words of Hannah's prayer are not necessary from the point of view of the flow of the story. Second, the prayer does not very directly relate to Hannah's situation of having been miraculously given a son. Only in verse 5 is reference made to barrenness, and, even there, "seven" children are mentioned, not merely the one that Hannah in fact had. It may very well be that Hannah did not compose this prayer herself but, rather, prayed a prayer that already existed, that Eli or someone else suggested for her. Its contents only very generally fit her situation, but it was appropriate enough.

These facts suggest that the inclusion of the prayer here has less to do with Hannah's situation than with the author's interests. Rather than record that Hannah prayed a prayer of thanksgiving and moving along with his narrative, the author inserts the contents of her prayer. For the author, the salient feature of the prayer was not its somewhat vague applicability to Hannah's situation but its reference to the Lord's king and anointed one in verse 10. By inserting this hymn with its references to the king at the beginning of the book, the author is signaling at the outset one of his dominant themes.

The reference to a king is especially striking when we remember that, at this time, there was as yet no king at all. This hymn expresses a blessing on the king proleptically (i.e., in advance). It has its roots in the many earlier assurances about a king that we have noted above.

We find a second reference to God's anointed one in the same chapter, in the words of the man of God in 2:35. Thus, the inclusion of two such references reinforces this point. As Brevard Childs notes, this entire chapter reveals the books' theocentric perspective: "The focus on God's chosen king, his anointed one, David, appears right at the outset, and reveals the stance from which the whole narrative is being viewed."[57]

When we move to the end of 2 Samuel, we find that the work comes full circle to this theme sounded at the outset. That is because, in David's final hymn of praise to the Lord, we find a remarkable echo of 1 Samuel 2:10: "He gives his king great victories; he shows unfailing kindness to his anointed, to David and his descendants forever" (2 Sam. 22:51). Both the "king" and the "anointed one" of Hannah's prayer are mentioned here. But now, at the end of the work—now that the story has unfolded and we know that it was David who was the righteous and rightful king—we find an additional datum added: reference is made to David and the Davidic Covenant in the last clause of 2 Samuel 22:51. This verse, then, dramatically brings us back to where we started, but with a fuller knowledge of the king and his place in God's plan.

57. Brevard S. Childs, *IOTS*, 273.

We can note here that, just as Hannah's prayer was not integral to the flow of the narrative, neither is David's hymn in 2 Samuel 22. The reference to Saul in verse 1 indicates that it may have been first sung many years earlier, and thus it might have been more appropriately included in 1 Samuel, not 2 Samuel. However, no doubt David sang it more than once, and its inclusion here serves as an appropriate wrap-up of David's life (note the reference to "all his enemies" in v. 1). More significantly, it serves well the author's purposes of highlighting David's kingship.

Furthermore, just as the reference to God's anointed one in 1 Samuel 2:10 is reinforced by a similar reference in 2:35, so also here we find a second reference to David as God's anointed. It occurs in the introduction to the "last words of David" (2 Sam. 23:1–7), when David is mentioned as "the man anointed by the God of Jacob" (23:1).

Thus, in addition to the various indications within 1 & 2 Samuel that God was pleased with David and that He was giving the Davidic monarchy as a blessing to His people, we see that the final shape of the book(s) makes this point very clearly. That is, the author selected material for inclusion that made this point, both on the basis of the content of the material and on the basis of his placement of it.

THE EFFECTS OF SIN

The theme of sin's effects can be seen in almost every biblical book, but it is especially striking in the books of Samuel. All of 1 & 2 Samuel can be seen to be built upon different characters' declines juxtaposed against others' rises.[58] Each character's decline is due in some way to his sin.

For example, early in 1 Samuel, Eli and Samuel are contrasted. Eli's decline is seen in large part as having been due to his sons' wickedness. The section (chaps. 2–3) is built upon a framework of favorable comments about Samuel's ministering or growing before God. These occur at 2:11, 18, 21, 26, 3:1, 19.

The six references to Samuel's development bracket five blocks of narrative material, four of which deal with the evil in Eli's house (the exception being 2:18–21). The import of this is clear: divine blessing and legitimation would accrue to Samuel for his (and his mother's) faithfulness to God; Eli's household was doomed because of the apostasy of his sons. This foreshadows the trouble David was to have with his sons at the end of his life, told in the last half of 2 Samuel.

---

58. John A. Martin ("The Literary Quality of 1 and 2 Samuel," 131–45) makes a similar point and develops it further; he terms it the "reversal-of-fortune motif." See also Fokkelman (*The Crossing Fates,* and his "Saul and David: Crossed Fates," 20–32) on this, and on Saul and David in particular.

2:11	"The boy [Samuel] ministered before the Lord under Eli the priest."
2:12–17	*The sins of Eli's sons*
2:18a	"Samuel was ministering before the Lord."
2:18b–21a	*God's gracious blessing upon Hannah*
2:21b	"The boy Samuel grew up in the presence of the Lord."
2:22–25	*Eli's wicked sons*
2:26	"And the boy Samuel continued to grow in stature and in favor with the Lord and with men."
2:27–36	*The prophecy against Eli's house*
3:1	"The boy Samuel ministered before the Lord under Eli."
3:2–18	*Samuel's call and a further prophecy against Eli's house*
3:19	"The Lord was with Samuel as he grew up."

Samuel, however, was not immune to the effects of sin either. Later, the wickedness of his sons (along with his improper appointment of them as judges) was the immediate catalyst for the request for kingship (1 Sam. 8:1–5).

Early in his kingship, Saul appears as a very commendable character (chaps. 9–11). Soon after he becomes king, however, Saul disqualifies himself from the office by *his* sins (13:13–14; 15:22–29). After David is anointed king (chap. 16), the rest of the book of 1 Samuel is devoted to the interplay of the rising fortunes of David and the declining fortunes of Saul. In almost every encounter between the two of them, David emerges with his reputation enhanced, while Saul's has suffered further.

Even David, however—who was God's chosen king, whose rise in fortunes occupies all of 1 Samuel 16–31 and 2 Samuel 1–5, and whose reign is marked by great successes early on (2 Samuel 6–8)—suffered a decline and much trouble with his sons (chaps. 12–24), after his great sins against Bathsheba and Uriah (chap. 11). His first son by Bathsheba died (chap. 12); another son, Amnon, raped David's daughter Tamar (chap. 13); yet another son, Absalom, killed Amnon (chap. 13); Absalom rebelled against his father (chaps. 15–18); and another son, Adonijah, seized the kingship from his brother Solomon (1 Kings 1). David seems to have lost most of his moral authority and much of his stature by that point in his life. For example, in 1 Kings 1:6, he is judged for never having disciplined his son Adonijah, and in 2 Samuel 13:21 the Old Greek and Qumran versions add the statement, "[David] would not punish his son Amnon, because he loved him, for he was his firstborn" (NRSV).

Thus, the two books serve to indicate that God still maintained standards, against which even individuals chosen for special tasks and status were to be measured.[59] Individuals or nations could not violate God's standards with impunity, expecting such violations to have no effect.

GOD'S SOVEREIGNTY

A thread that runs through all the discussions of kingship and of the effects of sin, as well as through the stories of David's exploits, is that of God's sovereignty. In the end, it is He who is in control of all. He gave the Philistines and the Ammonites into the hands of Samuel (1 Sam. 7:9–14), Saul (11:6, 13), Jonathan (14:12, 15, 23), and countless times into David's hands. His choice of David as king was backed up by His providential care over David in the face of many adversities. Indeed, the intricate details of intrigue and escape that we see when David was a fugitive—which get confusing and tedious at times—serve to show David's rise in popularity and God's hand of protection upon him again and again (chaps. 18–30).

OUTLINE OF 1 & 2 SAMUEL

The Rise of Samuel (1 Samuel 1–7)
The Birth of Samuel (1:1–2:10)
   Samuel's Birth (1:1–28)
   Hannah's Song (2:1–10)
Samuel and the House of Eli: Rise and Decline (2:11–4:1a)
Israel, the Philistines, and the Ark (4:1b–7:1)
   Loss of the Ark and Eli's Death (4:1b–22)
   The Ark in Philistia (5:1–12)
   Return of the Ark to Kiriath-Jearim (6:1–7:1)
Samuel the Judge (7:2–17)

The Advent of Kingship (1 Samuel 8–15)
The Demand for a King (8:1–22)
Anointing and Choosing of Saul (9:1–10:27)
Saul's First Victory (11:1–15)
Covenant Renewal (12:1–25)
Saul Rejected as King—A (13:1–15a)
Saul's and Jonathan's Military Exploits (13:15b–14:52)
Saul Rejected as King—B (15:1–35)

59. In a tangential, but related vein, John A. Martin ("The Structure of 1 and 2 Samuel," 28–42) argues that the books' central purpose has to do with the motif of fertility/infertility as a consequence of obedience/disobedience. Viewed in this way, the books focus not so much on one man as on the Lord's covenant and individuals measuring up to it.

David's Rise to Power (1 Samuel 16:1–2 Samuel 5:10)
David Anointed as King at Bethlehem (1 Sam. 16:1–13)
David's Arrival at the Royal Court (1 Sam. 16:14–23)
David and Goliath (1 Sam. 17:1–18:5))
Threats to David (1 Sam. 18:6–20:42 [MT 21:1])
  Saul's Jealousy Aroused (18:6–9)
  Saul's Madness: The Evil Spirit from God (18:10–11)
  David Succeeds in Everything He Does (18:12–16)
  David and Merab, Saul's Daughter (18:17–19)
  David and Michal, Saul's Daughter (18:20–30)
  David's Flight (19:1–20:42 [MT 21:1])
David the Fugitive (1 Sam. 21:1 [MT 2]–30:31)
  David and Ahimelech, the Priest of Nob (21:1–9 [MT 2–10])
  Miscellaneous Travels (21:10 [MT 11]–22:5)
    David and Achish, King of Gath (21:10–15 [MT 11–16])
    David's Followers (22:1–2)
    David in Moab (22:3–5)
  Saul Kills the Priests at Nob (22:6–23)
  David on the Run (23:1–29 [MT 24:1])
    David at Keilah (23:1–13)
    Interlude: David and Jonathan (23:14–18)
    David in the Wildernesses of Ziph and Maon (23:19–29
      [MT 24:1])
  David Spares Saul Near En-gedi (24:1–22 [MT 2–23])
  David, Nabal, and Abigail (25:1–44)
  David Spares Saul Again in the Wilderness of Ziph (26:1–23)
  David Returns to Achish, King of Gath (27:1–28:2)
  Saul and the Medium at En-dor (28:3–25)
  David Leaves Achish, King of Gath (29:1–11)
  A Kinglike Hero (30:1–31)
The Death of Saul (1 Sam. 31:1–2 Sam. 1:27)
  Death and Burial of Saul (1 Sam. 31:1–13)
  Aftermath of Saul's Death (2 Sam. 1:1–27)
    Report of Saul's Death (1:1–16)
    David's Lament (1:17–27)
Judah's Anointing of David as King at Hebron (2 Sam. 2:1–11)
A Rival King (2 Sam. 2:12–4:12)
All Israel's Anointing of David as King at Hebron (2 Sam. 5:1–5)
David's Capture of Jerusalem (2 Sam. 5:6–10)

David's Consolidation of Power (2 Samuel 5:11–8:18)

Material Successes—A (5:11–25)
Spiritual Successes (6:1–7:29)
    Return of the Ark to Jerusalem (6:1–23)
    The Davidic Covenant (7:1–29)
Material Successes—B (8:1–18)

David's Decline (2 Samuel 9–24)

David and Mephibosheth (9:1–13)
The Ammonite War—A (10:1–19)
The Bathsheba Affair (11:1–12:25)
The Ammonite War—B (12:26–31)
Two Rebellious Sons (13:1–18:33 [MT 19:1])
    Amnon Rapes Tamar (13:1–22)
    Absalom Kills Amnon (13:23–39)
    Absalom Restored (14:1–33)
    Absalom's Revolt (15:1–18:33 [MT 19:1])
David's Restoration (19:1 [MT 2]–20:26)
    David's Return to Jerusalem (19:1–43 [MT 2–44])
    Shimei's Revolt (20:1–22)
    David's Administration (20:23–26)
David's Last Deeds (2 Samuel 21–24)
    The End of Saul's Family (21:1–14)
    Philistine Wars (21:15–22)
    A Psalm of David (22:1–51)
    The Testament of David (23:1–7)
    David's Mighty Men (23:8–39)
    The Census Plague (24:1–25)

6

1 & 2 KINGS

Turn from your evil ways. Observe my commands and decrees, in accordance with the entire Law that I commanded your fathers to obey and that I delivered to you through my servants the prophets. (2 Kings 17:13)

Nevertheless, for the sake of his servant David, the Lord was not willing to destroy Judah. He had promised to maintain a lamp for David and his descendants forever. (2 Kings 8:19)

The books of Kings chronicle the ebb and flow in the fortunes of, first, a united Israel, then a divided Israel and Judah, and finally a solitary Judah. On the surface, they contain little more than prosaic accounts of the achievements—mainly in the spiritual realm—of each succeeding king of Israel and Judah, punctuated with interesting stories about certain prophets. On the whole, they seem to present a relentless litany of wicked kings, and an unremittingly negative view of life in these kingdoms.

However, underneath this first impression lies a living message fraught with hope for God's people. The roots of the message of these two books lie in God's great promises to David in 2 Samuel. The lesson for God's people during the period of the Exile in Babylonia and afterward—which is the time period addressed by the author of these books—is threefold: (1) that Israel should learn a lesson from the mistakes of its forebears and listen to God's mouthpieces, the prophets, in order to avoid such severe punishment again; but (2) that God nevertheless is a good and gracious God, still ready to forgive when people truly repent; and (3) that He still holds out hope for His people, regardless of how dire their circumstances.

The books open with King David old and feeble, and power being passed on to his son Solomon, who is the subject of extended attention thereafter. Solomon's sins led to the division of the kingdom into two rival nations, and the bulk of the work alternates between the two, presenting and evaluating their histories. After the fall of the northern kingdom, the southern kingdom's history is chronicled until it, too, fell, as a result of its sin. The books end on a forward-looking note, with a hint of hope that God was still with His people.

TITLE AND PLACE IN THE CANON[1]

Like the books of Samuel, the books of Kings were originally one book. In Hebrew the title for the unified work is *mĕlākîm*, "Kings." The division into two books was for practical convenience and first appears in the Greek versions of the Septuagint. The Greek versions called the books "Third and Fourth Reigns"; the first two "Reigns" books were 1 & 2 Samuel. The English title—"Kings"—comes from Jerome's Latin version, the Vulgate, where these two books were called "Third and Fourth Kings."

These early titles reflect the fact that the division between 1 & 2 Samuel and 1 & 2 Kings is somewhat artificial. The story of David, which is the subject of almost all of 2 Samuel, does not end until his death is recorded in 1 Kings 2:10–11. Indeed, some Greek manuscripts place the end of 2 Samuel precisely here (at 2:11), whereas others place it after 1 Kings 2:46a, which is the point at which Solomon gains secure control of the kingdom. The division of the books of Samuel and Kings into two books is not attested in Hebrew manuscripts until the fourteenth or fifteenth century A.D. Daniel Bomberg's rabbinic Bible of 1516–17 A.D. divided the books in two with a marginal note explaining that the division was due to non-Jews (lit., "those speaking a foreign tongue").

The division between 1 & 2 Kings likewise is artificial and was most likely done for the convenience of fitting each book on one scroll. The account of Ahaziah, king of Israel, which begins in 1 Kings 22:51, does not end until 2 Kings 1:18. Also, the account of Elijah the prophet's ministry, which begins in 1 Kings 17, is not concluded until 2 Kings 2.

The books of Kings are the last of the Former Prophets in the Hebrew Bible. The "Latter Prophets" (Isaiah, Jeremiah, Ezekiel, and "the Twelve") consist of very different material, but they have at least two things in common with 1 & 2 Kings: (1) the books of Kings provide the historical framework into which the ministries of almost all the writing prophets may be fitted; (2) we can see duplication of several texts between 1 & 2 Kings and the prophets (most notably 2 Kings 18:13–20:19 // Isaiah 36–39 and 2 Kings 24:18–25:30 // Jeremiah 52).

---

1. See the brief summaries in R. K. Harrison, *Introduction to the Old Testament*, 719; E. Ball, *ISBE* 3, s.v. "Kings, Books of."

AUTHORSHIP AND DATE OF COMPOSITION

The books of Kings do not give any indication as to their author, nor does any other biblical book indicate this. Rabbinic tradition in the Talmud ascribes their authorship to Jeremiah (*Baba Bathra* 15a). That is primarily because the last chapter of the book of Jeremiah (chap. 52) is identical to the last portion of 2 Kings (24:18–25:30) and because of the need evidenced in the Talmud to ascribe every book's authorship to a prophet.[2] We should note that a strong prophetic outlook does permeate the book (see below), so the suggestion that the book's author may have been a prophet is plausible enough in this case. However, in the last analysis, it is impossible to know who the author was.

We use the term *author* advisedly. That is, we assume that the books, in their final form, were written by one person. However, the author used many sources (as discussed below), and in many cases he probably incorporated these into his work verbatim. But his additions, his creation of a coherent and consistent framework, the very process of selection and omission of materials, and the integrated viewpoints throughout his work give this person a rightful claim as "author," not merely "editor," "compiler," or "redactor."[3]

The last event referred to in the book of 2 Kings is the release from a Babylonian prison of King Jehoiachin in the thirty-seventh year of the Exile (25:27–30), namely, 561 B.C.[4] This means that the final form of the book must date after that time, regardless of the dates of the earlier sources.

The phrase "to this day" or "until now" occurs fourteen times in 1 & 2 Kings.[5] Each of these speaks of some event causing a state of affairs that continued until the time of writing. Most of these could easily have been written by the final author of 1 & 2 Kings some time after 561 B.C., but they do not give any further clue as to the time of writing. Two of the references are somewhat problematic, as they would seem to point to an earlier, preexilic time. The first is in 1 Kings 8:8, which states that the poles for carrying the ark that was in Solomon's Temple were still there "to this day." The statement presupposes that the Temple was still standing, which it was not after 586 B.C. This is either a statement from the "Book of the Acts of Solomon" (11:41) that was carried over unchanged into the final form of the book,[6] or it is a much later addition. The statement is not found in the origi-

---

2. See Harrison (*Introduction*, 719–20) on this latter point.
3. In this regard, see the trenchant comments of Burke O. Long, *1 Kings*, 14–21.
4. Edwin R. Thiele, *Mysterious Numbers of the Hebrew Kings*, 189–90.
5. "To this day" (*'ad hayyôm hazzeh*): 1 Kings 8:8; 9:13, 21; 10:12; 12:19; 2 Kings 2:22; 8:22; 10:27; 14:7; 16:6; 17:23, 34, 41; "until now" (*'ad 'attāh*): 2 Kings 13:23.
6. So C. F. Keil, *The First Book of Kings*, 121. The statement is also found in 2 Chronicles 5:9.

nal Greek versions, which lends credence to the latter suggestion. The second reference is in 2 Kings 13:23, which states that "the Lord was unwilling to destroy [Israel] or send them away from his presence, until now" (author's translation). Since Israel was indeed destroyed and banished in 723/22 B.C., this too poses a potential problem. What this undoubtedly means, however, is that God had been patient with Israel for a while, but by the time of writing (after 561 B.C.) His patience had ended and He *had* destroyed them by then.[7]

Martin Noth suggested a date during the Exile, shortly after 561 B.C., namely, ca. 550 B.C., for the writing of 1 & 2 Kings.[8] His suggestion accords well with the internal data of 1 & 2 Kings, and it will be used as a working assumption here.

DATE OF THE EVENTS

First Kings opens at the end of David's reign, ca. 970 B.C., and 2 Kings ends with a reference to King Jehoiachin dating to 561 B.C. Thus, these books span more than four hundred years. (For details of the chronologies of individual kings, see "Chronology in 1 & 2 Kings" below. For details of the events in 1 & 2 Kings in their ancient Near Eastern context, see chapter 7 under "Israel and Its Neighbors in 1 & 2 Kings.")

PURPOSE

Describing the contours and message of 1 & 2 Kings is a relatively easy task: as noted earlier, these books detail the fortunes of the kingdoms of Israel and Judah and their respective kings. However, the purpose for which an author expended so much energy is less clear. As G. H. Jones states, "it is far more difficult to give a clear definition of the author's dominant theme and to specify his intention."[9] J. G. McConville agrees: "The meaning of the Books of Kings is, it seems to me, one of the areas of Old Testament interpretation which has been least well served by Old Testament criticism."[10]

Martin Noth suggested that the author's purpose was essentially a negative one: to give an accounting for the present disastrous state of affairs during the Exile.[11] This is an overly pessimistic rationale for writing such an account, however, and it ignores the fact that Israel still survived as an identifiable entity during the Exile, one that needed words of hope and instruc-

---

7. So also Robert Hubbard, *First and Second Kings*, 190.
8. Martin Noth, *The Deuteronomistic History.*
9. G. H. Jones, *1 and 2 Kings*, 1:78.
10. J. G. McConville, "Narrative and Meaning in the Books of Kings," 31.
11. Noth, *Deuteronomistic History.*

tion. John Van Seters sees a purely historiographical purpose: These books represent the respective kingdoms' rendering of an account to themselves of their past.[12] Such a view, however, ignores the genuine religious stamp that is seen throughout the books.

Much more likely is some statement of purpose that takes into account Judah's exilic situation—one in which God's people needed not only to be reminded of their past sin but one in which a note of hope for the future was sounded. The writing of 1 & 2 Kings was during roughly the same period that the people asked Ezekiel, "Our offenses and sins weigh us down, and we are wasting away because of them. How then can we live?" (Ezek. 33:10). God's answer through Ezekiel was that they needed to repent of their evil ways, and so it is in 1 & 2 Kings.

The sins of the kings and the people are recorded in great detail, not out of a perverse delight in sin and punishment—and certainly not for "secular historiographical" purposes—but rather as reminders of the people's sins, as warnings to the present exilic generation. These catalogues of failings are interspersed with God's gracious promises, which were all fulfilled, and with reminders that there was still hope for God's people if they repented. In the end, the books of Kings look to the future—a future in which God's people have turned to Him and in which God remained faithful to His own promises, both to His people and to the household of David. (See further below under "Theology of 1 & 2 Kings.")

The Composition of 1 & 2 Kings

Concerning the composition of the books of Kings, three issues present themselves. The first involves the *sources* used by the author of 1 & 2 Kings to compose his work. The second involves *how the author incorporated these* into his writing, especially in creating a framework around which he built the work. Both of these issues involve analysis at levels below the book level. The third issue involves *the place of 1 & 2 Kings in the larger "Deuteronomistic History,"* which involves analysis at levels above the book level.

THE USE OF SOURCES IN 1 & 2 KINGS

The author of the books of Kings (along with the author of 1 & 2 Chronicles) depends more explicitly on written sources than does any other author of the Bible. He repeatedly mentions three sources, and it is likely that he used other, unnamed sources as well.

---

12. John Van Seters, *In Search of History.*

Sources named in 1 & 2 Kings. The first named source is mentioned once—the "Book of the Acts of Solomon" (1 Kings 11:41)—and it was the author's source for most or all of 1 Kings 3–11. These chapters include a great deal of diverse information, ranging from delightful stories about Solomon that illustrate his great wisdom (3:3–28; 4:29–34; 10:1–13) and his great speech and prayer of dedication (8:14–61) to mundane bureaucratic records (4:1–6, 7–19, 22–28) and exhaustive details concerning the Temple and the king's palace (6:1–7:51). It is impossible to tell whether the Book of the Acts of Solomon contained all of this material, or whether it was merely the source of some of it. The notice in 11:41 would seem to indicate that it contained more, rather than less, since it mentions "all that he did, and his wisdom."

The second source is called "the Book of the Daily Deeds [or Annals][13] of the Kings of Israel," and it is mentioned eighteen times.[14] It appears in the death notices of seventeen of the twenty kings of Israel[15] as the source the reader could consult to find more complete information about the kings. Typically the following is stated: "Now, the rest of the deeds of [king's name], and all that he did, are they not written in the Book of the Daily Deeds of the Kings of Israel?" (author's translation).

The third source is called "the Book of the Daily Deeds [or Annals] of the Kings of Judah," and it appears fifteen times.[16] Formulaic death notices are missing for five monarchs (Ahaziah, Athaliah, Jehoahaz, Jehoiachin, and Zedekiah), including any reference to this source. When it is mentioned, the reference to this source follows the same pattern as the one for Israel.

These sources appear to have been very much like a genre common in Assyria and Babylonia called "chronicles" (or "chronographic texts"), which consisted of lengthy lists of kings.[17] Each year that the king reigned was recorded, usually with a notice of some significant political, military, or religious event. The information in the Mesopotamian chronicles was brief for each king, ranging from two or three words, recording the king's name and length of reign, to several short sentences detailing highlights for each year of the king's reign. It would appear that several of the short notices in 1 & 2 Kings (such as those for Zechariah, Shallum, Menahem, Pekahiah, and Pekah in 2 Kings 15), which average less than five verses apiece, could have been taken almost verbatim from such chronicles.

---

13. RSV has "Chronicles" and NIV "annals" for Hebrew *dibrê hayyāmîm.* These are not the biblical books of Chronicles, however.
14. First Kings 14:19; 15:31; 16:5, 14, 20, 27; 22:39; 2 Kings 1:18; 10:34; 13:8, 12; 14:15, 28; 15:11, 15, 21, 26, 31.
15. It is missing for Tibni, Joram, and Hoshea, whereas it is mentioned twice in connection with Jehoash (2 Kings 13:12; 14:15).
16. First Kings 14:29; 15:7, 23; 22:45 [MT 46]; 2 Kings 8:23; 12:19 [MT 20]; 14:18; 15:6, 36; 16:19; 20:20; 21:17, 25; 23:28; 24:5.
17. See *ANET,* 274, 301–15, 564–66; A. K. Grayson, *Assyrian and Babylonian Chronicles.*

We should remember, however, that official court records, as those found in Mesopotamia (and presumably in Israel and Judah), did not include the religious evaluations of the kings that we find in 1 & 2 Kings. So we must assume that these court records were added to by the final author of 1 & 2 Kings. A further assumption is that these records were "published" versions of (usually inaccessible) court documents, since we find the repeated statements that they were available for public consultation.

A fourth source is mentioned in the Greek text of 1 Kings 8:53 (which is 8:12–13 in Hebrew): "the Book of the Song." By a slight modification of the presumed underlying Hebrew (*šîr*, "song," to *yāšār*, "Jashar") we get the "Book of Jashar," which is known from Joshua 10:13 and 2 Samuel 1:18. This is the source for the brief poem uttered by Solomon in 1 Kings 8:53 of the Greek versions, but the source is not attested in the Hebrew manuscripts of 8:12–13.

Sources not named in 1 & 2 Kings. Besides the three sources named in 1 & 2 Kings, it is likely that the author used other sources in composing his work.

Despite the highly structured nature of the books, a certain unevenness and imbalance in its treatment of different subjects prevails. Thus (to cite but one example), Omri, one of the most politically significant and powerful kings in Israel, one who is mentioned in several extrabiblical texts, is allotted a mere eight verses (1 Kings 16:21–28), whereas the prophet Elisha, who is unknown in contemporary documents outside the Bible, is prominent in seven chapters (2 Kings 2–8). We also find a special emphasis upon such kings as Solomon (1 Kings 3–11), Jeroboam (1 Kings 11–14), Ahab (1 Kings 16–22), Jehu (2 Kings 9–10), Hezekiah (2 Kings 18–20), and Josiah (2 Kings 22–23), upon such prophets as Elijah (1 Kings 17–19, 21; 2 Kings 1), Micaiah (1 Kings 22), Elisha (2 Kings 2–8), and Isaiah (2 Kings 19–20), and upon the process of transition from David to Solomon (1 Kings 1–2). In the case of the combined Hezekiah/Isaiah narratives (2 Kings 18–20), 2 Kings 18:13–20:19 is almost exactly parallel to Isaiah 36–39.[18] Presuming that the Isaianic passage was written earlier than the 2 Kings one,[19] here is a good example of the author of 2 Kings depending on a source that he does not mention by name.

Scholars have proposed a wide variety of sources that may have lain behind the unevenness of the present text, and many of these are plausi-

---

18. Isaiah's prayer in Isaiah 38:9–20 is omitted in 2 Kings, and there are minor differences in wording throughout.

19. This assumption is disputed by most critical scholars; for a defense of this position, see C. Hassell Bullock, *An Introduction to the Old Testament Prophetic Books,* 147; John N. Oswalt, *The Book of Isaiah: Chapters 1–39,* 699–703.

ble.[20] There is nothing in the texts themselves to preclude our postulating the existence of an early text or tradition dealing with Elijah, Elisha, or Hezekiah, for example, that may have been used in the composition of the final work. More comprehensive proposals that postulate larger documents, such as a "Succession Narrative" (2 Samuel 9–20; 1 Kings 1–2; see chapter 5 in this book), or a "Prophetic Record" (extending from 1 Samuel 1 to 2 Kings 10),[21] also have certain inherent plausibilities.

The identification of such hypothetical sources involves the use of several disciplines, including form criticism (to isolate different genres of texts within 1 & 2 Kings), tradition history (to isolate larger "traditions" that may have been passed down and incorporated into 1 & 2 Kings), and redaction criticism (to identify how the forms and traditions may have been incorporated into the larger whole). On the level of form criticism, the many larger sources have been analyzed in terms of even more, smaller structural units, such as "chronicle," "biography," "farewell speech," "genealogy," "oracle," "prayer," and so forth.[22] Several of these are very small, and usually were part of larger sources, but a few may have been used directly by the author of 1 & 2 Kings in writing the work.

In the last analysis, however, we should remember that these are hypothetical sources, and due caution must be exercised in speaking of them. More important, however, in the cases of both types of sources (named and unnamed), we should remember that they, by themselves, were not Scripture. Rather, the books of Kings were—and are. It is the final composition of the inspired author that should be the ultimate focus of anyone interested in the *message* of these Scriptures.

THE FRAMEWORK OF 1 & 2 KINGS

The pattern. The material in 1 & 2 Kings is organized around the reigns of the kings, beginning with David and Solomon, continuing through the divided monarchies, and ending with the last kings of Judah. After the division of the kingdom (1 Kings 12–14), the author uses a predictable framework with which to introduce his material. The framework begins with a patterned notice of a king's accession and ends with a similarly structured notice of the king's death. The patterns diverge slightly for each kingdom. The typical pattern is as follows:[23]

---

20. For representative surveys, see Otto Eissfeldt, *The Old Testament, An Introduction*, 286–97; Georg Fohrer, *Introduction to the Old Testament*, 232–36; and especially E. Ball, *ISBE* 3, s.v. "Kings, Books of," 30–33, and Simon J. DeVries, *1 Kings*, xxxviii–lii.
21. Anthony F. Campbell, *Prophets and Kings.*
22. The most comprehensive form-critical analysis of 1 & 2 Kings is that of Burke O. Long, *1 Kings, 2 Kings.* Long identifies no fewer than 126 different genres in these two books.
23. On this, see Richard Nelson, *The Double Redaction of the Deuteronomistic History,* 29–42; Steven W. Holloway, *ABD* 4, s.v. "Kings, Book of 1–2."

Accession notice: Synchronism (until Hoshea)
Age at accession (Judah only)
Length of reign
Capital city
Name of queen mother (Judah only)
Theological verdict

Death notice: Source citation
Death and burial
Notice of succession

Typically, this pattern for Israel was expressed thus:

> **Accession notice:** In the Xth year of PN [personal name], king of Judah, PN
> son of PN began to reign over all Israel at Tirzah/Samaria and reigned for X
> years. He did what was evil in the Lord's eyes.
>
> **Death notice:** Now the rest of the deeds of PN, and all that he did, are they
> not written in the Book of the Daily Deeds of the Kings of Israel? And PN slept
> with his fathers and was buried at Tirzah/Samaria; and PN (his son) reigned in
> his place.

The typical pattern in Judah was expressed thus:

> **Accession notice:** PN son of PN [his father, the king] began to reign over
> Judah in the Xth year of PN king of Israel. PN was X years old when he began
> to reign, and he reigned X years in Jerusalem. His mother's name was PN
> daughter of PN. And PN did what was good/evil in the Lord's eyes.
>
> **Death notice:** Now the rest of the deeds of PN, and all that he did, are they
> not written in the Book of the Daily Deeds of the Kings of Judah? PN slept with
> his fathers and was buried with his fathers in the city of David his father; and
> PN his son reigned in his place.

We should notice that, in addition to the extra information in the Judahite formulas (king's age and name of his mother), Judahite kings received
mixed verdicts—some were good and some evil—whereas in Israel the
judgment was consistent: all were evil. Also, the order of presentation is
slightly different in the respective accession notices. Furthermore, a dynastic succession is visible throughout Judah's history (i.e., sons succeeded
fathers), but in Israel that was true in only half the cases.

Theological significance of the pattern. As noted, official court records
probably formed the basis for most of the information in the framework, but
not all of it. For one thing, the synchronistic notices (i.e., the matching up of
a king's accession with the corresponding year in the sister nation) were

probably not a part of the official records of each nation; it would have been enough to have an internally consistent chronology. Indeed, it is difficult to imagine official records of such hated rivals as Israel and Judah acknowledging each other in this way. Second, the theological evaluation of each king's reign was probably not part of the official court records. That very likely came from the pen of the author of 1 & 2 Kings.

The framework's pattern has several significant implications. First, the close attention to such precise records indicates the author's desire to write an accurate, comprehensive history. He intended to write a *history*, not *fiction*.[24] The author reinforces this in his use of synchronisms with the ancient Near East (i.e., references to Egyptian, Assyrian, and Babylonian kings), as well as his challenges to his readers to verify matters themselves by appeal to the official court records. Israel's and Judah's history could be verified, just like anyone else's.

Second, however, this was not a dispassionate, "balanced" history, "history for history's sake"; it was a *theological* history. The author cast his history in a certain theological light, first, by evaluating each king theologically (in the brief formulas), and, second, by giving greatly expanded narratives about some kings and some prophets.

Third, the author intended his work to be part of the larger history of Israel's experience as a nation.[25] The cumulative effect of the detailed chronologies is to show a nation with a long history. When that is added to the date early in the book that ties the beginning of the building of the Temple to the Exodus—1 Kings 6:1 states that it came 480 years after the Exodus—this entire history is linked with that great formative event at the beginning of Israel's history, making the point that even these sinful kingdoms were nevertheless linked with the covenant people of the Exodus.[26]

Fourth, the careful synchronisms for each king's reign with the dates of the sister nation's king indicates the author's desire to represent the histories of Israel and Judah as the history of one people, not two.[27] The two kingdoms were inextricably related to each other, not only by chronology and the historical events of this period but also by their previous history as one people under God, both of whom still were accountable to Him.

24. This point is also made by Brevard S. Childs, *IOTS*, 298–99.
25. Ibid., 297.
26. William Barnes (*Chronology of the Divided Monarchy of Israel*, 146–47) makes the intriguing point that, according to the Judahite *regnal totals* in 1 & 2 Kings, it was exactly 480 years from the original coronation of David over Judah to the last date in the work (561 B.C.), the 37th year of the last-named king in the work (2 Kings 25:27–30), although the actual "historical" total was only 449 years, since David acceded to the throne in ca. 1010 B.C. (not 1041); see chapter 5 under "Date of the Events."
27. Childs, *IOTS*, 298.

1 & 2 KINGS AND THE "DEUTERONOMISTIC HISTORY"

Discussion of the questions of authorship and composition of 1 & 2 Kings is inseparable from the question of the so-called Deuteronomistic History. This is a lengthy, hypothetical literary composition stretching from Deuteronomy to 2 Kings. As understood by most scholars, the final author(s) of 1 & 2 Kings were the final author(s) or editor(s) of the entire Deuteronomistic History.

This hypothetical construct was first proposed by Martin Noth in 1943.[28] Noth contended that it was the work of a single theologian, the "Deuteronomist," who wrote after the fall of Jerusalem and who sought to explain the events of 723/22 and 586 B.C. (the destructions of Samaria and Jerusalem). He saw this work as attempting to demonstrate that these events were the direct consequence of Israel's unrepentant following after other gods and her failure to obey God. As such, it had essentially a negative purpose. This author used many traditions available to him in his own day, and his work was added to in minor ways, but, essentially, the entire corpus was the work of one author. Noth rejected the work of those who saw any of the Pentateuchal "documents" (JEDP) in Joshua or any later books.

For Noth, there are several basic themes in the Deuteronomistic History: (1) the graciousness of God's covenant and the special bond between God and His people; (2) the evils of idolatry and a decentralized cult; (3) the inevitability of reward and punishment, according to obedience or disobedience; and (4) the keeping of the Mosaic Covenant, which is expressed not so much by sacrificial observances as by obedience to the stipulations of the law and by worship, which includes reading and keeping of the law.[29]

In the years since Noth, his construct has received a remarkable degree of acceptance in almost all scholarly circles.[30] Many scholars have modified it or proposed alternatives, but it has remained the starting point for all subsequent discussion of the issue. The primary criticisms have been at two points: (1) his assessment of the overall message is too negative; (2) his postulate of a single, exilic author is too simplistic.

Concerning the first point, several scholars have identified more positive themes or subthemes in the Deuteronomistic History than Noth did.

---

28. The English translation is Martin Noth, *The Deuteronomistic History*.
29. Noth, *Deuteronomistic History,* 134–45.
30. Recent reviews of the extensive work on the Deuteronomistic History since Noth may be found in Gerald Gerbrandt, *Kingship According to the Deuteronomistic History,* 1–18; Steven L. McKenzie, *The Trouble With Kings,* 1–19; *ABD* 2, s.v. "Deuteronomistic History."

Gerhard von Rad first identified the great promises to David and the portrait of David as the righteous king par excellence as integral parts of the Deuteronomistic History's themes,[31] and he has been followed in this by many scholars. For example, Hans Walter Wolff has stressed the importance of repentance and forgiveness as a model put forth by the author,[32] and Walter Brueggemann has stressed the importance of God's graciousness (expressed in the motif of "goodness").[33] More recently, J. G. McConville has stressed that the Deuteronomistic History communicates the ideas of hope and God's grace in significant ways.[34]

Concerning the second criticism of Noth, many scholars have identified more than one author or editor of the Deuteronomistic History. These range from those who postulate two or three authors/editors to those who postulate many more (e.g., Rainer Stahl argues for nine levels of editing, and Mark O'Brien argues for at least seven).[35]

The most important modification of Noth's theory—both in terms of identifying themes and of identifying author(s)—has come from Frank Cross and was developed by Richard Nelson.[36] Cross and Nelson argue for two editions of the Deuteronomistic History, a first composed in the reign of Josiah (640–609 B.C.), and a second during the Exile. For Cross, two themes dominate the first edition: first, an emphasis upon the sins of Jeroboam I, and, second (with von Rad), an emphasis upon God's choice of David and Jerusalem. These two contrast sharply with each other; the first theme ends with an analysis of the destruction of Samaria (2 Kings 17), whereas the second climaxes in the great reforms of Josiah (2 Kings 22–23). For Cross, the second (exilic) edition lays the blame for Judah's downfall on Manasseh in 2 Kings 21:2–15, a section that closely parallels 2 Kings 17. The first edition was more hopeful, containing as it did the great themes of God's choice of David and Jerusalem, whereas the second edition was more downbeat, explaining why Judah itself, the tribe of the Davidic line, fell.

There are some obvious strengths to an approach that sees a large, unified composition of the type Noth proposed. First, there *is* a strong "Deuter-

31. Gerhard von Rad, "The Deuteronomistic Theology of History in the Books of Kings," 74–91; see also his *Old Testament Theology,* 334–54.
32. Hans Walter Wolff, "The Kerygma of the Deuteronomic Historical Work," 83–100, 141–43.
33. Walter Brueggemann, "The Kerygma of the Deuteronomistic Historian," 387–402.
34. McConville, "Narrative and Meaning in the Books of Kings," 31–49; "1 Kings VIII 46–53 and the Deuteronomic Hope," 67–79; *Grace in the End: A Study in Deuteronomic Theology.*
35. For two authors, see, e.g., Alfred Jepsen, *Die Quellen des Königsbuches*; for three, see, e.g., Iain W. Provan, *Hezekiah and the Books of Kings*; for more authors, see, e.g., Rainer Stahl, *Aspekte der Geschichte deuteronomistischer Theologie* (a 1982 dissertation cited in McKenzie, *The Trouble With Kings,* 18); Mark A. O'Brien, *The Deuteronomistic History Hypothesis: A Reassessment.*
36. Frank Moore Cross, *Canaanite Myth and Hebrew Epic,* 274–89; Richard D. Nelson, *The Double Redaction of the Deuteronomistic History.*

onomistic" influence found throughout Joshua–2 Kings, one that is not nearly so visible in Genesis–Numbers. Thus, there can be some value in speaking of a "Deuteronomistic" philosophy of history (i.e., one in which there is a strong—and almost always immediate—correlation between obedience/disobedience and reward/punishment) or a "Deuteronomistic" history (i.e., a corpus of books that reflects the same viewpoints that are found in Deuteronomy).

Second, the theory of consecutive, discrete blocks of literary materials joined together at various "seams" (as Noth envisioned) is much easier to countenance than is the older "documentary" theory of various intertwined strands coming together.

Third, on the whole, there is more of a unity, both in content and in outlook, to Deuteronomy–Kings than there is to the so-called Hexateuch, i.e., Genesis–Joshua. Thus, if large, hypothetical compositions are to be posited, a Deuteronomistic History is much more plausible than is a Hexateuch (or a Heptateuch or Octateuch!).[37]

However, there are some deficiencies in this approach. First, the approach usually assumes that Deuteronomy was not written by Moses but by a person or group during the time of Josiah in the seventh century B.C. or during the Exile in the sixth century. This assumption does not take seriously the biblical witnesses to Deuteronomy's provenance at a far earlier period in Israel's history.[38]

Second, the removal of Deuteronomy from Genesis–Numbers leaves that corpus as a torso; the resulting "Tetrateuch" is most unsatisfactory—and unconvincing—as a literary unit. This has led some scholars to postulate even larger units that would incorporate all of the material from Genesis to 2 Kings into one large, unified document.[39] This is a helpful approach, emphasizing as it does the essential unity of this entire corpus, but it still begs the question of the authorship or composition of the smaller units.

Third, Noth's essentially negative understanding of the Deuteronomist's purpose has not been generally accepted. As Childs notes, "It is hard to imagine a negative cause as sufficient reason to compose and preserve the tradition."[40]

Fourth, the various revisions of Noth that postulate two or more editions, while exhibiting a sensitivity to changes in emphasis or perspective in the corpus, nevertheless usually do not deal adequately with the message

---

37. On the "Hexateuch," see chapter 2; on the "Heptateuch" and "Octateuch," see Eissfeldt, *Introduction*, 279, 288; Fohrer, *Introduction*, 103–4.
38. For a defense of Mosaic authorship of the Pentateuch, see Herbert Wolf, *An Introduction to the Old Testament Pentateuch*, 51–78.
39. E.g., David Noel Freedman, *IDBSup*, s.v. "The Deuteronomic History."
40. Childs, *IOTS*, 237.

and thrust of the organic whole. In the last analysis, the final author(s) must be given pride of place in considering the overall message of any book or larger corpus.

With some refinements and qualifications, however, the idea of a Deuteronomistic History can indeed be helpful. Surely the historical books do reflect the theology of Deuteronomy in significant ways. The term *Deuteronomistic* can thus be used in a more neutral, descriptive way to refer to those books or ideas reflective of the distinctive viewpoints found in Deuteronomy —with no conclusions concerning authorship of Deuteronomy or the other books inherent in the use of the term. This is the understanding of the term when it is employed in the present work.

In terms of the composition of 1 & 2 Kings, any discussion of the Deuteronomistic History must deal seriously with the authorship and shape of these two books. In the present work, the assumption is that the author of 1 & 2 Kings was indeed a single person, writing during the Exile (ca. 550 B.C.?), who integrated diverse sources to present a coherent picture of the life of Israel and Judah during their histories and to point to a hope for them, even in exile. This author's relationship with the earlier materials is more difficult to judge, but his work certainly is of a piece with the books of Joshua, Judges, and 1 & 2 Samuel (and Deuteronomy), both in terms of style and outlook, and it is perhaps possible to speak of him as the "author" of Joshua, Judges, and 1 & 2 Samuel as well, in the sense spoken of above (see "Authorship and Date of Composition" above).

CHRONOLOGY IN 1 & 2 KINGS

In no book of the Bible is chronology a matter of greater concern than in the books of Kings. An impressively large number of texts in these two books record chronological data: close to sixty such texts exist,[41] more than one per chapter. Furthermore, these are not scattered at random: the very books themselves are structured around a careful chronological framework. A repeated and fairly predictable pattern is found at the beginning and end of each successive king's reign, a pattern that includes careful dating information.

The chronological data can be studied on two levels. First, it is a matter of some interest and importance to establish an accurate absolute chronology of the books, that is, to be able to assign fixed dates to the events and reigns in the books. (This is dealt with in the present section.) Second, the function of the chronological data in the overall message or theology of

41. Leslie McFall, "A Translation Guide to the Chronological Data in Kings and Chronicles," 3–45.

the books must also be considered. (This has been dealt with above, under "The Framework of 1 & 2 Kings: Theological Significance of the Pattern.")

THE CHRONOLOGICAL SCHEME OF 1 & 2 KINGS[42]

Dating of events in the Bible is of two types: relative and absolute. *Relative dating* (or "internal" dating) involves dating of events with reference to some other period or event. This is illustrated in the repeated formulas for kings' accession to the throne, such as the notice concerning Azariah in 2 Kings 15:1: "In the twenty-seventh year of Jeroboam king of Israel, Azariah the son of Amaziah, king of Judah, began to reign." Here, King Azariah's accession in Judah is synchronized with the years of the Israelite king's (Jeroboam's) reign.

Absolute dating (or "external" dating) involves dating of events with reference to the known calendar, such that a specific year can be assigned a particular event. This may be illustrated by the "fourteenth year of Hezekiah's reign," mentioned in 2 Kings 18:13, being commonly assigned by scholars to the year 701 B.C. This date is known because it was the year that Sennacherib, king of Assyria, invaded Judah, an event mentioned both in the Bible (2 Kings 18:13) and in Sennacherib's own annals.[43] The Assyrians kept accurate records that could be correlated with astronomical phenomena (especially solar and lunar eclipses), which, through mathematical extrapolation, can be determined down to the very day.

Unfortunately, on the surface, the chronological data in 1 & 2 Kings are filled with difficulties, both internal and external. These difficulties are of several different types.[44] First, sometimes contradictory dates are given for certain facts. For example, 2 Kings 1:17 states that Jehoram became king of Israel in the second year of another Jehoram's reign in Judah, but 2 Kings 3:1 states that he became king in the eighteenth year of *Jehoshaphat's* reign (Jehoshaphat was the father of Judah's Jehoram). Furthermore, 2 Kings 8:16 reverses the information found in 1:17: this text states that Jehoram of Judah became king *after* Israel's Jehoram,[45] whereas 1:17 states that Jehoram of Judah came to power first.

Second, sometimes summary dates for a king's reign do not match up with the synchronisms established with the dates in the other kingdom.

---

42. The literature on this question is immense. It may be accessed via the bibliographies in the following: Edwin R. Thiele, *The Mysterious Numbers of the Hebrew Kings*; John H. Hayes and Paul K. Hooker, *A New Chronology for the Kings of Israel and Judah*; William Hamilton Barnes, *Studies in the Chronology of the Divided Monarchy of Israel.*
43. *ANET,* 287–88; *TANE,* 199–201; *DOTT,* 64–69.
44. See Thiele (*Mysterious Numbers,* 36–39) for these and other examples.
45. This particular problem is further complicated by the confusion of having two contemporary kings with the same name ("Jehoram"), both of whom are also called "Joram." The NIV distinguishes between the two by calling the Israelite king "Joram" and his Judahite counterpart "Jehoram."

Thus, for example, 1 Kings 16:23 states that Omri became king of Israel in the thirty-first year of Asa, king of Judah, and that he reigned twelve years. However, verses 28–29 state that Omri's son Ahab succeeded him after his death, in the *thirty-eighth* year of Asa, which would give Omri a reign of only seven years (not twelve).

A third type of problem comes when numbers that are added up to fill a certain time period do not match up with each other. Thus, we know that Jeroboam I of Israel and Rehoboam of Judah came to power at the same time, when the kingdom split (1 Kings 12–14). Many years later, Jehu of Israel and Athaliah of Judah assumed power in the same year, with the deaths of Joram of Israel and Ahaziah of Judah (2 Kings 9:23–27). Thus, this period was identical in both Israel and Judah. Yet, computing the lengths of these two periods from the individual data given for the reigns in each kingdom yields ninety-eight years for Israel, but only ninety-five years for Judah.

A fourth type of problem comes when external synchronisms are attempted with known dates. Thus, the year 701 b.c. is known to be the year in which Sennacherib invaded Judah, and this is stated to have been Hezekiah's fourteenth year (2 Kings 18:13). Thus, Hezekiah should have acceded to power in 715 b.c. However, 2 Kings 18:1 states that Hezekiah became king of Judah in the third year of Israel's King Hoshea, which was 729 b.c. Hoshea himself was deposed in 723/22 with the destruction of Samaria. Thus, there is a discrepancy of fourteen years in the internal and external data.

The problem is reflected in the earliest sources. The problems noted above come from the Hebrew MT itself, and several early Greek versions— most notably, Codex Vaticanus and the Lucianic recension—have markedly different chronological schemes, as does the Jewish historian Josephus.[46] Early and late rabbinic sources also recognized difficulties in the biblical data.[47] Early Christian scholars such as Jerome noted the difficulties, and a seemingly endless string of modern scholars has wrestled with them.

Modern solutions usually begin with observation of a few fixed (i.e., "absolute") dates, with which the biblical data can then be correlated. Absolute dates can be recovered from many ancient documents; among the most important are Assyrian and Babylonian king lists and chronicles. Edwin R. Thiele relies most heavily on the date of the battle of Qarqar in 853 b.c. (from which he derives the death of Ahab in that year and the accession of Jehu in 841) and the date of Sennacherib's invasion of Judah in 701 b.c.

46. Thiele, *Mysterious Numbers*, 167–227; J. D. Shenkel, *Chronology and Recensional Development in the Greek Text of Kings*.

47. Hayim Tadmor, "The Chronology of the First Temple Period: A Presentation and Evaluation of the Sources," 368–83, 408–11, esp. p. 370. (This is reprinted from *WHJP* 4.1, 44–60, 318–20.)

He then extrapolates the rest of the biblical dates from these fixed dates.[48] Hayim Tadmor gives a total of twenty fixed dates that can be synchronized with biblical data, all from Assyrian and Babylonian sources.[49] William Barnes analyzes several additional dates from Phoenician and Egyptian sources.[50]

Almost every attempt to resolve the difficulties has been forced to argue that the present Hebrew text is mistaken in one or more places. Some argue for the priority of the Greek traditions over the Masoretic one,[51] while others argue for the superiority of the Masoretic tradition.[52] Even among the latter, however, almost all argue that the present Hebrew text is mistaken in several or many instances. The most conservative scholar on this point is Edwin Thiele, who has championed the uncanny reliability of the Hebrew text, but even he argues that the final editors of the books of Kings were mistaken in several dates in 2 Kings 17–18.[53]

Thiele's efforts have been the most comprehensive and sustained, and his chronological scheme, while still criticized from numerous quarters, has won more acceptance than any other. Its greatest strength is that it accounts for almost every date in the Hebrew text,[54] namely, that it "works." On the whole, it demonstrates the internal consistency of the biblical data. Perhaps its greatest weakness is its complicated nature. This has intimidated many students and rendered many scholars skeptical. Thiele's scheme rests upon several principles that are not always clear in the text. These include the following:[55]

1. In Israel, years were reckoned from the month of Nisan (roughly equivalent to April), whereas in Judah they were reckoned from Tishri (roughly equivalent to October).

2. Israel and Judah used different systems for counting the first year of a king's reign (by some methods of counting, it would have overlapped the previous king's last year and thus counted twice); furthermore, each nation changed its system at least once during its history.

48. See Thiele (*Mysterious Numbers*, 67–78) for his discussion of absolute dating.
49. Tadmor, "Chronology of the First Temple Period," 377–78.
50. Barnes, *Chronology of the Divided Monarchy*.
51. Shenkel, *Chronology and Recensional Development*; Childs, *IOTS*, 296–97; Barnes, *Chronology of the Divided Monarchy*.
52. Thiele, *Mysterious Numbers*; Tadmor, "Chronology of the First Temple Period"; Hayes and Hooker, *A New Chronology*. See also the following responses to Shenkel: D. W. Gooding, "Review of J. D. Shenkel, *Chronology and Recensional Development*," 118–31; Thiele, "Coregencies and Overlapping Reigns Among the Hebrew Kings," 174–200.
53. Thiele, *Mysterious Numbers*, 134–37, 168, 174–75, 198–205.
54. Except for the ones in 2 Kings 17–18 that claim that Hoshea's and Hezekiah's reigns overlapped, which he disbelieves.
55. See Thiele, *Mysterious Numbers*, 43–65. The best nontechnical introduction to the entire question of chronology is Thiele's popular presentation, *A Chronology of the Hebrew Kings*; see pp. 14–22 for these principles.

3. Israel and Judah each counted the other's years using their own systems.

4. Both nations employed a system of "coregencies," in which a king's son may have been installed as king before his father died; the overlapping years were then usually counted twice.

Despite its complicated nature, Thiele's system does show the biblical text to be internally consistent, down to the exact year (except with reference to Hoshea and Hezekiah in 2 Kings 17–18), and it is based on indications in the text itself, some explicit and some implicit. Several conservative scholars have noted that Thiele's system would be completely consistent if he had merely applied one of his own principles, namely, coregency, to Hezekiah: the extant data suggest that Hezekiah had a fourteen-year coregency with his father Ahaz, which thus allows for the overlap between Hezekiah and Hoshea that the Bible affirms in 2 Kings 17–18.[56]

Because of its plausibility and internal consistency, along with its widespread acceptance, Thiele's system is followed in the present work. Thiele's dates are listed on page 187 (modified to show Hezekiah's coregency).[57]

THE KINGS OF ISRAEL AND JUDAH

Looking at the chart below, we can see that there were twenty monarchs in both nations. However, that the kingdom of Judah lasted 135 years longer than did Israel demonstrates the higher level of political instability in the north. Indeed, seven Israelite kings died by assassination, to be replaced by their assassins: Nadab, Elah, Joram, Zechariah, Shallum, Pekahiah, and Pekah. An eighth—the unfortunate Zimri, who reigned but seven days!—burned his palace down around himself when he realized he was doomed (1 Kings 16:18).

In Judah, the dynasty of David continued unbroken from beginning to end. In Israel, the longest dynasties were those of Omri (four kings) and Jehu (five kings). Jehu's family's relatively long tenure on the throne was due to his having rid Israel of the abomination of Baal worship by killing the entire household of Ahab (2 Kings 10:30; 15:12).

In Israel, out of a total of twenty kings, none was judged to have been good by the author of 1 & 2 Kings. Jehu came the closest: he was anointed king by Elisha at the Lord's command (2 Kings 9:1–13), and he was commended by God for his destruction of the enormously wicked house of Ahab

---

56. J. N. Oswalt, *ISBE* 3, s.v. "Chronology of the Old Testament"; T. C. Mitchell and K. A. Kitchen, *NBD*, s.v. "Chronology of the Old Testament"; Eugene Merrill, *Kingdom of Priests*, 402–5; Leslie McFall, "Did Thiele Overlook Hezekiah's Coregency?" 393–404.
57. See the charts in Thiele, *Mysterious Numbers*, 217; *Chronology of the Hebrew Kings*, 75; for extended discussion, see *Mysterious Numbers*, 79–138, 173–92.

The Kings of Israel and Judah

ISRAEL		JUDAH	
1. Jeroboam I	930–909	1. Rehoboam	930–913
2. Nadab	909–908	2. Abijam	913–910
3. Baasha	908–886	3. Asa	910–869
4. Elah	886–885		
5. Zimri	885		
6. (Tibni)	885–880*		
7. Omri	885–874		
8. Ahab	874–853	4. Jehoshaphat	872–848
9. Ahaziah	853–852	5. Jehoram	
10. Joram	852–841	(Joram)	853–841
		6. Ahaziah	841
11. Jehu	841–814	7. (Athaliah)	841–835*
12. Jehoahaz	814–798	8. Joash	
13. Jehoash		(Jehoash)	835–796
(Joash)	798–782	9. Amaziah	796–767
14. Jeroboam II	793–753	10. Azariah	792–740
15. Zechariah	753		
16. Shallum	752		
17. Menahem	752–742	11. Jotham	750–732
18. Pekahiah	742–740		
19. Pekah	752–732	12. Ahaz	735–715
20. Hoshea	732–723/22	13. Hezekiah	729–686
		14. Manasseh	697–642
		15. Amon	642–640
		16. Josiah	640–609
		17. Jehoahaz	609
		18. Jehoiakim	609–598
		19. Jehoiachin	598–597
		20. Zedekiah	597–586

* The author of 1 & 2 Kings does not regard either of these two as legitimate monarchs. Tibni was a rival to Omri (1 Kings 16:21–22), whereas Athaliah, Ahaziah's mother, usurped power that legitimately belonged to Joash (2 Kings 11:1–20). Significantly, there are no accession formulas or formal death notices for either.

(10:30). However, in the final analysis, he did not turn away from the sins of Jeroboam, who set the standard of iniquity in the northern kingdom (10:29, 31).

In Judah, there were *eight good kings: Asa, Jehoshaphat, Joash, Amaziah, Azariah, Jotham, Hezekiah, and Josiah.* Of these, the first six neglected to remove from the land the symbols of Canaanite pagan practices, the high places. Only Hezekiah and Josiah received unreserved praise.

Yet, in the end, even the greatness of these kings was not enough to spare Judah from destruction. Ironically, Manasseh, one of Judah's most wicked kings, followed one of its greatest kings, his father Hezekiah. We are told that it was "because of the sins of Manasseh" that God finally allowed Judah to be destroyed (24:3–4). Ultimately, the survival of the Davidic line was not due to his or anyone else's inherent goodness. Rather, it was due to God's grace (see below, under "Theology of 1 & 2 Kings").

Prophets and Prophecy in 1 & 2 Kings

Prophets and prophecy play an important part in the books of Kings. The portrayal of these generally fits into what we know of prophets from elsewhere in Scripture, but a few characteristic features stand out here more sharply than they do elsewhere.[58]

PROPHETIC TITLES

Prophets were often called God's "servants." The prophets Ahijah and Jonah are called this (1 Kings 14:18; 2 Kings 14:25), and the term *my/his servants the prophets* often was used in a general way (2 Kings 9:7; 17:13, 23; 21:10; 24:2). These terms show God's claim upon them as His mouthpieces. A second general term for a prophet—used sixty times in 1 & 2 Kings—was *man of God.* This refers most often to Elijah and Elisha, but also it designates Shemaiah (1 Kings 12:22) and an anonymous prophet (chap. 13). A third general term is *sons of the prophets,* and it is used exclusively in Elijah's and Elisha's day (see below).

---

58. For general introductions to prophecy, see Bullock, *An Introduction to the Old Testament Prophetic Books,* esp. pp. 11–36; Edward J. Young, *My Servants the Prophets;* Gary V. Smith, *ISBE* 3, s.v. "Prophecy, False," and "Prophet; Prophecy"; John F. A. Sawyer, *Prophecy and the Prophets of the Old Testament;* Carl E. Armerding and W. Ward Gasque, eds., *A Guide to Biblical Prophecy;* Walter C. Kaiser, Jr., *Back Toward the Future;* Willem A. Van-Gemeren, *Interpreting the Prophetic Word,* esp. pp. 15–99; John J. Schmitt and John Barton, *ABD* 5, s.v. "Prophecy." Two more specialized (and technical) studies are Robert R. Wilson, *Prophecy and Society in Ancient Israel;* David L. Petersen, *The Roles of Israel's Prophets.*

Two terms used of prophets elsewhere, *rō'eh* ("seer") and *ḥōzeh* ("one who sees visions"), are not found in 1 & 2 Kings, but the common word "prophet" (*nābî'*) does. It is used fifty-four times in these books, referring to twelve different individuals as well as to large groups, such as the prophets of Baal and Asherah (1 Kings 18:19), Ahab's four hundred false prophets (1 Kings 22:6), and the "companies of the prophets" that Elisha encountered (e.g., 2 Kings 2:3ff.).

The basic idea behind the word *prophet* was that this was a spokesperson or mouthpiece for God. Prophets *spoke* words from God. The repeated phrase "Thus says the Lord" in the prophetic books makes this point clearly. So does the remarkable reference in Exodus 7:1, where God said to Moses, "See, I have made you like God to Pharaoh, and your brother Aaron will be your prophet. You are to say everything I command you and your brother Aaron is to tell Pharaoh to let the Israelites go." Here Aaron functions as the mediator between Moses and Pharaoh, a mediator who passes along a message, a message received from a superior. Amos associated prophecy with speaking words from God (Amos 3:8), and the author of 1 Samuel affirms that Samuel was a prophet whose words were effective: The Lord "let none of his words fall to the ground" (1 Sam. 3:19–20).

The author of 1 & 2 Kings speaks of the importance of prophetic words in this last way twice: (1) he states that everything Moses promised concerning God's rest was fulfilled, that "not one word has failed" (lit., fallen; 1 Kings 8:56); (2) he affirms that nothing Elijah said concerning Ahab would "fall to the ground" (2 Kings 10:10).

CHARACTERISTICS AND FUNCTIONS OF PROPHETS

True prophets were commissioned, or "called," by God to speak for Him. In 1 & 2 Kings, we see God's call of Elisha through the prophet Elijah (1 Kings 19:16–21). Elsewhere, we have accounts of the calls of Samuel (1 Samuel 3), Isaiah (Isa. 6:1–13), Jeremiah (Jer. 1:4–10), Ezekiel (Ezek. 1:1–3), Hosea (Hos. 1:2–9; 3:1–5), and Amos (Amos 3:3–8; 7:10–17). These "call experiences" were important validations for the prophets themselves, their hearers, and their readers that God's hand was indeed upon them.

True prophets were to reflect high moral character. That is clear from such passages as Ezekiel 13 and Jeremiah 23. It is hard to imagine Nathan, for example, effectively rebuking David for sin if he himself were not a man of high moral character or Elijah condemning Ahab's Baal worship if he himself were a secret idol worshiper.

An important function of prophets was to foretell future events to God's people. According to J. Barton Payne's estimates, more than one-fourth of the entire Bible consists of predictive matter of all types,[59] and the prophets were the major vehicles for communicating such predictions.

In 1 & 2 Kings, a special concern was the correspondence between a prophecy and its fulfillment. Whereas in the prophetic books, the fulfillment of most prophecies is not indicated, the opposite is the case in 1 & 2 Kings: the words of every true prophet in 1 & 2 Kings are shown to have come to pass.[60] Von Rad identified eleven such cases, where a prophecy is given and its fulfillment is explicitly detailed, to which several more can be added.[61] These are stated to be in fulfillment of "the word of the Lord" or of a prophet speaking for the Lord.

Related to this, the idea of the "word of the Lord" is very important in 1 & 2 Kings. This phrase occurs forty-four times in the two books. The "word of the Lord" is presented in 1 & 2 Kings as effecting change: it is something that causes people to act, and it always comes true.

Biblical prophecy was no mere fascination with the future for its own sake, however. Many scholars have emphasized that the prophets' primary task was not foretelling, but "forthtelling," i.e., to proclaim God's word publicly. They were to "explain the past, elucidate the present, and disclose the future."[62] First and foremost, they were mouthpieces for God, declaring His message to His people in their own times. Thus, the bulk of the messages of Elijah and Elisha, for example, was directed to the abominable conditions of their own day.

VARIETIES OF PROPHETS IN 1 & 2 KINGS

The phenomenon of prophecy was not evenly distributed throughout Israel's history; rather, prophets tended to arise more during certain periods than during others. Previous to Samuel, for example, prophecy had been relatively sparse: "In those days the word of the Lord was rare; there were not many visions" (1 Sam. 3:1). The time period covered by 1 & 2 Kings was the time of prophets par excellence. Most of the prophetic books have this period of the monarchies as their backdrop, and prophets are very prominent in 1 & 2 Kings, as we have seen. Prophets spoke especially to kings and to the nations through these kings.

59. J. Barton Payne, *Encyclopedia of Biblical Prophecy,* 681.
60. George Savran, "1 and 2 Kings," 161.
61. G. von Rad, "Deuteronomistic Theology of History," 78–81. The passages are 2 Samuel 7:13 // 1 Kings 8:20; 1 Kings 11:29ff. // 1 Kings 12:15; 1 Kings 13:2 // 2 Kings 23:16–18; 1 Kings 14:6ff. // 1 Kings 15:29; 1 Kings 16:1ff. // 1 Kings 16:12; Joshua 6:26 // 1 Kings 16:34; 1 Kings 22:17 // 1 Kings 22:35ff.; 1 Kings 21:21ff. // 1 Kings 21:27–29 (cf. 2 Kings 9:7); 2 Kings 1:6 // 2 Kings 1:17; 2 Kings 21:10ff. // 2 Kings 24:2 (cf. also 23:26); 2 Kings 22:15ff. // 2 Kings 23:30. Von Rad does not mention the following cases: 1 Kings 13:3 // 1 Kings 13:5; 1 Kings 21:23 (and 2 Kings 9:10) // 2 Kings 9:30–37.
62. Kaiser, *Back Toward the Future,* 42.

Court prophets. One type of prophet particularly typical of the period of the monarchy was the court prophet, i.e., a prophet who had easy access to the king himself. Some court prophets would not have been true prophets of the Lord; they had been employed by the king, and they tended to tell the king only what he wanted to hear. The parade example of this is the four hundred prophets Ahab consulted about going to war against Syria (1 Kings 22). They told Ahab what he wanted to hear, whereas a true prophet of the Lord—Micaiah—did not. Ahab hated Micaiah precisely for this reason: "I hate him, for he never prophesies good concerning me, but evil" (1 Kings 22:8). Ahab also employed the 450 prophets of Baal, whom Elijah opposed (18:20–40).

True prophets of the Lord with access to kings in 1 & 2 Kings include Nathan (chap. 1),[63] an anonymous "man of God" (chap. 13), Jehu, son of Hanani (16:1, 7), Elijah (chaps. 17–19, 21), Micaiah (chap. 22), Elisha (2 Kings 2–9, 13), and Isaiah (chaps. 19–20).[64] These prophets usually confronted kings—at great personal risk—with messages they did not want to hear.

Prophetic groups. The typical prophet of the Lord appears as a lone figure, courageously confronting king and society about their ills. However, in two periods, we see a variety of prophets living and working in groups. The first is in the days of Samuel, when we see a "company" of prophets prophesying together (1 Sam. 10:5, 10), and a different group living at Ramah with Samuel (19:18–24). We are not told much about their particular activities vis-à-vis the general public, except that they sang and "prophesied."

The second period is in the days of Elijah and Elisha. Here the prophets are called "the sons of the prophets" (1 Kings 20:35).[65] They lived in groups at Gilgal and elsewhere. In 2 Kings 4:38, 42–43, they are seen living in a group of a hundred men and eating a common meal, which suggests that they also lived in a common house. This is confirmed by 2 Kings 6:1, where mention is made of where they dwelled and their desire to build a new dwelling place. First Kings 18:13 mentions Elijah's hiding of groups of fifty of the Lord's prophets from Jezebel's clutches. However, some prophets maintained private residences (14:4: Jeroboam's wife went to Shiloh "and came to the house of Ahijah"), and some even married and had families

---

63. Although Nathan spoke with more divine authority on earlier occasions (2 Samuel 7, 12) than he did here. (See David M. Howard, Jr., *ABD* 4, s.v. "Nathan.")
64. Other court prophets in this period not mentioned in 1 & 2 Kings include Gad, in David's day (2 Sam. 24:11; 1 Chron. 21:9; 2 Chron. 29:25); Iddo, in Solomon's and Rehoboam's reigns (2 Chron. 9:29; 12:15); Hanani, in Asa's and Jehoshaphat's day (2 Chron. 16:7; 19:2); and anonymous seers, in Manasseh's day (2 Chron. 33:18).
65. The term is used eleven times in the OT, all in 1 & 2 Kings. Except for the first reference, all occur in connection with Elisha: 1 Kings 20:35; 2 Kings 2:3, 5, 7, 15; 4:1, 38, 38; 5:22; 6:1; 9:1.

(2 Kings 4:1: a widow of one of the sons of the prophets speaks to Elisha about her and her two sons' destitute condition).

The precise nature of these prophetic groups has provoked much discussion.[66] Many scholars envision these as formal, prophetic "guilds," where prophets were trained in their craft.[67] The association even has been made with medieval monasteries, although the prophetic groups were much more public in their activities than were the medieval monks, and so the analogy cannot be pressed. However, it is also argued that these—at least those in Elisha's day—were informal groups of "lay supporters" of Elisha.[68] They are not found after Elisha's day, so the analogy of "training schools" for prophets is inappropriate as a general description of prophetic activity in later periods, if at all.

Writing prophets. The "writing prophets" are those whose writings are collected in the prophetic books of the OT. Of these, two are mentioned in 1 & 2 Kings. Isaiah figures prominently in the story of Hezekiah and Sennacherib (2 Kings 19–20), and a prophecy by Jonah is mentioned in 14:25.[69] The use of both of these prophets' prophecies fits the author's purpose of showing the pattern of prophecy and fulfillment mentioned above.

ELIJAH AND ELISHA

The Elijah and Elisha narratives. The narratives about the prophets Elijah and Elisha play an important part in the unfolding of the narrative of 1 & 2 Kings.[70] These two prophets appear during the Omride dynasty in Israel, at a time when the Israelite kings were openly pursuing the worship of Baal. The stories about Elijah are found in 1 Kings 17–19, 21, and 2 Kings 1–2, whereas Elisha's are found in 1 Kings 19 and 2 Kings 2–9, 13. The activities of these two prophets are emphasized more than those of any prophet after Moses in the OT.[71]

In the chapters where these prophets appear, the emphasis shifts away from chronicling the dates and events of the kings' reigns and focuses

---

66. For representative discussions, see C. F. Keil, *The First Book of Samuel,* 199–206; Wilson, *Prophecy and Society in Ancient Israel,* 140–41, 202–6; T. R. Hobbs, *2 Kings,* 25–27.
67. E.g., G. von Rad, *Old Testament Theology,* 2:26–27.
68. E.g., Hobbs, *2 Kings,* 25–27.
69. The "Obadiah" in Ahab's household who helped Elijah (1 Kings 18) was not the prophet Obadiah, nor was the "Zephaniah" of 2 Kings 25:18 the prophet Zephaniah. These were common names in Hebrew society.
70. They have been studied extensively, usually as independent narratives. See the bibliographies in Jerome T. Walsh, *ABD* 2, s.v. "Elijah"; Keith W. Whitelam, *ABD* 2, s.v. "Elisha"; and two recent works: Alan J. Hauser and Russell Gregory, *From Carmel to Horeb: Elijah in Crisis;* Rick Dale Moore, *God Saves: Lessons from the Elisha Stories.*
71. The exception to this is Jeremiah, whose message was inextricably bound up with his life story at many points (see Jeremiah 26–29, 32–45), but he was not a miracle worker like Elijah and Elisha were.

on the prophets and their words and activities. Elijah's activities revolve around confrontation of the king, whereas Elisha's sphere of activity is mainly among the common people. The presence of such extensive material devoted to prophetic activities is an important element in the overall prophetic perspective of 1 & 2 Kings.

The accounts of Elijah are all linked with his opposition to pagan idol worship, mainly of Baal. First Kings 17–19 are the most important in this regard. The section begins with Elijah's word of prophecy that no rain will come upon the land until God decrees it (17:1–7). This anticipates the climactic confrontation with the prophets of Baal in chapter 18, since Baal was the Canaanite storm god. In 17:8–24, we find two episodes where Elijah performs miracles on behalf of a widow, from Zarephath, which was in Phoenician territory, near Sidon (the land from which worship of Baal was imported into Israel). The prophecy about the rain is reiterated (17:14), and in both episodes "the word of the Lord" in the mouth of Elijah is affirmed (17:16, 24). These episodes serve to establish Elijah's credentials as a bona fide prophet from God.

The climax of these narratives comes in chapter 18 with the dramatic confrontation between Elijah and 450 of Baal's prophets on Mount Carmel. Baal's prophets are humiliated, since they cannot induce him to send fire onto the altar, nor have they been able to induce their storm god to produce rain for three years prior to this (v. 1). The import of this humiliation is heightened when we remember that Baal was the Canaanite storm god: Canaanite texts about him extol his attributes over precisely the forces that are challenged in 1 Kings 18: "the seasons of his rains will Baal observe . . . and he will peal his thunder in the clouds, flashing his lightnings to the earth."[72] It is God, however, who controls the rain, and He sends it after Baal's prophets have been executed (vv. 41–46).

In the aftermath of this confrontation, Elijah flees to the desert and is provided for by God (chap. 19). He spends forty days and nights fasting and meets God at Mount Horeb, where Moses had met God many years earlier. God appears, not in the wind, earthquake, or fire, which are reminiscent of Baal's failed spheres of supposed influence, but through a still, small voice (19:9–18). Elijah is encouraged, and he meets Elisha, who will become his successor in a way reminiscent of Joshua's succession of Moses (19:16–21; cf. Num. 27:18–23, Deut. 34:9). Many scholars have noted the parallels between Moses and Elijah (and even Elisha).[73] Elijah is presented as a second Moses in many ways, and both Elijah and Elisha were God's representatives in a critical time of great opposition, just as Moses had been.

---

72. *ANET,* 133.
73. See Walsh (*ABD* 2, s.v. "Elijah") for extensive details; see also Whitelam, *ABD* 2, s.v. "Elisha."

In 1 Kings 21, the confrontation between Elijah and the king does not so much revolve around idol worship but around Ahab's arrogance in office, demonstrated by his stealing of Naboth's vineyard. Even here, however, Ahab's idol worship is condemned (21:25–26).

The next episode in which Elijah figures concerns Ahab's son, Ahaziah, who also was a Baal worshiper: he sent to inquire of Baal-zebub, a Philistine god associated with Baal (2 Kings 1). Elijah effectively condemned Ahaziah as well. The mantle of prophecy is then passed from Elijah to Elisha in 2 Kings 2, and Elijah is taken up to heaven in a whirlwind.

The stories of Elisha are even more extensive than the Elijah stories. Elisha performs numerous miracles, which cluster in 2 Kings 2:19–6:7.[74] Here, three extended narratives focusing on the activities of certain individuals are found: (1) Joram of Israel, Mesha of Moab, and Elisha (3:4–27); (2) Elisha, the Shunammite woman, and her son (4:8–37); and (3) the Syrian general Naaman and Elisha (5:1–27). These extended narratives are interspersed with brief accounts of other miraculous acts of Elisha: (1) Elisha and the poisonous water, Elisha and the jeering boys (2:19–25); (2) Elisha and the widow's oil (4:1–7); (3) Elisha and the poisonous stew, Elisha and the provision of food (4:38–44); (4) Elisha and the axe head (6:1–7).

All of these miracles function to confirm Elisha's authority as a prophet of the Lord, serving well to legitimate him for the tasks that lay ahead, when he became involved in the affairs of nations (2 Kings 6:8–7:20; 8:7–9:13). First, he was involved in two incidents involving Israel's enemy, Syria (6:8–7:20). In the first incident, Elisha acted on Israel's behalf in capturing Syrians and leading them into Samaria (6:8–23). In the second, he accurately prophesied that the siege of Samaria would be lifted (6:24–7:20). Then, he prophesied that Hazael would become king of Syria (8:7–15), and, through his servant, he anointed Jehu as king of Israel (9:1–13).

These stories about Elisha's authority are confirmed by the prominence of his dealings with the Shunammite woman. After he helped her and her son (4:8–37), she testified to the king on his behalf at a crucial moment (8:1–7), which further increased Elisha's stature. The stories of Elisha end with the account of his death and burial (13:14–21). He died prophesying, and even in death he was responsible for a miracle: a dead man who came into contact with his bones was revived.

Many scholars have posited the existence of independent "cycles" of stories involving Elijah and Elisha, documents or traditions that were preserved by northern (i.e., Israelite) prophetic groups.[75] Elisha is seen as leader of a prophetic "guild" called "the sons of the prophets" (see above).

---

74. See J. H. Stek (*ISBE* 2, s.v. "Elisha") on the patterning here.
75. See Eissfeldt, *Introduction*, 290–96; Fohrer, *Introduction*, 232–34; and especially Wilson, *Prophecy and Society in Ancient Israel*, 192–206.

Elijah is the only prophet in Scripture who is recorded as having designated his successor, and this is said to have been a characteristic of Israelite (i.e., northern) prophetic circles. Despite the plausibility of many such proposals, however, they remain hypotheses. Even if true, their ultimate importance lies in how the Elijah-Elisha narratives are used in the books of Kings.

We are on safer ground when we note some of the characteristics of these stories. These two prophets arose during a time of great crisis in Israel, when the worship of Baal (and his consort, Asherah) was first introduced into the nation on the official level. That is, the king himself now, for the first time, sanctioned and sponsored pagan idol worship within Israel (1 Kings 18:18–19). The extensive dual emphasis upon fulfilled prophecy and (especially) miracles in this section legitimates these prophets as true (along with Micaiah, the brave, lone prophet in chap. 22), in contrast to the hundreds of "official" prophets of Baal and other false prophets employed by the king. In Ahab's and his son's day, the nation was in great danger of losing its identity as a nation called apart to be God's special people (cf. Ex. 19:4–6). This time, the threat was internal and officially sanctioned by the king, which made it all the more insidious. The king's function was to be immersed in the Law of the Lord and to lead his people in obedience to it (Deut. 17:18–20), not to be leading them in Baal worship (1 Kings 18) or in listening to innumerable false prophets (chap. 22).

SPECIAL ISSUES IN 1 & 2 KINGS

ELIJAH, ELISHA, AND MIRACLE "CLUSTERING" IN THE BIBLE

The Bible is well known for its chronicling of many miracles. However, what is not as much noticed is that the miracles are not evenly spread out; they tend to occur in clusters. They were separated in time by many hundreds of years. One such cluster is here in 1 & 2 Kings, through the human agency of Elijah and Elisha.

Two other major clusters may be found in the Bible. The first is during the time of Moses, both in Egypt (the plagues) and in the wilderness (provision of manna, water, and so on). The second is in the NT, during the ministry of Jesus and in the early church period.[76]

Each of these periods was one of major transition or crisis. The Mosaic period was crucial for the life of God's people, and many authenticating miracles were performed by God through Moses. Jesus' miracles also served to authenticate his (new) message at another crucial time of transition, and the miracles in the book of Acts performed the same function. The

---

76. Another such period is during the days of Daniel in Babylon, but the number of miracles recorded is much smaller than during any of the other three.

time of Elijah and Elisha was not as dramatic a transition, but it was a critical time of decision for the nation of Israel, whether to follow pagan worship or to remain faithful to the Lord.

This pattern may be relevant for those interested in observing miracles in postbiblical times, including the present. When it is remembered that miracles were clustered into certain time periods (and even in certain locations, such as the northern kingdom or Babylonia), similar patterns—i.e., when miracles abound in certain times and places and are scarce in others—throughout history and today may not be so perplexing.

GOD AND THE LYING SPIRIT

In 1 Kings 22, the prophet Micaiah tells of a vision in which he saw the Lord in the heavenly councils, and He sent a prophet who volunteered to go and deceive Ahab (22:19–23).[77] Some have questioned the morality of God's seeming to sponsor evil here by sending a lying prophet to Ahab. However, two points must be made in response.

First, this fails to account for primary and secondary causes. God would allow the already-existent evil to run its course, but that would not excuse the perpetrator(s) of the evil at all. An analogy is found in the NT in Judas's situation. Here, Jesus Himself said to Judas, "What you are about to do, do quickly" (John 13:27). This does not mean that Jesus thereby became the sponsor of the evil perpetrated upon Him any more than God sponsored the evil when He commanded the prophet in Micaiah's vision to go ahead with his plan to lie (1 Kings 22:21b). Nevertheless, it is ironic (and fitting) that Ahab, who had lived his life by consulting false (and lying) prophets and rejecting true prophets, now faced the possibility that he might be led to his death by listening to a false prophet.

Second, and more to the point, we must note that this all comes in Micaiah's *vision* (vv. 18–22). None of it actually took place on the human stage; Ahab went to his death on the basis of following the advice of his four hundred court prophets and ignoring Micaiah's words, whom he knew very well to be a true prophet (see v. 8). Also note, most importantly, that ultimately God did *not* deceive Ahab, since *the content of the vision was revealed to Ahab.* He was given full warning and was given a chance not to be deceived. He chose not to heed the warning. His downfall, then, was entirely of his own choosing.

---

77. See Walter Kaiser, *Hard Sayings of the Old Testament,* 119–21. See Keil (*The First Book of Kings,* 276–77) for a similar view, but he differs with Kaiser vis-à-vis God's working of evil: "According to the Scriptures, God does work evil, but without therefore willing it and bringing forth sin" (p. 277).

THEOLOGY OF 1 & 2 KINGS

THE KINGDOM OF GOD AND THE DAVIDIC KINGDOM

From the moment one reads the title of 1 & 2 Kings until the time of reading about the last of Judah's kings, the motif of kingship stands out in bold relief. The books trace the development of the monarchies, first in Israel, then in Israel and Judah, to their destructions by foreign powers.

However, the concern with these two kingdoms is not a concern with political entities as such. As C. F. Keil stated, "The historical development of the monarchy, or, to express it more correctly, of the kingdom of God under the kings, forms the true subject matter of our books."[78] The books carefully trace the spiritual fortunes of the two nations and show how their political fortunes were tied to their spiritual conditions.

The figure of David the king casts a long, impressive shadow across the pages of 1 & 2 Kings. He is physically present in only the first two chapters of 1 Kings (and he is weak there), but 1 Kings clearly intends to pick up where 2 Samuel leaves off. The high point of that book is found in 2 Samuel 7, where the prophet Nathan announces the promises of the Davidic Covenant. As noted in the previous chapter, these were unconditional promises to David of a perpetual dynasty, which introduce the concept of the king as the "son" of God Himself.

The books of Kings are concerned to show how these promises to David were carried out in history. Thus, we see that, despite many assassinations in Israel and the repeated introduction of new family lines in that kingdom, in the kingdom of Judah and in the line of David the family lines continued unbroken. The typical formula in Judah concluding each king's reign makes reference to the king's having been buried with "David his father." Many of David's descendants were wicked, to be sure, but God's promises to David always continued unbroken.

Furthermore, the author of 1 & 2 Kings was particularly concerned to show this unbroken continuity, not only in the continuous genealogical connections that are visible but also in explicit references.[79] Numerous times, the author speaks of God's acting graciously for the sake of His servant David.[80] On other occasions, David's having received the promises from God is mentioned.[81]

78. Keil, *The First Book of Kings,* 5.
79. See Gerbrandt, *Kingship,* 165–69.
80. See 1 Kings 11:12, 13, 32, 34, 36; 15:4–5; 2 Kings 8:19; 19:34; 20:6.
81. First Kings 2:33, 45; 5:5; 8:15, 19, 24, 26; 11:38; 2 Kings 21:7.

The physical kingdoms of Israel and Judah—especially Judah—were symbols of God's own kingdom. The king—as the "son" of God (2 Sam. 7:14)—was God's vice-regent on earth. As the king went, so went the nation.

Thus, as the spiritual and political fortunes of the Davidic kingdom went, so in a very real sense went the fortunes of God's kingdom upon the earth. That is not because of any special merit in David or his kingdom per se but because of God's having chosen him and it as the means of accomplishing His purposes in the world. Throughout most of 1 & 2 Kings, the sad fact was that the spiritual fortunes of this kingdom suffered.

GOD'S GRACE AND HOPE FOR THE FUTURE

The message of hope. Related to the idea of the kingdom of God in 1 & 2 Kings is the idea of God's grace. Contrary to Martin Noth (see above), the message of 1 & 2 Kings is not merely a negative one, explaining the cause of the downfall of both kingdoms. Rather, a strong, positive message pervades these books, one that can be expressed in various ways, such as G. von Rad's affirmations of a "messianic" motif, H. W. Wolff's emphasis on calls to repentance, W. Brueggemann's statements about God's graciousness, or J. G. McConville's formulations about hope (see nn. 31–34).

For example, the books' emphasis on the gracious promises to David constitute a true message of hope for God's people, especially the idea that the promises were "forever" (2 Sam. 7:13, 16; 1 Kings 2:45; 9:5; 2 Kings 8:19). David would always have a "lamp" before the Lord in Jerusalem in the person of one of his descendants (1 Kings 11:36; 15:4; 2 Kings 8:19).

The message of hope was not tied exclusively to David, however. In an important signal early in 1 Kings, Solomon (in his great Temple dedication prayer) acknowledges that exile would come some day (8:46–53) and asks for God's mercy. He does not do this on the basis of God's promises to David but twice refers back to the days of Moses and Israel's status as God's chosen people from that time forward (vv. 51, 53).

The ending of the work (2 Kings 25:27–30) is most significant in the matter of the message of hope for the future. Whereas 2 Kings ends on a predominantly negative note (in recounting the destruction of Jerusalem), in the last analysis this note is not completely devoid of hope. That is because the last four verses of the book show Jehoiachin, the Judahite king who had been taken into exile years earlier, being released from prison and treated well by the Babylonian king. In fact, he was given a place of honor above that of any other king who also had been exiled to Babylon (25:28). Many scholars discount this final appendix as being insufficiently "weighty" to counter the predominantly negative tone seen throughout most of 1 & 2

Kings.[82] However, it cannot be discounted completely, and it must be seen as offering a glimmer of hope to people in exile—that their king was still alive and that the great promises to David were not completely dead.[83]

Conditionality and unconditionality in 1 & 2 Kings. We can see a tension in 1 & 2 Kings between emphasis on God's unconditional promises to David and the conditions imposed on the Davidic kings in order to experience God's fullest blessings. We must take seriously those passages granting David the kingdom "forever" and the statement in 2 Samuel 7:15–16: "But my love will never be taken away from him, as I took it away from Saul, whom I removed from before you. Your house and your kingdom will endure forever before me; your throne will be established forever."[84]

Yet, on the other hand, there are many indications in 1 & 2 Kings of a conditional element to these promises. Beginning with the statement in 2 Samuel 7:14—"When [David's son] does wrong, I will punish him with the rod of men, with floggings inflicted by men"—we see that God's promises were not given carte blanche to the kings to do whatever they pleased. This is especially visible in the conditional "Solomonic Covenant," where the promises to David are repeated to Solomon but with important provisos about integrity, righteousness, and obedience being conditions for maintaining the land (1 Kings 9:2–9; see also 2:4). If Israel repeatedly disobeyed, if it violated the terms of the Mosaic Covenant, it could lose the land. Some individual kings did reject God and some were punished. Also, both Israel and Judah ultimately did lose their land, which the author attributed to their unfaithfulness (2 Kings 17:7–23; 24:3–4).

The confluence between the unconditional Davidic Covenant and the predominantly conditional Mosaic Covenant comes in the requirements that the individual kings were responsible to keep the covenant in order to secure God's blessings for themselves.[85] However, the promises themselves would never be invalidated; God's purposes would still be accomplished, ultimately through the survival of the Davidic line, and 1 & 2 Kings also make this clear.

---

82. E.g., Noth, *Deuteronomistic History,* 117, 143; John Gray, *I and II Kings,* 773; M. Cogan and H. Tadmor, *II Kings,* 329–30.
83. See Jon D. Levenson, "The Last Four Verses in Kings," 353–61; R. A. Carlson, *David, the chosen King,* 263–67; so also, in differing ways, the scholars in nn. 31–34 above.
84. Frank Moore Cross (*Canaanite Myth and Hebrew Epic,* 251–64) and Walter C. Kaiser, Jr. (*Toward an Old Testament Theology,* 156–57 and passim), are two scholars (among many) who develop the idea of the unconditionality of these promises in some depth.
85. See David M. Howard, Jr. ("The Case for Kingship in Deuteronomy and the Former Prophets," 113–14), on the merging of these divergent covenants in the "Deuteronomistic History."

The presence of a member of the Davidic line in 2 Kings 25 gives hope to Israel, but his weakened, vassal status serves as a powerful reminder that, ultimately, it is God in whom Israel was to place its trust. It was only through God's grace that Jehoiachin (or any other king, for that matter) survived.

CONCERN FOR THE COVENANT

As just noted, the kings (and the people) were expected to keep the covenant that God had made with Israel at Sinai. That was stated as far back as Deuteronomy 17:18–19 with reference to kings, and it was a matter of continuing concern throughout the monarchies. Solomon was exhorted to keep the covenant (1 Kings 3:14), and the fall of the northern kingdom is explicitly tied to its disobedience to the covenant (2 Kings 17:7–23; 18:12).

The highest praise given to any of the kings in 1 & 2 Kings belongs to Hezekiah and Josiah. Of both, it is said that they kept the requirements of the law of Moses:

> Hezekiah trusted in the Lord, the God of Israel. There was no one like him among all the kings of Judah, either before him or after him. He held fast to the Lord and did not cease to follow him; he kept the commands the Lord had given Moses. (2 Kings 18:5–6)

> Neither before nor after Josiah was there a king like him who turned to the Lord as he did—with all his heart and with all his soul and with all his strength, in accordance with all the Law of Moses. (2 Kings 23:25)[86]

The judgment about Josiah is especially significant. The exact wording used here—"with all his heart and with all his soul and with all his strength"—is found in only one other passage in the entire OT: Deuteronomy 6:5, where God urges His people to "Love the Lord with all your heart and with all your soul and with all your strength." As Gerald Gerbrandt notes, Josiah was being commended with "language which came from the very core of Israel's understanding of what God expected from Israel. God expected Israel to obey the law as summarized by the command in Deut. 6:5 to love the Lord with one's whole being."[87] Josiah read from the Book of the

---

86. The apparent contradiction between these two passages is easily resolved, as Gerald Gerbrandt correctly points out, by noting the basis of the author's praise in each passage: "Whereas there 'was none like' Hezekiah in that he 'trusted in the Lord the God of Israel,' Josiah was incomparable in that he 'turned to the Lord . . . according to all the law of Moses.' Thus each was the greatest in his own particular way" (*Kingship According to the Deuteronomistic History,* 53). He helpfully points to a similar passage not often noted in this regard—1 Kings 3:12—where another king, Solomon, is also presented as incomparable, in this case with respect to wisdom.
87. Gerbrandt, *Kingship,* 55.

Covenant (2 Kings 23:2), he renewed the covenant (23:3), and he celebrated the Passover according to the instructions in the Book of the Covenant (23:21).

Alongside the important concern with the kings of Israel and Judah in 1 & 2 Kings, an equally important emphasis is upon the prophetic perspective. (See also the section above entitled "Prophets and Prophecy in 1 & 2 Kings.") Indeed, a recent influential work postulates a large document called the "Prophetic Record," extending from 1 Samuel 1–2 Kings 10, so prominent are prophetic perspectives in this section of Scripture.[88]

The term *prophet(s)* occurs ninety-four times in 1 & 2 Kings, and "man of God" (a prophetic title) sixty times. Prophets appear on the scene regularly to condemn the kings, and they act as God's mouthpieces to them and to others. The fulfillment of their words is also an important part of the message of 1 & 2 Kings.

Prophetic condemnations. The popular stereotype of biblical prophets involves an angry man condemning the powerful establishment surrounding the king, and many prophets in 1 & 2 Kings certainly fit that mold. Beyond this, the prophets consistently brought God's word to bear on a particular situation. Examples include Ahijah the prophet, who announced to Jeroboam that he would inherit the ten tribes of Israel (1 Kings 11), and then condemned him for his disobedience (chap. 14); Elijah, who fearlessly opposed Ahab and Jezebel on several occasions (chaps. 17–19, 21); and Micaiah, who also stood up to Ahab, despite overwhelming opposition (chap. 22). These prophets condemned the kings for failing to adhere to the standards of the Mosaic Covenant about obedience and single-minded faithfulness to God.

Beyond the glimpses of individual prophets in these books, we see the author of 1 & 2 Kings evaluating the kings in terms reminiscent of these prophets' words. The downfall of both kingdoms is clearly expressed in such terms (2 Kings 17:7–23; 24:3–4), and the individual kings were consistently evaluated as to whether they did right in the eyes of the Lord or whether they followed after the ways of their wicked fathers and pursued other gods.

Prophetic fulfillment. We have already noted the importance of the prophetic word and its fulfillment in 1 & 2 Kings (see under "Characteristics and Functions of Prophets" above, and nn. 60 and 61). The proclamation of God's word through the prophets, and the explicit notices of its fulfillment, are an important part of the theology of 1 & 2 Kings.

88. Campbell, *Of Prophets and Kings.*

JUDGMENT AND REPENTANCE

One cannot come away from a reading of 1 & 2 Kings without being impressed with the central role that judgment plays in the books. The once-unified Israel was wrenched apart into two kingdoms as a judgment upon Solomon for his unfaithfulness to God (1 Kings 11), and the two kingdoms both fell to foreign powers as judgments for their sins (2 Kings 17:7–23; 24:3–4). The history of the two nations followed a long, downward trajectory. To scholars such as Martin Noth, this downward trend and the strong motif of judgment accompanying it form the *raison d'être* for the writing of the books. As we have seen, however, that is an overly pessimistic view.

Accompanying the motif of judgment is a pronounced emphasis upon repentance.[89] The Hebrew root usually translated "repentance" (*ŠWB*) denotes a "turning" away from evil and toward the good. In key passages in 1 & 2 Samuel and 1 & 2 Kings, we find that idea coming to the fore.

For example, in Samuel's farewell speech, he exhorts the people to follow the Lord (1 Sam. 12:14–15), and he urges them not to "turn away from the Lord" and not to "turn away after useless idols" (vv. 20–21). In Solomon's great Temple prayer (1 Kings 8), five times (vv. 33, 35, 47, 48, 58) he mentions the people turning back to God (i.e., "repenting"). A repeated motif in this prayer is the request that God be attentive to His people when they turn and cry out to Him: seven times (vv. 30, 32, 34, 36, 39, 43, 45) he asks God to "hear from heaven" and be gracious to them.

In his great reflective summary as to why Israel fell to Assyria, the author reiterates what God had repeatedly said to His people: "Turn from your evil ways. Observe my commands and decrees, in accordance with the entire Law that I commanded your fathers to obey and that I delivered to you through my servants the prophets" (2 Kings 17:13). And, in high praise for Josiah, the author tells us that there was no one like this king who "turned" to the Lord with his entire being (23:25).

The call to repentance has its roots in God's graciousness, or, to put it another way, in God's goodness. That is, Israel must have something to turn *to*, and the object of Israel's turning is God and the goodness He represents. Walter Brueggemann has shown how the motif of God's goodness is found at critical points throughout Deuteronomy and the following books.[90]

In 1 & 2 Kings, Solomon affirms God's "good promises" (lit., "every good word") and how not one word of them has failed (1 Kings 8:56), a sentiment that was already expressed in Joshua's day (Josh. 21:45; 23:14–15). In Solomon's declaration, the "good word" was not merely oriented toward

---

89. See especially Wolff, "The Kerygma of the Deuteronomic Historical Work."
90. Brueggemann, "The Kerygma of the Deuteronomistic Historian."

the past; verse 57 looks to the future: "May the Lord our God be with us as he was with our fathers; may he never leave us nor forsake us."

Brueggemann notes that God's "good word" is expressed in visible ways through the Davidic line in 1 & 2 Kings,[91] which brings us back to the motif of the Davidic kingdom and the kingdom of God discussed above. God not only said "good words" to Israel but also did "good things," and this was a source of joy and gladness to His people (1 Kings 8:66). Even at the end of 2 Kings, we see the Babylonian king speaking "kindly" to Jehoiachin (2 Kings 25:28); the word in question is literally "good." As Brueggemann notes, "The Davidic house is still the bearer of Yahweh's 'good.'"[92]

OUTLINE OF 1 & 2 KINGS

David's Reign Concluded (1 Kings 1:1–2:46)

The Book of the Acts of Solomon (1 Kings 3–11)
Solomon's Wisdom (3:1–28)
Solomon's Greatness—A (4:1–34)
Building of the Temple (5:1–7:51)
Dedication of the Temple (8:1–66)
The "Solomonic Covenant" (9:1–9)
Solomon's Greatness—B (9:10–10:29)
Solomon's Decline (11:1–43)

The Divided Kingdoms of Israel and Judah (1 Kings 12–2 Kings 17)
Division of the Kingdom (1 Kings 12:1–20)
Jeroboam's Evil Reign over Israel (12:21–14:20)
Rehoboam's Evil Reign over Judah (14:21–31)
Abijam's Evil Reign over Judah (15:1–8)
Asa's Good Reign over Judah (15:9–24)
Nadab's Evil Reign over Israel (15:25–31)
Baasha's Evil Reign over Israel (15:26–16:7)
Elah's Evil Reign over Israel (16:8–10)
Zimri's Evil Reign over Israel (16:11–20)
Omri's Evil Reign over Israel (16:21–28)
Ahab's Evil Reign over Israel (16:29–22:40)
Jehoshaphat's Good Reign over Judah (22:41–50)
Ahaziah's Evil Reign over Israel (22:51–53; 2 Kings 1)
Joram's Evil Reign over Israel (2 Kings 1:17–9:26)
Jehoram's Evil Reign over Judah (8:16–24)

91. Ibid., 397–401.
92. Ibid., 400.

Ahaziah's Evil Reign over Judah (8:25–9:28)
Jehu's Evil Reign over Israel (chaps. 9–10)
Queen Athaliah's Evil Reign over Judah (11:1–20)
Joash's Good Reign over Judah (11:21–12:21)
Jehoahaz's Evil Reign over Israel (13:1–9)
Jehoash's Evil Reign over Israel (13:10–14:16)
Amaziah's Good Reign over Judah (14:1–21)
Jeroboam's Evil Reign over Israel (14:23–29)
Azariah's (Uzziah's) Good Reign over Judah (14:22; 15:1–7)
Zechariah's Evil Reign over Israel (15:8–12)
Shallum's Evil Reign over Israel (15:13–16)
Menahem's Evil Reign over Israel (15:17–22)
Pekahiah's Evil Reign over Israel (15:23–26)
Pekah's Evil Reign over Israel (15:27–31)
Jotham's Good Reign over Judah (15:32–38)
Ahaz's Evil Reign over Judah (chap. 16)
Hoshea's Evil Reign over Israel (chap. 17)
　Introductory Formula (17:1–2)
　The Fall of Samaria (17:3–6)
　Evaluation of the Kingdom of Israel (17:7–23)
　Rise of the "Samarians" (17:24–41)

The Kingdom of Judah (2 Kings 18–25)
Hezekiah's Good Reign (chaps. 18–20)
Manasseh's Evil Reign (21:1–18)
Amon's Evil Reign (21:19–26)
Josiah's Good Reign (22:1–23:30)
Jehoahaz's Evil Reign (23:31–34)
Jehoiakim's Evil Reign (23:34–24:7)
Jehoiachin's Evil Reign (24:8–16)
Zedekiah's Evil Reign (24:17–25:7)
The Destruction of Jerusalem (25:8–21)
Gedaliah's Governorship (25:22–26)
Jehoiachin's Release from Prison (25:27–30)

7

HISTORICAL AND CULTURAL CONTEXT FOR 1 & 2 KINGS

But as for Hezekiah, the Jew, who did not bow in submission to my yoke, forty-six of his strong walled towns and innumerable smaller villages in their neighbourhood I besieged and conquered by stamping down earth-ramps and then by bringing up battering rams, by the assault of foot-soldiers, by breaches, tunnelling and sapper operations. (Sennacherib's Annals, *ANET,* 288)

That night the angel of the Lord went out and put to death a hundred and eighty-five thousand men in the Assyrian camp. When all the people got up the next morning—there were all the dead bodies! So Sennacherib king of Assyria broke camp and withdrew. He returned to Nineveh and stayed there. (2 Kings 19:35–36)

More than in any other book in the OT, the events in 1 & 2 Kings are tied in with international events. That is partly because of the long history covered by these books (more than four hundred years) but especially because the books deal mainly with the affairs of the nations of Israel and Judah *as nations*; the focus is not so much upon great individuals (as in 1 & 2 Samuel, for instance). It is also because the period covered by these books is extraordinarily well documented in extrabiblical sources, and various kings of Israel and Judah are mentioned numerous times in these sources. Furthermore, the record of material remains in Palestine and Mesopotamia is extremely rich, and excavations in great cities such as Samaria, Jerusalem, Nineveh, and Babylon have yielded much information about the period. For all these reasons a separate chapter is now devoted to the historical context of 1 & 2 Kings. It includes overviews of the neighboring peoples mentioned prominently in these books, discussion of the most prominent extrabiblical texts that relate to 1 & 2 Kings, and a special discussion of Jerusalem, that all-important city, both historically and theologically.

ISRAEL AND ITS NEIGHBORS IN 1 & 2 KINGS

During the time of the first kings of Israel, the great international powers of Mesopotamia and Egypt were not overly concerned with events in Canaan. Thus, on a political level, the way was open for the expansion of the kingdom of Israel under David and Solomon. Solomon's influence—directly or indirectly—reached as far as the Euphrates River in the northeast (1 Kings 4:24) and to the "Brook of Egypt" in the southwest (8:65).[1] The international relations of the early kings of Israel were mainly with the rulers of small neighboring states.

Solomon was extremely wealthy (4:20–28; 10:14–29), and he built a fleet of trading ships at the southern tip of his kingdom, at Ezion-geber on the Gulf of Aqaba, the eastern branch of the Red Sea (9:26–28). He imported such things as gold, silver, ivory, apes, and baboons (10:22), and kings came from many lands, bringing him such tribute as silver, gold, garments, myrrh, spices, horses, and mules (10:25). He impressed the queen of Sheba, who came hundreds of miles from the area of the southwestern Arabian peninsula to visit him (10:1–13).[2]

The small nation-states that had contact with Israel and Judah during this time included "Phoenicia," Moab, Edom, and Aram. Israel and Judah also were inevitably affected by the activities of the large empires of Egypt, Assyria, and Babylonia.

THE PHOENICIANS

The Phoenicians[3] were the people who lived along the eastern coast of the Mediterranean Sea, in the areas today occupied by Lebanon and Syria. They arose as a discernible entity after 1200 B.C. and retained an identity for hundreds of years, until the Greco-Roman era. There never was a political entity called "Phoenicia"; rather, the Phoenicians were organized into city-states, and Phoenicians identified themselves by their cities, i.e., "Tyrians," "Sidonians," and so on.

1. See Barry J. Beitzel, *The Moody Atlas of Bible Lands,* 121–25; Carl G. Rasmussen, *NIV Atlas of the Bible,* 116–23.
2. See J. B. Pritchard, ed., *Solomon and Sheba.*
3. Convenient introductions to the Phoenicians may be found in the following: M. Liverani, *ISBE* 3, s.v. "Phoenicia"; Brian Peckham, *ABD* 5, s.v. "Phoenicia, History of" and Philip C. Schmitz, *ABD* 5, s.v. "Phoenician Religion"; William A. Ward, "The Phoenicians," *POTW.* Longer treatments are Donald Harden, *The Phoenicians,* and Sabatino Moscati, *The World of the Phoenicians.*

The Divided Kingdom and Surrounding Nations

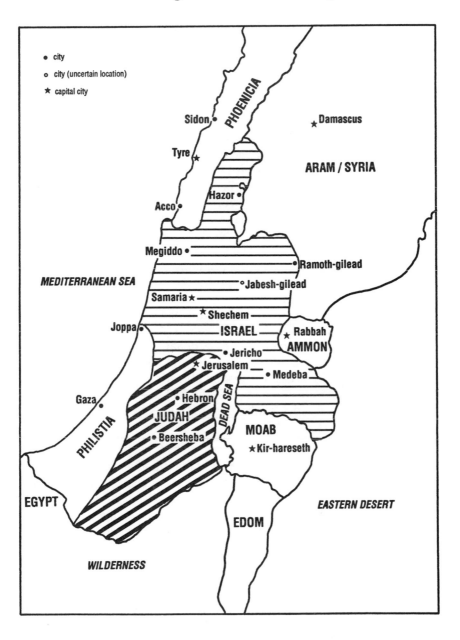

The Phoenician language was very similar to Hebrew, and Phoenician religion drew upon the common religious foundation known throughout ancient Canaan; it stood in continuity with the Canaanite religion known from Ugarit in an earlier period. The Phoenician pantheon of gods was even more fluid than the Ugaritic one. Baal was worshiped in many localities, but in early periods the gods Resheph, Dagon, and Elyon are found, and later such gods as Melqart and Eshmun are apparent; in Greco-Roman times, Adonis was worshiped. Most of these names were manifestations of fertility gods, upon whom sustenance from the land depended.

The Phoenicians are best known for their commerce and travel. They developed into expert seamen and established trading colonies as far away as Spain and sites in England and on the western coast of Africa.

In 1 & 2 Kings, Phoenicia figures in two periods: the days of David and Solomon and the days of Ahab. Both David and Solomon had good relations with the long-lived Hiram, king of Tyre, who helped David at the beginning of his reign and then helped Solomon with the building of the Temple (2 Sam. 5:11; 1 Kings 5:1–12 [MT 15–26]). Later in his reign, Solomon gave twenty "cities" (or villages) in northern Galilee to Hiram, apparently in exchange for 120 talents of gold. This strained relations between the kings because Hiram judged them to be worthless, calling the area "Cabul," which means "good for nothing" (9:10–14).

After Hiram, we have no record of any official relations between any Phoenician city and Israel or Judah. However, Ahab's wife Jezebel was a Phoenician princess, the daughter of Ethbaal, "king of the Sidonians" (16:31). His Phoenician name was Ittobaal, and he ruled over Tyre and Sidon ca. 887–856 B.C.[4] Jezebel was responsible for the importing of the official worship of Baal into Israel; indeed, the first time Baal is mentioned in 1 & 2 Kings is when Jezebel is introduced (1 Kings 16:31).

THE MOABITES

The Moabites[5] were distant cousins of the Israelites, having descended from Lot, Abraham's nephew (Gen. 19:37). They occupied the high plateau east of the Dead Sea. An identifiable nation-state existed there starting in the Late Bronze Age (ca. 1400–1200 B.C.) and continuing into the Persian period, ca. 500 B.C. The kingdom's relations with Israel were usually not very friendly (see, e.g., Numbers 21; Judges 3; Jeremiah 48). Their high god was Che-

---

4. John Gray, *I & II Kings*, 368–69.
5. On the Moabites, see J. R. Bartlett, "The Moabites and Edomites," *Peoples of Old Testament Times*, 229–58; J. R. Kautz, III, *ISBE* 3, s.v. "Moab"; W. S. LaSor, *ISBE* 1, s.v. "Chemosh"; J. Maxwell Miller, *ABD* 4, s.v. "Moab"; Gerald L. Mattingly, "The Moabites," *POTW.* Standard in-depth studies are A. H. Van Zyl, *The Moabites*; and Andrew Dearman, ed., *Studies in the Mesha Inscription and Moab.*

mosh, and they worshiped a variety of other deities as well. The author of 1 & 2 Kings tells us that Solomon had built shrines for this god Chemosh and others (1 Kings 11:7; 2 Kings 23:13).

In the period of the monarchies, the most significant contacts between Israel and Moab came during the dynasty of Omri. Second Kings records that Moab rebelled against Israelite control—which had forced him to pay tribute of a hundred thousand lambs and the wool of a hundred thousand rams—after Omri's son Ahab's death and that Omri's grandson Joram warred against Mesha, king of Moab (1:1; 3:4–27). Mesha's rebellion appears to have spanned the reigns of both sons of Ahab—Ahaziah and Joram (1:1; 3:5).[6] Joram allied himself with Jehoshaphat of Judah and the king of Edom and marched against Mesha (3:6–12). After assurances from the prophet Elisha, they gained a great victory over the Moabites (4:13–25), only to have its impact dissipated at the last minute by Mesha's sacrifice of his oldest son and Israel's adverse reaction to this (4:26–27). Moab suffered the same fate at the hands of the Babylonians as did Judah, ca. 586 B.C.

THE EDOMITES

The Edomites[7] were the Moabites' southern neighbors, in the area south and east of the Dead Sea. Their heritage went back to Esau, Jacob's brother (e.g., Gen. 36:8–9). Their land was a forbidding place, with parched deserts and treacherous gorges leading up out of both sides of the Rift Valley south of the Dead Sea. The Edomites denied the Israelites passage through their land in an early period (Num. 20:14–21), and David warred against them in a later time (2 Sam. 8:13–14; 1 Kings 11:15–16). Their national god was named Qaus, although he is not mentioned in the Bible. Not as much is known about the Edomites as about other peoples because almost no Edomite texts have been found.

During the time of the monarchies, the Edomites appear mainly as adversaries, rebellious subjects, of Israel and Judah. Hadad the Edomite rebelled against Solomon as part of God's punishment to the latter (1 Kings 11:14); Edomites rebelled against Jehoram of Judah a century later (2 Kings 8:20–22); and it appears that Amaziah of Judah subjugated Edom as well (2 Kings 14:10). At least once the Edomites found themselves allied with Israel and Judah: they were part of the coalition that opposed Moab under Mesha (2 Kings 3). Like their neighbors, they lived under the shadow of the Assyrians, and they met their end as a kingdom at the hands of the Babylonians about the same time Jerusalem was destroyed.

---

6. Mesha gives us his own version of his rebellion against Israel in the so-called Moabite Stone, a long and important text. See below for more on this inscription.
7. See B. MacDonald, *ISBE* 2, s.v. "Edom; Edomites"; J. R. Bartlett, *ABD* 2, s.v. "Edom in History"; Kenneth G. Hoglund, "The Edomites," *POTW*.

THE ARAMEANS

These peoples,[8] located in present-day Syria, northeast of Israel, made their first appearance on the ancient Near Eastern stage during the Late Bronze Age, ca. 1100 B.C. Their language, Aramaic, was closely related to Hebrew, and it became the international language of diplomacy and trade in the Near East during most of the first millennium B.C. The Arameans' ancestry is traced back to one "Aram," a descendant of Shem, in Genesis 10:22–23. They worshiped many of the same gods their neighbors did, but they named their high god Hadad. Their kingdom, whose capital was Damascus, came into intermittent conflict with Israel over a period of three centuries, beginning in Saul's day. Saul defeated the kings of Zobah, a powerful Aramean city-state in southwestern Syria and central Lebanon (1 Sam. 14:47), and David defeated Hadadezer, king of Zobah, thereby extending his territory to the Euphrates River (2 Sam. 8:3). It was finally overrun at the end of the eighth century B.C. by the Assyrians.

In 1 & 2 Kings, the Arameans were the most active local adversaries of Israel and Judah. Rezon was a king in Damascus who plagued Solomon, as Hadad the Edomite had (1 Kings 11:23–25). Later, Ben-Hadad I of Aram allied with Asa of Judah against Baasha of Israel (15:16–22). After this, a Ben-hadad (II?) of Aram[9] twice attacked Samaria, where Ahab was king, and twice God delivered Ahab, having promised victories through his prophets (chap. 20). Ahab eventually was killed in an ill-advised venture against Aram (chap. 22). The years following Ahab's death saw continued conflict between Israel and Aram under its kings Ben-Hadad (II?), Hazael, and Ben-Hadad (III?) (2 Kings 6–8, 12–13). The last king of the Arameans was Rezin, who allied himself with Pekah of Israel against Ahaz of Judah; he was killed by the Assyrians, who took his people away as captives, ca. 732 B.C. (15:37–16:9).

THE EGYPTIANS

Egypt[10] is mentioned in 1 & 2 Kings for the first time since the book of Exodus as a political entity with which the Israelites had any contemporary

---

8. See Merrill F. Unger, *Israel and the Aramaeans of Damascus*; A. Malamat, "The Aramaeans," in *Peoples of Old Testament Times*, 134–55; A. R. Millard, *ABD* 1, s.v. "Arameans"; Wayne T. Pitard, "The Arameans," *POTW.*
9. Some scholars argue that this king was the same as the one in Asa's day, whereas others argue that they were two different kings. See Unger, *Israel and the Arameans*, 59–61; Eugene Merrill, *Kingdom of Priests*, 330 and nn. 32–33; K. A. Kitchen, *NBD*, s.v. "Ben-Hadad"; R. K. Harrison, *ISBE* 1, s.v. "Ben-Hadad."
10. Brief introductions to Egypt are W. S. LaSor, *ISBE* 2, s.v. "Egypt"; James K. Hoffmeier, "The Egyptians," *POTW*; for more detail, see Margaret A. Murray, *The Splendour That Was Egypt*; K. A. Kitchen et al., *ABD* 2, s.v. "Egypt, History of."

interaction. In general, during the period of the monarchies in Israel and Judah, Egypt was a weak power, and it certainly did not have the ability to threaten Israel and Judah in the way that Assyria and Babylonia did. The zenith of its power came during the Eighteenth and Nineteenth Dynasties (ca. 1550–1200 B.C.). A dramatic example of Egypt's relative weakness after 1200 is seen in a famous literary text dating to the early eleventh century B.C., which chronicles the journey of an Egyptian official named Wen-Amon into Phoenicia: Wen-Amon is insulted and ignored, reflecting the low status to which Egypt had sunk.[11]

Israelite and Judahite relations with Egypt during the period of the monarchies were minimal. Nevertheless, we find that Solomon made marriage alliances with several foreign kings, including the king of Egypt (1 Kings 3:1; 11:1–3). This Egyptian king captured Gezer from the Canaanites and gave it to Solomon as a dowry (9:16); the king's name is unknown, but several scholars identify him with the Pharaoh Siamun (ca. 978–959 B.C.),[12] who made several incursions into Palestine.[13]

Several other Egyptian contacts are mentioned in 1 & 2 Kings. First, the pharaoh Shishak (Sheshonk) invaded Judah in Rehoboam's fifth year (ca. 925 B.C.) and looted the Temple treasuries (1 Kings 14:25–26). Later, Israel's last king attempted to look for help against Assyria from the otherwise-unknown Egyptian pharaoh So (2 Kings 17:4).[14] Then, Pharaoh Neco II made his influence felt during the last years of Judah (23:29–35).

THE ASSYRIANS

Like Egypt, Assyria[15] was a major power over a period of many centuries; it arose as a political power in the mid-second millennium B.C. Unlike Egypt, however, Assyria's greatest power came precisely during the period of the Israelite and Judahite monarchies. Assyria posed a threat to Israel starting in the middle of the ninth century B.C., and we find Israelite and Judahite kings mentioned by name in a number of Assyrian texts from this time forward.

11. *ANET,* 25–29; *TANE,* 16–24.
12. Dates from Anthony Spalinger, *ABD* 2, s.v. "Egypt, History of (Dyn. 21–26)."
13. Gray, *I & II Kings,* 119–20; Simon J. DeVries, *1 Kings,* 50.
14. Attempts to identify this pharaoh in Egyptian and Assyrian records are legion; see Edmund S. Meltzer, *ABD* 6, s.v. "So."
15. Accessible introductions to the Assyrians may be found in D. J. Wiseman, *ISBE* 1, s.v. "Assyria"; William C. Gwaltney, Jr., "The Assyrians," *POTW;* for more detail, see A. Kirk Grayson, "History and Culture of Assyria," *ABD* 4, 732–55, and "Assyria: Ashue-dan II to Ashur-Nirari V (934–745 B.C.)," 238–81; J. A. Brinkman et al., "Assyria and Babylonia," 1–321; A. Leo Oppenheim, *Ancient Mesopotamia;* H. W. F. Saggs, *The Might That Was Assyria.*

Shalmaneser III (858–824 B.C.)[16] was the first Assyrian king in this period to be interested in westward expansion, and the annual campaign by the king or his commander-in-chief became a standard feature under him.[17] He was repelled in a significant battle (not mentioned in the Bible) at Qarqar in 853 B.C., in northern Syria (just east of Ugarit, on the Orontes River), by a coalition of twelve western kings, including "Ahab the Israelite." Shalmaneser claims a great victory,[18] but the evidence suggests differently.[19]

Several years later (in 841 B.C.), Shalmaneser collected tribute from several kings in western Asia, including "Hazael of Damascus" and "Jehu, son of Omri."[20] The only contemporary pictorial representation of an Israelite in antiquity depicts Jehu's submission to Shalmaneser. It comes from Shalmaneser's "Black Obelisk," which shows Jehu bowing before the king. The accompanying inscription reads as follows:

> The tribute of Jehu, son of Omri; I received from him silver, gold, a golden *saplu*-bowl, a golden vase with pointed bottom, golden tumblers, golden buckets, tin, a staff for a king, (and) wooden *puruhtu*.[21]

There was a general decline in Assyrian fortunes, particularly in the west, following the defeat at Qarqar. This decline lasted the better part of a century, although there was a brief resurgence of power under Adad-Nirari III (810–783 B.C.). It reached its low point in the middle of the eighth century B.C.[22]

It was precisely at this time—in the first half of the eighth century B.C.—that Israel and Judah experienced a political and economic stability unknown since the days of Solomon. In Israel, Jeroboam II (793–753 B.C.) had a long, prosperous reign (see 2 Kings 14:23–29). In Judah, Azariah (Uzziah) (792–740 B.C.) did likewise (14:22–23; 15:1–7; 2 Chron. 26:1–23). This all was especially possible because of the relative power vacuum to the north and east.

The rise of Tiglath-Pileser III (744–727 B.C.) marked the resurgence of Assyria, this time with a vengeance. As William Hallo states, "[Tiglath-

---

16. Dates for Assyrian kings' reigns in this section are from A. Kirk Grayson, *ABD* 4, s.v. "Mesopotamia, History of (Assyria)"; see also J. A. Brinkman, "Mesopotamian Chronology of the Historical Period," in Oppenheim, *Ancient Mesopotamia*, 345–46. These dates often differ by one year from those in Hallo and Simpson, *ANEH*, 123–49.
17. Hallo and Simpson, *ANEH*, 127.
18. *ANET*, 278–79; *TANE*, 188–91; *DOTT*, 47.
19. Hallo and Simpson, *ANEH*, 127–28; Merrill, *Kingdom of Priests*, 348–49.
20. *ANET*, 280; *TANE*, 191.
21. *ANET*, 281; *ANEP*, plate 355; *TANE*, 192 and plate 100. See John Bright (*History of Israel*, 254 n. 64) and Baruch Halpern ("Yaua, Son of Omri, Yet Again," 81–85) for discussion of the reading of Jehu's name here.
22. Hallo and Simpson, *ANEH*, 129–32; Grayson, "Assyria," 276–79.

The Last Kings of Assyria

Shalmaneser III	858–824
Shamshi-Adad V	823–811
Adad-Nirari III	810–783
Shalmaneser IV	782–773
Ashur-Dan III	772–755
Ashur-Nirari V	754–745
Tiglath-Pileser III	744–727
Shalmaneser V	726–722
Sargon II	721–705
Sennacherib	704–681
Esarhaddon	680–669
Assurbanipal	668–627
Ashur-etel-ilani	
Sin-shumu-lishir	
Sin-shar-ishkun	–612
Ashur-uballit II	611–609

The dates are from J. A. Brinkman, "Mesopotamian Chronology in the Historical Period," in Oppenheim, *Ancient Mesopotamia*, 346. Shalmaneser III was the 102d king in a line that extended back to the third millennium B.C., and the last king, Ashur-uballit, was the 117th.

Pileser] and his two successors changed the whole balance of power in the Near East, destroying Israel among many other states and reducing the rest, including Judah, to vassalage."[23]

Tiglath-Pileser's first great campaign in 743–738 B.C. was westward. Assyria is mentioned for the first time in 1 & 2 Kings in connection with this campaign: we read that Menahem, king of Israel (752–742 B.C.) paid tribute to Tiglath-Pileser (2 Kings 15:19–20).[24] Tiglath-Pileser states that he received tribute from many kings, including "Menahem of Samaria," as well as an "Azriau of Iaudi." "Azriau" may well have been the contemporary Judahite king Azariah, although this identification is not undisputed.[25] His second western campaign came in 734–732 B.C.[26] This campaign was even

23. Hallo and Simpson, *ANEH*, 132–37; quote from p. 133. See also Merrill, *Kingdom of Priests*, 393–95.
24. He is called "Pul" here.
25. For Menahem, see *ANET*, 283; *DOTT*, 54, and 57 n. (a). For Azriau, see *ANET*, 282; *DOTT*, 54 and 56 n. (a); Bright, *History*, 270 nn. 1–2; M. Cogan and H. Tadmor, *II Kings*, 165–66.
26. Hallo and Simpson, *ANEH*, 136–37.

more successful than the first, and he established control over all of the eastern Mediterranean. This campaign also is mentioned in 2 Kings, as well as in Isaiah and 1 & 2 Chronicles.

Tiglath-Pileser's main focus in this campaign initially was Rezin of Damascus. At this time, Rezin had allied with Pekah, king of Israel (752–732 B.C.), against Judah and its king, Ahaz (735–715 B.C.; see 2 Kings 16:5–6; Isa. 7:1–2). In response to Ahaz's appeal for help, Tiglath-Pileser came against Syria and Israel and captured much territory, killing Rezin and taking many people away to Assyria (2 Kings 15:29; 16:7–9; see also 1 Chron. 5:26; 2 Chron. 28:16). That is the deliverance for Ahaz about which the prophet Isaiah gave assurances (Isaiah 7–8). Pekah was assassinated by Hoshea (2 Kings 15:30), who was Israel's last king (732–723 B.C.) and who took a pro-Assyrian stance. Indeed, Tiglath-Pileser claimed to have installed Hoshea as king himself in the same year that Damascus fell (732 B.C.).[27]

Shalmaneser V (726–722 B.C.) succeeded Tiglath-Pileser. Not much is known of his reign, but he captured Samaria, according to 2 Kings 17:1–7; 18:9–11. His successor, Sargon II, claimed the victory,[28] but this indicates no more than that he was the second-in-command at the time or that he was taking undue credit for this conquest. Indeed, the Babylonian Chronicles attribute Samaria's fall to Shalmaneser.[29] Sargon (721–705 B.C.) continued the aggressive, expansive policies of his predecessors. He is not mentioned in the historical books of the Bible, but he launched three western campaigns into Syria-Palestine between 720 and 712 B.C. The rest of his reign was occupied with southern campaigns.[30]

Sennacherib (704–681 B.C.) followed Sargon, and he invaded Palestine in 701 B.C., an event given much attention in the Bible. (See below for a fuller discussion of the biblical and extrabiblical texts describing this campaign.) He described this campaign at length in his own words, including his siege of Jerusalem. He also depicted his siege of Lachish during this campaign in graphic reliefs that were found at Nineveh. These show dramatically the terrors in store for a city that dared resist the powerful Assyrians.

According to the biblical text, Sennacherib was murdered by two of his sons (2 Kings 19:37). He was succeeded by his son Esarhaddon (680–669 B.C.), who turned out to be a very able ruler. He consolidated his political position at home, then routed Egyptian troops of Tirhakah in 671 and occupied Memphis. He died on the march back home.

27. *DOTT,* 55; *ANET,* 284. See Cogan and Tadmor (*II Kings,* 174–75) on Tiglath-Pileser's activities in Israel.
28. He did so in several different inscriptions. See *ANET,* 284–87; *TANE,* 195–98; *DOTT,* 59–62.
29. See H. Tadmor, "The Campaigns of Sargon II of Assur," 22–40, 77–100; also see Hallo and Simpson, *ANEH,* 138.
30. On Sargon, see Hallo and Simpson, *ANEH,* 138–41.

During this time, Hezekiah's son Manasseh was king of Judah during a long reign (697–642 B.C.). The author of 2 Kings harshly condemns his disloyalty to the Lord (2 Kings 21), but he does not mention Manasseh's relations with Assyria. Second Chronicles 33 tells us that he was captured and carried away to Babylon by the Assyrians, but there he repented and was released to return to Jerusalem (2 Chron. 33:10–13).[31] This incident is not mentioned directly in any Assyrian records, but Manasseh *is* mentioned in Esarhaddon's annals as being among a group of vassal kings in Palestine whom he forced to transport large quantities of building materials (i.e., tribute) to Nineveh.[32]

Esarhaddon's son and successor, Ashurbanipal (668–627 B.C.), also lists Manasseh as a loyal vassal who paid heavy tribute.[33] Ashurbanipal pressed his father's campaign against Egypt, which had not given up easily, and he marched south up the Nile to Thebes, the ancient capital, and destroyed it in 663.

However, things were never to be this good again for Assyria. Psammeticus I (664–610 B.C.), an Egyptian spared by Ashurbanipal, gradually won back most of Egypt, and ca. 655 (or shortly thereafter) he withheld tribute and made himself formally independent. Internal threats also weakened the Assyrian empire, and its northern and eastern frontiers were threatened increasingly by the Medes and other Indo-Aryan groups. Eventually the Assyrian capital of Nineveh fell in 612 B.C. to Nabopolassar, king of Babylon (625–605 B.C.).[34] The Assyrians continued resisting on the western front until 609 but could accomplish nothing, and they never again figured as significant players on the world stage.

It was against this backdrop of Assyrian decline that Josiah reigned in Judah (640–609 B.C.). During this period of relative independence, he was able to concentrate on religious matters, and he instituted his sweeping reforms (2 Kings 22–23).

THE BABYLONIANS

On the political level, the rise of Babylon[35] under Nabopolassar spelled

---

31. The extrabiblical book, "The Prayer of Manasseh," which is found in the Apocrypha, purports to be the text of the penitential prayer mentioned in 2 Chronicles 33:12–13. Even though it dates to a period much later than Manasseh's time, and undoubtedly does not come directly from Manasseh, it nevertheless is a beautiful prayer in its own right.
32. *ANET,* 291; *TANE,* 201–2; *DOTT,* 74–75.
33. *ANET,* 294; *TANE,* 201; *DOTT,* 73–75.
34. Dates for Babylonian kings' reigns in this section are from Grayson, *ABD* 4, s.v. "Mesopotamia, History of (Babylonia)."
35. Brief introductions to Babylonia are D. J. Wiseman, *ISBE* 1, s.v. "Babylonia"; Bill T. Arnold, "The Babylonians," *POTW;* for more detail, see Grayson, "History and Culture of Babylonia," *ABD* 4, 755–77; J. A. Brinkman et al., "Assyria and Babylonia," 1–321; H. W. F. Saggs, *The Greatness That Was Babylon.*

the beginning of the end for Judah. After the death of Josiah in 609 B.C., Judah was caught in the disputes between Babylon and Egypt. The Egyptian pharaoh Neco II (610–594 B.C.), son of Psammetichus I, had allied with the remnants of Assyria, and he marched with a large force against the Babylonians at Carchemish on the Euphrates. Josiah foolishly met him and resisted at Megiddo, and he was killed (2 Kings 23:29–30; 2 Chron. 35:20–24).

Neco took an active part in events in Judah. He captured Josiah's son Jehoahaz after he had reigned only three months and took him to Egypt. He installed Jehoiakim, another of Josiah's sons as king (2 Kings 23:31–35). He exacted heavy tribute from the land. Jehoiakim continued as a vassal of Neco until 605 B.C., when the Egyptians were routed by the Babylonians under Nebuchadnezzar II (604–562 B.C.) at Carchemish. This battle marked a significant turning point in ancient Near Eastern history, since it marked the end of effective Egyptian power in Syria and Palestine (cf. 24:7).[36] It would appear that an initial deportation from Judah to Babylon took place at this time (Dan. 1:1).[37]

The Kings of the Neo-Babylonian Dynasty

Nabopolassar	625–605
Nebuchadnezzar II	604–562
Evil-Merodach	561–560
Neriglissar	559–556
Labashi-Marduk	556
Nabonidus	555–539

The dates are from J. A. Brinkman, "Mesopotamian Chronology in the Historical Period," in Oppenheim, *Ancient Mesopotamia*, 340.

From that point on, Judah lived out its last days under the long shadow of Babylonian power under Nebuchadnezzar. In 601, Jehoiakim rebelled against this king (2 Kings 24:1), who eventually came and captured Jerusalem and Jehoiakim in 598/597 B.C. Rather than remove Jehoiakim into exile, it appears that Nebuchadnezzar allowed him to stay in Jerusalem, where he died, but the Babylonian king looted the Temple and took many treasures back to Babylon (2 Chron. 36:6–7).

Jehoiachin's tenure was brief (three months), and he was taken captive by Nebuchadnezzar in 597. The looting was more extensive this time,

36. R. Youngblood, *ISBE* 1, s.v. "Carchemish"; Bright, *History*, 326–27.
37. Gleason L. Archer, Jr., "Daniel," 31–32; C. Hassell Bullock, *An Introduction to the Old Testament Prophetic Books*, 281–82.

and many people of the elite of the land were carried away to Babylon with their king (2 Kings 24:10–16). Nebuchadnezzar installed Jehoiachin's uncle, Zedekiah, in his place, but within ten years, he returned and crushed Jerusalem altogether, taking Zedekiah captive in 586 B.C., along with more captives and booty (25:1–17). The Exile lasted until after the fall of the Babylonian Empire in 539 B.C.

The last reference to a foreign king in 2 Kings is to the Babylonian Evil-Merodach, who dealt graciously with Jehoiachin, still alive at the time, in 561/60 B.C. (25:27–30). It is interesting to note that some administrative texts from the tenth to the thirty-fifth years of Nebuchadnezzar (595–570 B.C.) were discovered in Babylon that mention generous provisions of oil for many of the captives at the time. Four of these texts specifically mention Jehoiachin and his sons as being among the recipients.[38]

EXTRABIBLICAL TEXTS AND 1 & 2 KINGS

The years covered in 1 & 2 Kings are well represented by texts in most lands of the Bible. In Mesopotamia, thousands of tablets have been uncovered in the past two centuries of exploration and excavation. In Palestine, textual remains are much more meager, but many important texts have been uncovered, written in Hebrew, Moabite, Phoenician, Aramaic, and Ammonite. Even a few Edomite inscriptions (mostly names) have been found.

Most of these texts do not mention Israel or Judah specifically, but they do give insight into life in the lands of their provenance. Some do mention people or events discussed in the Bible, and several of them have been discussed above. The texts in Hebrew are of special interest, since these are the only extrabiblical examples of the language—i.e., "Classical Hebrew"—spoken during the time of the monarchies. Of the non-Hebrew texts, two deserve special treatment because of their length and the close correlation they display with biblical accounts: the Moabite king Mesha's account of his relations with Israel, and the Assyrian king Sennacherib's account of his siege of Jerusalem. Finally, the apocryphal book of Tobit is set against the backdrop of the books of 1 & 2 Kings as well.

HEBREW INSCRIPTIONS

In Palestine during the monarchies, much writing was done on perishable materials such as papyrus and leather parchment, so very few original literary texts remain. The documents containing the lengthy compositions that make up the Bible have all long since disappeared.

38. *ANET,* 308; *TANE,* 205; *DOTT,* 86; see also W. F. Albright, "King Joiachin in Exile," 49–55.

Nonetheless, some Hebrew texts have survived that were inscribed on more durable materials, mostly clay, such as potsherds (ostraca), tablets, and pots and bowls. The following is a sampling of the most important Hebrew inscriptions during the time of 1 & 2 Kings.[39]

The Gezer Calendar. The earliest Hebrew inscription discovered to date was found at Gezer. It is a short agricultural calendar inscribed on a soft limestone tablet, dating to the end of the tenth century B.C. (i.e., shortly after Solomon's time). It begins as follows: "Two months of it are ingathering; two months of it are sowing; two months of it are late sowing; a month of it is flax cutting."[40] The word translated "ingathering" here appears in the Bible in connection with the Feast of Ingathering (or "Tabernacles"); it shows that the agricultural calendar began in the fall (September-October).

The Kuntillet Ajrud finds. In the mid-1970s, excavations at Kuntillet Ajrud in the northern Sinai desert yielded some remarkable inscriptions and drawings dating to the ninth-seventh centuries B.C.[41] In several inscriptions, various gods are mentioned, including Baal and the Bible's God, Yahweh. On one storage jar, a painted drawing depicts three figures: on the right, a seated woman is playing a lyre; in the center, the god Bes (of Egyptian origin) stands, legs apart, with his tail (or genitals) visible between his legs; on the left, a similar, unidentified figure stands. Both look like bulls. Above this last figure's head is an inscription that reads in part, "I bless you by Yahweh of Samaria and his Asherah (i.e., consort)."

This is a remarkable find for several reasons. First, if the identification of Yahweh in the inscription is correct, then we see here a text that links Him with a specific city, much like the Bible does with Baal, in the name "Baal of Peor" (Num. 25:3); see also the place names that include Baal's name: Baal-Gad (Josh. 11:17); Baal-Hermon (Judg. 3:3); Baal-Hamon (Song 8:11). Second, if the inscription above the third figure's head is related to the picture (as seems likely), we have here a remarkable example of a pictorial representation of Israel's God, Yahweh, in direct violation of the commandment against such representations (Ex. 20:4–5). Third, assuming that the inscription and the picture go together, we can see that some Israelites assigned Yahweh a "wife." This fit the practices in the cultures surrounding

39. Accessible translations of most of these may be found in *ANET, TANE,* and *DOTT.* See also John C. L. Gibson, *Textbook of Syrian Semitic Inscriptions*; G. I. Davies, *Ancient Hebrew Inscriptions.*
40. Translations in this section are the author's own unless otherwise indicated. Other translations may be found in the works in n. 39.
41. See Zeev Meshel, "Did Yahweh Have a Consort?" 24–34; J. A. Emerton, "New Light on Israelite Religion: The Implications of the Inscriptions from Kuntillet 'Ajrud," 2–20; David Noel Freedman, "Yahweh of Samaria and his Asherah," 241–49; Meshel, *ABD* 4, s.v. "Kuntillet Ajrud."

Israel: all the major gods had wives. This text and picture show us a prime example of the religious syncretism (i.e., importing of pagan beliefs) that the prophets continually railed against.

The Yavneh Yam Letter. A relatively lengthy inscription was discovered in 1960 on an ostracon at Yavneh Yam, a site on the Mediterranean. It dates to ca. 630 B.C. (the time of Josiah), and it is a letter addressed by a member of a work gang to the official overseeing the work, complaining about a co-worker's or a low-level official's taking of his coat. The letter writer asks for the coat to be returned. The subject matter is revealing of one aspect of everyday life at the time, and it might reflect the biblical provision of taking garments as security pledges, as laid out in Exodus 22:26–27, since the letter writer protests that he is guiltless of any crime or debt.

The Baruch and Jerahmeel seals.[42] In the mid-1970's, two seal-impressions surfaced from the time of Jehoiakim that represent the first objects discovered that can be identified with almost absolute certainty as having belonged to a biblical character. These are small bullas, which are small, flat clay objects used to seal letters written on papyrus, into which a stamped impression was pressed.

The inscription on one of these seal-impressions reads as follows: "Belonging to Berechiah [i.e., Baruch], son of Neriah, the scribe." This undoubtedly refers to Jeremiah's scribe, who is referred to in Jeremiah 36 as "Baruch, son of Neriah." He wrote at Jeremiah's dictation and took his book to the king, Jehoiakim, who burned the scroll.

The inscription on the other seal-impression reads, "Belonging to Jerahmeel, the king's son." An official of the king is identified in exactly the same way in Jeremiah 36:26: "Jerahmeel, the king's son." He was dispatched by the king to arrest Baruch and Jeremiah.

The Lachish Letters. Twenty-one ostraca were found at Lachish in the 1930s, dating to the years immediately before the destruction of Jerusalem. Several of these invoke Yahweh's name; they tell of the Babylonian siege of Lachish at the same time Jerusalem was under siege (see 2 Kings 25:1–2). Jeremiah 34:7 states that Jerusalem, Lachish, and Azekah were the only remaining Judahite cities holding out against the Babylonians. In one dramatic letter (#4), the writer states that he is watching especially closely for the fire-signals of Lachish, since "we cannot see Azekah" (i.e., it had now fallen to the Babylonians). In another letter (#6), the writer accuses officials from Jerusalem of subverting the Judahite cause: "The words of the princes are not good, (but they) weaken your hands and slacken the hands of the (men)." Strikingly, these are the exact same charges leveled against Jeremiah,

---

42. Nahman Avigad, "Jerahmeel and Baruch," 114–18.

who was in Jerusalem at the time: "He is discouraging the soldiers who are left in this city, as well as all the people, by the things he is saying to them. This man is not seeking the good of these people, but their ruin" (Jer. 38:4). That is because Jeremiah (accurately) prophesied the capture of Jerusalem, not its deliverance.

THE MOABITE STONE: MESHA'S REVOLT AGAINST ISRAEL

One of the most important extrabiblical correlations with events in 1 & 2 Kings is the account that the Moabite king Mesha gives in the "Moabite Stone," a black basalt stone discovered intact by scholars in 1868. The inscription is in Moabite, and it is the longest inscription discovered in the eastern Mediterranean coastlands from this period (some thirty-four lines long). It is largely taken up with Mesha's boasts about his rebellion and victories against Israel, his close relationship with his god Chemosh, and his building projects. Here are two relevant sections that deal with Israel:

> Omri was king of Israel, and he had oppressed Moab for many days, for Chemosh was angry with his land. His son succeeded him, and he too said, "I will oppress Moab." In my days he spoke thus. But I triumphed over him and over his house, and Israel utterly perished forever. And Omri took possession of the land of Medeba and dwelt in it during his days and half the days of his son, forty years. . . . Then Chemosh said to me, "Go, seize Nebo from Israel." So I went by night and I fought against it from the break of dawn until noon. And I took it and killed all of it: 7000 men and male aliens and women and female aliens and female slaves, for I had devoted it to Ashtar-Chemosh. And I took from there the vessels of Yahweh and I dragged them before Chemosh. . . .[43]

Mesha's statements about Omri's and his son's oppressing Moab and Mesha's rebellion against Israel accurately reflect the statements in 2 Kings 1:1 and 3:4–5. Furthermore, the enigmatic statement in the biblical text about Mesha's offering his oldest son as a sacrifice, which caused Israel to withdraw (3:27), may well accord with Mesha's boasts about his victories over Israel. We should note that Mesha claims more victories than the Bible mentions, however. These claims may well have some truth behind them, since the account in 2 Kings is only concerned with Mesha in the context of the Elisha stories, when Elisha provided a prophetic word to the Israelite

---

43. Lines 4–8, 14–17, author's translation. The Mesha Inscription has been widely translated and studied. Accessible translations are in *ANET*, 320–21; *TANE*, 209–10; *DOTT*, 195–99; P. D. Miller, Jr., *ISBE* 3, s.v. "Moabite Stone." See also the several studies in Dearman, ed., *Studies in the Mesha Inscription and Moab.*

and Judahite kings; Moab very well could have prevailed over Israel in several other battles, which the author of 1 & 2 Kings chose to ignore.

Reconciling the chronology in 2 Kings and the Mesha Inscription is somewhat difficult. Mesha claims that Omri and his son occupied Moab for forty years and that this only extended halfway into Omri's son's reign. Since Omri and Ahab together only reigned thirty-two years (Omri, 885–874 B.C.; Ahab, 874–853 B.C.), this poses a problem. Furthermore, 2 Kings 1:1 and 3:5 explicitly say that Mesha rebelled *after* Ahab's death, whereas Mesha claims that he triumphed over Omri's son (Ahab)and his house.

These difficulties can be resolved in at least two ways. First, Mesha's forty years may be taken as a round number, signifying a generation or so. Or (a better solution), the mention of Omri's "son" may in fact refer to one of his grandsons (Ahaziah reigned in 853–852, and Joram in 852–841). Forty years from early in Omri's reign would end midway through Joram's reign and bring Mesha's text into accord with the biblical data. Mesha's revolt could have been against only Joram, then, or perhaps it began shortly before Ahab died (this, then, being the "son" of Omri mentioned by Mesha) but coming to full fruition a year or so later under Joram.[44]

SENNACHERIB'S ANNALS: THE SIEGE OF JERUSALEM

One of the most important extrabiblical correlations with events in 1 & 2 Kings is between Sennacherib's account of his third military campaign in 701 B.C., during which he came into Judah and besieged Jerusalem, and three biblical accounts of that same campaign found in 2 Kings 18:13–19:37; 2 Chron. 32:1–22; and Isaiah 36–39. This is the only extended account in the OT for which there are three versions, so it obviously was of some considerable importance.

Sennacherib described his campaign at length, including his siege of Jerusalem.[45] As noted above, he also depicted his siege of Lachish during this same campaign in reliefs found at Nineveh.[46] Here is a portion of Sennacherib's own words about this campaign:

> But as for Hezekiah, the Jew, who did not bow in submission to my yoke, forty-six of his strong walled towns and innumerable smaller vil-

---

44. See also Miller, *ISBE* 3, s.v. "Moabite Stone"; B. Oded, "Neighbors on the East," 256–57; Bayla Bonder, "Mesha's Rebellion Against Israel," 82–88. Despite various reasonable solutions, many scholars are skeptical about the possibility of reconciling the two sources. See J. A. Dearman, "Historical Reconstruction and the Mesha Inscription," in Dearman, ed., *Studies in the Mesha Inscription and Moab,* 196–208.
45. *ANET,* 287–88; *TANE,* 199–201; *DOTT,* 66–68. The translation excerpt below is from *ANET.*
46. *ANEP,* plates 371–74; *TANE,* plates 101–2.

lages in their neighbourhood I besieged and conquered by stamping down earth-ramps and then by bringing up battering rams, by the assault of foot-soldiers, by breaches, tunnelling and sapper operations. I made to come out from them 200,150 people, young and old, male and female, innumerable horses, mules, donkeys, camels, large and small cattle, and counted them as spoils of war. He himself I shut up like a caged bird within Jerusalem, his royal city. I put watch-posts strictly around it and turned back to his disaster any who went out of its city gate. . . . As for Hezekiah, the awful splendour of my lordship overwhelmed him. . . . Together with 30 talents of gold, 800 talents of silver, precious stones, antimony, large blocks of red stone, ivory (inlaid) couches, ivory arm-chairs . . . , all kinds of valuable treasures, as well as his daughters, concubines, male and female musicians he sent to me later to Nineveh, my lordly city.

The account in 2 Kings 18–19[47] correlates in several remarkable ways with Sennacherib's account, but it also differs in places, and it includes extended descriptions of conversations between Assyrian and Judahite officials that are not found in Sennacherib's text. Portions of the account relating most closely to Sennacherib's are as follows:

In the fourteenth year of King Hezekiah's reign, Sennacherib king of Assyria attacked all the fortified cities of Judah and captured them. . . . And the king of Assyria exacted from Hezekiah king of Judah three hundred talents of silver and thirty talents of gold. . . . The king of Assyria sent his supreme commander, his chief officer and his field commander with a large army, from Lachish to King Hezekiah at Jerusalem. . . . That night the angel of the Lord went forth, and put to death a hundred and eighty-five thousand men in the Assyrian camp. When the people got up the next morning—there were all the dead bodies! So Sennacherib king of Assyria broke camp and withdrew. He returned to Nineveh and stayed there. (2 Kings 18:13, 14, 17; 19:35–36)

Both accounts mention Hezekiah, Sennacherib's campaign against many cities, Hezekiah's tribute of thirty talents of gold and several hundred[48] talents of silver, the siege of Jerusalem itself, and Sennacherib's return to Nineveh. We should also notice that, amidst Sennacherib's bombastic claims, he carefully avoids mentioning that he actually captured Jerusalem or Hez-

47. See James D. Newsome, Jr., ed. (*A Synoptic Harmony of Samuel, Kings, and Chronicles,* 223–41), for a full and convenient layout of the parallels and differences among the three biblical accounts.
48. This number differs in the two accounts; *ANET* (p. 288) has "800," whereas the Bible has "300." The larger number may be due to inclusion of the silver from elsewhere in the Temple (vv. 15, 16). (So also Cogan and Tadmor, *II Kings,* 229.)

ekiah, and he avoids any mention of his defeat there. This is in keeping with the practice throughout most of the ancient world (and much of the modern world!), whereby only military victories are recorded, or defeats are recast as victories.

Several problems in the data present themselves, however, and these (and other considerations) have led some scholars to propose two campaigns of Sennacherib against Jerusalem, one in 701 B.C. (described in 2 Kings 18:13–16) and one later (described in 18:17–19:37).[49] In this view, the accounts of the two have been telescoped into one. One problem concerns the mention of Tirhakah, king of Ethiopia, in 2 Kings 19:9. Since Tirhakah did not become king until 690 B.C., this indicates to some that part of the account deals with a campaign later than 701 B.C. Another concerns the contradictory claims of victory in both the Assyrian and the biblical accounts. Another problem is that Sennacherib did not die until 681 B.C., whereas the biblical account makes it appear that he died in 701 (19:36–37).

However, despite the strong arguments advanced for two campaigns, there is no direct evidence of two campaigns against Judah or Jerusalem, either in the biblical records or in Sennacherib's own annals (which do record five campaigns after 701 B.C.). The problems noted above (and others) are capable of other explanations.[50] The first discrepancy is easily solved by noting that Tirhakah would have been a young general in 701 B.C., whereas the second can be explained by noting the differing literary tendencies in the two accounts. The third is resolved by understanding a twenty-year gap between verses 36 and 37 in 2 Kings 19; the author's concern was with the events of 701, and so a detailed recording of events following this was unnecessary for his purposes. The weight of scholarly opinion—both among Assyriologists and biblical scholars (conservative and nonconservative alike)—favors only one campaign into Judah by Sennacherib, and, despite many difficulties, that is the conclusion favored here.

THE BOOK OF TOBIT

The apocryphal book of Tobit preserves stories about the families of its two heroes, Tobit and Sarah, who supposedly lived in the eighth and seventh centuries B.C., during the time of such Assyrian kings as Shalmaneser, Sennacherib, and Esarhaddon, and Nebuchadnezzar of Babylon (sixth century) and Ahasuerus of Persia (fifth century). Both were righteous heroes who

---

49. Bright, *History,* 298–309; William H. Shea, "Sennacherib's Second Palestine Campaign," 401–18.
50. See Kenneth A. Kitchen, *Ancient Orient and Old Testament,* 82–84; and *The Bible in Its World,* 113–14; Richard D. Patterson and Hermann J. Austel, "1, 2 Kings," 263–64; Cogan and Tadmor, *II Kings,* 246–51.

were helped by the angel Raphael. Tobit was healed of blindness and Sarah rid of a demon, and they were married and lived a long, satisfying life.

The book of Tobit is not a good historical source for the periods mentioned in the book.[51] Scholarly consensus places its writing in the second century B.C., long years after these events, and there are many historical errors in them. However, the book does draw on many biblical themes and quotes several times from the Bible, including one reference to Nahum's prophecy about Nineveh (Tobit 14:4).

It appears to have been written in Hebrew or Aramaic, and it is found among the Qumran manuscripts; it was later translated into several Greek versions. It tells a delightful story about God's providential care of His people. Despite its popularity, however, its value lies not in providing any reliable historical backdrop for 1 & 2 Kings but, rather, in showing how many biblical concepts were developed in the intertestamental period.

JERUSALEM IN 1 & 2 KINGS

The history and theology of Jerusalem play an important part in 1 & 2 Kings. The city provides the stage for almost all the characters and activities in these two books. Many people have become interested in Jerusalem because some of the most dramatic archaeological finds in Palestine have come from there. However, it is prominent in the Bible not only as the physical capital of the land but as the spiritual symbol of God's kingdom.

JERUSALEM: HISTORICAL CITY[52]

David was the first to make Jerusalem into a truly Israelite city: he captured the city, established it as his capital, and began certain building projects (2 Sam. 5:6–11), and he set about the work of providing for a Temple to be built there (chap. 7; 24:18–25). Several scholars believe that the "Millo" of 5:9 (NASB, RSV; "supporting terraces," NIV) was the large stepped stone terraced structure uncovered in recent excavations.[53]

However, it was under Solomon that building projects truly grew in size and number. His greatest achievement, from the writer of 1 & 2 Kings'

---

51. See P. L. Redditt (*ISBE* 4, s.v. "Tobit") and Carey A. Moore (*ABD* 6, s.v. "Tobit, Book of") for good introductions to the book, and p. 866 and pp. 587–88, respectively, on the book's historical problems.
52. Good introductions to the city's history and the excavations there are Hershel Shanks, *The City of David*; Benjamin Mazar, *The Mountain of the Lord*; Nahman Avigad, *Discovering Jerusalem*; Yigal Shiloh, *Excavations the City of David, I, 1978–1982*; Hershel Shanks, "The City of David After Five Years of Digging," 22–38; W. Harold Mare, *The Archaeology of the Jerusalem Area*; Donald Ariel et al., *Excavations at the City of David 1978–1985*; David Tarler and Jane M. Cahill, *ABD* 2, s.v. "David, City of"; Philip J. King, *ABD* 3, s.v. "Jerusalem."
53. See Shanks, "The City of David After Five Years of Digging," 28; Shiloh, *Excavations*, pp. 27, 29.

The Solomonic Temple

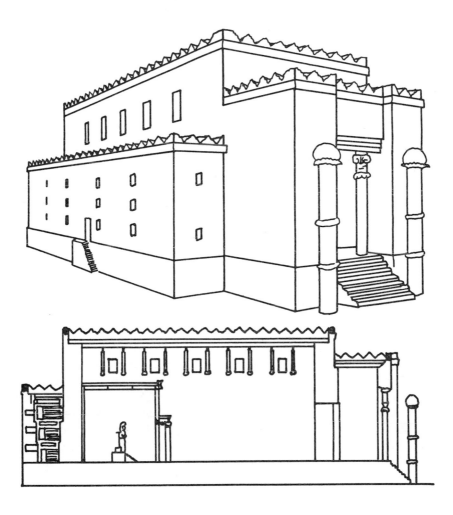

perspective, was his building of the Temple.[54] The Temple—including preparations for it and its contents—is described in much greater detail in 1 & 2
Chronicles due to the Chronicler's greater interest in ritual and sacrificial
matters, but it nevertheless occupies an important place in 1 & 2 Kings.

Solomon began building the Temple in the fourth year of his reign (ca.
966 B.C.; 1 Kings 6:1, 37), and it took seven years in the building (6:38). Its
actual building is described in detail in 6:1–38; 7:12–51 (and in 2 Chron.
3:1–4:22), and the author of 1 & 2 Kings includes a lengthy account of its
dedications (1 Kings 8).

Solomon completed the process of gathering building materials with the
help of his father's friend, Hiram, king of Tyre (5:1–18 [MT 15–32]; 7:13–14; cf.
2 Chron. 2:1–18 [MT 1:18–2:17]). The chief craftsman was another Hiram,
whose mother was an Israelite from the tribe of Naphtali and whose father was
a Phoenician. He was skilled in the use of many valuable materials (1 Kings
7:13–14). Stone was the basic building material, but it was overlaid on the
inside with wood so that it could not be seen (6:15, 18), and it was prepared
in an apparently novel way: ready-made at the quarry, so that the sound of
iron tools was not heard in the Temple itself (6:7). The Temple probably
was oriented to the east: Josephus states this (*Antiquities* 8.3.2), and the
placement of the Temple singers in 2 Chronicles 5:12 and 29:4 hints at it.[55]

The floor plan was tripartite. It had an outer porch, which was flanked
by (or contained) two pillars. The nave, or holy place, was the first inner
room, and the holy of holies was the innermost part. Inside the holy place
were the altar of incense, the table of the Presence, the lampstands, and numerous utensils used in the worship (1 Kings 7:45, 48–50). Inside the holy
of holies was the ark, flanked by the two large cherubim (6:19–20, 23–28).

The two pillars in the outer porch had names: Jachin ("he will establish") and Boaz ("in it/him is strength") (7:15–22).[56] These were eighteen
cubits high (7:15; Jer. 52:21), and it appears that the pillars were freestand-
ing, perhaps with fire-bowls at the top (1 Kings 7:16). According to Jeremiah
52:21 they were hollow. These were dismantled in the destruction of Jerusalem, and the metal was carried away (2 Kings 25:13; Jer. 52:20–23). Outside, in the courtyard, were several prominent features. First Kings mentions
only the great bronze sea, serviced by ten (wheeled) lavers (1 Kings 7:23–39).[57]

---

54. Good introductions into all aspects of the Temple may be found in G. Ernest Wright, "Solomon's Temple Resurrected," 17–31; André Parrot, *The Temple of Jerusalem*; J. Gutmann,
  ed., *The Temple of Solomon*; S. Westerholm, *ISBE* 4, s.v. "Temple"; Carol Meyers, *ABD* 6,
  s.v. "Temple, Jerusalem." The definitive work is T. Busink, *Der Tempel von Jerusalem.*
55. See further, H. Van Dyke Parunak, "Was Solomon's Temple Aligned to the Sun?"
56. See R. B. Y. Scott ("The Pillars Jachin and Boaz," 143–49) on these two terms for the pillars.
57. Second Chronicles adds mention of the great bronze altar (4:1) and a raised bronze platform on which Solomon stood (or knelt) when he addressed the Lord at the dedication ceremony (6:12–13).

South of the Temple was a palace complex consisting of several buildings and halls (1 Kings 7:1–8). It was likely larger than the Temple, as it took almost twice as long—thirteen years—to complete (7:1).

Surrounding the Temple and palace complexes were courtyards. The walls of these are not specifically mentioned in the Bible, but the courts are. The walls were built with stone and cedar (6:36; 7:12). A large, outer court (the "Great Court") surrounded both the Temple and the palace complex (7:9). Two inner courts stood next to each other, the "Priests' Court," surrounding the Temple (6:36; 7:12), and the "Other Court," surrounding the palace complex (7:8).

Solomon also built the city walls (3:1), although we do not know exactly where they were. The assumption is that they now enclosed the northern sections of the city that he had expanded and that he used the Jebusite walls around the old city.

Solomon also rebuilt the "Millo," the supporting terraces in the City of David, according to several references (9:15, 24; 11:27; 2 Kings 12:20 [MT 21]). These references may mean that he expanded or repaired it, as it seems to have been in existence in David's time (2 Sam. 5:9).

Only scattered reference is made to Jerusalem or its architecture during the ninth and eighth centuries in 1 & 2 Kings. Building activity and Temple repair were important during different periods: 2 Kings mentions the work of Joash (Jehoash) (835–796 B.C.) in repairing the Temple and replacing many of its utensils (2 Kings 12:4–16 [MT 5–17]) and also the work of Jotham (750–732 B.C.) on the Temple's upper gate and on the walls (15:35).[58]

Hezekiah did extensive work in Jerusalem, but this is emphasized much more in 2 Chronicles. In 2 Kings, the only reference to this is in 20:20: "He made the pool and the tunnel by which he brought water into the city." The pool was at the south end of the impressive tunnel that he built through the rock under the City of David.[59]

This tunnel is one of the most dramatic archaeological features ever found in Jerusalem. It was built in response to the Assyrian threat under Sennacherib in 701 B.C., to bring water into the city from the Gihon Spring, in the event of a siege, since the spring was outside the city walls. The tunnel follows sweeping S-curves, and drops seven feet from the Gihon Spring to the Pool of Siloam. Its length is some 1750 feet long, though the straight-line distance is only 1050 feet. It was dug by two crews digging toward each

58. Azariah (Uzziah: 792–740 B.C.) engaged in several ambitious building projects, both in Jerusalem and throughout the land, but these are mentioned only in 2 Chronicles 26.
59. Another pool, called the "Upper Pool," is mentioned in 2 Kings 18:17, but its location is uncertain (Cogan and Tadmor, *II Kings*, 230.)

other, and it took some eight months to build.[60] The surface was more than 150 feet above the diggers. The tunnel itself is as much as nineteen feet high near the south end and as low as five feet in parts of the northern half. Edward Robinson first crawled through the length of the tunnel in 1838, and Charles Warren followed him in 1867.[61] An inscription describing the work of the digging crews and the completion of the tunnel was found in 1880.[62] It was cleared of rubble and debris by the Parker Mission in 1909–11,[63] and today it can be enjoyed by visitors to Jerusalem.

After Hezekiah, the only significant references in 2 Kings to Jerusalem before its destruction come in the days of Josiah (640–609 B.C.). Josiah undertook to repair the Temple and institute various reforms (chaps. 22–23). The "Second District" encountered here (22:14) was the area of the city where Huldah the prophetess lived. This most likely was the area west of the City of David, on the "Western Hill," which was included in Jerusalem under the westward expansion of the city in Hezekiah's day.

Jerusalem was sacked and finally destroyed by the Babylonians under Nebuchadnezzar. It appears that there were three attacks and deportations—one in 605 B.C. (mentioned in Dan. 1:1), one in 597 B.C. (mentioned in 2 Kings 24), and the final one in 586 B.C. (mentioned in 2 Kings 25). The Babylonians destroyed most of the city, including the Temple, and carried off its utensils and the two large bronze pillars. No traces of this Temple have survived for modern discovery.

JERUSALEM: SPIRITUAL SYMBOL

Jerusalem is important in the Bible not only as the physical city where many OT and NT events took place, or as the capital of the Davidic kingdom, but also as a symbol of the kingdom of God.[64] An impressive theology of Jerusalem (or Zion) can be traced in such books as the Psalms, Isaiah, Jeremiah, Ezekiel, Zechariah, and Revelation.

The importance of Jerusalem as a spiritual symbol is emphasized in 1 & 2 Kings at several crucial points as well. In the first place, it was the place where the Temple was built, and the ark of the covenant of the Lord was brought there in a great celebratory festival (1 Kings 8). Furthermore, God's

---

60. Shanks, *City of David,* 115 n. 25, citing L. H. Vincent, *Underground Jerusalem* (London, 1911), 23.
61. Shanks, *City of David,* 58–60.
62. Ibid., 55–57; for the complete text of the inscription, see p. 55, or *ANET,* 321.
63. Shanks, *City of David,* 61.
64. Good introductions to the theology of Jerusalem include J. J. M. Roberts, "Zion in the Theology of the Davidic-Solomonic Empire"; Moshe Weinfeld, "Zion and Jerusalem as Religious and Political Capital: Ideology and Utopia"; William J. Dumbrell, *The End of the Beginning,* 1–34; Ben C. Ollenburger, *Zion: The City of the Great King*; Gordon McConville, "Jerusalem in the Old Testament."

choice of Jerusalem as His own "capital" went back at least as far as Moses' day, when the Israelites were instructed to worship only at "the place the Lord your God will choose from among all your tribes to put His Name there for his dwelling" (Deut. 12:5; cf. vv. 11, 13–14). This idea of Jerusalem as God's chosen city, the city where He would place His name (i.e., where He would identify His reputation) is echoed explicitly in 1 Kings 11:13, 32, 36, where God allowed one tribe to remain to the line of David when the kingdom split, for the sake of David His servant and for the sake of Jerusalem, His chosen city. This promise of God is also referred to in 2 Kings 21:4, 7; 23:27.

God pledged Himself to protect this city, and the theme of the inviolability of Jerusalem is important in 1 & 2 Kings. Much attention is given to wall building and repair under various kings, a symbol of protection for the city. More importantly, however, God Himself made Jerusalem strong (1 Kings 15:4). An important theme in the account of Sennacherib's siege of Jerusalem is the question of in whom should Hezekiah's trust rest: God or Sennacherib (2 Kings 18:13–19:37). The security of Jerusalem is at issue here (18:35; 19:10). Isaiah's prophecy concerning the deliverance of the city (19:20–34) affirms that God would defend it for His own sake and for the sake of His servant David (v. 34).

In the end, even this city of God was destroyed because of the people's sin. Yet, Isaiah had affirmed that there would come out of Jerusalem a remnant (19:31). It is left to the prophetic books and the Psalms to develop in depth the ideas of the return from exile, the rebuilding of city and Temple, and of the glorious future for both.

8

1 & 2 CHRONICLES

I will raise up one of your offspring to succeed you, one of your own sons . . . and I will establish his throne forever. . . . I will be his father, and he will be my son. I will never take my love away from him. . . . I will set him over my house and my kingdom forever; his throne will be established forever. (1 Chron. 17:11–14)

If my people, who are called by my name, will humble themselves and pray and seek my face and turn from their wicked ways, then I will hear from heaven and will forgive their sin and heal their land. (2 Chron. 7:14)

The books of Chronicles are wonderful. They possess a richness of texture and an exegetical challenge that surpasses that of most OT historical books. Part of their richness derives from the fact that they parallel other biblical books so closely: fully 50 percent of 1 & 2 Chronicles is the same material as found in 1 & 2 Samuel and 1 & 2 Kings. However, most of that richness lies in the other 50 percent, partly because of its content and partly because of the ways in which the author has added to and deleted material from his sources. Coming at the end of the OT period, these books contain deposits of almost every theological idea that has been developed in all the previous books. Concerning their content, Simon DeVries has a similar verdict: "I [now] regard Chronicles as one of the richest mines of spirituality in all of Scripture."[1]

These books are concerned with the progress of God's kingdom as it was represented by the Davidic kingdom in Israel (initially) and Judah (later). After an extensive genealogical introduction (nine chapters!) that highlights an interest in Judah, the Davidic dynasty, and the institution by David of centralized worship at Jerusalem and the Temple, David himself is the fo-

1. S. J. DeVries, *1 and 2 Chronicles*, xiv.

cus of the remainder of 1 Chronicles and his son Solomon of the first part of 2 Chronicles. The remainder of the work focuses on the fortunes of the kingdom of Judah, the heir of the promises of the Davidic Covenant. The books end with an upbeat look into the future—the release from exile of the Jews. In the process of presenting this history of God's kingdom, the author introduces many important truths about God Himself, about His workings in the world, and about proper ways to relate to God.

TITLE AND PLACE IN THE CANON

TITLE

The earliest known title for the book is *Paraleipomenōn*, which means "things left out." It is found in the Old Greek versions (Septuagint) and Jerome's Vulgate (in Latin), and obviously refers to the fact that 1 & 2 Chronicles supplement much material from 1 & 2 Samuel and 1 & 2 Kings. This has led to disparagements of its value and originality, which undoubtedly has contributed to its relative neglect within the church.

A disparaging view of the books' historicity has also arisen. Wilhelm De Wette (1807) believed that the Chronicler "reworked, altered, and falsified" his earlier sources to such an extent as to render the work useless as a historical document.[2] A similar, even more extreme, example is C. C. Torrey's comment:

> No fact of Old Testament criticism is more firmly established than this; that the Chronicler, as a historian, is thoroughly untrustworthy. He distorts facts deliberately and habitually; invents chapter after chapter with the greatest freedom; and, what is most dangerous of all, his history is not written for its own sake, but in the interest of an extremely one-sided theory.[3]

The view of 1 & 2 Chronicles that it consists merely of "things left out," however, does an injustice to the work. It ignores the obvious fact, for example, that 1 & 2 Chronicles contains much material quoted almost verbatim from 1 & 2 Samuel and 1 & 2 Kings, and it does not take into account the very important task of selectivity involved in compiling, arranging, and supplementing the sources. The title does show, however, that the books retrace and supplement the path trod by earlier biblical books.

The Hebrew title is *dibrê hayyāmîm*, "the affairs of the days" (i.e., "daily matters" or "daily deeds"), which is to be understood as "annals" or

---

2. Quoted in Brevard S. Childs, *IOTS*, 642.
3. C. C. Torrey, *The Composition and Historical Value of Ezra-Nehemiah* (Giessen: J. Ricker'sche, 1896), 252, 274, as cited in Leslie McFall, "Was Nehemiah Contemporary With Ezra in 458 BC?" 265–66.

"chronicles." Indeed, we get our English title from Jerome: "the chronicle (*chronikon*) of the whole of sacred history."[4] Jerome, who wrote in Latin, used a Greek word here, indicating that he saw it as a title.[5] Jerome's is a well-justified characterization, since the work extends from Adam (1:1) to Cyrus (2 Chron. 36:22–23).

The same phrase (*dibrê hayyāmîm*) occurs thirty-three times in 1 & 2 Kings, usually translated as "annals" by the NIV. It is always preceded by "book" and is usually followed by some qualifying phrase, such as "the kings of Judah" (1 Kings 15:7).[6] These "chronicles" are just various Israelite court records, however, not the canonical books, because (1) 1 & 2 Chronicles were written roughly a century after 1 & 2 Kings, and (2) 1 & 2 Kings sometimes appeal to the *dibrê hayyāmîm* to refer to some events not recorded at all in 1 & 2 Chronicles (e.g., 1 Kings 14:19; 15:31). (For a discussion of these sources, see chapter 6 under "The Use of Sources in 1 & 2 Kings.") Note also that *dibrê hayyāmîm* occurs once within 1 & 2 Chronicles itself (1 Chron. 27:24, referring to "the annals of King David"). The importance of this title is that it shows what the book is about, namely, the affairs of the kings, interpreted from a specific theological slant.

PLACE IN THE CANON

In today's Protestant canon, the books of Chronicles immediately follow 1 & 2 Kings and immediately precede Ezra and Nehemiah, which is the place that they occupy in the earliest description of the canonical ordering (Josephus's).[7] The Old Greek (Septuagintal) versions have the same ordering. Thus, they are part of the "historical" section of the canon. This reflects a proper chronological sequencing, since the events in Ezra and Nehemiah follow those in 1 & 2 Chronicles, and those in 1 & 2 Chronicles extend beyond the end of 2 Kings.

In the Hebrew canon, however, 1 & 2 Chronicles are part of the third section of the canon, the "Writings," and they are the last books in that section, making them the last books of the OT. The books of Ezra and Nehemiah immediately precede them. This reflects the almost unanimous witness of rabbinic tradition and ancient manuscripts,[8] even though it reverses the natural chronological ordering of events.

4. This title is found in his *Prologus galeatus* (H. G. M. Williamson, *1 and 2 Chronicles*, 3–4).
5. Williamson, *1 and 2 Chronicles*, 3–4.
6. But it is not so modified in Nehemiah 12:23; Esther 2:3; 6:1.
7. Josephus, *Against Apion*, I.7–8; J. B. Payne, "1, 2 Chronicles," 312; R. Beckwith, *The Old Testament Canon of the New Testament Church*, 451.
8. Beckwith, *Old Testament Canon*, 452–64. However, see the evidence of many medieval manuscripts, which place 1 & 2 Chronicles *first* in the Writings, before Psalms, and Ezra-Nehemiah last (Beckwith, *Old Testament Canon*, 458–59).

Various explanations for the reverse ordering of the Hebrew canon are given.[9] Some historical explanations have been offered, such as the suggestion that Ezra and Nehemiah may have been recognized as canonical earlier than 1 & 2 Chronicles and thus included in the developing canon in a location before the latter. Cyrus Gordon spoke of deliberate misplacement of these books so that the Hebrew Bible might end on the optimistic, positive note of Cyrus's decree releasing the Jews from captivity, which is found in the last two verses of 2 Chronicles.[10] The message, then, would be that all who follow (and who read this Scripture) will be "free" in the same sense. The reason might be even broader than this, however, reflecting the importance of the entire work—not just the ending—in the canonizers' minds and the importance of the books' themes, especially when they speak of the glories of the Davidic line and kingship. This accords well with Roger Beckwith's observation that "Chronicles is placed last as a recapitulation of the whole biblical story."[11] In either case, the OT canon ends on a generally upbeat note, much more appropriate for ending the OT than the sometimes tortuous specifics of failures and reforms seen in Ezra and Nehemiah.

It would appear that the Hebrew ordering was fixed and known in Jesus' day.[12] This is supported by Jesus' reference to two martyrs in Matthew 23:35 (cf. Luke 11:51): "from the blood of righteous Abel to the blood of Zechariah son of Berekiah," who was killed "between the temple and the altar." The canonical prophet Zechariah was the son of Berekiah (Zech. 1:1), but we do not know anything from the OT about his death. A Zechariah, son of Jehoiada, was killed in the temple courtyards (2 Chron. 24:20–22), and many scholars plausibly argue that this Zechariah was the one Jesus referred to, Jehoiada perhaps being his grandfather.[13] If so, Jesus' reference to martyrs ranging from Abel to Zechariah cites people mentioned in the first and last books of the Hebrew canon: Genesis and 2 Chronicles. It is the equivalent of a Christian saying that something is true "from Genesis to Revelation."

AUTHORSHIP

The work is anonymous, and nowhere in the Bible is any author specified for the work. According to the Talmud (*Baba Bathra* 15a), Ezra wrote it. There is a certain logic to this since 1 & 2 Chronicles ends as Ezra begins. Also, much vocabulary and style are similar (see below, esp. n. 20). Recent-

---

9. See R. K. Harrison, *Introduction to the Old Testament*, 1136.
10. Cited by ibid.
11. Beckwith, *Old Testament Canon*, 159.
12. R. L. Harris, however, argues for the priority of the Septuagintal ordering of 1 & 2 Chronicles before Ezra-Nehemiah ("Chronicles and the Canon in New Testament Times," 75–84).
13. See D. A. Carson, "Matthew," 485–86; Beckwith, *Old Testament Canon*, 212–22.

ly, however, many scholars have argued that Ezra was not the author (see "Relationship of 1 & 2 Chronicles to Ezra and Nehemiah" below). Others have suggested that a Levite or a member of the musicians' guild of Asaph wrote the work.[14] However, in the end, judgments about authorship are conjectures, so hereafter the author will simply be referred to as "the Chronicler."

DATE

DATE OF THE EVENTS

The genealogy that opens 1 Chronicles begins with Adam, and the narrative in 2 Chronicles ends with Cyrus's decree of 538 B.C., releasing the Jews from their exile in Babylon. Thus, the books of Chronicles cover a longer time frame than any other historical book in the OT. The main historical narrative portions of the books, however (1 Chronicles 10–2 Chronicles 36), cover the monarchies in Israel and Judah, beginning with Saul and David in the eleventh century B.C. and ending, as noted, in the mid-sixth century B.C.

DATE OF COMPOSITION

Scholarly opinion concerning the date of composition of 1 & 2 Chronicles ranges from the early postexilic period to ca. 200 B.C.[15] Hugh Williamson tentatively suggests some time in the fourth century B.C., perhaps 350.[16] Roddy Braun believes that the work was first written ca. 515 B.C., then revised and updated until it reached its final form ca. 350–300 B.C. John Sailhamer dates it early in the fifth century, in the second or third generation after the Exile.[17] Many date it to ca. 450 or 400 B.C. on the basis of assuming Ezra's authorship of the books.[18]

Considering the genealogy in 1 Chronicles 3:17–24, where "Jeconiah" (i.e., Jehoiachin) and Zerubbabel are mentioned, along with descendants at least two generations removed, it would seem impossible to date the writing too close to the end of the Exile. Assuming twenty to thirty years per generation, that would place the books' writing no sooner than early in the fifth century B.C. (the early 400s). No biblical evidence compels us to fix a late date for the writing, so there seems to be little reason to date it any later than 400 B.C.

14. Harrison, *Introduction*, 1154.
15. See the surveys of opinions in ibid., 1153–57; Williamson, *1 and 2 Chronicles*, 15–17.
16. Williamson, *1 and 2 Chronicles*, 16.
17. Braun, *1 Chronicles*, xxvii–xxix; John Sailhamer, *First and Second Chronicles*, 13.
18. E.g, W. F. Albright (cited by Harrison, *Introduction*, 1153–54); J. B. Payne, "1, 2 Chronicles," 306.

Purpose

The books of Chronicles intend to retell the story of God's people for an audience late in their history, several decades after the Exile, with special emphasis on the Davidic Covenant, the proper place of worship, and the certainty of God's punishment. A primary focus on Judah as the vehicle of God's outworking of His promises does not obscure the vision in these books of a people of God that includes all the faithful of both Israel and Judah.

Historical and Cultural Context for 1 & 2 Chronicles

Since the books of Chronicles cover the same time frames and much of the same ground as the books of 2 Samuel and 1 & 2 Kings, the reader is referred to the discussions of the historical and cultural backgrounds to those books (chapters 5 and 7). On the last two verses of 2 Chronicles, where Cyrus, the Persian king, is mentioned, as well as for the situation at the time of the writing of 1 & 2 Chronicles, see the chapter on Ezra-Nehemiah (chapter 9).

Relationship of 1 & 2 Chronicles to Ezra-Nehemiah

The books of Ezra and Nehemiah pick up the narrative thread of the Jews' story where 2 Chronicles leaves off. That the material in 1 & 2 Chronicles is in some way related to that in Ezra-Nehemiah may be hinted at, in the first place, by their positions adjacent to each other, in both the Hebrew and Protestant canons.

A more important indicator of their close relationship, however, is the fact that Ezra begins exactly as 2 Chronicles ends. That is, the last two verses of 2 Chronicles (36:22–23) are repeated essentially verbatim in Ezra 1:1–3a. They contain the words of Cyrus's decree releasing the Jews to return to Jerusalem. This makes the obvious point that the book of Ezra picks up where 2 Chronicles leaves off. Beginning with the German scholar L. Zunz in 1832 and continuing until the present day, this repetition has suggested to many scholars that both 1 & 2 Chronicles and the book of Ezra were written by the same author, most likely Ezra himself.[19]

A second argument in favor of common authorship is drawn from the apocryphal book of 1 Esdras, which was written in Greek. (See chapter 9 for more on the books of Esdras.) This work includes 2 Chronicles 35–36, then continues by reproducing the entire book of Ezra, and concludes with Nehemiah 7:38–8:12, breaking off in the middle of a sentence about Ezra's reforms. This too has suggested to many scholars that the original Hebrew books were by the same author.

---

19. H. G. M. Williamson, *Israel in the Books of Chronicles*, 7–11. See pp. 5–70 for Williamson's detailed evaluation of the entire relationship between these two works.

Third, many similarities in vocabulary and style between 1 & 2 Chronicles and Ezra-Nehemiah have suggested common authorship to many scholars.[20]

Fourth, many similarities have been noted in the two works in terms of general outlook, interests, and theology. Both 1 & 2 Chronicles and Ezra-Nehemiah were postexilic works, and both display strong interests in matters of Temple worship, religious officials, and genealogical continuities.

However, beginning with a work by Sara Japhet in 1968, the scholarly consensus has been moving toward the view that 1 & 2 Chronicles and Ezra-Nehemiah were written by different authors.[21] Japhet's work was primarily a detailed study of vocabulary that pointed toward different authorship. Hugh Williamson has added the observation that 1 Esdras does not exactly reproduce 2 Chronicles 35–36 but rather uses portions of it, along with portions of other Scriptures, notably 2 Kings 23. Thus, the shape of 1 Esdras does not necessarily argue that 1 & 2 Chronicles and Ezra-Nehemiah were originally one connected work. Williamson further shows that, in several key areas of outlook and theology, the books of Chronicles and Ezra-Nehemiah have markedly different concerns. These include their respective treatments of (1) mixed marriages (strongly condemned in Ezra-Nehemiah, whereas seemingly tolerated in 1 & 2 Chronicles), (2) the early history of Israel (more emphasis on Moses and the Exodus in Ezra-Nehemiah, and more emphasis on David and kingship in 1 & 2 Chronicles), (3) the fall of the northern kingdom (essentially ignored in 1 & 2 Chronicles, whereas echoed in Ezra 4), (4) the doctrine of immediate retribution for sin (present in 1 & 2 Chronicles, absent in Ezra-Nehemiah), and (5) the ways in which their histories were written (prophets and miracles abound in 1 & 2 Chronicles but are absent in Ezra-Nehemiah).[22]

Concerning the tag-line at the end of 2 Chronicles and the beginning of Ezra, this is not as persuasive an argument for unity as some would posit.[23] That is because other OT books that almost certainly shared the same author—such as 1 & 2 Samuel or 1 & 2 Kings, or even, perhaps, 2 Samuel and 1 Kings—do not have such a tag-line. The repetition in 2 Chronicles and Ezra is the only such repetition in the Bible, and it can be just as easily

20. In an earlier day, S. R. Driver (*Introduction to the Literature of the Old Testament*, 534–40) and E. L. Curtis and A. A. Madsen (*Commentary on the Books of Chronicles*, 27–36) compiled detailed lists of similar vocabulary and style.
21. S. Japhet, "The Supposed Common Authorship of Chronicles and Ezra-Nehemiah Investigated Anew," 330–71. See also Williamson, *Israel in the Books of Chronicles*, 5–70; and *1 and 2 Chronicles*, 6–11; Roddy Braun, "Chronicles, Ezra, and Nehemiah: Theology and Literary History," 52–64; and *1 Chronicles*, xix–xxi.
22. Williamson, *Israel in the Books of Chronicles*, 60–69.
23. See Menahem Haran ("Explaining the Identical Lines at the End of Chronicles and the Beginning of Ezra," 18–20) and Williamson's response ("Did the Author of Chronicles Also Write the Books of Ezra and Nehemiah?" 56–59).

explained by imagining a different author adding it to his work (to make sure his work was understood in relation to its companion work).

We may sum up by noting that there are clear affinities and continuities between 1 & 2 Chronicles and Ezra-Nehemiah and that these books complement each other in important ways. However, the continuities do not require us to postulate single authorship for both works; indeed, the weight of evidence—in what is admittedly a very subjective endeavor[24]—points to separate authorship.[25]

SOURCES IN 1 & 2 CHRONICLES

The Chronicler mentions no fewer than thirty-two different sources in his work, almost all of which are no longer extant.[26] These are discussed in the present section. However, he does not mention explicitly the most important sources he used, sources that are from the Bible itself, mainly 2 Samuel and 1 & 2 Kings. These are discussed more fully in the next section.

The thirty-two sources the Chronicler identifies form a remarkable contrast to the sources used by the author of 1 & 2 Kings, who named only three: the "Book of the Acts of Solomon," "the Book of the Annals of the Kings of Israel," and "the Book of the Annals of the Kings of Judah" (see chapter 6 under "The Use of Sources in 1 & 2 Kings"). This is all the more remarkable when we remember that the author of 1 & 2 Chronicles heavily depended upon 1 & 2 Kings.

Of the thirty-two sources identified by the Chronicler, most fall into one of three categories: official annals, genealogical records, and prophetic records.

The *official annals* include the following:

- the book of the annals of King David (2 Chron. 27:24)
- the book of the kings of Israel and Judah (27:7; 35:27; 36:8)
- the book of the kings of Judah and Israel (16:11; 25:26; 28:26; 32:32)
- the book of the kings of Israel (1 Chron. 9:1; 2 Chron. 20:34)
- the annals of the kings of Israel (33:18)
- the annotations ("midrash") on the book of the kings (24:27)
- the directions written by David king of Israel and by his son Solomon (35:4)

24. See Peter R. Ackroyd ("Chronicles-Ezra-Nehemiah: the Concept of Unity," 189–201) on this point.
25. A recent attempt to resurrect the single-author hypothesis is impressive, yet ultimately not convincing: David Talshir, "A Reinvestigation of the Linguistic Relationship between Chronicles and Ezra-Nehemiah," 165–93.
26. Jacob Myers, *1 Chronicles*, XLVI–XLVIII.

Official *genealogical records* are referred to for the descendants of Simeon (1 Chron. 4:33); Gad (5:17); Benjamin (7:9); Asher (7:40); and Rehoboam (2 Chron. 12:15). A genealogy of "all Israel" is recorded in 1 Chronicles 9:1; and one for the doorkeepers is mentioned in 9:22.

The *prophetic records* include the following:

- the records of Samuel the seer (1 Chron. 29:29)
- the records of Nathan the prophet (29:29; 2 Chron. 9:29)
- the records of Gad the seer (1 Chron. 29:29)
- the prophecy of Ahijah the Shilonite (2 Chron. 9:29)
- the visions of Iddo the seer (9:29)
- the records of Shemaiah the prophet (12:15)
- the records of Iddo the seer (12:15)
- the annotations ("midrash") of the prophet Iddo (13:22)
- the annals of Jehu son of Hanani, which are recorded in the book of the kings of Israel (20:34)
- events of Uzziah's reign . . . recorded by the prophet Isaiah son of Amoz (26:22)
- the vision of the prophet Isaiah son of Amoz in the book of the kings of Judah and Israel (32:32)
- the records of the seers (33:19)

From such passages as 2 Chronicles 20:34 and 32:32, it would appear that the prophetic records were understood to have been earlier documents that were later incorporated into the official annals of the kings and that the Chronicler was accessing them via the official annals, not directly.

Furthermore, a comparison of where such source citations occur in 1 & 2 Chronicles vis-à-vis the source citations in 1 & 2 Kings reveals that in almost every case[27] the Chronicler refers to these sources at precisely the same location that the author of 1 & 2 Kings cites his sources.[28] Conversely, the Chronicler does not add references to such sources where sources are not already referred to in 1 & 2 Kings (except in 1 Chron. 29:29).

This would suggest that most of the Chronicler's many "sources" are not independent sources at all but rather variant names for the two major sources mentioned in 1 & 2 Kings: "the book of the annals of the kings of

27. The exceptions are 1 Chronicles 29:29 and 2 Chronicles 35:26–27. The former is added with no parallel in 1 Kings, whereas the latter is merely displaced from its true parallel location in 2 Kings (see 2 Kings 23:28). .
28. The discussion in this section parallels Williamson's (*1 and 2 Chronicles*, 17–21), to whom I am indebted for several points.

Israel" and "the book of the annals of the kings of Judah." This hypothesis is reinforced by observing those passages where the author of 1 & 2 Kings cites the official records of the kings of Judah. The following chart shows that, in the parallel passages, the Chronicler used widely divergent terms in referring to these sources.

Parallel Source Citations in 1 & 2 Kings and 2 Chronicles

1 & 2 KINGS*	2 CHRONICLES
1 Kings 14:29	the records of Shemaiah the prophet and of Iddo the seer (2 Chron. 12:15)
1 Kings 15:7	the annotations of the prophet Iddo (2 Chron. 13:22)
1 Kings 15:23	the book of the kings of Judah and Israel (2 Chron. 16:11)
1 Kings 22:45	the annals of Jehu son of Hanani, which are recorded in the book of the kings of Israel (2 Chron. 20:34)
2 Kings 14:18	the book of the kings of Judah and Israel (2 Chron. 25:26)
2 Kings 15:6	"recorded by the prophet Isaiah son of Amoz" (2 Chron. 26:22)
2 Kings 15:36	the book of the kings of Israel and Judah (2 Chron. 27:7)
2 Kings 16:19	the book of the kings of Judah and Israel (2 Chron. 28:26)
2 Kings 20:20	the vision of the prophet Isaiah son of Amoz in the book of the kings of Judah and Israel (2 Chron. 32:32)
2 Kings 21:17	the annals of the kings of Israel (2 Chron. 33:18)
2 Kings 23:28	the book of the kings of Israel and Judah (2 Chron. 35:27)
2 Kings 24:5	the book of the kings of Israel and Judah (2 Chron. 36:8)

* The references in 1 & 2 Kings in every case are to "the Book of the Annals of the Kings of Judah."

This chart reveals that sometimes the Chronicler referred only to a prophetic record and sometimes to royal annals. However, in every case of the latter, the Chronicler has modified the name of the annals to include the

name "Israel." This could refer to independent sources that bear these additional names, but the more probable answer is that the Chronicler wanted to
emphasize the place of "Israel" in God's plan and added this name to a
source that in 1 & 2 Kings did not have it.[29] The inclusion of Israel in the
Chronicler's scheme is an important theme in the work, usually noted by
scholars on other grounds (see below). This inclusion of Israel even in the
source citation formulas serves to make the point even more strongly.

It would appear, then, that the Chronicler's major sources were the
biblical books of 2 Samuel and 1 & 2 Kings, supplemented by smaller portions quoted from other biblical books (at least Isaiah, Jeremiah, Psalms,
Lamentations).[30] His genealogical information would have come from other
sources, and he had independent knowledge of—if not access to—various
prophetic records. But the major sources for his direct citations would appear to have been the biblical books just noted.

The citation of the prophetic records in relation to the royal annals
suggests that the Chronicler did not have an interest in these as independent records, but only as they were part of the received body of authoritative
Scripture. If that is so, this reinforces another point made below: that the
Chronicler had a very high view of Scripture, since it was primarily (or exclusively)[31] to Scripture that he made reference. We may also notice in connection with these prophetic records that the Chronicler only cites them
when he is referring to a good king of Judah, never when discussing a wicked king.[32] That may be his way of reinforcing the positive messages that the
prophets had to offer: that things would go well when the kings and the people turned to God rather than away from Him.

One final "source" deserves mention here. The remarkable hymn sung
on the day of dedication of the ark (1 Chron. 16:8–36) is composed of several sections found verbatim in the book of Psalms.

> 1 Chronicles 16:8–22 = Psalm 105:1–15
> 1 Chronicles 16:23–33 = Psalm 96:1–13
> 1 Chronicles 16:34 = Psalm 106:1
> 1 Chronicles 16:35–36 = Psalm 106:47–48

These relationships have suggested to many scholars that the Chronicler borrowed portions from the various psalms and composed his own

---

29. Indeed, the variant names may have been the Chronicler's way of referring to the canonical
books of 1 & 2 Kings, and not to any sources behind these (see below).
30. A convenient reference work listing the parallels in the books of Samuel, Kings, and Chronicles, along with other passages, is James D. Newsome, Jr., *A Synoptic Harmony of Samuel, Kings, and Chronicles.*
31. Williamson argues that "the Chronicler drew on *no* source other than Kings" (*1 and 2
Chronicles*, 18; italics added).
32. Williamson, *1 and 2 Chronicles*, 19.

hymn, claiming that it represented words actually sung by David. However, the Chronicler states, "That day David first committed to Asaph and his associates this psalm of thanks to the Lord" (v. 7), so it is equally as plausible to suggest that the words of this hymn were passed down over the centuries, used in certain psalms, and incorporated in their entirety by the Chronicler.[33]

THE CHRONICLER'S HERMENEUTICS

After the two questions of what were the sources the Chronicler used and how he referred to them are considered, the next logical question concerns how the Chronicler *used* these sources. As mentioned, roughly 50 percent of 1 & 2 Chronicles consists of verbatim reproduction of material from 2 Samuel, 1 & 2 Kings, and elsewhere. The answer to this question has important implications for how one understands the message of these books.

SOME SUGGESTED APPROACHES

In the past, 1 & 2 Chronicles have been disparaged as unimaginative history (since they copied so much from other sources) or, as noted above, "falsified" history (since so much is different in 1 & 2 Chronicles from its sources). As a result, the books of Chronicles have stood relatively neglected in the study of the Scriptures.

Several reasons have been proposed to account for the differences between 1 & 2 Chronicles and their sources. Some differences are merely the result of textual variations between the manuscripts the Chronicler used and the manuscripts the authors of 1 & 2 Samuel and 1 & 2 Kings used.[34]

Many scholars argue that the books of Chronicles are an independent work, written during the late OT period to tell of the history of Israel from its own, distinctive perspective.[35] Sometimes this has been called a "redactional" approach, namely, one in which the differences are accounted for by appeal to different literary development and different purposes.[36]

THE CHRONICLER AS EXEGETE

Other scholars (especially recently) argue that, rather than being a new, independent work, 1 & 2 Chronicles represent an interpretive effort, one that is attempting to interpret for its own day earlier authoritative Scrip-

---

33. For a full exploration of the issues surrounding this hymn, see Jonathan Boyd, "'Sing an Old Song to the Lord': First Chronicles 16:8–36, the Psalter, and the Chronicler's Historiography."
34. H. G. M. Williamson, "Introduction," in Martin Noth, *The Chronicler's History*, 17.
35. DeVries, *1 and 2 Chronicles*, 17–18; Tomotoshi Sugimoto, "Chronicles as Independent Literature," 61–74.
36. John H. Sailhamer, "1 Chronicles 21:1—A Study in Inter-Biblical Interpretation," 37.

tures. That is, the Chronicler sees himself as an *exegete* of his sources, not an independent historian or theologian.[37]

This approach captures some important truths about the relationship between 1 & 2 Chronicles and their sources. It is clear that, in many cases, the Chronicler's purpose is to expound upon (i.e., to interpret, or to "exegete") his source material. However, for this idea to be meaningful, we must understand the concept of exegesis in a much broader way than is usually understood. That is because of the large number of extensive additions the Chronicler makes to his sources. When he adds material that extends over several chapters (e.g., 1 Chronicles 22–29), the added material is "exegesis" of his sources only in the broadest sense.[38] Nevertheless, to understand the work in this way reveals exciting new truths in the texts of both 1 & 2 Chronicles and its sources, and helps to clear up many misunderstandings of the past.

THE CHRONICLER'S EXEGETICAL TECHNIQUES

Brevard Childs has grouped the exegetical techniques used by the Chronicler into four categories: harmonization, supplementation, typology, and coherence of action and effect.[39]

Harmonization. In a number of instances, the Chronicler adds or emphasizes material in order to harmonize texts in Samuel-Kings with the Pentateuch. For instance, Deuteronomy 10:8 specifies that the Levites are to carry the ark of the covenant. Yet, in the account in 2 Samuel 6 of the moving of the ark from Kiriath-Jearim to Jerusalem in David's day, we find no mention of the Levites at all. Thus, when the Chronicler recounts the same episode, we find that he specifically mentions the Levites as bearers of the ark (1 Chron. 15:26–27).[40] In some way, the Chronicler has independent knowledge of the Levites' participation in this event, and he highlights it, making sure that his hero David is shown doing things "by the book."

Or, when 2 Samuel tells of David's building an altar and his offerings to the Lord when he bought the threshing-floor of Araunah, we are told of

---

37. Childs, *IOTS*, 644–53; Williamson, *1 and 2 Chronicles*, 21–22; Sailhamer, "1 Chronicles 21:1"; see also Peter R. Ackroyd, "The Chronicler as Exegete."
38. It is such additions, as well as the many changes of material in parallel passages, that have convinced many scholars that this is a truly independent work.
39. Childs, *IOTS*, 647–53. Childs's fourth category may in fact be treated better as a "theme" of 1 & 2 Chronicles, and it is discussed at length in the subhead "Reward and Punishment" under "Theology of 1 & 2 Chronicles."
40. Childs mentions "15.1ff" as being the harmonizing text (*IOTS*, 648). However, strictly speaking, verses 1–24 are supplementation (Childs's second category), and verses 26 and 27 are the ones that function as harmonizations, since they add reference to the Levites and the ark in a closely parallel passage.

the oxen for the burnt offerings and fellowship offerings and of the threshing sledges and ox yokes for the wood (vv. 22, 25). In the parallel passage, the Chronicler adds reference to "the wheat for the grain offering" (1 Chron. 21:23). This is probably influenced by the instructions in Numbers 15:1–4, which mention that a grain offering is to be brought with any offering by fire.

Supplementation. The Chronicler often adds material as a supplement to his primary sources, possibly taken from other (noncanonical) sources that were nevertheless understood to be accurate and authoritative. Thus, for example, in the account of Hezekiah's reign (2 Chronicles 29–32; 2 Kings 18–20), the Chronicler adds in great detail the account of the celebration of the Passover and other reforms (2 Chron. 29:3–30:27). Or, when David had the ark brought to Jerusalem, 1 Chronicles 15:1–24 is all new material, and we find that it goes into great detail concerning David's ordering of the liturgical service. We also find several more references to the Levites carrying the ark (vv. 2, 13–15), which reinforce the harmonization effort we noted above.

Typology. Often the Chronicler describes and records characters and events in ways that recall earlier characters and events. One of the most studied in this regard is Solomon.[41] Many scholars have noted, for example, that the transfer of leadership from David to Solomon is described in ways that recall the transfer of leadership from Moses to Joshua. Some of the parallels are as follows:[42]

1. Moses and David are both disqualified from achieving their main goals— Moses of entering the land and David of building the Temple—and this is related to the appointment of their successors, who fulfill these goals (Deut. 1:37–38; 31:2–8; 1 Chron. 22:5–13; 28:2–8).
2. Parallels in genre and even phrases between Joshua's and Solomon's accessions. See such phrases as "Be strong and of good courage"; "Do not fear and do not be dismayed"; "The Lord your God is with you"; "He will never leave you nor forsake you"; and the stress on prospering through obeying the law (most of these are in 1 Chronicles 22 and 28, and echo phrases found in Joshua 1).
3. Both Moses and David announce their successors privately first (Deut. 1:23; 1 Chron. 22:6), then publicly (Deut. 31:7–8;[43] 1 Chron. 28:20).

41. The Chronicler's portrayals of Asa, Jehoshaphat, and Hezekiah also have been studied typologically: see R. B. Dillard, "The Reign of Asa (2 Chr 14–16)," 207–18; "The Chronicler's Jehoshaphat," 17–22; and "The Chronicler's Hezekiah," in his *2 Chronicles*, 226–29, and bibliographies therein.
42. E.g., Childs, *IOTS*, 651; Dillard, *2 Chronicles*, 3–4; Williamson, "The Accession of Solomon in the Books of Chronicles," 351–61, esp. pp. 351–56.
43. Dillard (*2 Chronicles*, 3) has Deuteronomy 31:2 here; 31:7–8 is more appropriate, however.

4. Both Joshua and Solomon enjoy the immediate and enthusiastic support of the people (Deut. 34:9; Josh. 1:16–18; 1 Chron. 29:23–24).

5. God "magnified"[44] both Joshua and Solomon (Josh 3:7; 4:14; 1 Chron. 29:25; 2 Chron. 1:1).

Not only is Solomon portrayed as a worthy successor to David in the same way that Joshua is to Moses, he is also portrayed as a "second David" in his own right.[45] This portrayal makes the point that, like David, Solomon too was chosen by God, designated as the king through whom the blessings would follow, and that he was even more blameless than David.

Furthermore, there are striking parallels between Solomon and his craftsman Huram-abi in their work on the Temple and Bezalel and his helper Oholiab in their work on the Tabernacle.[46] These parallels show Solomon in the important role as the wise, skilled, and faithful builder of the Temple.

These typologies are not merely inventions by the Chronicler. Rather, his choice of information to communicate and the manner in which he communicates it, reveal a conscious patterning of later figures after earlier ones. This helps him to make the important point that these righteous kings were doing things right, that they were faithful to God and were blessed by God in ways similar to these earlier men, who were paradigms of virtue.

Interbiblical interpretation. The above exegetical techniques described by Childs and others often range far and wide in drawing out the parallels between persons or events in 1 & 2 Chronicles and such persons or events in earlier materials. Related to these are approaches that more closely stay with the parallel texts at hand and help to interpret via small, subtle, but important shifts of wording.[47]

A recent proposal concerning the difficult passage in 1 Chronicles 21:1 illustrates this close, "interbiblical" interpretive approach.[48] This passage and its parallel in 2 Samuel 24 read in the NIV as follows:[49]

---

44. The Hebrew is the piel of the root *GDL* in all four cases.
45. For details, see R. Braun, "Solomonic Apologetic in Chronicles," 503–16, esp. 506–14; Dillard, *2 Chronicles*, 2–3.
46. For details, see Dillard, "The Chronicler's Solomon," 296–99; *2 Chronicles*, 4–5.
47. These approaches are seen in the body of most recent commentaries on 1 & 2 Chronicles. See especially those by Williamson, Braun, and Dillard. The programmatic work on the exegetical approach in general is Thomas Willi's *Die Chronik als Auslegung* ["The Chronicles as Exegesis"].
48. John Sailhamer, *First and Second Chronicles*, 53; and "1 Chronicles 21:1—A Study in Inter-Biblical Interpretation," 33–48.
49. The line breaks are artificially added here to show the parallels between corresponding portions of the two verses.

Satan rose up
against Israel
and incited David
to take a census of Israel.

1 Chron. 21:1

Again the anger of the Lord burned
against Israel,
and he incited David
against them, saying,
"Go and take a census of Israel and Judah.

2 Sam. 24:1

Most traditional interpreters reconcile the differences in the first line by speaking of God's permissive will, which permits Satan free rein to tempt David, or by seeing Satan as God's instrument for tempting David.[50] Others see Satan's presence here as reflective of "the commonly held piety of the day, which hesitated to speak of God as the direct cause of evil."[51]

However, close exegetical attention to the terminology used here shows that the Chronicler was actually trying to explain how the burning of the Lord's anger incited David to number the people. Almost all scholars have noted that the term translated "Satan" is in fact a generic noun (*sāṭān*) meaning "adversary." Of the twenty-seven occurrences of the term, seventeen times (all in Job 1–2; Zech. 3:1–2) it occurs with the definite article ("*the* adversary"), referring to one specific adversary, who in these cases is a celestial being. As such, it is legitimately rendered as a proper name (Satan). However, the remaining ten occurrences of the term *sāṭān* (Num. 22:22, 32; 1 Sam. 29:4; 2 Sam. 19:22 [MT 23]; 1 Kings 5:4 [MT 18]; 11:14, 23, 25; 1 Chron. 21:1; Ps. 109:6) do not have the definite article. In these cases, the translation is usually "an adversary."

The term in 1 Chronicles 21:1 occurs without the article; thus, for consistency, it should more properly be rendered "an adversary." However, every major English Bible version and almost every commentator—on essentially groundless assumptions that *sāṭān* (without the definite article) is a proper name—renders it as "Satan" in this verse, too. Consistency with the linguistic pattern of usage, however, would demand a translation of "an adversary."

The implications of this can be seen when the term *adversary* is surveyed in the sources available to the Chronicler. These almost always occur in contexts where enemies stand up against God's people to pose a military threat. Note especially the following references:

50. E.g., C. F. Keil, *The Second Book of Samuel*, 503; Walter C. Kaiser, Jr., *Hard Sayings of the Old Testament*, 129–32.
51. Roddy Braun, *1 Chronicles*, 217.

1 Kings 11:14:	"Then the Lord raised up against Solomon an *adversary*, Hadad the Edomite."
1 Kings 11:23:	"And God raised up against Solomon another *adversary*, Rezon son of Eliada."
1 Kings 11:25:	"Rezon was Israel's *adversary* as long as Solomon lived."

The Chronicler's method in referring to a human "adversary" (not Satan) inciting David to number the people—substituting it for "the anger of the Lord" in 2 Samuel 24:1—becomes clear when it is remembered that often the Lord's anger burning against a people will result in an enemy (i.e., an adversary) rising up against them (Num. 22:22; Judg. 2:14, 20; 3:8; 10:7; 2 Kings 13:3; 23:26). See especially the following references (as they appear in the NASB):[52]

Judges 2:14:	"So the anger of the Lord burned against Israel, and He gave them into the hands of plunderers . . . and He sold them into the hands of their enemies around them."
Judges 3:8:	"Then the anger of the Lord was kindled against Israel, so that He sold them into the hands of Cushan-Rishathaim, king of Mesopotamia."
Judges 10:7:	"And the anger of the Lord burned against Israel, and He sold them into the hands of Philistines, and into the hands of the sons of the Ammonites."
2 Kings 13:3:	"So the anger of the Lord was kindled against Israel, and He gave them continually into the hand of Hazael king of Syria, and into the hand of Ben-hadad the son of Hazael."

Note especially the following reference, where the burning of the Lord's anger and His standing as an adversary are explicitly linked: "But God was angry because [Balaam] was going, and the angel of the Lord took his stand in the way as an adversary against him" (Num. 22:22).

---

52. In each case, the Hebrew root *HRR* is used; it is translated as "burned," "was kindled," or "was angry" in the NASB.

Thus, we see that, in the narrative texts of the Pentateuch and Former Prophets, when God's anger burned against a people, He gave them over to an adversary of some type. The Chronicler, then, merely was reading the reference in 2 Samuel 24:1 in that light and substituted "an adversary rose up" for "Again the anger of the Lord burned" in his source. A final note should be made concerning the third line of 2 Samuel 24:1: the NASB is more correct than the NIV here when it states that "it incited David against them." That is, "it" refers to the Lord's burning anger—and, by extension, to the adversary that appeared to threaten David—not to the Lord Himself.

Thus, we can render the two verses in question as follows:

> An adversary rose up
> against Israel
> and incited David
> to take a census of Israel.
>
> 1 Chron. 21:1

> Again the anger of the Lord burned
> against Israel,
> and it[53] incited David
> against them, saying,
> "Go and take a census of Israel and Judah."
>
> 2 Sam. 24:1

We have here, then, a fine illustration of how the Chronicler was "exegeting," i.e., explaining/clarifying, the text that he was dealing with and doing so using understandings of terms within the larger confines of that very text. In the process, a classic "problem text" is explained in a simple, straightforward manner.

Summary. All of the above methods could be classified as exegetical in the broadest sense. However, we should note that some scholars understand *exegesis* in a more limited sense and refer, for example, to what Childs calls "typology" as "paradigmatic patterning." This is seen as something different from pure exegesis.[54] Regardless of the terminology used, however, what remains clear is the extent to which the Chronicler attempted to use his canonical and noncanonical sources, either in clarifying their meanings in various ways or in modeling people or events in his work after earlier people or events. The Chronicler's work, then, far from being an inferior, unimaginative, or erroneous history of Israel and Judah, displays a

---

53. I.e., the appearance of an enemy, brought on by the Lord's anger, who nonetheless remains unidentified in the text.
54. E.g., Williamson, *1 and 2 Chronicles*, 22–23.

masterful command of earlier canonical and noncanonical material, used to bring their message alive for his own—later—time.

THE GENEALOGIES IN 1 CHRONICLES 1–9

The book of 1 Chronicles opens with the most extensive genealogical section in the Bible, covering nine chapters. The genealogies here cover the entire range of OT history: they begin in chapter 1 with Adam and move into the postexilic community in chapter 9. The genealogies end with Saul's line, who is the subject of chapter 10. The shaping of these genealogies highlights the interest in Judah, the Davidic dynasty, and the institution by David of centralized worship at Jerusalem and the Temple. Yet, the fact that they begin with Adam, rather than, say, Abraham or Jacob, indicates that the Chronicler saw that redemption was not merely limited to the house of David or to Judah or even to Israel as a whole; rather, ultimately, it was available to the entire human race.

Despite his prominence in the books, David per se is not even the object: the Davidic genealogy in chapter 3 takes us beyond the kings of Judah into the Exile and postexilic period (in 3:19–24). This makes the point that God's faithfulness is the real point at issue. The pale shadow that was the postexilic Davidic "dynasty" was a far cry from the splendor of the preexilic kingdom, yet the Davidic descendants were still alive and accounted for, and God's promises still obtained.

INTRODUCTION TO GENEALOGIES

Terminology. The genealogies in 1 Chronicles 1–9[55] are very complex, the most complex found anywhere in the Bible.[56] In general (here and elsewhere), genealogies can be *broad* (e.g., "These are the sons of Israel: Reuben, Simeon, Levi, Judah . . ."—1 Chron. 2:1) or *deep* ("The sons of Solomon: Rehoboam, Abijah his son, Asa his son . . ."—3:10). If a genealogy is only deep, it is called *linear.* The most common depth for linear genealogies is four to six generations; the minimum is obviously two generations, and they rarely extend beyond ten to twelve generations. If a genealogy displays breadth as well as depth, it is called a *segmented* genealogy. If the genealogy proceeds from parent to child, it is called *descending* (e.g., 9:39–44; see also Matthew's genealogy of Jesus in Matt. 1:1–16);

55. A good introduction to the genealogies in 1 Chronicles is Braun, *1 Chronicles*, 1–12. In more depth, see M. D. Johnson, *The Purpose of the Biblical Genealogies*, 37–82; W. L. Osborne, *The Genealogies of 1 Chronicles 1–9.* A good introduction to genealogies in general is R. K. Harrison, *ISBE* 2, s.v. "Genealogy."
56. I am indebted in this section mainly to Braun (*1 Chronicles*, 1–3), for most of the next few paragraphs, who derives much of his presentation from Robert R. Wilson, *Genealogy and History in the Biblical World.*

if it proceeds from child to parent, it is called *ascending* (e.g., 1 Chron. 9:14–16; see Luke's genealogy of Jesus in Luke 3:23–37).

Linear and segmented genealogies have very different functions. The *linear genealogy* has as its object the legitimization of the last-named person(s) in the list. The lists of kings in the Bible and in the ancient Near East are good examples of this, as is Moses' and Aaron's genealogy in Exodus 6:14–26.

The *segmented genealogy* primarily attempts to show the relationships existing among those listed, and they typically will not point toward one individual per se. The emphasis here is on inclusivity. (Note that the genealogy of Moses and Aaron just mentioned begins in a segmented fashion [Ex. 6:14–16], before moving into its true function, a linear one, of showing the heritage of these two men.) In both types of genealogy, however, the emphasis is upon "kinship relations between various individuals and groups."[57]

Purposes of genealogies. M. D. Johnson identifies nine purposes for the OT genealogies:[58]

1. To demonstrate existing relationships between Israel and neighboring tribes by tracing lines back to common ancestors. This shows at one and the same time a degree of kinship and also a degree of distinction between Israel and its neighbors. Examples include the descendants of Lot (Gen. 19:36–38), Nahor (22:20–24), Keturah (25:1–6), Ishmael (25:12–16), and Esau (chap. 36).

2. To bring together previously "isolated" (*sic*) elements "concerning Israelite origins by the creation of a coherent and inclusive genealogical system."[59] A good example of this, according to Johnson, is the Genesis "Toledoth book."[60]

3. To bridge gaps in the narrative records. Good examples are in Genesis 5 and 11, and Ruth 4:18–22. (These are the ancient literary equivalents to the "fast-forward" function on modern videocassette recorders.)

4. To perform a limited chronological function, such as establishing dates for the Flood (Genesis 5) or the birth of Abraham (chap. 11), or dividing all of preexilic history into half (by assigning twelve priests from the Exo-

57. Braun, *1 Chronicles*, 2.
58. Johnson, *Purpose of the Biblical Genealogies*, 77–82.
59. Ibid., 78. On this point, Johnson reveals a distrust (along with many biblical scholars) that the relationships claimed in the genealogies were in fact true kinship relationships; he (and others) would claim that many such relationships are fictional creations in service of a larger sociological purpose—that of bringing together these unrelated elements.
60. On this "Toledoth" theory, see Herbert Wolf, *An Introduction to the Old Testament Pentateuch*, 56–57.

dus to Solomon's Temple and twelve from the Temple to the Exile in 1 Chronicles 5:27–41 (Eng. 6:1–15). However, since many genealogies were selective, this is only a rough tool for chronological reckoning.[61]

5. To perform a military function of numbering the warriors. A good example is Numbers 26. (See especially v. 2: "Take a census of the whole Israelite community by families—all those twenty years old or more who are able to serve in the army of Israel.")

6. To legitimate individuals (or to enhance their statures). A good example is the genealogy of Moses and Aaron in Exodus 6:14–26, as noted above.

7. To establish and preserve the homogeneity of the Jewish community, found only in lists in Ezra-Nehemiah (and in rabbinic tradition).

8. To demonstrate the continuity of the people of God through great calamity (i.e., that they survived, despite exile). Good examples of this are found in both the genealogical lists in 1 & 2 Chronicles and Ezra-Nehemiah.

9. To express a "priestly" concern for order and arrangement, and the conviction that "the course of history is governed and ordered according to a pre-arranged plan."[62]

Selectivity of genealogies. As just noted, biblical genealogies are not always exhaustive or all-inclusive. Exodus 6:14–26 presents a five-generation genealogy of Moses and Aaron whose function is to legitimate Moses and Aaron in the new roles and duties they are about to assume in leading the Israelites.

However, there is a problem of chronology here. There are only five generations in this genealogy—Jacob (v. 14); Levi (v. 16); Kohath (v. 16); Amram (v. 18); Moses and Aaron (v. 20)—whereas we know from 1 Chronicles 7:23–27 that there were at least ten generations from Joseph to Joshua, not five. We also know that the period of slavery in Egypt was to be 400 years (Gen. 15:13) or 430 years (Ex. 12:40–41), too long for a normal span of five generations. The answer as to why the Exodus 6 genealogy is so short is that it is selective, since it has a limited purpose—that of legitimating Moses and Aaron—and is not concerned with being a comprehensive genealogy at all (note even that only the three oldest sons of Jacob are mentioned).[63]

61. See "Selectivity of genealogies" below, and Wolf, *An Introduction to the Old Testament Pentateuch*, 96–97.

62. Johnson, *Purpose of the Biblical Genealogies*, 81.

63. On selectivity in genealogies, see K. A. Kitchen, *Ancient Orient and Old Testament*, 35–41, 54–55; and *The Bible in Its World*, 31–34; R. K. Harrison, *Introduction*, 145–52; and *ISBE* 2, s.v. "Genealogy"; A. R. Millard, *NBD*, s.v. "Genealogy."

THE GENEALOGIES OUTLINED

The following outline shows the progress of the genealogies in these chapters:

Introduction
    1:1–2:2   Adam to Israel

Judah (Southern Tribes)
    2:3–55   Judah—A
    3:1–24   David
    4:1–23   Judah—B
    4:24–43   Simeon[64]

Eastern Tribes
    5:1–10   Reuben
    5:11–17   Gad
    5:18–23   Transjordan Tribes (narrative)
    5:23–26   East Manasseh

Levi
    6:1–15 [MT 5:27–41]   High Priests
    6:16–30 [MT 1–15]   Levites
    6:31–53 [MT 16–38]   Levites and Priests appointed by David
    6:54–81 [MT 39–66]   Levitical Cities

Northern Tribes
    7:1–5   Issachar
    7:6–12   Benjamin—A
    7:13   Naphtali
    7:14–19   East and West Manasseh[65]
    7:20–29   Ephraim
    7:30–40   Asher
    8:1–40; 9:1a   Benjamin—B

Postscript
    9:1b–34   Postexilic Jerusalem
    9:35–44   The Line of Saul

64. Simeon is undoubtedly included here because it was assimilated into Judah's territory: Joshua 19:1b states that "[Simeon's] inheritance lay within the territory of Judah."
65. This is a very complicated list. Keil (*The Books of the Chronicles*, 135) thinks it is only of West Manasseh, but it devotes considerable attention to Machir and Gilead (vv. 14–17), which were east of the Jordan.

The introductory section (chap. 1) moves quickly from Adam to Jacob ("Israel"), then the body of the genealogical section (chaps. 2–8) focuses in depth upon Jacob's descendants, mostly from the preexilic period, and particularly from the time of David. It begins with a rapid survey of twelve generations between Judah and David (2:3–15), then moves to Davidic (3:1–24) and Judahite (4:1–23) genealogies proper before proceeding to list the other Israelite tribes, with an eye to showing that they all were a legitimate and loyal part of a united Israel. David, as the first king of a truly united Israel, and with whom the major narrative portions following the genealogies are preoccupied, is constantly in the background—and sometimes explicitly mentioned—even in these lists. The next-to-last section (9:1–34) is of the postexilic Jerusalem community, particularly those involved in the Temple service that David had inaugurated. The lists here also serve to emphasize the continuity between the postexilic people of God and preexilic "Israel."[66] The final section (9:35–44) shows Saul's line, since Saul is the subject of chapter 10.

Note that no genealogy is given at all for Dan and Zebulun and that Naphtali is only mentioned in one verse. Note also that only for the royal house of David (3:1–24) and the high-priestly line of Eleazar (6:4–15) does the genealogy reach down to the Exile or beyond; all the others are relatively short. This reinforces the judgment, made on other grounds as well, that David and priestly concerns figure prominently in the Chronicler's estimation.

THEOLOGY OF 1 & 2 CHRONICLES

THE UNITY OF GOD'S PEOPLE: ALL ISRAEL

The author of 1 & 2 Chronicles has a concern to show that God's people are still a unity, even in his own day, which is many decades after the Exile of Judah and several centuries after the fall and disappearance of the northern kingdom of Israel. Though he does not chronicle the events or the fate of the northern kingdom per se, he does show a concern to demonstrate that "all Israel" still is a viable entity.[67]

Several factors indicate this feeling that the north must be included:[68]

---

66. Williamson, *1 and 2 Chronicles*, 38 (p. 38 is transposed with p. 2 in early editions); and *Israel in the Books of Chronicles*, 87–140; Johnson, *Purpose of the Biblical Genealogies*, 80.
67. See especially Johnson, *Purpose of the Biblical Genealogies*, 47–55; Williamson, *Israel in the Books of Chronicles*, 87–140; R. L. Braun, "A Reconsideration of the Chronicler's Attitude Toward the North," 59–62; Japhet, *The Ideology of the Book of Chronicles*, 267–351.
68. For this list, see Johnson, *Purpose of the Biblical Genealogies*, 48–49; for more depth, see Williamson, *Israel in the Books of Chronicles*, 87–140.

1. "All Israel" and "all the elders of Israel" came to anoint David as king at Hebron (1 Chron. 11:3, 4, 10); 1 Chronicles omits any reference to David's anointing at Hebron over only Judah (which we find in 2 Sam. 2:1–4).

2. Great numbers from all twelve tribes (not just Judah) are mentioned as having come for this purpose (1 Chron. 12:23–27), and they were united in purpose in making David king (12:38).

3. The priests and Levites who "were in all Israel" defected to Judah and Jerusalem in the days of Jeroboam I, because of religious intolerance in the north (2 Chron. 11:13–14).

4. Much later, great numbers deserted from Ephraim, Manasseh, and Simeon to Asa, when "they saw that the Lord his God was with him" (15:8–9). Note that Simeon is actually (historically) an extinct tribe by this time; the point is that Simeon is very much "alive" in the Chronicler's mind (see also factor 7 on 2 Chron. 34:6–7).

5. Jehoshaphat gathered people "from Beersheba to the hill country of Ephraim and turned them back to the Lord, the God of their fathers" (19:4). Note that Jehoshaphat lived in Jerusalem (v. 4) and that he appointed Levites and priests and "heads of Israelite families" to judge in Jerusalem (19:8).

6. Hezekiah invited people from "all Israel and Judah," including Ephraim and Manasseh, as far as Zebulun, to come to Jerusalem to celebrate the Passover (30:1, 6, 10). Some came from several of the northern tribes: Asher, Manasseh, Zebulun (30:11), and Ephraim, Manasseh, Issachar, and Zebulun (30:18). These then went throughout "all Judah and Benjamin and in Ephraim and Manasseh" (i.e., the two major tribes of north and south) to destroy pagan cult sites and apparatus (31:1).

7. Josiah's reform extended to "the towns of Manasseh, Ephraim, and Simeon, and as far as Naphtali . . . throughout all the land of Israel" (34:6–7 RSV). Note that the northern kingdom was extinct by now and that Simeon had been extinct for a longer period of time. The Temple was repaired with monies collected "from the people of Manasseh, Ephraim and the entire remnant of Israel and from all the people of Judah and Benjamin and the inhabitants of Jerusalem" (34:9).

A look at the specific phrase "all Israel" and how the Chronicler used it relative to his sources in 2 Samuel and 1 & 2 Kings is instructive in showing us this interest. The following chart[69] illustrates the Chronicler's use of this phrase:

Uses of the Phrase "all Israel" in 1 & 2 Chronicles

SAME IN CHRONICLES AS IN SOURCES	CHANGED IN CHRONICLES	NEW IN CHRONICLES
1 Chronicles	1 Chronicles	1 Chronicles
18:14	11:1	9:1
19:17	11:4	11:10
	13:5	12:38 [MT 39]
	13:6	15:3
	13:8	28:4
	14:8	28:8
	15:28	29:21
	21:4	29:23
	21:5	29:25
		29:26
2 Chronicles	2 Chronicles	2 Chronicles
7:8	10:3	1:2a
9:30	10:16b	1:2b
10:1	11:3	7:6
10:16a		11:13
		12:1
		13:4
		13:15
		29:24a
		29:24b
		30:1
		31:1
		35:3

The term *all Israel* occurs at least 105 times in biblical Hebrew. Almost 40 percent of these references occur in 1 & 2 Chronicles: forty times! This statistic alone shows the prominence of this idea in the two books.

---

69. This list contains forty references. According to Johnson (*Purpose of the Biblical Genealogies*, 47), the phrase occurs thirty-four times in 1 & 2 Chronicles, and the list in Abraham Even-Shoshan (*A New Concordance of the Bible*, 535) also includes thirty-four occurrences. The additional references are to occurrences of the phrase "all Israel" with an additional Hebrew particle attached to the word (*'et-kol-yiśrā'ēl* or *běkol-yiśrā'ēl* or *lěkol-yiśrā'ēl*). The NIV renders the Hebrew phrase as "all Israel" in only thirty-two cases.

In addition, in about half as many cases, we find a construct phrase of the following type: "all the elders of Israel," "all the congregations of Israel," "all the tribes of Israel," "all the lands of Israel," "all the kings of Israel," and so on.[70]

An even more revealing statistic comes from noticing that in only six cases does the Chronicler use the phrase exactly as it appears in his sources. In twelve cases the Chronicler, in using the phrase "all Israel," changes his underlying source slightly. The underlying phrase usually is something such as "Israel" or "all the tribes of Israel," which the Chronicler has changed to the more standardized "all Israel." In twenty-two cases, the Chronicler uses the phrase on his own, so to speak; it comes in material he has added, that is not found in 2 Samuel or 1 & 2 Kings. Sometimes, it is only a small insertion (of a verse or even a phrase), and the phrase "all Israel" is found within the insertion. The data may be summarized as follows:

> No change from sources: 6 times
> Change to "all Israel": 12 times
> New in 1 & 2 Chronicles: 22 times.

Strikingly, fourteen of the references to "all Israel" come in 2 Chronicles 10–36, after the death of Solomon, when "Israel" was no longer a unified entity. Even more strikingly, five references come in chaps. 29–36, after the fall of the northern kingdom, when there was no political entity called "Israel" at all. This shows that the term's use is more than merely accidental in referring to the united kingdom; it is an integral part of the Chronicler's vision of things. He conceived of "Israel" as an indivisible unity, which was God's people in its entirety, and one that still had a place in God's plans for the future.

The Chronicler reminds us that the Davidic kingdom embraced all twelve tribes, and he regularly shows the remnant from the north remaining loyal to the Davidic king and to the Jerusalem cult. Even extinct tribes, such as Simeon, Benjamin, and all northern tribes after the fall of the north, are remembered. Thus, we see that one of the Chronicler's burdens was to keep the memory of "all Israel" alive, even if it did not exist as a socio-political reality in his day. This echoes some of the prophets' insistence upon a future restoration of the entire nation.

DAVIDIC KINGSHIP

The figure of David dominates 1 & 2 Chronicles.[71] Indeed, almost all scholars agree that the books of Chronicles have David and the Davidic dy-

---

70. Johnson, *Purpose of the Biblical Genealogies*, 47–48.
71. On David as historical individual and as theological symbol, see David M. Howard, Jr., *ABD* 2, s.v. "David."

nasty as a central theme or motif.[72] Typical is R. North's comment in a section entitled "Davidism"—"The person and dynasty of David forms the heartbeat of all the Chronicler's theology"[73]—or that of P. R. Ackroyd:

> The centrality of the David material . . . appears from 1 Chron. 10 to 2 Chron. 9 explicitly, and implicitly also to the end of 2 Chron. . . . The elaboration of the Davidic genealogical material [1 Chronicles 1–9] . . . would seem to point to an even greater concern with the Davidic ideal.[74]

As we have noted above, the genealogies in 1 Chronicles 1–9 highlight David and his line. Following this, David himself is the focus of the remainder of 1 Chronicles (chaps. 10–29) and his son Solomon of the first part of 2 Chronicles (chaps. 1–9). The remainder of the book focuses on the fortunes of the kingdom of Judah, the heir of the promises of the Davidic Covenant (chaps. 10–36). In particular, the importance of David and Solomon as ones who established the Temple and the true religious service in Jerusalem is an important theme in 1 & 2 Chronicles. David and Solomon were both chosen by God as His royal representatives in Israel,[75] as were their descendants. The promises to David and Solomon were in perpetuity, and the work ends with a clear note of hope (2 Chron. 36:22–23), introducing the reestablishment of the centralized worship in Jerusalem that David and Solomon had initiated.

Much of 1 Chronicles parallels the accounts in 1 & 2 Samuel, but it has its own selective omissions and additions, and its own distinctive slant. Specifically, 1 Chronicles omits the entire story of David's rise to power (1 Sam. 16–2 Sam. 5), except for a cursory look at Saul (1 Chronicles 10), the list of David's sons (2 Sam. 3:1–4), his anointing at Hebron (11:1–3), and his capture of Jerusalem (11:4–9). Most of the material related to his consolidation of power is included (chaps. 5–8), but almost all of the story of his decline (2 Sam. 9–1 Kings 2) is missing (including the story of his sins related to Bathsheba), except for his Ammonite war (2 Sam. 19:1–20:3) and some of the material from the Samuel "Appendix" (chaps. 21–24).

72. The following are representative: A. C. Welch, *The Work of the Chronicler*; D. N. Freedman, "The Chronicler's Purpose," 436–42; R. North, "Theology of the Chronicler," 369–81; P. R. Ackroyd, "The Theology of the Chronicler," 101–16; H. G. M. Williamson, "Eschatology in Chronicles," 115–54; and *1 and 2 Chronicles*; Braun, *1 Chronicles*.
73. North, "Theology of the Chronicler," 376.
74. Ackroyd, "Theology of the Chronicler," 112.
75. On the importance of Solomon along with David in 1 & 2 Chronicles, see R. L. Braun, "Solomonic Apologetic in Chronicles," 503–16; and "Solomon, the Chosen Temple Builder: The Significance of 1 Chronicles 22, 28, and 29 for the Theology of Chronicles," 581–90; Dillard, "The Chronicler's Solomon," 289–300.

New information about David. First Chronicles does provide us with some significant, new information concerning David not found elsewhere. Significant additions include an expanded listing of David's supporters (chap. 12); an extended psalm (16:4–42); and—in one of the most extended sections of new material in either 1 or 2 Chronicles—details of David's preparations for building of the Temple; Levitical and priestly responsibilities; instructions for musicians, gatekeepers, keepers of the treasuries, officers, judges, and other officials; and David's last words to Solomon and the people, in which he encouraged them particularly in building the Temple and in following their God (22:2–29:22a).

The picture of David that emerges in 1 Chronicles is one of a true "man after God's own heart" (cf. 1 Sam. 13:14; Acts 13:22). His extended flight from Saul, and his sins and his difficulties with his household after that, all are omitted, presumably because they would detract from the picture of David that the Chronicler desired to present. The Chronicler emphasized, rather, David's devotion to God, especially as expressed through his preparations for the future Temple and everything associated with it, and his place as God's favored king, the head of the Judahite (and messianic) dynasty. The notice of his death shows him to have had a full, honorable, and honored life (1 Chron. 29:28, 30).

The Davidic Covenant. Of central importance to any consideration of Davidic kingship is 1 Chronicles 17, which tells of the important Davidic Covenant. This chapter's parallel in 2 Samuel 7 has aptly been called "the theological highlight of the Books of Samuel . . . if not of the Deuteronomistic History as a whole,"[76] because of its significant content and its importance in later texts. As noted above, in the discussion of 2 Samuel 7, the Davidic Covenant forms the basis for the rich theology of messianic kingship that arises more clearly in later OT (and NT) texts. (See chapter 5 for a broad discussion of the terms and importance of the covenant in the OT.)

The chapter is essentially parallel with 2 Samuel 7.[77] Mostly, 1 Chronicles omits small phrases, the net effect of which is to strip the account of minor matters extraneous to the author's purposes. See, e.g., the omission in 1 Chronicles 17:1 of the matter of "rest" (a recurring theme in Joshua–2 Kings) from 2 Samuel 7:1 or the change from "your offspring after you, who shall come forth from your body" (2 Sam. 7:12) to "your offspring after you, one of your own sons" (1 Chron. 17:11). The wording change to "sons" emphasizes David's lineage, which of course is a major concern in Chronicles. The major omission of significance is in verse 13, where the following clause about chastening—found in 2 Samuel 7:14—is omitted: "When he commits iniquity, I will chasten him with the rod of men, with the stripes of the sons of men."

76. A. A. Anderson, *2 Samuel*, 112.
77. See the parallel layout in Newsome, *Synoptic Harmony*, 37–40.

As we noted in the discussion of 2 Samuel 7, the question of conditionality or unconditionality of the Davidic Covenant is the subject of much debate. The clause about chastening in 2 Samuel 7:14 seems to give it a conditional aspect. However, in 1 Chronicles 17, the emphasis is clearly upon its unconditionality, since this clause is omitted. Williamson notes that many later references in 1 & 2 Chronicles (e.g., 1 Chron. 22:6–10; 28:2–10; 2 Chron. 6:15–17; 7:17–18) emphasize the "eternal" aspect of the covenant, despite various conditional tendencies there and in the texts in 2 Samuel and 1 & 2 Kings underlying them. Also, other references show that the Chronicler did indeed regard the dynasty as eternally established (2 Chron. 13:5; 21:7; 23:3).[78]

Eschatology in 1 & 2 Chronicles. Many scholars question whether indeed the Chronicler felt that the Davidic dynasty had a place in the future plans of God for Israel or whether its importance in 1 & 2 Chronicles was limited to the age of the monarchies. Did the Chronicler have a "theocratic" or an "eschatological" perspective?[79] If his perspective was theocratic, he would have seen the Davidic dynasty as having failed (by the time of the Chronicler), and thus of no abiding significance for the future, except in the roles of David and Solomon as ones who established the religious service and Temple worship, which were now to be regarded as the true expressions of God's rule. For most scholars who see the Chronicler as taking this position, the present order—i.e., the end of the fifth century B.C., after the Ezra-Nehemiah reforms, when the Temple and the religious service were now well established—represented the culmination of past history and prophecy. An earthly king or kingdom was of no further value, since these had exhausted their usefulness in establishing the religious service.

If the Chronicler had an eschatological perspective, he would have seen the Davidic dynasty as continuing beyond his own time, with an abiding significance in God's rule. In this understanding, the promises about the perpetuity of the dynasty were still in effect in the Chronicler's time, despite its absence from the political scene at the time. Most scholars who see the Chronicler as taking this position speak of a "Davidic messianism," the expectation that one day in the future a Davidic descendant would rise to reestablish the kingdom.

In light of the plainly eschatological views of the Davidic line elsewhere in the Bible—especially in the prophetic corpus, the Psalms, and the

78. Williamson, *1 and 2 Chronicles*, 133–34. See further his "Eschatology in Chronicles," 115–54; and "The Dynastic Oracle in the Books of Chronicles," 305–18. See also the references in n. 82 below.

79. The debate may be entered via J. D. Newsome, Jr., "Toward a New Understanding of the Chronicler and His Purposes," 201–17; Williamson, "Eschatology in Chronicles"; Magne Saebø, "Messianism in Chronicles?" 85–109; W. J. Dumbrell, "The Purpose of the Books of Chronicles," 257–66; J. G. McConville, "Ezra-Nehemiah and the Fulfillment of Prophecy," 205–24.

NT—it is appropriate to ask whether the books of Chronicles are outside the mainstream of biblical thought in this matter. A majority of scholars would affirm that these two books are indeed out of step, based on what they perceive as a relatively closed view of the future in the books.[80]

Many scholars, however, have argued convincingly that the Chronicler was indeed at least somewhat eschatological in outlook.[81] First, it is difficult to avoid the conclusion that the Chronicler saw the Davidic dynasty as a perpetual one, given the consistent descriptions of it as "forever."[82] Second, several references equate the earthly throne with God's throne: (1) Second Chronicles 13:8, which refers to "the kingdom of the Lord in the hands of the sons of David," is a very important reference, since it asserts that God's kingdom—about which there is no question as to its permanence—is now expressed on earth via the Davidic dynasty in Israel. The permanence of the latter is indicated in verse 5, with the reference to the covenant of salt, which was an eternal covenant (see also Num. 18:19). (2) First Chronicles 28:5 mentions a similar idea, that of Solomon sitting on "the throne of the kingdom of the Lord over Israel." (3) First Chronicles 29:23 also states this thought: "Solomon sat on the throne of the Lord as king in place of his father David" (see also 2 Chron. 9:8).

Although to say he lacks the great eschatological vision found especially in the prophets and the NT is not to say that the Chronicler was closed to the future—even a future in which the Davidic dynasty figured in some way. That his vision of the reestablishment of this dynasty may have been more limited than that of some writers does not negate his having such a vision. After all, this dynasty was not important for its own sake; it was important as the symbol of the kingdom of God (see, e.g., 1 Chron. 17:14; 28:5; 29:11–12, 23; 2 Chron. 9:8).[83]

---

80. See Williamson ("Eschatology in Chronicles," 116–20) for a review of these.
81. See Williamson ("Eschatology in Chronicles," 120–33) for a review of these, and pp. 133–54 for his own argument that there was indeed an eschatological outlook in 1 & 2 Chronicles. See also his "The Dynastic Oracle in the Books of Chronicles," in which he develops the argument more fully; and Martin Selman, "The Kingdom of God in the Old Testament," 163–71; Saebø, "Messianism in Chronicles?"; Japhet, *Ideology of the Book of Chronicles*, 493–504.
82. See 1 Chronicles 17:12, 14, 17, 23, 24, 27; 22:10; 28:4, 7, 8; 2 Chronicles 9:8; 13:5, 8; 21:7. For a discussion of the Hebrew phrase in most of these references ('ad-'ôlām), see D. M. Howard, Jr., "The Case for Kingship in the Old Testament Narrative Books and the Psalms," 29 n. 38.
83. See Williamson ("Eschatology in Chronicles," 133–54) for extended support. See also W. C. Kaiser, Jr., *Toward an Old Testament Theology*, 258–61; Sailhamer, *First and Second Chronicles*, 11, 32–33, 66–68; Dillard, *2 Chronicles*, 72, 108, 161.

THE TEMPLE AND WORSHIP

The Temple and the rituals of worship surrounding it are prominent in 1 & 2 Chronicles.[84] The importance of the Temple is that it symbolizes God's presence with His people. It is modeled after the Tabernacle, which also is a symbol of God's presence. Indeed, the word for "Tabernacle" is *miškān*, which means "dwelling place."[85]

The Temple was closely linked with concern for the city in which it stood: Jerusalem. Jerusalem was the capital, the center, the focus of all of the land of Israel and Judah. It was God's dwelling place (1 Chron. 23:25), and it was the sole legitimate place of worship (2 Chron. 6:6; 33:7; see also 30:3, 11; 36:14).

The Temple was to be built according to the pattern given to David (1 Chron. 28:11–21), which was modeled after the pattern of the Tabernacle. The Tabernacle's pattern had been shown to Moses by God on the mountain (Ex. 25:9, 40; cf. also Num. 8:4). Hebrews 8:5 quotes from Exodus 25:40, also mentioning the "pattern" (*túpon*). The pattern (or "plan") of the Temple is mentioned four times in 1 Chronicles 28: verses 11, 12, 18, 19. Of special significance is verse 19: "All this . . . I have in writing from the hand of the Lord upon me, and he gave me understanding in all the details of the plan."

The Temple was the place God promised to set His name (2 Chron. 6:10–11, 20; cf. Deut. 12:11). And Jerusalem was "the city the Lord had chosen out of all the tribes of Israel in which to put his Name" (2 Chron. 12:13).

The entire thrust of Solomon's great prayer of dedication of the Temple (6:14–42) was that God was greater than this Temple, that He was not confined to it (see esp. 6:18) but that His presence was to be found here, and He was to listen—"hear from heaven (your dwelling place)" (6:23, 25, 27, 30, 33, 35, 39)—and respond to His people when they prayed toward this place.

The ark was the specific place of God's dwelling within the Temple. It was God's very throne (1 Chron. 13:6; cf. 1 Sam. 4:4; 2 Sam. 6:2), the actual place where God would meet with His people and from which He would speak to them (Ex. 25:22). It contained three items: (1) the Ten Commandments, (2) a pot of manna, and (3) Aaron's rod (Ex. 25:16; 40:20; Deut. 10:1–5; Heb. 9:4).

Because of the importance of the Temple, its establishment and maintenance were dominant. A large proportion of the account of David in

---

84. See Williamson, *1 and 2 Chronicles*, 28–31; Braun, *1 Chronicles*, xxix–xxxi, esp. the bibliography on p. xxix.; Japhet, *Ideology of the Book of Chronicles*, 199–266.

85. See the incarnational development of this idea in John 1:14: "and the Word became flesh and dwelt [lit. 'tabernacled'] among us."

1 Chronicles (chaps. 21–29) is devoted to preparations for Temple building (i.e., an emphasis on David as Temple builder). The same is true for Solomon in 2 Chronicles 2–7. It is also true for the later kings, whose success or failure in God's eyes often is stated in terms of their regard for the Temple and its religious service. This perspective is best exemplified in King Abijah's words to Jeroboam I, his adversary, in 2 Chronicles 13:10–12:

> As for us, the Lord is our God, and we have not forsaken him. The priests who serve the Lord are sons of Aaron, and the Levites assist them. Every morning and evening they present burnt offerings and fragrant incense to the Lord. They set out the bread on the ceremonially clean table and light the lamps on the gold lampstand every evening. We are observing the requirements of the Lord our God. But you have forsaken him. God is with us; he is our leader. His priests with their trumpets will sound the battle cry against you. Men of Israel, do not fight against the Lord, the God of your fathers, for you will not succeed.

Indeed, all of the good kings in Judah are commended for their activities in purging the land of idolatry and reinstituting true worship in some way. In the cases of five of these kings, they are specifically said to have rebuilt or repaired the Temple in some way, and usually they reinstituted the accompanying worship rituals.

> *Asa* repaired the altar of the Lord in front of the Temple (15:8).
> *Joash* restored the Temple (24:4–14).
> *Jotham* built the upper gate of the Temple (27:3).
> *Hezekiah* repaired, cleansed, and rededicated the Temple (chaps. 29–31).
> *Josiah* repaired the Temple and celebrated the Passover (34:8–35:19).

The emphasis upon the Temple is important in and of itself, in the sense that it focuses upon proper worship of God. Beyond this, however, it is important as a symbol of the heavenly Temple spoken of in the NT. In Hebrews, much is made of the inadequate, earthbound nature of the Tabernacle (Heb. 8:1–7; chap. 9), and much more of the inadequacy of the Aaronic-Levitical priesthood (Hebrews 5–10).

The NT makes another point concerning the Temple, stating that Christ, the ultimate son of David, was to build the Temple. See the reference in John 2:19—"Destroy this temple, and I will raise it again in three days" —and John's comment in verse 21: "But the temple he had spoken of was his body." Note also John's comment in Revelation 21:22: "I did not see a temple in the city, because the Lord God Almighty and the Lamb are its temple." This, then, is the ultimate fulfillment of the promise that David's son would build a "house" for the Lord (2 Sam. 7:13; 1 Chron. 17:12).[86]

REWARD AND PUNISHMENT

One of the major theological motifs in 1 & 2 Chronicles is that of God's reward for obedience and punishment for sin. The theme is especially prominent in 2 Chronicles 10–36 (after the split in the kingdom). Roddy Braun states that "retribution is the major, if not the sole, yardstick used in writing the history of the post-Solomonic kings."[87] Explicit expression of this idea is given in David's words to Solomon in 1 Chronicles 28:9: "If you seek [the Lord], he will be found by you; but if you forsake him, he will reject you forever." This idea is repeated almost verbatim on three later occasions, to Rehoboam and his officials (2 Chron. 12:5), to Asa (15:2), and to the people in Joash's day (24:20). Other passages in which the same idea is articulated in slightly different terms include the great assurances from God to Solomon (7:13–14) and Jehoshaphat's words to the people (20:20).[88]

Several concrete examples of people suffering for their sins confront the reader: Saul's death, which is attributed to his unfaithfulness and his consulting a medium (1 Chron. 10:13); Uzziah's leprosy, attributed to his offering incense illegitimately in the Temple (2 Chron. 26:16); and Josiah's death, attributed to his not listening to God's words spoken through the Egyptian pharaoh Neco (35:22).

Another example is Rehoboam's, which is especially instructive, since it shows the interplay between sin and retribution, repentance and deliverance (chap. 12). Here, Rehoboam is first promised that God would abandon him to the Egyptian pharaoh Shishak because Rehoboam had abandoned God (v. 5). Then, when Rehoboam and his officials repented, God promised that he would not utterly destroy them but would spare them in some measure from Shishak (vv. 6–12).

Raymond Dillard sees 7:14 as a key verse in this regard—a "charter," in fact, for the rest of Israel's history: "If my people, who are called by my name, will humble themselves and pray and seek my face and turn from their wicked ways, then I will hear from heaven and will forgive their sin and heal their land." Dillard points out how specific terminology from this verse, such as "seeking God," "humbling oneself," "turning," and "healing" occur frequently, and at critical junctures. He also shows how these words' ant-

---

86. It may be that the book of Hebrews' lack of mention of the Temple per se—as opposed to the Tabernacle—is because of a consciousness of Christ's being the "New Temple."
87. Braun, *1 Chronicles*, xxxvii.
88. Recent treatments of this theme include Williamson, *1 and 2 Chronicles*, 31–33; Childs, *IOTS*, 651–53; Braun, *1 Chronicles*, xxxvii–xxxix; Dillard, "Reward and Punishment in Chronicles: The Theology of Immediate Retribution," 164–72; and *2 Chronicles*, 76–81.

onyms—such as "abandon, forsake" and "be unfaithful, rebellious"—carry much of the Chronicler's message when they are applied to the wicked.[89]

The general pattern in 2 Chronicles tends to show the validity of the principle of retribution, aside from the explicit expressions of it. Generally throughout, acts of piety and obedience are rewarded with (1) success and prosperity, (2) building programs, (3) victory in warfare, (4) progeny, (5) popular support, and (6) large armies. Conversely, disobedience and unfaithfulness bring (1) military defeat, (2) disaffection of the population, and (3) illness.[90]

We should note, however, that even the Chronicler, despite all of his great interest in this theme, is not slavishly devoted to it as a "barren and unalterable law."[91] For example, not every attack on Judah is due to its sins (see 16:1; 25:13; 32:1), and punishment occasionally is delayed until the prophets have had time to confront kings and offer chances for repentance (e.g., 12:5). Thus, 1 & 2 Chronicles stand, in the main, in the tradition of Deuteronomy, where obedience and blessing, disobedience and cursing, are closely linked. Yet, it also is sensitive, in a small way at least, to the tradition represented by Job and Habakkuk, where suffering is not always seen as being directly linked to punishment.

ATTITUDES OF THE HEART

The term *heart* occurs about 850 times in the OT. It occurs 63 times in 1 & 2 Chronicles—19 times in 1 Chronicles and 44 times in 2 Chronicles. Roddy Braun rightly sees "The Disposition of the Heart" as one of the themes in 1 & 2 Chronicles.[92] He notes that mere outward obedience to the letter of the law is not enough for the Chronicler; what is important is that obedience be done with a willing, generous, perfect, and joyful heart. Braun notes that the phrase "with a perfect heart" or "with all the heart" occurs 21 times, only three of which come from the parallel in 1 & 2 Kings, which demonstrates the Chronicler's special interest in this idea.[93]

A note of joy is struck frequently in connection with attitudes of the heart. The books of Chronicles uses the term *ŚMḤ*, "be glad, rejoice," fifteen times without parallel in Samuel-Kings. In 1 Chronicles, see especially 12:38–40 [MT 39–41], where David's fighting men volunteered willingly and joyfully to follow him and make him king, and the people throughout Israel rejoiced and gave generously, as well as 1 Chronicles 29:9, 22, where the

89. Dillard, *2 Chronicles*, 77–78.
90. Ibid., 78–80.
91. Ibid., 80.
92. Braun, *1 Chronicles*, xl–xli. See also Japhet, *Ideology of the Book of Chronicles*, 247–65.
93. Braun, *1 Chronicles*, xl.

people gave willingly and joyfully to the building of the Temple. In 2 Chronicles, see especially the Hezekiah narrative, where Levites, singers, and laity alike rejoiced greatly at Hezekiah's reforms (29:30, 36; 30:21, 23, 25). However, the Chronicler almost never passed up a chance to note joyful celebrations in religious ceremonies.[94] This is reminiscent of similar notes of joy struck in Ezra-Nehemiah (see Ezra 3:13; 6:22; Neh. 8:12, 17; 12:27).[95]

A related item is the people's generosity in supporting the monarchy and the religious service. This is especially visible in 1 Chronicles 29, where David invites the people to give gifts for the building of the Temple, and they do so, evoking memories of a similar phenomenon in Exodus with respect to the Tabernacle (Ex. 35:20–29). It also is very much visible in 2 Chronicles 29 and 31, where people give abundantly of animals for the sacrifices (29:30–36; 31:5–12), following King Hezekiah's own example (31:3).

We find a special emphasis on the concept of a properly disposed heart in the account of Hezekiah's reign: the term *heart* occurs eleven times in 2 Chronicles 29–32. In *none* of these occurrences in chapters 29–32 is the reference to the heart found in the parallel in 2 Kings, which again shows us the Chronicler's special concern with this idea (quotes from RSV):

29:10:	Hezekiah: "Now it is in my *heart* to make a covenant with the Lord."
29:31:	People brought burnt offerings with a "willing *heart.*"
29:34:	"The Levites were more upright in *heart* than the priests in sanctifying themselves."
30:12:	There was a unity in Judah—"one *heart*"—to do what God commanded.
30:19:	Speaks of the people setting their *heart* to seek God.
30:22:	Hezekiah spoke "encouragingly" (so RSV; lit., "to the *heart*") to the Levites.
31:21:	Hezekiah's every work in the service of the Temple was done "with all his *heart.*"
32:6:	Hezekiah spoke "encouragingly" (so RSV; lit., "to the *heart*") to the people.
32:25:	Hezekiah did not repent, "for his *heart* was proud."
32:26:	"Hezekiah humbled himself for the pride of his *heart.*"
32:31:	God left Hezekiah to himself, "in order to try him and to know all that was in his *heart.*"

94. See references in ibid.
95. Ibid.

As is obvious from these references, the attitudes of the heart are of paramount importance in relating to God: a proud heart was unacceptable to God, while a humble, willing, and whole heart were what pleased God.

PRAYER

Prayer plays an important role in 1 & 2 Chronicles. We find five major prayers (whose contents are given) included in the books. These prayers are all by good kings—David (2), Solomon, Jehoshaphat, and Hezekiah—and their inclusion performs at least two functions: first, they reinforce the positive picture that the Chronicler wants to paint of these kings; second, their contents provide us with rich insights into God Himself, His desires for His people, and ways of properly relating to God.

The noun "prayer" occurs twelve times in 1 & 2 Chronicles, all in 2 Chronicles (6:19 [twice], 20, 29, 35, 39, 40; 7:12, 15; 30:27; 33:18, 19), whereas the verb "to pray" occurs fifteen times, mostly in 2 Chronicles (1 Chron. 17:25; 2 Chron. 6:19, 20, 21, 24, 26, 32, 34, 38; 7:1, 14; 30:18; 32:20, 24; 33:13). In addition to the five major prayers discussed below, four additional prayers are mentioned, without their contents being revealed:

> The people's prayer in Hezekiah's day: 2 Chronicles 30:27
> Hezekiah's two prayers: 2 Chronicles 32:20, 24
> Manasseh's prayer: 2 Chronicles 33:13[96]

The five major prayers whose contents are preserved in 1 & 2 Chronicles are as follows.

David's prayer of response (1 Chron. 17:16–27). David's response to God's promises of the Davidic Covenant was a heartfelt prayer of gratitude. It is a good model for prayer, as its essential thrust is praise to God for how great He is. This passage is paralleled in 2 Samuel 7:18–29; there are minor differences in wording, but the thrust is the same in both. The prayer has three emphases:

1. David begins by reviewing what God has done in making this covenant and emphasizing his own insignificance (17:16–19; see also 17:25–26).

2. Then David praises God for who He is and what He has done for Israel (17:20–22).

3. Finally, David asks Him to establish what He has promised and to establish His name (17:23–24, 27).

---

96. A beautiful, moving prayer of confession purporting to be this prayer is found in the Apocrypha; it is entitled "The Prayer of Manasseh." Although it was written much later than Manasseh's day, it nevertheless can serve in its own right as a model for earnest prayer.

David's prayer of dedication (1 Chron. 29:10–19). This prayer is a dedication of the gifts brought for the building of the Temple. It is not paralleled in 2 Samuel. David had the right perspective on the Temple: it "is not for man but for the Lord God" (29:1b). This perspective is amply manifested in David's prayer. He begins by praising God (vv. 10–13), and then by acknowledging that all gifts come from God; they are not deserved (vv. 14–16). It ends with an acknowledgement that God desires inward purity and with a prayer for Solomon, that he would indeed keep the law with a whole heart and build the Temple in the same spirit (vv. 17–19).

Solomon's prayer of dedication (2 Chron. 6:12–42). This lengthy prayer was uttered on the occasion of the dedication of the Temple in Jerusalem. It is a mature and wide-ranging prayer of praise and petition.

It begins with praise of God (vv. 14–15), then asks God to remember and honor the Davidic Covenant (vv. 16–17). In verses 18–21 it changes topics, looking to the future, asking God to be faithful to this place where He had promised to place His name and to hear His people's requests. Then Solomon, continuing his look into the future, anticipates occasions of crisis when God's people would petition Him for help, and it repeatedly asks God to "hear from heaven" and to respond accordingly (vv. 22–40). The prayer concludes by repeating the early requests, asking God to take His place in the Temple and not to forget His steadfast, faithful love for His anointed one, His servant David (vv. 41–42). The last line of verse 42 closely parallels the important promise found in Isaiah 55:3b: "I will make an everlasting covenant with you, my faithful love promised to David."[97]

A glittering jewel of theological insight is found in the rhetorical question and answer given in verse 18: "But will God really dwell on earth with men? The heavens, even the highest heavens, cannot contain you. How much less this temple I have built!" Both here and in 1 Kings 8:27 (where the same words are found), we see the magnificent Temple that Solomon built placed in its proper perspective: regardless of how great it was—and it was great indeed!—the God who was condescending to identify with this place was infinitely greater.

This passage is paralleled in 1 Kings 8:22–53, although there are some omissions, and the end is taken from Psalm 132, not 1 Kings 8.[98] Second Chronicles adds two blocks of material and deletes one.

The first addition is in verse 13, where 2 Chronicles adds the information that Solomon knelt on a small bronze platform during his prayer. Some

---

97. On this reading, see Williamson, "'The Sure Mercies of David': Subjective or Objective Genitive?" 31–49; and *1 and 2 Chronicles*, 220–21; Walter C. Kaiser, Jr., "The Unfailing Kindnesses Promised to David: Isaiah 55:3," 91–98.
98. James D. Newsome, *Synoptic Harmony*, 117–21.

scholars suggest that this is to avoid the impression that Solomon was usurping priestly functions in front of the altar. Many scholars, however, believe that this verse was originally in Kings and has been lost in the transmission of the text (by *homoioteleuton*, since the phrase at the end of both verses 12 and 13 is "he spread forth his hands," and a scribe's eye easily could have jumped from the first to the second, causing him to omit v. 13 entirely).[99]

The second addition is in verses 40–42. Verses 41–42 are taken from Psalm 132. Verse 41 is close to Psalm 132:8–9, but verse 42 reverses the order of the two lines of Psalm 132:10 (and perhaps borrows from Ps. 132:1). Verse 40 is typical of other portions of Solomon's prayer, asking God to be attentive to a prayer from this place.

Between verses 39 and 40, 2 Chronicles omits four verses found in 1 Kings, which speak in some detail about the captivity and mention Egypt twice (1 Kings 8:50–53). The de-emphasis of Egypt in 2 Chronicles and the additions from Psalms at the end of the prayer serve to highlight David and the Davidic Covenant, in keeping with one of the Chronicler's main interests.

Jehoshaphat's prayer (2 Chron. 20:5–12). Jehoshaphat prayed a moving prayer in the Temple in response to a threat to Judah from Moabites, Ammonites, and others (vv. 1–4). It is not paralleled in 2 Kings. This prayer echoes Solomon's prayer in many ways. It is a model of affirming who God is and waiting expectantly on Him (see esp. v. 12: "We do not know what to do, but our eyes are upon you"). It also affirms that God's presence is in the sanctuary, where He had placed His name, just as Solomon had affirmed (vv. 8–9).

Hezekiah's prayer (2 Chron. 30:18–19). This prayer is short and specific, and it is not paralleled in 2 Kings. Many of the northerners who had been invited down for the Passover had not properly cleansed themselves before participating in the Passover. So Hezekiah prayed for them, asking God to overlook this minor, ceremonial violation. He emphasized the importance of a true heart, rather than "the sanctuary's rules of cleanness" (RSV). The implication here is that it was a proper and effective prayer, because "the Lord heard Hezekiah and healed the people" (v. 20).

THE AUTHORITY OF SCRIPTURE

It should be obvious that the Chronicler held the Scriptures in high regard. As noted above, he took great pains to reconcile or harmonize the Pentateuch with the historical works he was dealing with. His attitude was

---

99. See Dillard, *2 Chronicles*, 46, 48.

that, in the last analysis, Scripture would not flatly contradict Scripture; he saw part of his task to be that of finding the continuities in passages that stood in tension with each other, bringing them into some degree of meaningful and legitimate harmony. This is an important tenet—and, by some estimates, the defining tenet—of an evangelical approach to the Scriptures.

Also, we see the Chronicler's high regard for the Scriptures in that he undertook his work in the first place. That is, he used the canonical books of 2 Samuel and 1 & 2 Kings as his primary sources, and supplemented them with many other canonical sources. He gave these Scriptures pride of place and used them as springboards for addressing the needs of his own day.

Furthermore, it appears that the Chronicler assumed that his readers had knowledge of Israel's history in general through the written Scriptures, and sometimes he seems to have assumed specific knowledge of the passages in his sources that he was referencing. A small, but revealing, example of this assumption is found in 1 Chronicles 29:22b, where we are told that Solomon was made king "a second time." In 1 Chronicles, there has been no reference made prior to this to Solomon's having been made king a "first" time,[100] so this reference to "a second time" is somewhat surprising. The first time was probably the impromptu and semi-private ceremony that is described in one of the Chronicler's sources—1 Kings 1:32–40.[101] The reference to a "second" time shows that the Chronicler assumed that his readers knew of the events earlier, through their own reading or hearing of the Scriptures, even though he himself did not write of them.[102]

Outline of 1 & 2 Chronicles

Genealogies (1 Chronicles 1–9)
Introduction: Adam to Israel (1:1–2:2)
The Tribe of Judah (Southern Tribes) (2:3–4:43)
  Judah—A (2:3–55)
  David (3:1–24)
  Judah—B (4:1–23)
  Simeon (4:24–43)

---

100. The reference in 23:1 to David making Solomon king is a summary title for the rest of the book (along with the listing in 23:2), and not an independent reference to another coronation. So also Williamson, *1 and 2 Chronicles*, 159; Sailhamer, *First and Second Chronicles*, 56.
101. So also Williamson, *1 and 2 Chronicles*, 187; Sailhamer, *First and Second Chronicles*, 64.
102. R. D. Culver ("Peculiarities and Problems of Genealogical Method and of Text in the Book of Chronicles") agrees on this general point: "Previous knowledge of earlier portions of Scripture or of other information is assumed. Without it many statements are not only inexplicable but misleading" (first page). [The pages are not numbered.]

Transjordan Tribes (chap. 5)
  Reuben (5:1–10)
  Gad (5:11–17)
  Transjordan Tribes—summary narrative (5:18–23)
  East Manasseh (5:23–26)
The Tribe of Levi (6:1–81 [MT 5:27–6:66])
  High Priests (6:1–15 [MT 5:27–41])
  Levites (6:16–30 [MT 1–15])
  Levites and Priests Appointed by David (6:31–53 [MT 16–38])
  Levitical Cities (6:54–81 [MT 39–66])
Northern Tribes (7:1–9:1a)
  Issachar (7:1–5)
  Benjamin—A (7:6–12)
  Naphtali (7:13)
  East and West Manasseh (7:14–19)
  Ephraim (7:20–29)
  Asher (7:30–40)
  Benjamin—B (8:1–40; 9:1a)
Postscript: Postexilic Jerusalem and the Line of Saul (9:1b–44)

David: A Great Leader (1 Chronicles 10–31)
  The Death and Burial of Saul (chap. 10)
  David's Rise (chaps. 11–12)
    David Anointed King by All Israel (11:1–3)
    David Captures Jerusalem (11:4–9)
    David's Mighty Men (11:10–47)
    David Attracts Many Supporters (12:1–40)
  David, the Ark, and the Cult (chaps. 13–16)
    The Ark Moved from Kiriath-Jearim (chap. 13)
    The Greatness of David (chap. 14)
    Preparations and Celebrations (15:1–16:3)
      David Assembles Priests and Levites (15:1–10)
      Priests and Levites Sanctified (15:11–15)
      David Appoints Singers, Musicians, Gatekeepers (15:16–24)
      Celebration of the Ark's Return (15:25–29)
      Offerings for the Ark (16:1–3)
    Celebrations and Praise (16:4–43)
  The Davidic Covenant (chap. 17)
    The Covenant Proper (17:1–15)
    David's Prayer of Response (17:16–27)

David's Wars (chaps. 18–20)
  Overview of David's Victories (18:1–13)
    Over Philistines (18:1)
    Over Moabites (18:2)
    Over King of Zobah and the Arameans of Damascus (18:3–8)
    Tribute from the King of Hamath (18:9–11)
    Over Edomites (18:12–13)
  Administration of the Kingdom (18:14–17)
  Victories over the Ammonites (19:1–20:3)
  Victories over the Philistines (20:4–8)
A Place for the Temple (21:1–22:1)
  The Census and the Punishment (21:1–17)
  A Place for the Temple (21:18–22:1)
David's Preparations for Temple Building (22:2–19)
  Materials Gathered (22:2–5)
  Encouragement and Instructions for Solomon (22:6–16)
  Encouragement and Instructions for Leaders (22:17–19)
David's Organization of the Leaders of Israel (chaps. 23–27)
  David's Commissioning of Solomon and Leaders (23:1–2)
  The Levites (23:3–19)
  The Priests (24:1–19)
  The Rest of the Levites (24:20–31)
  The Musicians (25:1–31)
  The Gatekeepers (26:1–19)
  The Treasurers (26:20–28)
  Officers and Judges (26:29–32)
  Other Officials: Military and Civil (27:1–34)
David's Last Words and Solomon's Accession (chaps. 28–29)
  Public Commissioning of Solomon (28:1–10)
  The Plan of the Temple (28:11–21)
  Gifts for the Temple (29:1–9)
  David's Prayer (29:10–19)
  Solomon's Accession to the Throne (29:20–25)
  Evaluation of David's Reign (29:26–30)

Solomon: David's Successor (2 Chronicles 1–9)
  Solomon's Greatness—A (chap. 1)
  The Building of the Temple (2:1–5:1)
  The Dedication of the Temple (5:2–7:22)
  Solomon's Greatness—B (8:1–9:28)
  Solomon's Epitaph (9:29–31)

Kings of Judah (2 Chronicles 10–36)

Rehoboam's Reign (chaps. 10–12)
   The Split of the Kingdom (10:1–11:4)
   Rehoboam's Kingdom Established (11:5–23)
   Shishak's Invasion (12:1–12)
   Rehoboam's Epitaph (12:13–16)
Abijah's Reign (13:1–14:1 [MT 13:1–23])
Asa's Reign (14:2–16:14 [MT 14:1–16:14])
   Asa's Greatness (14:2–8 [MT 1–7])
   Asa's Victory Over Zerah (14:9–15 [MT 8–14])
   Asa's Religious Reforms (15:1–19)
   Asa's War Against Israel (16:1–10)
   Asa's Epitaph (16:11–14)
Jehoshaphat's Reign (17:1–21:1)
   Summary of Jehoshaphat's Reign (17:1–6)
   Jehoshaphat's Greatness and Faithfulness (17:7–19)
   Jehoshaphat and Ahab (18:1–19:3)
   Jehoshaphat's Judicial Reforms (19:4–11)
   Jehoshaphat's Military Victories (20:1–30)
   Jehoshaphat's Epitaph (20:31–21:1)
Jehoram's Reign (21:2–20)
Ahaziah's Reign (22:1–9)
Athaliah's Reign (22:10–23:21)
   Athaliah's Seizure of Power (22:10–12)
   Jehoiada's Revolt (23:1–21)
Joash's Reign (chap. 24)
Amaziah's Reign (chap. 25)
Uzziah's Reign (chap. 26)
Jotham's Reign (chap. 27)
Ahaz's Reign (chap. 28)
Hezekiah's Reign (chaps. 29–32)
   The Temple Cleansing and Rededication (29:1–36)
   The Passover Celebration (30:1–27)
   Hezekiah's Provisions for Temple Worship (31:1–21)
   Hezekiah's Rewards (32:1–31)
   Hezekiah's Epitaph (32:32–33)
Manasseh's Reign (33:1–20)
Amon's Reign (33:21–25)
Josiah's Reign (chaps. 34–35)
The End of the Kingdom of Judah (36:1–21)
Cyrus's Edict of Return (36:22–23)

9

EZRA-NEHEMIAH

Praise be to the Lord, the God of our fathers, who has put it into the king's heart to bring honor to the house of the Lord in Jerusalem in this way and who has extended his good favor to me before the king and his advisers and all the king's powerful officials. Because the hand of the Lord my God was on me, I took courage and gathered leading men from Israel to go up with me. (Ezra 7:27-28)

Remember me for this, O my God, and do not blot out what I have so faithfully done for the house of my God and its services. (Neh. 13:14)

The books of Ezra and Nehemiah record the last events, chronologically, in the OT period. The early chapters of Ezra present the glorious and happy return from Babylonian Exile and the excitement of the rebuilding of the Temple. Later, we read of another, equally happy return under Ezra, who held a commission from the Persian king to teach the law. Nehemiah returned a few years later with an administrative commission to rebuild Jerusalem's walls. The walls were rebuilt, the law was read, and joyful celebrations were held.

However, everything was not altogether promising. Both Ezra and Nehemiah found that God's people were defiling themselves and threatening Israel's survival as an ethnic and spiritual entity by intermarrying with pagans. Nehemiah found many other abuses as well. Furthermore, we read of stiff local opposition to the efforts of Temple rebuilding in Ezra and of wall rebuilding in Nehemiah. And throughout both books, the Jews were still in slavery to the Persians, albeit a very tolerant form of servitude. The books end on a rather plaintive note, with Nehemiah's brief prayer: "Remember me with favor, O my God" (Neh. 13:31).

These books are tightly packed with spiritual messages waiting to be extracted. They communicate a rich spirituality during times when things were not overwhelmingly positive for God's people. They are concerned with lists that show the unity of God's people. The importance of spiritual disciplines such as prayer, fasting, sacrificing, and reading of the Scriptures is exemplified throughout both books. There is much we can learn in them.

TITLE

The books of Ezra and Nehemiah get their respective titles from their main characters. Each man was the author of what have been called his "memoirs," which form a significant portion of each book (see below). Ezra's name is a shortened form of "Azariah," which means "Yah[weh] helps"; Nehemiah's name means "Yah[weh] comforts." Neither book makes a point of any message inherent in these names, however.[1] In those lists and traditions in which the books were considered as one (see "Unity" below), the unified work was called "Ezra."

PURPOSE

The books' immediate purpose is to present the life of God's people as it unfolded in the postexilic period, both immediately after the Exile and many years later. This is done through a religious lens so that the Temple and religious ceremonies are of paramount importance. Because of the trauma of the Exile—during which there was no Temple nor sacrifices, and the very existence of God's people was in question—the unity and purity of God's people is of major concern in these books. They are written, then, to show that God was still faithful and gracious to His people and that this people, who had their origin centuries earlier, still was alive and attempting to continue in the faithful traditions laid down by Moses.

PLACE IN THE CANON

ORDER

These two books always appear together, with Ezra preceding Nehemiah, in all lists and manuscript traditions. In present English versions, they immediately follow 1 & 2 Chronicles as part of the "historical" section of the canon. This ordering reflects that assumed by Josephus[2] and found in the Old Greek versions (Septuagint). It also reflects a proper chronological sequencing, since the events in Ezra and Nehemiah follow those in 1 & 2 Chronicles.

1. See F. Charles Fensham (*The Books of Ezra and Nehemiah*, 23–27) on names in Ezra-Nehemiah, and p. 24 on this specific point.
2. Josephus, *Against Apion* 1.8. (See Roger Beckwith, *Old Testament Canon of the New Testament Church*, 451; R. K. Harrison, *Introduction to the Old Testament*, 1135.)

In the Hebrew canon the two books are found among the "Writings," the third section of the canon, immediately preceding 1 & 2 Chronicles. This reflects the almost unanimous witness of rabbinic tradition and ancient manuscripts,[3] even though it reverses the natural chronological ordering of events. (See chapter 8 for a discussion of this reverse ordering.)

UNITY

Originally, Ezra and Nehemiah were considered to be one book. They appear as one in all Hebrew manuscripts until the fifteenth century A.D. The Jewish scribes, the Masoretes, who included total word counts of each book in the OT at the end of the books, gave one total for both books at the end of Nehemiah. There is also no gap in the Masoretic manuscript tradition between Ezra 10 and Nehemiah 1; they were treated as parts of one text. Furthermore, several early lists count the two books as one.[4]

The division into two books appears to have come from the Christian tradition. Origen (185–253 A.D.) seems to have been the first to distinguish between the two, and Jerome, in the fourth century, divided them into two books in his Latin translation, the Vulgate.[5] The first Hebrew Bibles that evidence a division into two books date to the late Middle Ages, and they do so under the influence of Christian versions.[6]

RELATIONSHIP TO 1 & 2 ESDRAS

Several noncanonical books bear Ezra's name. Of these, some closely parallel biblical materials and others do not. The two most commonly known are the books known as 1 & 2 Esdras in English versions.[7]

1 Esdras.[8] First Esdras reproduces the substance of 2 Chronicles 35–36, all of Ezra, and Nehemiah 7:38–8:12, breaking off in the middle of a sentence about Ezra's reforms. It especially emphasizes the contributions of Josiah, Zerubbabel, and Ezra to the reform of Israelite worship. It is in

---

3. Beckwith, *Old Testament Canon,* 452–64. In many medieval manuscripts, 1 & 2 Chronicles are found first in the Writings, before Psalms, and Ezra-Nehemiah last (Beckwith, *Old Testament Canon,* 458–59).
4. See H. G. M. Williamson (*Ezra, Nehemiah,* xxi) and D. J. A. Clines (*Ezra, Nehemiah, Esther,* 2) for these and other evidences of the books' unity.
5. Williamson, *Ezra, Nehemiah,* xxi–xxii; Edwin M. Yamauchi, "Ezra-Nehemiah," 572–73.
6. Clines, *Ezra, Nehemiah, Esther,* 2; Williamson, *Ezra, Nehemiah,* xxi.
7. Other noncanonical books bearing Ezra's name include the "Greek Apocalypse of Ezra," "Vision of Ezra," "Questions of Ezra," and "Revelation of Ezra." (See J. H. Charlesworth, ed., *The Old Testament Pseudepigrapha,* 1:561–604 on these.) In addition, the work known as the "Apocalypse of Sedrach" has many close ties with 1 Esdras (S. Agourides, "Apocalypse of Sedrach," in *The Old Testament Pseudepigrapha,* 1:607).
8. See "The First Book of Esdras," in B. M. Metzger, ed., *The Oxford Annotated Apocrypha,* 1–22; William R. Goodman, *ABD* 2, s.v. "Esdras, First Book of."

Greek, consists of nine chapters, and essentially duplicates biblical materials, but with numerous differences. Its underlying Hebrew or Aramaic text does not appear to have been the same as that underlying the MT, nor does it reproduce the Old Greek versions of Ezra-Nehemiah. Numerous small discrepancies exist, including rearrangement of material and the addition of a story of three young men in Darius's court not found in the Bible (3:1–5:6). Josephus followed 1 Esdras rather than the Old Greek versions of Ezra-Nehemiah in writing his history of the period.

This work is called 3 Esdras in the Latin Vulgate (Ezra and Nehemiah being 1 and 2 Esdras there), and Esdras Alpha in the Old Greek versions (Septuagint). Sometimes it is called "the Greek Ezra," to distinguish it from the canonical books of Ezra and Nehemiah.

2 Esdras.[9] Second Esdras is a very different type of book, being the only apocalyptic book in the Apocrypha. It denounces the wickedness of Rome ("Babylon") and wrestles with the question of theodicy (the vindication of God's justice). It appears to have been written originally in Hebrew or Aramaic, and translated into Greek; only scraps of the Greek translation remain. The extant versions are in Latin, Syriac, Coptic, Ethiopic, Arabic, Armenian, and Georgian. It is called 4 Esdras in the Vulgate and is also known as "the Apocalypse of Ezra."

Nomenclature. The following chart shows the relationships among the various books called "Ezra" or "Esdras":[10]

Relationship of Ezra with the Esdras Books

ENGLISH	VULGATE	SEPTUAGINT
Ezra	Esdras I	Esdras B (Beta)
Nehemiah	Esdras II	Esdras C (Gamma)
1 Esdras	Esdras III	Esdras A (Alpha)
2 Esdras	Esdras IV	———

AUTHORSHIP

Issues of authorship, composition, and date of Ezra and Nehemiah are more tangled for these books than for almost any other among the historical

9. See "The Second Book of Esdras," in *The Oxford Annotated Apocrypha*, 23–62; B. M. Metzger, "The Fourth Book of Ezra," in *The Old Testament Pseudepigrapha*, 1:516–59; Michael E. Stone, *ABD* 2, s.v. "Esdras, Second Book of."

10. See the charts in Jacob M. Myers, *Ezra-Nehemiah*, XXXVIII; Yamauchi, "Ezra-Nehemiah," 587; B. M. Metzger, "The Fourth Book of Ezra," in *The Old Testament Pseudepigrapha*, 1:516 (and discussion on p. 517).

books, and commentators' discussions of these issues are often tortuous and confusing. Only brief summaries can be undertaken here.[11]

According to the Talmud (*Baba Bathra* 15a), Ezra was the author of both 1 & 2 Chronicles and Ezra-Nehemiah. This view has many adherents even in recent scholarship.[12] Other scholars hold that the author of 1 & 2 Chronicles also wrote Ezra-Nehemiah (or edited them into a final form), but that this person was not Ezra.[13] Still other scholars hold that the author(s) of Ezra and Nehemiah was (were) different from the author of 1 & 2 Chronicles.[14] This is the most probable view. (For more detail on this entire question, see chapter 8 under "Relationship of 1 & 2 Chronicles to Ezra and Nehemiah.")

Ezra and Nehemiah differ from most OT books in that they both contain extensive sections written in the first person. These include Ezra 7:27–28, 8:1–34, 9:1–15; and Nehemiah 1:1–7:5; 12:27–43; 13:4–31 (or 13:1–31). Such first-person references naturally suggest that these sections, if not their entire respective books, were written by Ezra and Nehemiah themselves.

We should note that there appears to have been some editorial reworking of either Ezra or Nehemiah, or both. That is because the list of returnees from the Exile appears in both Ezra 2 and Nehemiah 7. Also, Ezra is the major figure in Nehemiah 8, whereas elsewhere in the book, Nehemiah is prominently highlighted. Williamson believes that, whereas Ezra and Nehemiah were responsible for their first-person sections, the books as they stand now came together under the hand of an editor a century later.[15] Others maintain that someone may have reworked both books, but only slightly, after they were essentially completed by Ezra and Nehemiah, respectively.[16]

COMPOSITION

In this section, we are considering how the writers compiled their works, not who wrote them. In their broadest contours, the books of Ezra and Nehemiah are organized around three major "sources": a historical

---

11. For authorship, see the following: Derek Kidner, *Ezra & Nehemiah*, 136–39; Fensham, *Ezra and Nehemiah*, 1–4; Clines, *Ezra, Nehemiah, Esther*, 9–12; Williamson, *Ezra, Nehemiah*, xxxiii–xxxv; Yamauchi, "Ezra-Nehemiah," 575–79.
12. Jacob M. Myers, *Ezra-Nehemiah*, LXVIII; Gleason L. Archer, Jr., *A Survey of Old Testament Introduction*, 405, 411.
13. Fensham, *Ezra and Nehemiah*, 3; Clines, *Ezra, Nehemiah, Esther*, 9–12.
14. Williamson, *Ezra, Nehemiah*, xxi–xxii; Yamauchi, "Ezra-Nehemiah," 579; Tamara C. Eskenazi, "The Structure of Ezra-Nehemiah and the Integrity of the Book," 641–56. For an extensive bibliography on this issue, see n. 21 in chapter 8.
15. Williamson, *Ezra, Nehemiah*, xxxiv–xxxvi.
16. So Harrison, *Introduction*, 1149–50; Yamauchi, "Ezra-Nehemiah," 579–80.

document, Ezra's "memoirs," and Nehemiah's "memoirs." Within these, many smaller sources can be seen.[17]

1. A historical review (Ezra 1–6). This consists of a typical historical narrative, mostly about events ca. 538–515 B.C., more than half a century before the time of Ezra. These events revolve around the return from Babylonian Exile and the rebuilding of the Temple.

2. Ezra's "Memoirs"—Part One (Ezra 7–10). This section deals with events in which Ezra himself was involved, taking place in the years following his return to Jerusalem in 458 B.C. The fact that in some portions of these "memoirs" he is referred to in the third person (7:1–26, 8:35–36; 10:1–44), whereas in the others he writes in the first person, has suggested to some that the material may have been edited after he wrote them.

3. Nehemiah's "Memoirs"—Part One (Nehemiah 1–7).[18] Here Nehemiah tells of his own labors in returning to Jerusalem in 445 B.C. and in rebuilding the walls of Jerusalem. Chapter 7 is a list found also in Ezra 2.

4. Ezra's "Memoirs"—Part Two (Nehemiah 8–10). Ezra (the man) reappears in Nehemiah 8, and some scholars add chapter 9 (and even chapter 10) to the "Ezra Memoirs."[19] In this section, Ezra leads the people in reading the law and in confession of sin.

5. Nehemiah's "Memoirs"—Part Two (Nehemiah 11–13). This final section of Nehemiah's "memoirs" includes several lists, and it tells of Nehemiah's labors in instituting various reforms. Occasionally Nehemiah appears in the third person (12:26, 47), but mostly these are his first-person version of the events.

Yamauchi notes that Nehemiah's memoirs seem more personal and that they probably were incorporated into the book almost unchanged, whereas Ezra's seem to have been edited to a greater degree.[20]

The smaller types of sources identified can be grouped into two general kinds: lists and letters.[21]

---

17. On the sources in Ezra-Nehemiah, see, briefly, Kidner, *Ezra & Nehemiah,* 134–35; Fensham, *Ezra and Nehemiah,* 4–5; Yamauchi, "Ezra-Nehemiah," 573–75; in more depth, see Clines, *Ezra, Nehemiah, Esther,* 4–9; Williamson, *Ezra, Nehemiah,* xxiii–xxxiii.
18. A more nuanced division of the "Nehemiah Memoirs" is given by Yamauchi ("Ezra-Nehemiah," 574): Nehemiah 1–6; 7:1–5; 11:1–2; 12:27–43; 13:4–31.
19. E.g., Fensham, *Ezra and Nehemiah,* 4–5.
20. Yamauchi, "Ezra-Nehemiah," 574.
21. A "source" referred to by some scholars as the "Aramaic Chronicle" (e.g., Clines, *Ezra, Nehemiah, Esther,* 8) is discussed below under "The Aramaic of Ezra."

Lists. Many lists are found in the two books, including genealogies and detailed records of participants in various events. These include the following:

1. Temple vessels (Ezra 1:9–11)
2. Returnees from exile (Ezra 2; Nehemiah 7)
3. Ezra's genealogy (Ezra 7:1–5)
4. Returnees under Ezra (8:1–14)
5. Offenders regarding mixed marriages (10:18–43)
6. Those rebuilding the walls (Nehemiah 3)
7. Those sealing the covenant (10:1–27)
8. Settlers in Jerusalem and surroundings (11:3–36)
9. Priests and Levites (12:1–26)

Letters. Numerous letters are included in Ezra:

1. Cyrus's decree (Ezra 1:2–4)
2. Rehum's accusation against the Jews (4:11–16)
3. Artaxerxes's reply (4:17–22)
4. Tattenai's report (5:7–17)
5. Memorandum of Cyrus's decree (6:2–5)
6. Darius's reply to Tattenai (6:6–22)
7. Artaxerxes's authorization to Ezra (7:12–26)

All but the first of these letters is written in Aramaic, and their authenticity—which had been questioned in an earlier time—is almost universally accepted today.[22] Indeed, the entire corpus of letters has been subjected to careful scrutiny by Cap Hensley, who concludes that "linguistically, stylistically, and historically the [Ezra Documents] correspond perfectly to the non-Biblical documents of the Achaemenid period."[23]

THE COMPOSITION OF EZRA 4

Many an unsuspecting reader has been tripped up by the composition of Ezra 4. That is because in this chapter we find three chronological horizons, two of which are out of place in Ezra 1–6. The main story line in Ezra 1–6 takes place between 538 and 515 B.C. (see below). That is the time frame for Ezra 4:1–5, 24, which detail opposition to the Jews' rebuilding of the Temple. However, the author has inserted a section (vv. 6–23) that is

---

22. Clines, *Ezra, Nehemiah, Esther,* 8.
23. Cap Hensley, "The Official Persian Documents in the Book of Ezra" (Ph.D. diss., Univ. of Liverpool, 1977), 233; cited in Yamauchi, "Ezra-Nehemiah," 573.

out of place chronologically. Verse 6 tells of (unspecified) opposition to the Jews during the days of Ahasuerus (486–464 B.C.), whereas verses 7–23 tell of opposition to an attempt to rebuild the walls of Jerusalem during the days of Artaxerxes (464–423 B.C.). These conflicts were prior to Nehemiah's labors to rebuild the walls, which began in 445 B.C. Many superficial readers, therefore, assume that the walls were rebuilt at the same time as the Temple or that Nehemiah was somehow involved in these earlier events because of the juxtaposition of diverse materials in this chapter.

As it stands, however, the chapter is about opposition to the Jews' work in Jerusalem (in whatever time period). It begins (vv. 1–5) by telling of the opposition during the time frame in which chapters 1–6 operate (the years immediately following 538 B.C.). The author, who obviously must have lived many years later, then diverges to tell of further opposition to the Jews in two later periods (vv. 6–23). The author returns to his original time frame in verse 24, with a "resumptive repetition,"[24] taking us back to the original time frame and mentioning Darius's second year (520 B.C.).

DATE

DATE OF THE EVENTS[25]

Traditional Dating. The date formulas in the books are fairly precise. The events in Ezra 1–6 begin (1:1) with Cyrus's decree in his first year (538 B.C.) and end (6:15) with the completion of the Temple in the sixth year of Darius's reign (early in 515 B.C.). As just noted, we are told in 4:24 of a hiatus in work on the Temple until Darius's second year (520 B.C.).

Later, we are told that Ezra returned to Jerusalem in the seventh year of King Artaxerxes (I), which was 458 B.C. (Ezra 7:7), and that Nehemiah returned in his twentieth year, which was 445 B.C. (Neh. 2:1). Furthermore, we are told that the first stage of Nehemiah's ministry was twelve years, until the king's thirty-second year, or 433 B.C. (Neh. 5:14). Also, we read that in this thirty-second year Nehemiah went back to Babylon on an official mission, after which he returned to Jerusalem again (13:6–7). Finally, we find that Ezra's public reading of the law was done in the seventh month of the year (7:73), which was undoubtedly the same year that Nehemiah arrived (cf. 6:15 and 2:1).[26]

Thus, according to the internal biblical data, Ezra's ministry extended at least thirteen years, spanning the period 458–445 B.C., whereas Nehemiah's was later, extending at least twelve years, 445–433 B.C.

24. The term is Williamson's (*Ezra, Nehemiah,* 57).
25. See Kidner, *Ezra & Nehemiah,* 134–39, 146–58; Fensham, *Ezra and Nehemiah,* 1–9; Clines, *Ezra, Nehemiah, Esther,* 4–24; Williamson, *Ezra, Nehemiah,* xxi–xliv; Yamauchi, "Ezra-Nehemiah," 573–86.
26. So C. F. Keil, *The Book of Nehemiah,* 227.

Scholarly challenges. However, beginning at the end of the nineteenth centuryand continuing since, this picture of the dating of Ezra (the man) to 458 B.C. has been challenged by many scholars. The dating of Nehemiah to 445 B.C. is relatively certain, especially since the discovery of the Elephantine Papyri. In one of these letters, dated to 407 B.C., two sons of Sanballat, Nehemiah's well-known opponent, are mentioned as officials in Samaria, while Sanballat is mentioned as still being governor.[27] This likely was near the end of Sanballat's life, and the biblical dates for Nehemiah thus fit well with this extrabiblical datum.

Postexilic Chronology

Cyrus II captures Babylon	539
Cyrus issues emancipation decree (Ezra 1:1)	538
Jews return to Palestine (Ezra 2)	538/537
Altar rebuilt (Ezra 3:2)	538/537
Temple foundations laid (Ezra 3:8–10)	536
Opposition encountered (Ezra 4:1–5, 24)	536–520
Temple completed (Hag. 1:14–15; Ezra 6:15)	520–515
Opposition to Jews in Jerusalem (Ezra 4:6)	485(?)
Esther and Mordecai rise in the Persian Court	484–465
Further opposition to Jews in Jerusalem (Ezra 4:7)	463–???
Ezra returns to Jerusalem (Ezra 7:1, 8)	458
Nehemiah returns to Jerusalem (Neh. 2:1)	445
Nehemiah visits Babylon and returns to Jerusalem (Neh. 13:6–7)	433

However, many scholars have questioned the traditional dating of Ezra to the reign of Artaxerxes I, assigning his return to Jerusalem instead to the seventh year of King Artaxerxes II, which would have been 398 B.C. This is for a long list of reasons, some more significant than others.[28] The most important are as follows.

First, many scholars note that, if Ezra and Nehemiah were contemporaries, they should have mentioned each other more often in their works. As

---

27. *ANET*, 492; *TANE*, 281; *DOTT*, 264–65.
28. The literature on the issue is vast. The discussion may be entered via Kidner, *Ezra & Nehemiah*, 146–58; Edwin M. Yamauchi, "The reverse order of Ezra/Nehemiah reconsidered," 7–13; and "Ezra-Nehemiah," 583–86; Clines, *Ezra, Nehemiah, Esther*, 16–24; Williamson, *Ezra, Nehemiah*, xxxix–xliv. All of these scholars support the traditional dating of Ezra's return in 458 B.C., and each makes most of the points and counterpoints below, although what follows here is especially indebted to Yamauchi and Kidner. (Note that Williamson, though supporting the 458 date for Ezra, does not believe that Ezra's and Nehemiah's ministries overlapped.)

it stands, they are specifically mentioned together only twice, in Nehemiah 8:9 and 12:26,[29] and many scholars see these texts as later glosses. However, the missions and interests of the two men were very different. Since Ezra's was primarily a religious commission, the administrative work of Nehemiah would not naturally have fit into his book. Also, since Nehemiah's account was so highly personal, revolving mainly around his own activities, his infrequent mention of Ezra should evoke little surprise. Furthermore, we find other OT contemporaries who also do not mention each other, such as Jeremiah and Ezekiel or Haggai and Zechariah.

Second, many scholars cannot understand why Ezra, who was commissioned to instruct people in the law (Ezra 7), did not actually read it publicly until thirteen years later (Nehemiah 8). Thus, they place Ezra some time after 445 B.C. However, this too narrowly focuses upon a single public reading and ignores the very real possibility (or probability) that Ezra was engaged in much teaching prior to this public event. Indeed, Ezra 7:10 states precisely that he had done this as a matter of course in Babylon, and we may readily assume that he continued this practice in Jerusalem. Furthermore, Nehemiah 8:1 states that the people "told Ezra the scribe to bring out the Book of the Law of Moses." This seems to indicate that this *public reading came* at others' initiative; presumably Ezra had made them aware of the law, and, when the appropriate time came, he was asked to read it in public. (Also, the quick response and confession of the people in Nehemiah 8–10 could indicate precisely that they had been prepared in advance for the public reading of the law.)

Third, many scholars note that both Ezra and Nehemiah had to deal with the issue of mixed marriages (Ezra 9–10; Neh. 13:23–28). Nehemiah's actions date to 433 B.C., whereas the precise date of Ezra's reforms is unknown. If Ezra were such a great leader, this would show him to have been a failure, since a further "purge" under Nehemiah was needed. Also, many scholars believe Ezra's harsher remedies more logically should have come later than Nehemiah's more humane remedies. However, both of these are purely subjective arguments. The first ignores the fact that many godly biblical characters were "failures" when judged by the standards of whether people followed their lead. The second is impossible to address in any meaningful way, since it reflects an arbitrary subjectivity. Indeed, the reverse could be argued on the basis of indications from other Scriptures— i.e., that harsher measures may have been appropriate in the first instance of an offense. For example, Sabbath breakers were stoned the first time they were encountered (Num. 15:32–36), whereas, later, Sabbath breakers were

29. Although Ezra appears a total of eleven times in the book of Nehemiah: 8:1, 2, 4, 5, 6, 9, 13; 12:13, 26, 33, 36.

not punished in this way (Amos 8:5–6); and the deaths of Ananias and Sapphira in punishment for their deception were instantaneous (Acts 5:1–11), whereas similar deceptions since their time usually has not resulted in similarly severe results.

Fourth, many scholars note that Ezra visited a priest named "Jehohanan, son of Eliashib" in Jerusalem (Ezra 10:6). A high priest by the name of Johanan, a son or grandson of Eliashib, is mentioned in Nehemiah 12:22–23. Yet one of the Elephantine Papyri mentions a high priest named Johanan,[30] who dates to 407 B.C. Many scholars assume that these are all the same person and that Ezra more probably visited him in 398 B.C. or thereafter. However, Ezra's Jehohanan is only a priest (not a high priest). Furthermore, he is a true son of Eliashib, whereas Nehemiah's Johanan appears to be a grandson of (another) Eliashib (cf. Neh. 12:10–11, 22).[31]

Fifth, many scholars note that when Nehemiah returned to Jerusalem he found the walls destroyed (Neh. 1:3; 2:13, 17), whereas Ezra thanked God for a "wall of protection in Judah and Jerusalem" (Ezra 9:9). However, Ezra's term for "wall" is *gādēr*, which usually refers to enclosures of fields of vineyards, not the common word for "wall" (*hômāh*). Furthermore, in its context it clearly is used metaphorically: the reference is to a wall "in Judah and Jerusalem," an unlikely reference to the actual walls of Jerusalem.

Conclusion. Whereas large numbers of scholars have argued for any number of dates for Ezra, most of them later than 458 B.C.,[32] the major arguments can easily be countered. Indeed, many critical scholars now seem to be moving in the direction of accepting the traditional date for Ezra.[33] The conclusion here is that the traditional dating scheme for both Ezra and Nehemiah is correct.

A recent (conservative) work argues for the traditional dating of Ezra's return (458 B.C.) and maintains that Ezra and Nehemiah were indeed contemporaries, but that Nehemiah's ministry began in 465 B.C. (not 445 B.C.).[34] The crux of this argument lies in understanding Artaxerxes's "twentieth year" (Neh. 2:1) as referring to his father Xerxes's twentieth year (i.e., the twentieth year from the start of the dynasty of which Artaxerxes was a part). This has the decided advantage of faithfulness to the Hebrew text and of retaining the traditional date for Ezra, while at the same time embracing the critical consensus that Nehemiah 8–10 belongs alongside Ezra 9–10. How-

---

30. *ANET,* 492; *TANE,* 280; *DOTT,* 263–65.
31. On this point, see especially Yamauchi, "Reverse order of Ezra/Nehemiah reconsidered," 8–9; Carl G. Tuland, "Ezra-Nehemiah or Nehemiah-Ezra?" 55–59.
32. Leslie McFall identifies no fewer than nine different proposed dates for Ezra, ranging from 515 B.C. to 367 B.C. ("Was Nehemiah Contemporary With Ezra in 458 BC?" 264–65).
33. Yamauchi, "Reverse order of Ezra/Nehemiah reconsidered," 13.
34. McFall, "Was Nehemiah Contemporary With Ezra in 458 BC?" 263–93.

ever, it is not altogether convincing: it rests on a questionable assumption about dating, which relies in the main on a somewhat dubious interpretation of a date formula in 2 Chronicles 16:1.

DATE OF COMPOSITION

Deciding upon the date of composition[35] of either Ezra or Nehemiah depends upon one's view of the authorship and composition of both works and of their relationship to each other. (These matters were considered in more depth under "Authorship" and "Composition.")

We must start with the assumption that the books' writing comes after the last events in them (since they profess to be historical narratives, not prophecies). There is little evidence in either book (or anywhere else in Scripture) that demands a writing very much later than the events in the books themselves. Accordingly, Clines puts the final writing ca. 400 B.C.[36] Yamauchi dates the Ezra materials to 440 B.C., the Nehemiah memoirs to 430 B.C., and the final writing somewhat later, perhaps 400 B.C.[37] Though both these authors assume that the Chronicler compiled the final form of Ezra-Nehemi-ah, and the judgment here is that he did not, their conclusion regarding the date of composition for Ezra-Nehemiah is nonetheless eminently reasonable. Kidner, one who sees a different authorship for 1 & 2 Chronicles and Ezra-Nehemiah, agrees: "The books could have been compiled at any time from the last years of Darius II (423–404) onward."[38]

HISTORICAL AND CULTURAL CONTEXT FOR EZRA-NEHEMIAH

The events in Ezra and Nehemiah fit into two general time frames: the immediate postexilic period (538–515 B.C.), and a later time (458–433 B.C.). Both periods unfolded against the backdrop of the Persian Empire (see below).

The events in the first period (Ezra 1–6) immediately followed the Exile, which was the most traumatic period in the nation's history. Gone were the Temple and its trappings, the religious service and the entire sacrificial system. Only the poorest of the land remained there (2 Kings 24:14; 25:12).

However, the books of Ezra and Nehemiah are upbeat, for the most part. Ezra opens with Cyrus's decree releasing the Jews to return to the land, and there was great joy when the altar and foundation to the Temple were

---

35. See Kidner, *Ezra & Nehemiah*, 138; Clines, *Ezra, Nehemiah, Esther*, 12–14; Williamson, *Ezra, Nehemiah*, xxxv–xxxvi; Yamauchi, "Ezra-Nehemiah," 579–80.
36. Clines, *Ezra, Nehemiah, Esther*, 14.
37. Yamauchi, "Ezra-Nehemiah," 580. Williamson has a similar analysis of the first-person "memoirs," but he places the composition of Ezra 1–6 much later and the final composition ca. 300 B.C. (*Ezra, Nehemiah*, xxxiv–xxxvi).
38. Kidner, *Ezra & Nehemiah*, 138.

built (Ezra 3:4, 11–13), although there were those who remembered the far greater glory of the former Temple (3:12). Opposition arose to the Jews' efforts, but a recurring motif in chapters 1–6 is the favor of the Persian government upon God's people.

In the later period, God's gracious hand still was on the people, but Ezra and Nehemiah had many problems they needed to address (see below). Nevertheless, they addressed the problems, and they were facilitated by the still-prevalent mood of toleration among Persian officialdom.

THE PERSIANS

The Persian empire[39] forms the backdrop to all the postexilic books in the OT, including 1 & 2 Chronicles, Ezra-Nehemiah, and Esther. It arose when the Persians toppled Babylon in 539 B.C. and ended with Alexander the Great's pillaging of the Persian capital Persepolis and the death of Darius III in 330 B.C.[40] Persia was east of Mesopotamia, in present-day Iran.

The Persians, an Indo-European people who were nomadic pastoralists, probably entered the Iranian plateau from the steppes to the north late in the second millennium B.C.[41] The Hebrew word *pāras* ("Persia") refers to the land of Persia itself; it occurs thirty-four times, in Ezekiel (twice), 2 Chronicles (only in chap. 36), Ezra, Esther, and Daniel. The word *Persian* occurs twice, once in Aramaic (Dan. 6:28 [MT 29]: "Cyrus the Persian") and once in Hebrew (Neh. 12:22: "Darius the Persian").

The Early Kings of the Persian Empire[42]

559–530	Cyrus II (the Great)
530–522	Cambyses
522–486	Darius I
486–465	Xerxes I (Ahasuerus)
464–423	Artaxerxes I
423–404	Darius II Nothus
404–359	Artaxerxes II Mnemon

39. See A. R. Millard, *NBD*, s.v. "Persia"; R. E. Hayden, *ISBE* 3, s.v. "Persian"; Pierre Briant, *ABD* 5, s.v. "Persian Empire"; Edwin M. Yamauchi, "The Persians," *POTW*; and *Persia and the Bible*; T. C. Young, Jr., et al., "Part I: The Persian Empire," *CAH* 4, 1–286.
40. Briant, *ABD* 5, s.v. "Persian Empire," 243.
41. Millard, *NBD*, s.v. "Persia."
42. K. A. Kitchen and T. C. Mitchell, *NBD*, s.v. "Chronology of the Old Testament." Dates will vary by a year in some cases; e.g., Artaxerxes is dated 464–424 B.C. by other scholars (e.g., Yamauchi, *Persia and the Bible*, 242).

The earliest traditions of the Persians are recorded in the Zend-Avesta, the sacred book of the Zoroastrians.[43] Their earliest kings ruled in Anshan, northwest of Susa. Achamenes, the founder of the Achamenid dynasty, probably reigned ca. 680 B.C. His grandson Cyrus I opposed Ashurbanipal of Assyria (ca. 668–627 B.C.), but later he submitted.

Cyrus II. Cyrus I's grandson, Cyrus II ("the Great"), acceded to power ca. 559 B.C., rebelled against his Median overlord (and his mother's father) Astyages, and took his capital Ecbatana (in northwestern Iran) ca. 550 B.C. He established the Persian (Achamenid) empire proper, taking the titles of "king of the Medes" and "king of Elam." Thereafter, Median language and culture had strong influences upon those of Persia, and Cyrus called himself the "king of the Medes and the Persians," as well as the "king of Elam."

Cyrus then went west and conquered Anatolia and Lydia (in Asia Minor), and returned east to conquer territories in northwestern India. By 540 B.C., he was strong enough to attack Babylon, which he finally conquered in October 539 B.C.

In his first year, Cyrus issued his famous decree, freeing subject peoples to return to their homelands. Versions of this decree are recorded in 2 Chronicles 36:22–23 and Ezra 1:1–4; another version survives in his own cylinder inscription, dated to 536 B.C. Here is the portion where Cyrus mentions his release of captive peoples:

> I (also) gathered all their (former) inhabitants and returned (to them) their habitations. Furthermore, I resettled upon the command of Marduk, the great lord, all the gods of Sumer and Akkad whom Nabonidus has brought into Babylon to the anger of the lord of the gods, unharmed, in their (former) chapels, the places which make them happy.[44]

Though, here, Cyrus gives credit to Marduk, his adopted Babylonian god, the Bible tells us that he gave credit to "the Lord, the God of heaven" (2 Chron. 36:23; Ezra 1:2). This discrepancy merely shows that Cyrus was a good "politician," adopting the god of whatever peoples he was dealing with. The text on the Cyrus Cylinder may represent the general decree, and the text in the Bible may represent a version that was sent to the Jews.

Cyrus was the dominant political figure for Judah in this period. Indeed, Cyrus had been mentioned years earlier by Isaiah (44:28; 45:1) as the Lord's anointed instrument for carrying out His plan. The Persian empire was divided under Cyrus into large regions ruled by satraps, taken from Persian or Median nobles, who had native officers under them (cf. Dan 6:1–3).

---

43. Zoroaster, the founder of this religion, lived in the seventh or sixth century B.C.
44. *ANET,* 316. For the entire text, see *ANET,* 315–16; *TANE,* 206–8; *DOTT,* 92–95.

Cyrus was succeeded as king by his son Cambyses (II) in 530 B.C. (who had already been coregent for some time). Cambyses conquered Egypt in 525 B.C. His successors, Darius I and Xerxes I, expended considerable energy trying to conquer the Greeks in the Pelopponesus Peninsula of Greece, almost the only area outside the control of the Persian empire in the known world. Darius was defeated in a critical battle at Marathon in 490 B.C., but it was not until 334–330 B.C., under Alexander the Great, that the Greeks were able completely to destroy the Persian empire.

In general, Persian policy toward its captive peoples was benign. This can be seen in Persian texts themselves,[45] as well as in the Bible. The Jews tended to flourish under Persian rule, since they were granted relative independence in Judah. This is apparent in Cyrus's decree and in the rights that the Jews enjoyed. (See the various letters and decrèes written on their behalf in the book of Ezra.) Even Jews in exile under the Persians were able to flourish. (See the ascendancy in the Persian courts of such persons as Daniel, Nehemiah, Esther, and Mordecai.)

Darius I and Darius the Mede. Several references are made in Ezra 4–6 to Darius king of Persia. This is Darius I, who ruled 522–486 B.C. and is known from extensive references outside the Bible. Darius I should not be confused with "Darius the Mede," the king mentioned several times in the book of Daniel (e.g., 5:31; 6:9, 25, 28; 9:1). Daniel's Darius is nowhere mentioned outside the Bible, and he does not fit (by that name) into the known chronology of the Persian kings outlined above. For this reason, many scholars have suggested that "Darius the Mede" never existed and that the author of Daniel was hopelessly confused concerning his identity.

However, at least two plausible suggestions have been advanced concerning his identity.[46] One is that "Darius the Mede" was an alternative title for Cyrus II (559–530 B.C.).[47] In this view the last part of the text in Daniel 6:28, "So Daniel prospered during the reign of Darius and the reign of Cyrus the Persian," should be understood to mean "the reign of Darius, that is, the reign of Cyrus" (see NIV marg. n.), which is certainly within the bounds of the Hebrew grammar of the passage. Perhaps the most plausible suggestion, however, identifies "Darius the Mede" with Gaubaruwa (Gubaru), a governor under Cyrus who conquered Babylon on his behalf and who ruled Babylon with royal authority (thus, his description in Daniel as "king").[48] The

---

45. See George G. Cameron, "Ancient Persia," 77–97.
46. See G. L. Archer, Jr., "Daniel," 16–19; Yamauchi, *Persia and the Bible*, 58–59; Klaus Koch, *ABD* 2, s.v. "Darius the Mede."
47. D. J. Wiseman, *Notes on Some Problems in the Book of Daniel*, 9–16; B. E. Colless, "Cyrus the Persian as Darius the Mede in the Book of Daniel," 113–26.
48. W. H. Shea, "Darius the Mede: An Update," 229–48; cf. John C. Whitcomb, *Darius the Mede*.

details of "Darius the Mede's" life fit those of Gaubaruwa very closely, and "Darius the Mede" may simply have been an alternative title for him.

THE "SAMARIANS"

Opposition to the Jews' rebuilding the walls of Jerusalem included people from "the city of Samaria" during the early days of Artaxerxes (Ezra 4:10, 17). These people had been deported from their own lands and resettled by an Assyrian king, Ashurbanipal (668–627 B.C.). Later, the opposition to Nehemiah's project of rebuilding the walls also involved "Samarians," led by Sanballat and "the army of Samaria" (Neh. 4:2).

In addition, "people of the land" also opposed them earlier, during the days of Zerubbabel's leadership, when they were rebuilding the Temple (Ezra 4:1–5; NIV has "the peoples around them" in v. 4). These "people of the land" stated that they had been living in the land since the days of Esarhaddon, Ashurbanipal's father (680–669 B.C.), who resettled them there (v. 2). A careful reading of the text shows that there was no connection between these people and the Samarians who opposed the Jews later.

The conflicts between the Jews and the "Samarians" in Ezra and Nehemiah have often been assumed to be the origins of the later conflict between the Jews and the group that came to be known as the "Samaritans" (see John 4:9). We do know that, in an earlier time, the Assyrian king Shalmaneser (726–722 B.C.) resettled people from throughout his empire in "the towns of Samaria" to replace the Israelites he deported in 723/22 B.C. when he took Samaria (2 Kings 17:24–26).

However, there is no concrete evidence to associate the Samaritans of the late intertestamental and NT periods with the "Samarians" of the OT period. Concerning the Jewish-Samaritan antagonisms, Williamson notes that "it is now widely agreed that that controversy arose very much later."[49] Therefore, since it is anachronistic to speak of "Samaritans" in Ezra and Nehemiah, their designation here is "Samarians."

THE ELEPHANTINE PAPYRI[50]

The Elephantine colony was a Jewish settlement (also called Yeb) on a small island in the Nile, at present-day Aswan, near the southern Egyptian border (550 miles south of Cairo). It was a military colony, probably of mercenaries originally, but by the fifth century B.C. wives and children lived there too.

---

49. Williamson, *Ezra, Nehemiah,* 49 (see also bibliography here).
50. See R. K. Harrison, *ISBE* 2, s.v. "Elephantine Papyri"; Bezalel Porten, *ABD* 2, s.v. "Elephantine Papyri."

Two caches of primarily legal and business texts, written in Aramaic on papyrus, were found in 1893 and later, and published between 1906–11 and in 1953. The letters show the existence of a Jewish temple dedicated to YHW ("Yaho"), which is a shortened form of God's personal name, YHWH ("Yahweh"). The temple apparently had been constructed before the invasion of Egypt by Cambyses in 525 B.C., but it had been destroyed by Egyptians in 410 B.C.

One of the most interesting letters speaks of this temple at some length.[51] It was addressed from the colonists to Bagoas, the Persian governor of Judea, in 407 B.C. It seems to have been a follow-up letter to an earlier complaint about the destruction of this temple (which apparently received no reply), and it complains about the desecration of the shrine and asks permission to rebuild it. It mentions requests for help made to the two sons of Sanballat, governor of Samaria; Sanballat himself may have been only a figurehead by this time.

The temple at Elephantine is an example of syncretistic Jewish practice at this time, which incorporated elements of pagan worship along with true worship. Its long list of contributors showed that they were honoring not only YHW, but also other deities: Ishua-bethel, Anath-bethel, Herembethel, and even Anath-YHW.[52] Some letters request the blessing of "the gods" along with more traditional biblical phrases, such as "God of heaven" and "Lord of hosts." Also, the fact that a temple outside of Jerusalem even existed shows the deterioration of biblical ideals in this Jewish community.

In many respects the Elephantine Letters are significant for the study of Ezra and Nehemiah. Their version of Aramaic is an early form of the Imperial Aramaic appearing in Ezra and Daniel. "The letters in Ezr. 4 particularly exhibit a great many of the characteristics of fifth-century B.C. Aramaic" (i.e., that of the Elephantine Letters).[53] They give insight into the language itself in Ezra, into formal characteristics of Persian letters, and into customs of the time, as well as into the individuals mentioned.

NEHEMIAH'S JERUSALEM

When Nehemiah returned to Jerusalem in 445 B.C., the major part of his mission was to rebuild the city's walls. We read of his overseeing this task in Nehemiah 2:9–20, and chapters 3–6. The walls were completed in the same year of his return, only six months later (6:15; 7:1)![54] He reestab-

---

51. *ANET*, 492; *TANE*, 279–81; *DOTT*, 260–65.
52. This Anath-YHW may have been a consort (i.e., "wife") of YHW. See the discussion of "Yahweh and his Asherah" on an ostracon at Kuntillet Ajrud (in chapter 7), for a similar example of earlier syncretism.
53. See Harrison, *ISBE* 2, s.v. "Elephantine Papyri," 61.

lished a sense of community, giving the people recognized political status and an honest administration. Jerusalem and the villages around it were resettled (chap. 11), the city walls dedicated (12:27–43), and Levites appointed for religious service (12:44–47).

The wall rebuilding provided Jerusalem with a measure of security against its enemies, one that deflated their opposition to the Jews (6:16). This physical separation complemented the Jews' social and spiritual separation from foreigners that formed an important part of the theology of both Ezra and Nehemiah (see below).

Regarding the size of Jerusalem in Nehemiah's day, the city walls are described three times in the book of Nehemiah: (1) 2:11–16: Nehemiah's night inspection tour; (2) chapter 3: the description of the work crews' efforts on each section of the wall; and (3) 12:31–43: the description of the locations of the two companies of people on the day of the walls' dedication (the dedication account begins in v. 27). These are detailed descriptions, but they do not give any clear picture concerning the size of the city.

Some scholars have argued that the extent of the city was large, the same size it had been in preexilic times, in the days of Hezekiah.[55] That is, it would have included the small "City of David," the large Temple Mount area north of that, and the "Western Hill" to the west. However, there is no archaeological evidence for occupation of the western hill during the Persian period (nor even the later Hellenistic period for that matter); thus, the scholarly consensus today holds that Nehemiah's city was smaller than the preexilic city.[56]

This minimalist picture should not be surprising, however. There were relatively few people returning from exile, and the population was greatly reduced.[57] Thus, the smaller City of David (on the southeastern hill) was more than enough for their needs. When Nehemiah 7:4 states that "the city was wide and large, but the people within it were few and no houses had been built," the words "wide and large" undoubtedly refer to the city's size relative to the small population.[58] This explains the need for resettling Jerusalem (chap. 11).

THE ARAMAIC OF EZRA

The book of Ezra has two sections written in Aramaic rather than Hebrew. Aramaic was the *lingua franca* of the first half of the first millennium

54. On date, see Kidner, *Ezra & Nehemiah*, 100–101.
55. W. S. LaSor, *ISBE* 2, s.v. "Jerusalem." See esp. pp. 1013, 1017, and his diagram on p. 1020. See chapter 7 in this volume on the extent of the city in Hezekiah's day.
56. For more on this "minimalist" position, see N. Avigad, *Rediscovering Jerusalem*, 61–63; Williamson, *Ezra, Nehemiah*, 188; and "Nehemiah's Wall Revisited," 81–88.
57. Yamauchi, "Ezra-Nehemiah," 566–68.
58. So also ibid., 717.

B.C. in the ancient Near East, i.e., it was the international language of trade and communication, much as English functions in the world today. A revealing episode into its usage during the period of the monarchies is found in the story of King Hezekiah's emissaries' negotiations with the Assyrian officials of Sennacherib in 2 Kings 18. Hezekiah's emissaries asked the Assyrians to speak to them in Aramaic—the language of diplomacy—not in Hebrew (literally "Judahite"), so that the people listening on the city walls could not understand. The Assyrians insulted them and, to spite them, responded in Hebrew to the assembled people (2 Kings 18:26–28).

Outside of Ezra, Aramaic is found in only three passages:

GENESIS 31:47: Two words here are in Aramaic, representing the name Laban gave to a place to which Jacob gave a Hebrew name.

JEREMIAH 10:11: This is a verse detailing words that Israel was to say to the nations in condemning their gods, using the international diplomatic language to do it.

DANIEL 2:4b–7:28: This is an extended section introduced by a story about King Nebuchadnezzar's astrologers' attempt to interpret his dream, and we are told, "Then the astrologers answered the king in Aramaic," following which the Aramaic begins. Joyce Baldwin notes, "The six chapters [Daniel 2–7] as a whole form a theology of history, addressed to the kings of the earth and therefore written in the international language."[59] The chapters that follow were addressed to the Jews, and they are in Hebrew.

The Aramaic in Ezra is found at 4:8–6:18 and 7:12–26. The transition to Aramaic in 4:7 is marked by the statement, "The letter was written in Aramaic script and in the Aramaic language." The Aramaic sections here consist largely of official documents. Of the sixty-seven verses of Aramaic, fifty-two are records or letters, and only fifteen are narratives.[60] It appears that the author merely copied the Aramaic documents, then linked them with connecting material of his own, also in Aramaic. This was the official language of the province of Judea, as well as being the international *lingua franca*. The dialect of Aramaic here is "Imperial Aramaic," which was common ca. 700–200 B.C. As referenced above (n. 23), the "Ezra Documents" correspond perfectly well to the language and history of contemporary Persian documents and letters.

Why was Aramaic used at all here? In the case of the international correspondence, the answer is fairly obvious: the language in which the letters

---

59. Joyce Baldwin, *Daniel*, 60.
60. Yamauchi, "Ezra-Nehemiah," 586–87.

and decrees were written is preserved intact. However, elsewhere in the OT, speech that was in another tongue is not preserved in that tongue but, rather, rendered in Hebrew. Furthermore, what of the narrative portions that link the letters and decrees? Many scholars propose that this section consisted of an independent document of an unknown king, called by some the "Aramaic Chronicle."[61] However, the contours of this "document" are somewhat strange: it does not cohere very well as an independent unit. Furthermore, this proposal does not explain the interruption in 6:19–7:11 of fifteen verses of Hebrew before a reversion to Aramaic for another fifteen verses.

Perhaps the most convincing explanation for the use of Aramaic is Daniel Snell's proposal that it lends a sense of authenticity to the work.[62] Snell states that the "motivation for Aramaic in the Bible can usually be discerned to be to give a sense of authenticity to the documents and stories by presenting them in the language in which they are likely first to have been composed."[63] Such a theory is persuasive, certainly with respect to the official documents in Ezra but equally so regarding the narrative bridges between them. That is, the author was showing by his command of Aramaic in his own narrative framework that he did indeed understand the Aramaic of the documents he was passing along. This would have functioned to authenticate him as an authoritative interpreter of the materials.

As to why the author returned to Hebrew for the last four verses of the first major section of his book (6:19–22), it seems that when the subject returns to religious matters as prescribed by the law (as it does here), specifically "as it is written in the book of Moses" (6:18), the natural language in which to proceed was the language in which those instructions had been given, namely, Hebrew.

The second use of Aramaic in the book is in the section about Ezra's own time, many years later. Here, the Aramaic consists only of one document, which can easily be explained in terms of its being preserved in its original language (7:12–26).

EZRA AND NEHEMIAH AND THEIR REFORMS

EZRA THE MAN

We do not learn anything about Ezra himself until the "Ezra Memoirs" begin in chapter 7 of his book. Here his genealogical credentials are presented in some detail in 7:1b–5. His priestly lineage is traced back through sixteen generations (including Zadok, priest in David's day) to Aaron, the high priest. This genealogy serves to show him genuinely qualified for the

61. Clines, *Ezra, Nehemiah, Esther*, 8–9; Kidner, *Ezra & Nehemiah*, 136.
62. Daniel C. Snell, "Why Is There Aramaic in the Bible?" 32–51.
63. Ibid., 32.

task at hand. (See chapter 8 under "The Genealogies in 1 Chronicles 1–9" on this function of genealogies.)

Ezra returned to Jerusalem from Babylonia, not Persia (7:6). He came with royal authorization to teach the law of the Jews and to take all necessary steps to reinstitute the sacrificial system (7:11–26). Besides being a priest, Ezra was also a scribe, "well versed"[64] in the law of Moses (7:6). Furthermore, he had "devoted himself to the study and observance of the law of the Lord, and to teaching its decrees and law in Israel" (7:10). An evaluative summary of Ezra calls him "the priest and teacher, a man learned in matters concerning the commands and decrees of the Lord for Israel" (7:11). Both the genealogy (which traces his roots to Aaron) and the comments about his grounding in the law of Moses show Ezra himself to be connected in important ways with the early history of Israel as a nation, a connection that is made in many other ways in the book as well (see below).

Ezra was a great figure in postbiblical Judaism, where he was placed on a par with Moses and credited—along with "the men of the Great Synagogue"—with the origins of the synagogue. However, most of these "facts," as well as the existence of a fixed institution known as "the Great Synagogue" and of a fixed synagogue service modeled after the reading of the law in Nehemiah 8:1–12, are matters of conjecture.[65]

EZRA'S REFORMS

In the book of Ezra, only one true reform is addressed—the problem of marriages to foreigners. Strictly speaking, then, we should speak of Ezra's "reform"—and not "reforms"—since his activities here are limited to one issue. However, in the book of Nehemiah, we see him involved in wider issues related to his commission as teacher of the law.

In Ezra 9, the Jewish leaders approached Ezra with a report of the problem, that Israelites—both clergy and laity—had not refrained from marrying foreigners (v. 1). The basis for the leaders' concern seems to have been the Pentateuchal prohibitions against mixing with peoples of the land of Canaan (vv. 1–2). Several passages strongly warn against mixing in any way with these peoples, and some even specifically refer to intermarriage:

---

64. The word is *māhîr*, which occurs only four times in the OT, only here in Ezra. It means "quick, prompt, ready, skilled" (BDB, 555). RSV has "skilled." It is striking to note the use of this root here, rather than the more common word *ḥākām.* ("wise, skilled"), which perhaps is the author's way of suggesting something about Ezra's character and his readiness to accomplish his tasks.
65. Daniel Sperber, *Encyclopaedia Judaica* 15, C. Roth and G. Wigoder, eds., (Jerusalem: Keter, 1971), s.v. "Synagogue, the Great"; M. R. Wilson, *ISBE* 4, s.v. "Synagogue, the Great"; Williamson, *Ezra, Nehemiah*, 281–82; Paul V. M. Flesher, *ABD* 2, s.v. "Great Assembly."

Exodus 34:11–16 (see v. 16 on intermarriage) and Deuteronomy 7:1–4 (see v. 3 on intermarriage; cf. also Deut. 20:10–18). The concern in these passages is with pollution of Israel's faith and religion. A dramatic example of how faith was polluted by intermarriage can be seen in Solomon (1 Kings 3:1; 11:1–8).[66]

Sometimes we see that several biblical heroes did take foreign wives, with no apparent censure by God or the biblical writers. For example, Abraham took Hagar, an Egyptian (Gen. 16:3); Joseph married Asenath, an Egyptian (Gen. 41:45); Moses married Zipporah, a Midianite (Ex. 2:21), and a Cushite woman (Num. 12:1); Boaz married Ruth, a Moabite (Ruth 4); David married Maacah, a Geshurite (2 Sam. 3:3). Some of these wives (e.g., Ruth) may have been converts to Israel's faith, but not all were.

Here in Ezra, eight groups of peoples are mentioned: Canaanites, Hittites, Perizzites, Jebusites, Ammonites, Moabites, Egyptians, and Amorites (9:1). This list especially recalls two passages cited above (in connection with intermixing): Exodus 34:11 mentions the Amorites, Canaanites, Hittites, Perizzites, Hivites, and Jebusites; Deuteronomy 7:1 mentions the Hittites, Girgashites, Amorites, Canaanites, Perizzites, Hivites, and Jebusites. This would seem to show the connections in the author's mind between the present problem and these earlier prohibitions.

The concern in verse 2 is that the "holy race" (lit., "holy seed") has been polluted. This recalls phrases describing Israel as a "holy nation" (Ex. 19:6) and a "godly seed" (Mal. 2:15), and especially Isaiah 6:13, where this precise term occurs again ("holy seed"), the only other place in the OT where the term occurs. The phrase in Malachi occurs in the context of mixed marriages, whereas the terminology in Isaiah refers to a holy remnant of God's people surviving.

Ezra's reaction was dramatic: it was one of distress and mourning, fasting and tearing out his own hair (9:3–5). He then prayed a heartfelt prayer of confession (9:6–15). It is a model prayer of a leader. In it can be found true confession and an attitude of repentance, as well as genuine identification with the sin of the people. Ezra himself was not guilty of intermarriage, yet he identified himself with the people in the prayer: he quickly shifted from "I" and "my" in 8:6a to "we" and "our" in 8:6b–15.[67]

After he persuaded all of the Israelites to deal with this problem (10:1–17), a list of offenders is given (10:18–43). The list is carefully ordered, starting with religious officials (10:18–24) and finishing with the laity (10:25–43). Kidner notes that this displays a certain forthrightness in that

---

66. As well as in the contemporary community at Elephantine. (See Yamauchi, "Ezra-Nehemiah," 677, for a good discussion of this.)
67. Williamson notes (*Ezra, Nehemiah,* 134) that several other leaders' prayers in the OT similarly identify with people's sins: for example, Nehemiah 1:6; 9:33; Daniel 9:5–19.

the clergy's sins are not in any way minimized.[68] Indeed, here they represent a higher percentage of the families than they had in the Ezra 2 list (15 percent vs. 10 percent); if this does not prove that they were *more* errant than the general population, at least it strongly suggests that they were not any *less* errant!

The list includes 27 clergymen and 84 laymen, a total of 111 persons altogether.[69] That is a very small portion of the population of almost 30,000 returned exiles. Several possibilities have been suggested to explain this. Some maintain that it may be only a partial listing, others that it may indicate that only a small percentage of people really did reform. Others suggest that the problem was not in actuality as serious as it appears on the surface.[70] The text does not indicate a reason for the apparently small number, although the list does have a certain air of comprehensiveness to it.

Beyond Ezra's activities recorded in his own book, we also see him involved with Nehemiah and presenting the law in its more positive aspects, as an enlightening force (Neh. 8:8) and as a "witness to God as liberator and provider (Ne. 8:9–18)."[71]

Regarding the "ethics" of the "divorce decree," the actions of Ezra and the people in taking these actions against foreign women, including some who had children (Ezra 10:44), seem harsh to many modern readers. Some have wondered about the fates of the cast-off women and children. Others have wondered whether the action violated the divorce law of Deuteronomy 24:1–4. That is, was this a mass divorce on grounds not provided for in the law?

In response to the first issue, the author's concern here is very much limited to treating the one question of the pollution within Israel. The urgency of protection of Israel's religious identity was the primary concern, not other, ancillary questions, however important. Indeed, the author is not even concerned with other, equally important religious issues, where deterioration in standards and obedience had indeed set in (as we see in the book of Nehemiah), so we may excuse the author for not satisfying our modern curiosity concerning these people's fates. As a conjecture, we might suggest that, knowing what we do of Ezra's special concern for the laws of the Pentateuch, he would have been well aware of the laws of provision for widows, orphans, and aliens within Israel (e.g., Ex. 22:21–24; Deut. 14:29; 16:11, 14; 24:17) and guaranteed that they were cared for in some way.

---

68. Kidner, *Ezra & Nehemiah*, 72.
69. So Myers, *Ezra-Nehemiah*, 87. Walter Kaiser (*Hard Sayings of the Old Testament*, 140–43, esp. p. 141) gives the totals as follows: 27 clergymen (17 priests, 6 Levites, 1 singer, and 3 porters) and 86 laymen, for a total of 113 persons.
70. See Myers (*Ezra-Nehemiah*, 87–88) for a review of these.
71. Kidner, *Ezra & Nehemiah*, 72.

However, if the relatively small number of offenders is indeed accurate, then we must at least place the "divorce decree" into proper perspective. Despite its seriousness, it had far less of an impact upon actual people who were put away than is often imagined; an innumerable underclass of thousands upon thousands of outcast women and children was not instantly created. Yamauchi shows that the total percentage of offenders is less than one percent of the population: 0.4 percent.[72]

Concerning the second issue, as to whether the action violates the divorce law of Deuteronomy 24:1–4, Walter Kaiser notes that this law did permit divorce for "something indecent" (NIV) found in a wife and that this could not have been adultery, since in that case the death penalty was called for (Deut. 22:22).[73] Thus, Ezra may very well have had this law in mind, and he may have understood these women's pagan (or at the very least, syncretistic) beliefs and practices as the "indecency" mentioned in that law.

NEHEMIAH THE MAN

Like Ezra, Nehemiah also returned to Judah with a commission from the Persian king, but his commission was a civil, not a religious, one. He was the king's cupbearer (Neh. 1:11), which afforded him access to the king and to many privileges, and the king authorized him to return to Jerusalem and rebuild the city (1:7–8).

As we read his "Memoirs," we see a gifted administrator, well prepared and equipped for his tasks. For example, when the king asked him concerning his proposal to return to Jerusalem, the conversation (2:6–8) reveals that Nehemiah had prepared himself well for this discussion (cf. also 1:4, 11b); he asked for several specifics: an amount of time for the project, as well as authorization for passage to Judah and for materials to be provided. The king readily acceded to the requests. Later, Nehemiah organized the people into groups whereby each man was responsible for repairing or rebuilding the walls of the city opposite the area in which he lived (chap. 3). Nehemiah organized defenses for the project when it was threatened by opposition (4:9, 13–23).

Nehemiah appears to have been full of self-confidence, as well as confident in God, and he combined the two in practical ways. A well-known verse illustrating this is 4:9, which tells of his response when he heard of the opposition to the rebuilding project: "We prayed to our God and posted a guard day and night to meet the threat." (Other examples of Nehemiah's

---

72. Yamauchi, "Ezra-Nehemiah," 676.
73. Kaiser, *Hard Sayings of the Old Testament*, 142.

combination of spiritual faith with practical actions are found at 2:4–5; 4:14, 20.) Nehemiah's self-confidence may also be illustrated by his response to men who married foreign women: he cursed them, beat them, and tore out their hair (13:25). Ezra's style was more low-key: when he heard similar news, he tore out his own hair (Ezra 9:3)!

Nehemiah also appears as a transparent man. He admitted to the Jews that he himself, and his household, had been engaged in lending practices that imposed hardships on people, practices he was urging the wealthy Jews to stop (Neh. 5:10). This confession, and his personal identification with those he was admonishing, set an example that was hard to ignore.

A late intertestamental Jewish tradition mentions a "library" founded by Nehemiah, which, given the chaotic conditions after the Exile, he may very well have done: "The same things are reported in the records and in the memoirs of Nehemiah, and also that he founded a library and collected the books about the kings and prophets, and the writings of David, and letters of kings about votive offerings" (2 Maccabees 2:13 NRSV).

NEHEMIAH'S REFORMS

Nehemiah was very active when he returned to Jerusalem. He surveyed the damaged city walls (Neh. 2:11–16), organized the rebuilding (chap. 3), and countered opposition to the rebuilding (chaps. 4 and 6). He also participated with Ezra in the reading of the law, celebration of the Feast of Tabernacles, separation from foreigners, and confession of sins (8:1-10:27). Beyond these measures, we find actual religious "reforms" being instituted on three occasions: 5:1–19; 10:28–39 [MT 29–40]; and 13:1–31.

Chapter 5. On the first occasion, various internal problems threatened the unity of the people. These problems revolved around various inequities among those who had become impoverished (5:1–13). An outcry arose among the people against other Jews (5:1). (This is reminiscent of the outcry that arose in Acts 6:1–6 concerning the inequities of treatment between the widows of the Grecian Jews and Hebraic Jews.) Three groups were represented, each with slightly different complaints, but all suffering from inequities that caused people to fall into a debt that they could not manage.

The first problem was life-threatening: many people were starving and apparently had no resources with which to purchase food (5:2). The second problem also arose out of the famine condition: some people did have resources, but they were forced to mortgage their properties in order to buy food (5:3). The third problem was that still others had to mortgage their properties to pay the king's tax (5:4), while some were even forced to sell their children into slavery to cover their debts (5:5).

The lending of money at interest per se was not illegal, nor was the practice of debt-slavery. Provision is made for these in such passages as Exodus 21:2–11; 22:25–27 [MT 22–24]; Leviticus 25:1–55; Deuteronomy 15:1–18; 24:10–13. However, here the matter was not one of legalistic hairsplitting but, rather, one of justice and the spirit of the law, since many people could not have survived much longer.

Nehemiah's response was quick and decisive, and he did so on his own authority, without invoking any specific legal authority (5:6–13).[74] Angered, he gathered the wealthy Jews who were holding the debts and lectured them, ordering them to release their holdings and the debts and promising that he would do the same (5:6–11). The lenders readily agreed to right the situation and followed through on this promise (5:12–13).

At this point, Nehemiah tells us of his own continued commitment to financial sacrifice (5:14–19). The thing that Nehemiah asked the wealthy Jews to do was very hard: to give up legally obtained properties voluntarily and with no compensation. The final section of the chapter covers a later period—the twelve years from Artaxerxes's twentieth to his thirty-second years (445–433 B.C.)—and it shows that he himself was willing to take on even more sacrifices than he asked of the people, since he already was divesting himself of the properties he had acquired (cf. 5:10–13). As governor of the province, he was legally entitled to live off the taxes from the province (cf. 5:14, 18: "the food allotted to the governor"). Yet, he did not avail himself of that opportunity, even though the requirements of his household were very great: one ox and six sheep per day, along with birds and much wine (5:18), which regularly served 150 men, not counting guests (5:17). He provided for these himself, in keeping with the spirit of generosity he had urged upon the wealthy Jews.

Chapter 10. A few months after the first set of reforms, Nehemiah participated with Ezra in reading the law and in a "covenant commitment" ceremony (chaps. 8–10). In this ceremony, the people committed themselves to various stipulations in the law. Some are found in the Pentateuch, whereas others are not, but the overall mood was one of a strong willingness to obey both the letter and spirit of the law.[75]

First, they separated themselves from foreigners, and forswore mixed marriages with foreigners (10:28–30).[76] The problem addressed by Ezra was visible again here.

---

74. Williamson, *Ezra, Nehemiah*, 239.
75. See Clines ("Nehemiah 10 as an Example of Early Jewish Biblical Exegesis," 111–17) for a discussion of how the new solutions here related to the Pentateuchal provisions.
76. The verse numbers for this chapter are cited from English versions; in the Hebrew Bible, the verse numbers are higher by one.

Second, they addressed problems of the Sabbath (10:31): foreigners were selling on the Sabbath, and the Jews were not to violate the Sabbath by buying from them. They also reaffirmed the provisions of the Sabbath year (see Ex. 21:2–6; 23:10–11).

Third, they promised to pay a "Temple tax" for support of the Temple and its ceremonies (Neh. 10:32–33). Strictly speaking, there is no such tax in the Pentateuch, but this commitment appears to build off of a law in Exodus 30:11–16.[77]

Fourth, they promised to bring wood offerings for the altar (Neh. 10:34). Here again, no law is found corresponding exactly to this commitment, but a related law is found in Leviticus 6:12–13 (MT 5–6), concerning the fire on the altar that was to be kept burning continually.

Fifth, they promised to support the Temple personnel, the priests and the Levites (Neh. 10:35–39).

The concluding statement brings most of the reforms together in a blanket summary commitment: "We will not neglect the house of our God" (10:39c).

Chapter 13. A final set of reforms is conveniently collected here, and a common thread in all of these is cleansing or purification.

First, the issue of separation from foreigners is addressed in 13:1–3, specifically in barring all foreigners from being admitted into the "assembly of God."[78] They were inspired by the book of Moses to do this, just as they had been inspired by the examples from the days of David to provide for the Temple service immediately prior to this (12:44–47).

Second, Nehemiah found that Eliashib the priest had violated the Temple by offering space in the storerooms to Tobiah for an "apartment" while Nehemiah was in Babylon. When he returned, he evicted Tobiah and purified the Temple (13:4–9).

Third, Nehemiah discovered that the Levites and Temple singers were reduced to working in the fields in order to survive (13:10–14). Nehemiah rebuked the people and had them bring their tithes, then set up treasurers of the storehouses to assure a regular flow of distribution to these Temple personnel (13:12–13).

Fourth, Nehemiah found the Sabbath being violated by Jews and foreigners alike. He again rebuked the leaders and issued orders to ensure that this would not happen again (13:15–22).

Fifth, the issue of mixed marriages again is raised (13:23–27). Nehemiah's initial reaction was a violent one, more aggressive than Ezra's had been

---

77. Williamson, *Ezra, Nehemiah*, 335.
78. This issue of mixing with foreigners is mentioned in the following passages in Nehemiah: 9:2; 10:28; 10:30; 13:1–3; 13:23–27.

to a similar problem (cf. Ezra 9:3–5). However, reading carefully between the lines, the text does not say that the foreign wives were put away (as they had been in Ezra), but only that Nehemiah had the people swear not to take foreign wives any more (Neh. 13:25).

Sixth, Nehemiah discovered that even the high-priestly line was being corrupted by intermarriage (13:28–29). It involved a marriage to Sanballat's daughter, of all people! Nehemiah chased the offender away.

The short conclusion to the book (13:30–31) sums up the essence of the entire work: purification from any contamination; establishment of correct worship; and provision for all things.

Special Issues in Ezra-Nehemiah

David and Royal Outlooks in Ezra-Nehemiah

Though David is a dominant figure in such books as 1 & 2 Samuel, 1 & 2 Kings, and 1 & 2 Chronicles, he does not have quite the same stature or place in Ezra-Nehemiah. He is mentioned three times in Ezra (3:10; 8:2, 20) and eight times in Nehemiah (3:15, 16; 12:24, 36, 37, 37, 45, 46). In Nehemiah, four of the references are topographical (to such things as the City of David).

Only once does David appear in a context that emphasizes his position as the chosen king of the Davidic Covenant, and that is in a genealogy, showing that the royal line was represented among the returnees in Ezra's day (Ezra 8:2; see also the reference to "David king of Israel" in 3:10).

Elsewhere, David's primary place seems to be as one who provided for the building of the Temple, and especially for the musical and other aspects of the Temple worship. Thus, we see in 3:10 that David appears as the sponsor of music; the celebrations of the Temple rebuilding were done "as prescribed by David king of Israel." In 8:20, David appears as the one who had set aside Temple servants to aid the Levites. In Nehemiah 12:24, the Levites performed their duties "as prescribed by David the man of God" (see the similar statement in 12:45). Nehemiah 12:36 mentions "the musical instruments prescribed by David the man of God," while 12:46 mentions singers and songs of praise and thanksgiving "in the days of David and Asaph of old."

These pictures of David that emphasize his role in the Temple worship recall similar emphases upon him and Solomon in 1 & 2 Chronicles. However, Ezra-Nehemiah have almost none of the emphasis upon these two men as heirs of the dynastic promises that is found in 1 & 2 Chronicles. This has led to the question of the place of these promises in Ezra-Nehemiah.

The usual scholarly consensus is that there is no interest in the royal line or messianic ideals by the time of these books. J. D. Newsome's comment is typical: "No breath of royalist or messianic hope stirs in Ezra-Nehemiah."[79]

However, a royalist interest is not entirely lacking in Ezra-Nehemiah. We have already noted the royal references to David in Ezra 3:10 and 8:2. Also, the prominence of Zerubbabel, David's descendant, in Ezra 1–6 attests to this interest as well.

Furthermore, there are indications in the books that—despite the relatively benevolent attitude of Persia toward the Jews and the restoration of the Temple and its religious service—all was not well even in this period and that there is more hope for the future than is commonly realized. Several scholars have made the point that even here one can see a perspective of hope and an openness to the future.[80]

This is done partly on the basis of dissatisfaction with the present state of affairs. It would include a statement such as Nehemiah's that "we are slaves today, slaves in the land you gave our forefathers" (Neh. 9:36). The context of this statement is that God always gave His people into slavery as a punishment for their sins (9:28–35). It would also include a statement such as Ezra's, that "because of our sins, we and our kings and our priests have been subjected to the sword and captivity, to pillage and humiliation at the hands of foreign kings, *as it is this day*" (Ezra 9:7; italics added). Both prayers, while they acknowledge God's graciousness, nevertheless reveal that things could be much better, i.e., in their own land under their own—not foreign—leadership.

See also the elders' lament when the foundation to the Temple was laid: they realized that the new Temple would fall far short of the glories of the former Temple (3:12–13). Also, notice the persistence of mixed marriages—and the fact that Nehemiah's book ends on the somewhat disheartening note of reforms repeated.

J. G. McConville notes parallels with several prophecies in the prophetic corpus that express a hope in the future—especially in Jeremiah and Isaiah—which indicate that the expectations in Ezra-Nehemiah did still look to the future, just as these prophecies did.[81] Note, for example, the reference to the "holy seed" (NIV "holy race") in 9:2 (the parallel in Isa. 6:13), where the holy seed is the stump that remains after the purging of Israel. Furthermore, the references in Ezra-Nehemiah to the restored remnant, including

79. James D. Newsome, Jr., "Toward a New Understanding of the Chronicler and His Purposes," 214.
80. K. Koch, "Ezra and the Origins of Judaism," 173–97; Williamson, *Ezra, Nehemiah*, li–lii; J. G. McConville, "Ezra-Nehemiah and the Fulfillment of Prophecy," 205–24.
81. McConville, "Ezra-Nehemiah and the Fulfillment of Prophecy," 214–23; he finds extensive allusions in Ezra 7–9, for example, to Jeremiah 31 and to motifs in Isaiah 40–66.

"Israel," "all Israel," and "Ephraim," point to an expectation of some type of restoration of the earlier kingdom.[82]

Finally, we should note that the emphasis on the Temple and the law is not incompatible with a "royalist" perspective and even an eschatological, messianic perspective, since among the king's responsibilities were keeping the law, worshiping correctly, and leading the people in doing so,[83] and it would be part of the future king's mission to reestablish these in some way.[84] Thus, we can conclude that the books of Ezra and Nehemiah are indeed compatible with the other historical—and prophetic—books that emphasize the importance for Israel of the Davidic Covenant and the hope for the future it portended.

THE IDENTITY OF SHESHBAZZAR

Considerable discussion has taken place over the question of the identity of Sheshbazzar. He is mentioned only four times in the Bible, all in Ezra (1:8, 11; 5:14, 16), and he is not known outside of the Bible. The issue at stake is that his and Zerubbabel's occupations and duties appear to overlap, and some have suggested that these are two names for the same individual.[85]

Sheshbazzar was commissioned by Cyrus to oversee construction of the Temple and to handle the treasuries sent back for that purpose (1:8, 11). He is called here the "prince of Judah," a title that is used nowhere else; it recalls references in Ezekiel to the Davidic "prince" that would come to restore Israel (e.g., Ezek. 7:27; 12:10, 12; 19:1; 21:25 [MT 30]; 34:24; 37:25).

On the basis of the Ezekiel references, some scholars believe that Sheshbazzar was a descendant of David. Thus, some have suggested that Sheshbazzar was the Shenazzar of 1 Chronicles 3:18, who was the fourth son of the king Jehoiachin, and the uncle of Zerubbabel, both of the line of David. However, linguistically, this suggestion does not stand up: "Sheshbazzar" is Hebrew for a Babylonian name, *šaššu-ab-uṣur* ("may *šaššu* [i.e., *šamaš*, the sun-god] protect the father"), while "Shenazzar" is Hebrew for a different Babylonian name, *sin-uṣur* ("may [the god] *sin* protect").[86]

---

82. McConville, "Ezra-Nehemiah and the Fulfillment of Prophecy," 222–23; Walter C. Kaiser, Jr., *Toward an Old Testament Theology*, 259.

83. See Gerald Gerbrandt, *Kingship According to the Deuteronomistic History*, 89–102.

84. See also Kaiser, *Toward an Old Testament Theology*, 261.

85. See Kidner, *Ezra & Nehemiah*, 139–42; Williamson, *Ezra, Nehemiah*, 5 n. 8, 17–19; W. White, Jr., *ZPEB* 5, s.v. "Sheshbazzar"; R. L. Pratt, Jr., *ISBE* 4, s.v. "Sheshbazzar." All of these scholars see Sheshbazzar and Zerubbabel as different individuals.

86. Williamson, *Ezra, Nehemiah*, 5 n. 8d.

Others have suggested that Sheshbazzar was indeed Zerubbabel him-self, the one being his personal name and the other his official name.[87] There is a certain attraction to this proposal in that both Sheshbazzar and Zerubbabel appear to have had Persian commissions to rebuild the Temple (Sheshbazzar: 1:8, 11; 5:14, 16; Zerubbabel: 2:2; 3:2, 8; 5:2). Both are called "governor": Sheshbazzar in Ezra 5:14 and Zerubbabel in Haggai 1:1. It is in-deed an attested phenomenon that people often had two names. Witness Solomon/Jedidiah, Azariah/Uzziah, and, in this period, witness Daniel/Bel-teshazzar and his three friends.

However, Ezra 5:14–16 seems to distinguish the two men, since Zer-ubbabel was present at that time (5:2), whereas Sheshbazzar seems to have been unknown to Tattenai: in 5:14, 16 he is mentioned as someone needing identification—"one whose name was Sheshbazzar" (v. 14); "this Sheshbaz-zar" (v. 16). Also, Sheshbazzar functioned under Cyrus (ca. 537 B.C.), where-as Zerubbabel did so under Darius (ca. 520 B.C.).

It also may be noted that there is no direct evidence that Sheshbazzar was a member of Judean royalty.[88] The term "prince" does not necessarily denote royalty, and he is not mentioned in the royal genealogy in 1 Chroni-cles 3, which seems to be aiming at comprehensiveness for the exilic and postexilic periods. Indeed, Sheshbazzar is given no family genealogy at all. He may not have been very prominent in Judah at all (but rather a Persian appointee).

Of Zerubbabel and Sheshbazzar, the former was clearly the more prominent. He was probably the true Jewish leader, in actual practice and function, while Sheshbazzar seems to have been only a titulary leader. Sheshbazzar was likely the Persian governor, appointed over Judah, not over all of Abar-Nahraim, as was Tattenai (5:3). This, and the fact that he was earlier (537 B.C.), may explain why the Jews spoke to Tattenai of Shesh-bazzar as if he would not have known him (or even of him).

As to why he was called the "prince of Judah," Williamson plausibly notes that it was the *author's* label for him, and not his actual title; his title was "governor" (5:14).[89] The reason for the author so labeling him was to call to mind elements of the Mosaic period, during which the Exodus from Egypt occurred. (This "second Exodus" motif is discussed under "Theology of Ezra-Nehemiah" below.) That is because in the accounts of the wilder-ness wanderings, especially in Numbers, several lists show various "princes" of the various tribes (Num. 2:3–31; 7:1–83; 34:18–28). Also, at Numbers 7:84–86, the "princes" of Israel were those who gave the gold and

87. Zerubbabel is referred to twenty-two times in the Bible: in 1 & 2 Chronicles, Ezra, Nehemi-ah, Haggai, and Zechariah.
88. See Williamson, *Ezra, Nehemiah*, 17, and references there.
89. Ibid., 17–18.

silver vessels for the altar's dedication. This association is probably what triggered the author's designation of Sheshbazzar as "prince" in 1:8, since here he is in charge of the inventory of articles of gold and silver.

This is a plausible explanation. But it remains to ask whether in fact the author was historically accurate in calling Sheshbazzar "prince of Judah." Since "prince of Judah" occurs only here, we do not have any evidence that it was a separate, special office. However, the use of the term "prince" in the book of Numbers does not refer to a separate, special office either. No canon of historical facticity is violated in this case by accepting the later author's license to make this designation of an earlier figure who was known in his own time as "governor." Thus, we conclude that Sheshbazzar and Zerubbabel were two separate individuals, both leaders of the people at different times, but the latter more prominent than the former.

THEOLOGY OF EZRA-NEHEMIAH

Several important themes reverberate throughout both Ezra and Nehemiah. Of these, the issues of the nature and identity of the people of God and of the importance of Temple worship are the most important.

GOD'S PEOPLE: AT ONE WITH PREEXILIC ISRAEL

Many strong indicators in Ezra and Nehemiah show that the people of God after the Exile were clearly to be understood as descended from God's people before the Exile and, as such, heirs to the promises to earlier generations. This was important, since the Exile had raised questions as to whether God's promises indeed were continuing, or whether God's people had a future at all.

A "second Exodus." The "exodus" from Babylon and the return home to Jerusalem as found in Ezra has many elements that are reminiscent of the Israelites' Exodus from Egypt and their first entry into the promised land.[90] For example, the returnees' neighbors bestowed upon them many valuable articles for their trip back (Ezra 1:6), which echoes the Egyptians' doing the same thing (Ex. 12:35–36). The original Temple vessels were restored to the Jews and carefully returned to Jerusalem (Ezra 1:7–11), reminding us of the original vessels that were made for the Tabernacle. Also, the Jews themselves gave freewill offerings for the building of the Temple (2:68–69), recalling similar freewill offerings for the Tabernacle (Ex. 35:20–29).

Faithfulness to the Mosaic Law. Many elements in Ezra and Nehemiah suggest a strong concern to do things in accordance with the Mosaic Law. Since the Exile had befallen the nation because of its unfaithfulness to God,

90. Ibid., li, 16.

strict obedience to the law now was a visible demonstration of the people's faithfulness. They were concerned to "get it right" this time.

Moses himself is referred to ten times in the two books, each time in connection with the law (Ezra 3:2; 6:18; 7:6; Neh. 1:7, 8; 8:1, 14; 9:14; 10:29; 13:1). In each of these cases, the reference to the law or instructions of Moses is in the context of the people's wanting to do things in accordance with the law. Thus, for example, some people could not eat sacred foods until a priest was present with the Urim and Thummim (Ezra 2:63). (The Urim and Thummim are mentioned in Ex. 28:30; Lev. 8:8; Num. 27:1.) Also, the people were in a hurry to build the altar of sacrifice—even before the Temple—so that they could offer sacrifices again (Ezra 3:2). Priests and Levites were installed in accordance with the law (6:18). Indeed, Ezra's entire commission was based upon his familiarity with the law (7:6). The public reading of the law—and the people's commitment to it—was an important event for the community, and both Ezra and Nehemiah were involved (Nehemiah 8–10). (For more on this, see the "The Importance of Scripture" below.)

One people of God. An important way in which both books speak of continuity with the past is in their inclusion of extensive lists of people. These lists give a general sense of connection with the past, especially since many names of people and places in these lists can be traced to known preexilic names. This is true in the list of returning exiles in Ezra 2 (duplicated in Nehemiah 7), as well as the names in the list of those returning many years later with Ezra (Ezra 8), and the list of new residents of Jerusalem in Nehemiah 11.

GOD'S PEOPLE: UNIFIED

The unity of God's people is an important motif in Ezra and Nehemiah. The extensive lists suggest this, conveying a sense of inclusiveness.[91] Also, people's generosity toward each other—from the many in Babylon who were staying behind and providing their neighbors with valuable gifts (Ezra 1:6) to the generous reaction to Nehemiah's suggestions about providing for the needy in Nehemiah 5—shows the shared community values. The combined actions of the entire community in rebuilding the Temple in the early postexilic period (Ezra 3; 6:13–18) and the walls of Jerusalem many years later (Nehemiah 3–4, 6) also illustrate this. Even the willingness of many people to move to Jerusalem from the surrounding countryside to repopulate the capital shows this generosity of community spirit (Nehemiah 11).

91. This point is also made by Tamara C. Eskenazi, "The Structure of Ezra-Nehemiah and the Integrity of the Book," 641–56.

GOD'S PEOPLE: SEPARATED

Essential to the well-being of the postexilic community was its remaining uncontaminated by contact with its unbelieving neighbors. Such contact had repeatedly been the cause of Israel's downfall and, in the end, led to the Exile. Thus, with the return from exile, the purity of the nation was essential.

This is demonstrated in a number of ways already spoken of above. In their concern for the law, for identification with preexilic Israel, and for unity in the community, the idea of Israel as a separate entity was being stressed. In addition, the reforms of both Ezra and Nehemiah demonstrated this. As noted, the separation from foreign wives under both men was a drastic measure to ensure the purity of Israel's religious practices. Part of the problem with foreign marriage was that Jewish children were no longer speaking their own language (Neh. 13:24). As seen so often in our own day as well, language is a powerful tool for nationalistic impulses.

Israel was certainly allowed to have *some* contacts with the outside world. God had promised great blessing to the nations through their contacts with Abraham and his descendants (Gen. 12:3), and we see many examples of positive contacts between Israelites and foreigners (e.g., Rahab, Ruth, Naaman, and the message of the book of Jonah). However, in this postexilic period, the greater imperative was the survival of Israel's religious faith. In that light, strict measures were required, and strict measures were taken.

TEMPLE WORSHIP

A major focus of attention in both books, especially in Ezra, is the Temple and the worship to be done there. The Temple had lain destroyed during the Exile, and no sacrifices were offered. Naturally, then, the early chapters of Ezra are preoccupied with the building of the Temple and the celebration of various religious ceremonies (Ezra 1–6). As soon as they returned, they began to offer regular sacrifices and celebrate the appointed festivals, such as the Feast of Tabernacles and the New Moon celebrations (3:3–6). When the Temple was completed, they dedicated it with a great celebration and installed the priests and Levites to care for it and its service (6:16–18). Then they celebrated the Passover (6:19–22).

At the same time that Ezra returned, many Temple personnel also returned (7:7). Yet Ezra found himself missing Levites on his journey, and he went no further until he was able to secure a full complement of Levites and others to help with the Temple service (8:15–20). They then offered sacrifices when they arrived (8:35).

The Temple vessels and treasuries were important as well. We see them carefully being brought back under Sheshbazzar in the first return (1:6–11; 2:68–69), and more treasures for the Temple were carefully returned under Ezra himself as well (8:24–34).

When Ezra and Nehemiah led the people in the great ceremony of reading the law, the people celebrated the Feast of Tabernacles as part of the occasion (Neh. 8:10–18). Even the attention to priests, Levites, and other Temple personnel in the various lists in both books attests to the importance of the Temple and its service.

THE IMPORTANCE OF SCRIPTURE

Obedience to the law of Moses is an important motif in both books of Ezra and Nehemiah, as noted above. The Mosaic Scriptures themselves are prominent in these books.[92] The reading of the Scriptures took its place alongside sacrificing as an essential part of the Jews' religious service. In addition to what we have already stated, we may add the following observations.

Public reading. Ezra read from "the Book of the Law of Moses"[93] in a prominent, public place, raised up on a specially designed wooden platform (Neh. 8:4–5). (Note the similar bronze platform used by Solomon at the dedication of the Temple in 2 Chron. 6:13.) The reading was done in the square in front of the Water Gate, on the east side of the city. It is interesting to notice Ezra's choice of site. Since it was not in front of the Temple proper, he may have been proclaiming the superiority of the law itself over the Temple or its sacrifices.[94] Note the contrast with Ezra 3:1–6, where the assembly was held in the Temple court.[95]

Significant date. This reading of the law was done on the first day of the seventh month (Neh. 8:2). The seventh month was "a feast month par excellence."[96] It was the month for the celebration of the Day of Atonement (Lev. 16:29; 23:27; 25:9), the Feast of Tabernacles (23:34, 39, 41), the Day of Trumpets (23:24; Num. 29:1), and other solemn days (Num. 29:7, 12ff.). It also was a month in which other significant events had transpired. For example, the ark was moved in Solomon's day from the city of David to the Temple at the feast of the seventh month (2 Chron. 5:3), and tithes were brought in between the third and seventh months (31:7).

92. See Eskenazi ("Ezra-Nehemiah: From Text to Actuality," 165–97) for an essay detailing the importance of the written text in the entire fabric of the community's life at this time.
93. On the identity of this book, and interaction with the critical position that it was a recent creation of Ezra's brought from Babylon, see Kidner, *Ezra & Nehemiah*, 104, 158–64.
94. So Ellison, quoted in Williamson, *Ezra, Nehemiah*, 287.
95. Kidner, *Ezra & Nehemiah*, 105.
96. Myers, *Ezra-Nehemiah*, 152.

Parallels to Temple building. The events in Nehemiah 8 and those in Ezra 3 reveal interesting comparisons between the laying of the foundations of the Temple and the reading of the law. Note especially the following (author's translation):

> Ezra 3:1: "And the beginning of the seventh month arrived, with the children of Israel in *the* towns, and the people gathered as one man at [Jerusalem.]"

> Nehemiah 7:73b–8:1a: "And the beginning of the seventh month arrived, with the children of Israel in *their* towns, and *all* the people gathered as one man at [the square before the Water Gate]."

The two texts are identical in Hebrew, except for the italicized portions. This similarity makes the obvious point that this reading of the law is to be understood in the same way as the rebuilding of the altar and Temple foundation some ninety years earlier. They both were great, significant, and happy occasions. This is supported, e.g., by the prominence of the "rejoicing" motif in both contexts (Ezra 3:10–13; Neh. 8:6, 12, 17).

Understanding the Scriptures. A key word in relation to the Scriptures is "understanding," which occurs six times in Neh. 8:1–12.[97] In two cases it denotes "explaining" (i.e., "causing to understand": 8:7, 9), and in the others it simply means "to understand." There is a remarkable cluster of related words in 8:8 as well: "They read from the Book of the Law of God, making it clear and giving the meaning so that the people could understand what was being read." The point is simple: when the law was read, the people understood it clearly, and this understanding formed the basis then for their confession, repentance, and reforms that followed.

The Levites had teaching responsibilities in "helping the people understand" (8:7; cf. 8:9: "the Levites who taught the people"), which fits a function that they had been given earlier. Deuteronomy 33:10 states, "They shall teach Thine ordinances to Jacob, and Thy law to Israel" (NASB). Second Chronicles 17:7–9 notes that Levites went through Judah teaching the law in the days of Jehoshaphat, while 2 Chronicles 35:3 mentions "the Levites who taught all Israel." Malachi 2:6–9 also stresses the importance of the teaching function for Levites.[98]

The Scriptures and celebrations. After the law was read, Ezra, Nehemiah, and the Levites collaborated in encouraging the people to rejoice and not mourn (Neh 8:9–12). The mourning was in response to their hearing of

---

97. Nehemiah 8:2, 3, 7, 8, 9, 12. The root is *BYN*. See the related word *ŚKL* ("to understand, to see") in Nehemiah 8:13; 9:20.
98. See Duane Garrett (*Rethinking Genesis*, 199–232) for a review of the Levites' teaching role.

the law, which they presumably realized they could not live up to. These leaders emphasized that it was a holy day (8:9, 10, 11), one for rejoicing (8:10, 12). Their rejoicing was because they had "understood" the words declared to them (8:12).

PRAYER

Along with the many other features of religious worship, prayer plays a prominent role in Ezra and Nehemiah. Three extended prayers of confession are recorded: Ezra's, on the occasion of discovering the mixed marriages (Ezra 9:6–15); Nehemiah's, when he heard about the poor conditions in Jerusalem (Neh. 1:5–11); and the people's, on the occasion of reading the law (9:5–37).[99]

Extended prayers. We have noted above that Ezra's prayer in Ezra 9 is a model prayer for a leader. We can see true confession and an attitude of repentance in it, as well as genuine identification with the sin of the people.

Nehemiah's prayer in Nehemiah 1 also is a good example of one whose heart is attuned to God. It confesses the people's sin, asking God for forgiveness, and also for grace in dealing with the Persian king.

The people's prayer in Nehemiah 9 is of a piece with several "historical" psalms: Psalms 78, 105, 106, 135, 136. All of these review Israel's history, with an eye to praising God for his deeds in the past and the present or confessing Israel's sins from the past and the present. The prayer here most closely parallels Psalms 106 and 135, which are of the latter type. (See also Stephen's speech in Acts 7.) The emphasis is upon God's graciousness and the people's rebelliousness.

Short prayers. Both books record short prayers as well, especially Nehemiah. Ezra tells of the people's praying for help on their journey homeward (Ezra 8:21–23). Nehemiah is famous for his short prayers, which give endearing pictures of Nehemiah the man. When King Artaxerxes asked him what he wanted, he records that "I prayed to the God of heaven, and I answered the king" (Neh. 2:4–5).

Frequently, we have the contents of Nehemiah's short prayers—which are uttered as "asides"—preserved for us. The first of these is at 5:19: "Remember me with favor, O my God, for all I have done for these people." The books ends with a similar request: "Remember me with favor, O my God" (13:31). In addition, we find such "remember" prayers at 6:9, 14; 13:14, 22, 29. We even see him uttering an imprecation against his enemies: "Hear us,

---

99. The Old Greek versions (Septuagint) have "And Ezra said" at the beginning of 9:6 (see RSV). NIV, NASB, and NJPSV do not translate it, understanding the prayer to be the people's. The public prayer probably begins in 9:5c (see NIV and NASB), since the first-person address to God begins there and continues in 9:6ff.

O our God, for we are despised. Turn their insults back on their own heads. Give them over as plunder in a land of captivity. Do not cover up their guilt or blot out their sins from your sight, for they have thrown insults in the face of the builders" (4:4–5).

GOD'S GRACE

The Lord's graciousness to His people is an important motif in Ezra and Nehemiah. The Persians' benevolent policies toward their subject peoples was one sign of God's grace (Ezra 7:6, 28; Neh. 2:8).

God's grace is also visible through His "good hand" or His "mighty hand." In these books, God's "hand" is mentioned nine times, six times in Ezra (7:6, 9, 28; 8:18, 22, 31) and three times in Nehemiah (1:10; 2:8, 18). Usually it is "the good hand" (or "the strong hand") of "our/my/his" God. In almost every one of these cases, we see people—whether Persian officials or others—helping the Jews. The point is repeatedly made that because of God's good hand things were done on the Jews' behalf.

Five times the phrase is literally "according to the hand of [the Lord or God]": Ezra 7:6, 9, 28; 8:18; Nehemiah 2:8. Williamson has noted that this expression is used in the sense of royal bounty elsewhere, such as at 1 Kings 10:13; Esther 1:7; 2:18.[100] In each of these cases, the phrase is exactly the same—"according to the hand of the king"[101]—and each time it refers to a king's generosity.

The references to God's good hand would then function as a low-key reminder that God Himself is still King and that the Persian kings' bounty was in reality the bounty coming from the "King of kings" to His people.

OUTLINE OF EZRA-NEHEMIAH

The Return from Exile (Ezra 1–2)
    Cyrus's Decree (1:1–4)
    The Return Under Sheshbazzar (1:5–11)
    The List of Exiles Who Returned (2:1–70)
        The Leaders (2:1–2)
            Zerubbabel
            Jeshua
        The Lay Israelites (2:3–35)
            Family/Clan Groupings (2:3–20)
            Hometown Groupings (2:21–35)

---

100. Williamson, *Ezra, Nehemiah*, 93.
101. Williamson neglects to mention that these three cases are the only ones outside of Ezra-Nehemiah in which this exact construction is found.

Further Preparations (8:21–30)
  A Fast (8:21–23)
  Provision for the Temple Treasures (8:24–30)
The Journey and Arrival at Jerusalem (8:31–36)

Ezra's Reform (Ezra 9–10)
The Problem: Mixed Marriages (9:1–5)
Ezra's Prayer of Confession (9:6–15)
Ezra's and the People's Response (10:1–6)
A Public Assembly (10:7–15)
The Legal Proceeding (10:16–17)
The List of Offenders (10:18–43)
Conclusion (10:44)

Nehemiah's Return to Jerusalem (Nehemiah 1–2)
News From Jerusalem (1:1–4)
Nehemiah's Prayer (1:5–11)
Nehemiah's Commission and Return to Jerusalem (2:1–10)
Nehemiah's Initial Actions in Jerusalem (2:11–20)
  Nehemiah and the Walls of Jerusalem (2:11–18)
    Nehemiah's Night Inspection Tour (2:11–16)
    Exhortation to Rebuild (2:17–18)
  Opposition (2:19–20)

Wall Rebuilding Begun (Nehemiah 3–4)
The Work on the Walls (3:1–32)
External Opposition: Point-Counterpoint (4:1–23 [MT 3:33–4:17])
  Verbal Opposition & Nehemiah's Response (4:1–6 [MT 3:33–38])
  Armed Opposition and Further Responses (4:7–15 [MT 1–9])
  Cautious Rebuilding (4:16–23 [MT 10–17])

Internal and External Problems (Nehemiah 5–7)
Internal Threats: Nehemiah's Initial Reforms (5:1–19)
  The Problem: Varieties of Inequities (5:1–5)
  Nehemiah's Response (5:6–13)
  Nehemiah's Own Sacrifice (5:14–19)
Further External Opposition (6:1–19)
  Sanballat's Intimidation (6:1–9)
  Shemaiah's Intrigue (6:10–14)
  The Walls Completed (6:15–19)
Officials for Jerusalem (7:1–3)
A New Crisis: Re–Population (7:4–73a)
  The Problem Discovered (7:4–5)
  The Former List of Returnees (7:6–73a)

10

ESTHER

On this day the enemies of the Jews had hoped to overpower them, but now the tables were turned and the Jews got the upper hand over those who hated them. (Est. 9:1b)

For if you remain silent at this time, relief and deliverance for the Jews will arise from another place, but you and your father's family will perish. And who knows but that you have come to a royal position for such a time as this? (Est. 4:14)

The book of Esther presents a delightfully told story of Jewish life in the Diaspora, i.e., among Jews who did not return from exile but who settled down and flourished in a foreign land. It tells of a Jewish girl's rise to become queen of Persia and of her intercession to save her people at a time of crisis. It shows things working out well for the Jews, beyond their fondest hopes.

Strikingly, this book has provoked some of the strongest reactions—both pro and con—of any book of the Bible. It has been denounced as a secularized, sub-Christian (or sub-Jewish) book at one extreme, and it has been elevated to a status essentially equal to the Torah's on the other.

Negative reactions to the book of Esther are primarily because of its lack of mention of God and its essentially secular nature, as well as its allegedly vindictive spirit and narrow Jewish nationalism. Thus, for example, Martin Luther wrote, "I am so hostile to [2 Maccabees] and to Esther that I could wish they did not exist at all; for they judaize too greatly and have much pagan impropriety."[1] Slightly less hostile was Samuel Sandmel, a Jewish scholar, who nonetheless stated, "If somehow or other the canon were

---

1. Martin Luther, quoted in Edwin M. Yamauchi, "The Archaeological Background of Esther," 111.

to become open in the twentieth century, I would be among those who would vote to exclude Esther."[2]

Positive reactions to the book have come for three main reasons. First, on a secular level, it shows a great triumph of the Jews, and it speaks of the survival of the Jewish people. Second, on a religious level, it displays God's providence in a low-key manner: it shows a steady force (i.e., God) in control of history by means of a series of extraordinary coincidences. Third, it contains instructions for the only biblical festival (Purim) outside the Pentateuch. Thus, for example, the Jerusalem Talmud states that, though the Prophets and the Writings may perish, the Torah and Esther will never do so.[3]

ESTHER: TITLE AND WOMAN

The name "Esther" occurs fifty-five times in the book and nowhere else in the Bible. Neither she nor anyone else in the book is mentioned elsewhere (except for Ahasuerus and possibly Vashti; see below). The book takes its name from its major character, although the character of Mordecai is in many ways just as important.

Esther's name is often said to have come from the Babylonian goddess of love, Ishtar, but it may also have come from the Persian word for "star" (*stâra*).[4] Her Hebrew name was Hadassah, which is mentioned only once (Est. 2:7). It is related to the Hebrew word for "myrtle" (a type of plant).[5]

As she appears in this book, Esther was a brave and beautiful woman upon whom fortune smiled again and again. She was chosen to be the king's queen over all the women in the kingdom (2:17), and the king valued her presence and advice (5:2–7; 7:1–8:8). She succeeded in bringing about a reversal of the Jews' fortunes in the book, but to do so she risked her own life (4:11, 16; 5:1–2). She received true authority from the king and was able to act with this authority (9:29–32).

AUTHORSHIP AND DATE OF COMPOSITION

Neither the author nor the date of composition of Esther is specified in the book. According to the Talmud, the men of the Great Synagogue (in Ezra's day) composed the book (*Baba Bathra* 15a). Josephus stated that Mordecai was the author (*Antiquities* 11.6.13). The author certainly displayed a familiarity with Persian words and names and with the geography of Susa, so he may have been a native of Persia. In the last analysis, however, the author's identity is unknown.

---

2. Samuel Sandmel, quoted in ibid.
3. F. B. Huey, "Esther," 784. See Anderson ("The Place of the Book of Esther," 33) for several statements concerning the rabbis' high regard for the book.
4. Carey A. Moore, *Esther,* LI n. 80; also p. 20.
5. F. W. Bush, *ABD* 3, s.v. "Hadassah."

The earliest possible date for the writing of the book would be some time after Ahasuerus's death (464 B.C.), since his death seems to be presumed by the summary of his reign in 10:2. Despite many proposals placing the latest possible date in the second (and even the first) century B.C., a date prior to the rise of the Greek empire in the east (ca. 330 B.C.) seems likely, since there is no trace of Greek influence upon the Hebrew of the book. Moore and others date the "first edition" to ca. 400 B.C. and the "final edition" to the late Persian or early Hellenistic (i.e., Greek) period.[6] An earlier date, rather than a later one, would better explain the author's familiarity with his surroundings, if we attribute this familiarity with his having lived in Persia.

We have no evidence of any written sources for the story of Esther itself, but the book does mention Persian royal annals several times (2:23; 6:1; 10:2). The last reference, which occurs in a summary of Ahasuerus's reign, is similar to the concluding formulas found in 1 & 2 Kings. It mentions his power and might and how all his acts were recorded "in the book of the annals of the kings of Media and Persia." (See chapter 6 under "Theological Significance of the Pattern" for a discussion of the theological significance of such a formula.)

CANONICITY AND PLACE IN THE CANON

In the present Hebrew Bible, the book of Esther appears between the books of Lamentations and Daniel, in the Writings.[7] It is the last of five *megillot* ("scrolls") in the Hebrew Bible—Ruth, Song of Songs, Ecclesiastes, Lamentations, Esther—which were used liturgically at the major festivals, and it is called *"the* Megillah" ("The Scroll") by Jews, because of its immense popularity.[8] Its appearance following Lamentations is logical enough, since it does speak of times of mourning (4:1–4, 16; 8:3), but its emphasis is upon celebrations and the turning of mourning into gladness. Thus, it offers hope after the gloomy situation depicted in Lamentations, which speaks of the Jews' enemies devastating Jerusalem. Esther, on the other hand, shows the Jews' enemies being routed. Esther's place before Daniel is logical as well, since these are the only two OT books that take place entirely in exile. They both show Jews rising high in foreign courts and depict God's providence in the lives of His people. In the Protestant canon, its appearance after Nehemiah, as the last "historical" book, reflects a rough (but not exact) chronological ordering.

---

6. Moore, *Esther,* LVII–LVIX; see also R. K. Harrison, *Introduction to the Old Testament,* 1087–90.
7. Esther's location in the many texts and lists of the Bible varies greatly, however (Moore, *Esther,* XXX; Roger Beckwith, *The Old Testament Canon of the New Testament Church,* passim).
8. Huey, "Esther," 776.

Esther is never cited in the NT (or elsewhere in the OT), and it is the only OT book not found among the Qumran scrolls. Considerable doubts concerning its canonicity have been expressed over the centuries, mainly concerning the nature of its inspired status or the reason(s) for its inclusion in the canon.[9] Among the rabbis, these doubts primarily concerned its apparently secular nature or its adding to the law by instituting a new festival. Among Christians, doubts centered primarily on its alleged "sub-Christian" values and its secularity. However, never was its place in the canon itself in serious question.

PURPOSE

It is difficult to discern the author's purpose with any degree of certainty. On one level, it can be said to tell a good story, one showing Jews flourishing in a foreign land amidst great hostility. On a deeper level, certainly the twin themes of God's providence and God's hiddenness are important components of the author's purpose. (See further under "Theology of the Book of Esther" below.)

HISTORY AND THE BOOK OF ESTHER

HISTORICAL AND CULTURAL CONTEXT

The events in the book of Esther take place in Persia, during the reign of Xerxes I (486–465 B.C.), who is known in Esther as "Ahasuerus." (For a postexilic chronology, see the chart in chapter 9.) As noted in chapter 9, the Persian empire stretched across the entire ancient Near East.[10] Xerxes was an ambitious, ruthless, and intolerant ruler, administrator over a vast empire, a brilliant warrior, and a jealous lover, according to Herodotus. This ancient Greek historian (ca. 484–424 B.C.) devotes fully one-third of his *History of the Persian Wars* (Books 7–9) to the years 481–479 B.C. of Xerxes' reign, the years of his landmark invasion of Greece. After some impressive initial victories, he suffered total defeat and was forced to retreat, never to venture beyond Asia Minor again. His reign marked the beginning of the end of the great Persian empire, which finally fell in 330 B.C. to Greece under Alexander the Great. Xerxes was assassinated in his bed chamber in 465 B.C.

Xerxes was a great builder, and he completed and improved the palaces of his father, Darius I. He was much less tolerant than his Persian pre-

---

9. Moore, *Esther*, XXI–XXX; Beckwith, *Old Testament Canon*, 288–97, 312–17, 322–23; D. J. A. Clines, *Ezra, Nehemiah, Esther*, 254–56.
10. See T. C. Young, Jr., et al. ("Part I: The Persian Empire," *CAH* 4, 1–286), for a thorough history of Persia ca. 525–479 B.C. See also Edwin M. Yamauchi (*Persia and the Bible*) for the entire Persian period.

decessors, however, who were renowned for their tolerance, religious and otherwise, and he was more harsh than they in his treatment of Egypt and Babylon.

The book of Esther gives us a unique glimpse into life among the Jewish exiles who did not return from Babylonia. Long after many of their compatriots had returned home to Jerusalem in the years following Cyrus's decree of 538 B.C., the Jews in this book lived and flourished in a foreign land.

HISTORICAL ACCURACY

More than the accuracy of most biblical books of the narrative genre (the possible exceptions are Jonah and Ruth), the historical accuracy of the book of Esther has been widely questioned.[11] This is for a variety of reasons, some fairly trivial and others much more weighty. That is ironic, however, since the book is also praised for its impressive knowledge of many of the details of Persian life and manners.[12] On the other hand, its historical accuracy has been ably defended as well.[13]

1. Points of Undisputed Accuracy.[14]

A. The book accurately depicts the extent of Xerxes's empire as reaching from India to Ethiopia (1:1; 8:9).

B. The banquet in Xerxes's third year (1:3) corresponds with the great council held to plan for the invasion of Greece in 483 B.C., which is mentioned by Herodotus (Book 7.8).

C. The four-year gap between 1:3 (when Xerxes had his banquet) and 2:16 (when Esther was summoned to his palace) would represent the time Xerxes was off fighting the Greeks (481–479 B.C.).

D. The author's knowledge of Susa, and especially the palace, is impressive (see 2:9, 14, 19; 4:11; 6:4; cf. also 1:5; 7:8). This palace was built by Xerxes's father Darius I (522–486 B.C.), and it was used by Xerxes. It was burned to the ground in the reign of his son Artaxerxes I (464–423 B.C.), but it was rebuilt by Artaxerxes II (403–359 B.C.), and it was essentially identical to the original. The ruins of this rebuilt temple have been excavated in modern times.[15]

11. See Moore, *Esther,* XXXIV–XLVI; L. B. Paton, *The Book of Esther,* 64–77.
12. Carey A. Moore, "Eight Questions Most Frequently Asked About Esther," 19–20.
13. J. S. Wright, "Historicity of the Book of Esther"; W. H. Shea, "Esther and History"; Huey, "Esther," 788–93; Joyce Baldwin, *Esther,* 16–24; cf. also R. Gordis, "Studies in the Esther Narrative," 382–88.
14. See Moore, *Esther,* XXXV–XLI; Clines, *Ezra, Nehemiah, Esther,* 260–61; and esp. Wright, "Historicity," 37–38.
15. See Yamauchi, "Archaeological Background of Esther," 110.

E. Many Persian terms for objects and Persian names are found in the book, almost all of which can be found in Old Persian texts, as well as other details of Persian life.[16]

2. Supposed "Inaccuracies."[17]

A. The book mentions 127 "satrapies" (*mĕdînôt*: 1:1; 8:9), whereas Herodotus (3.89) knows only 20. However, the satrapies were subdivided into smaller units. In such passages as Ezra 5:8; Neh. 1:3; and so on, the term *mĕdinâh* is used to refer to "Judah," which was but a portion of the larger satrapy of "Beyond the River" (Ezra 5:3, 6, etc.).

B. Mordecai's age is a problem for many scholars. According to many readings of Esther 2:5–6, Mordecai was exiled to Babylon with King Jeconiah (Jehoiachin) in 597/6 B.C. If this were he, then in 474 B.C., when he became prime minister, he would have been 122 years older! Since Esther was his *cousin*, this would have made her very old as well. The solution is rather simple, however. It is to read the antecedent of the relative pronoun *'ăšer* ("who") in 2:6a as "Kish," Mordecai's grandfather, not Mordecai himself (so also NIV). Kish, then (not Mordecai), was the one taken into captivity in 597/6 B.C.[18]

C. Many scholars hold that Esther could not have been queen to a Persian king, since the king had to choose his queen from among one of seven specific families, according to Herodotus (3.84). However, at least two Persian kings—Darius and Xerxes himself—in fact married outside the seven families. In Xerxes's case, his wife Amestris was herself not from one of these.[19]

D. The large size of Haman's gallows (50 cubits) is a problem for many (5:14; 7:9), especially since it appears to have been built in a relatively short time (5:14). However, we should note that its height is mentioned only on the lips of two protagonists (Haman's wife and friends in 5:14; Harbona, a eunuch in 7:9); it may well have been the exaggeration common in speech. The height is not specifically vouched for by the author of the book.[20]

E. The statements in 1:19 and 8:8 that the laws of Persia were unalterable (cf. also Dan. 6:8, 12 [MT 9, 13]) seem to have no extrabiblical corroboration. However, Wright notes a passage from Diodorus Siculus con-

---

16. Clines, *Ezra, Nehemiah, Esther,* 261; A. R. Millard, "The Persian Names in Esther and the Reliability of the Hebrew Text," 481–88.
17. For these and others, see Moore, *Esther,* XLV–XLIX; Huey, "Esther," 788–93; Wright, "Historicity," 38–40.
18. Wright ("Historicity," 38) cites 2 Chronicles 22:9 and Ezra 2:61 as places where the relative pronoun applies to the last name in a genealogy and also notes well that three *'ăšers* occur in Esther 2:6, all referring to their immediately preceding nouns.
19. Wright, "Historicity," 38–39.
20. Ibid., 39.

cerning Darius III that reads thus: "It was not possible for what was done by the royal authority to be undone."[21] Whereas the passage in Diodorus is not usually noted in discussions of Esther (or Daniel) and whereas it is open to an alternative interpretation, this understanding is nevertheless a legitimate option. If it stands, this affords an extrabiblical support of the statements in Esther and Daniel.

F. Perhaps the most serious historical problem is that Herodotus and Ctesius[22] mention only one queen as a wife of Xerxes: Amestris. Neither the name "Vashti" nor "Esther" is known outside of the Bible for this time period.

It may be that Xerxes had more than one wife but that Herodotus only mentioned one, perhaps the most prominent. Thus, Joyce Baldwin sees Esther as a secondary wife,[23] and David Clines believes that Xerxes easily may have had more than one queen.[24] He helpfully notes that Darius I, Xerxes's father, had at least three wives, who also were likely queens.

It may be that the biblical "Vashti" was Amestris herself. In that case, "Vashti" would have been her Hebrew name and "Amestris" her Persian name; the differences in the names is due to the difficulties of exact linguistic transmission across language boundaries. (As a case in point, we may note that "Xerxes," *'ăhašwērôš*, and "Ahasuerus" are Greek, Hebrew, and English forms, respectively, of a Persian name, which in Persian was *Khshayarsha*.)[25] The main linguistic problems in identifying Vashti with Amestris are two: the W/M interchange (Vashti's name begins with a W in Hebrew), and the R in "Amestris." W and M, however, are closely related phonetically, and the R may have been part of the name in Persian and dropped in Hebrew, or else not original, but added in (Herodotus's) Greek.[26]

There also are historical problems in identifying Amestris with Vashti, the main one being that Herodotus has Amestris accompanying Xerxes on his Greek campaigns, ca. 481–479 B.C., *after* Vashti has been deposed in the book of Esther.[27] Furthermore, Herodotus mentions her presence as the queen mother in Xerxes's son Artaxerxes I's reign.

Wright explains the first problem by noting that such a strong queen could not be deposed immediately and that her deposition was not finalized until Xerxes's return, whereupon he called for Esther.[28] On the second prob-

21. Ibid.
22. Herodotus lived ca. 484–424 B.C. and was a contemporary of Xerxes. His work was the *History of the Persian Wars*. Ctesias completed his *History of Persia* ca. 398 B.C. (Wright, "Historicity," 47 n. 4).
23. Baldwin, *Esther*, 21.
24. Clines, *Ezra, Nehemiah, Esther*, 259.
25. Wright, "Historicity," 41.
26. See ibid., 40–42; Shea, "Esther and History," 235–37.
27. Shea works out the chronology in detail to fit both the biblical and Herodotus's evidence ("Esther and History," 231–40).
28. Wright, "Historicity," 42–43.

lem, Herodotus is very sketchy on the later portions of Xerxes's reign. Certainly the fact that Amestris functioned as queen mother after Xerxes's death does not require us to see that she remained during his life as the principal queen.[29]

G. The actual existence of Mordecai has been questioned by many. His name does not appear in any Persian documents, and there are numerous problems with his name. However, a tablet discovered in 1904 contained the name "Marduka" as a high Persian official during the early years of Xerxes's reign, which corresponds to the time of Mordecai. In more recent years, more than thirty texts have been uncovered with the name Marduka (or Marduku), referring to up to four different individuals, one of whom could easily have been the biblical Mordecai.[30]

THE ADDITIONS TO THE BOOK OF ESTHER

The Old Greek translation (Septuagint) of Esther is a good one and relatively straightforward. Its underlying source for the Hebrew portions is substantially that of our MT.[31]

The most striking aspect of the Septuagint versions, however, is the presence of six substantial additions to the Hebrew text. The Hebrew text is 167 verses long; the Greek adds 107 verses to these! In Jerome's fourth-century Vulgate (Latin), they form chapters 11–15. They are helpfully included in italics in their rightful place in the modern Jerusalem Bible; see also the Revised English Bible and the NRSV (with Apocrypha), where they are clearly demarcated from the canonical text of Esther.

The six sections are as follows:

11:2–12:6:	Mordecai's dream and his foiling of the plot against the king
13:1–7:	The text of the king's first letter, ordering the massacre against the Jews
13:8–14:19:	The prayers of Mordecai and Esther
15:1–16:	Esther risks her life approaching the king
16:1–24:	The text of the king's second letter, denouncing Haman and ordering help for the Jews
10:4–11:1:	Mordecai's dream interpreted, and colophon attesting to the book's authenticity

---

29. See also Shea, "Esther and History," 240.
30. A recent work questioning the Marduka = Mordecai equation is D. J. A. Clines, "In quest of the historical Mordecai," 129–36. A response to Clines is E. Yamauchi, "Mordecai, The Persepolis Tablets, and the Susa Excavations," 272–75. An older work supporting the equation is S. H. Horn, "Mordecai, A Historical Problem," 14–25.
31. Moore, *Esther,* LXI–LXII.

The additions are universally judged to be later, and of little or no historical value. Their agenda is to give a religious slant to the book. They make frequent reference to God, they emphasize His choice of Abraham and Israel, and they emphasize prayer, all things that the book of Esther does not do.

THEOLOGY OF THE BOOK OF ESTHER[32]

In a strict sense, there is no "theology" (i.e., "study of God") in Esther, since God is not mentioned in the book. In addition, there is no reference to religious institutions or practices (except fasting), making the task of adducing a "theology" of the book doubly difficult. However, several assertions can be made that indeed point to a "theology" of the book of Esther.

GOD'S PROVIDENCE

Most discussions of the book place the theme of God's providence (i.e., His control of events) at the center of the book's theology. Many parallels exist between the story of Esther and that of Joseph in Genesis 37–48. Both concern ordinary, God-fearing individuals who find themselves in foreign lands, who rise to great prominence in the kingdoms of those lands and whose resultant influence is effective on behalf of their own people. In the book of Esther, these things happen to both Esther and Mordecai. A focus upon God's providential overseeing of these outcomes, rather than His direct intervention in spectacular ways, is the norm for the authors of both stories.

Several indicators point to God's presence (although hidden) in the book. For example, we see the Jews fasting because of the crisis at hand (4:3, 16–17); in the OT, fasting is almost always associated with praying, and the purpose is to move God to act. Furthermore, we also read of the assurance of Haman's wife and friends that he could not prevail against a Jew (6:13), which certainly expresses a knowledge of Israel's past history and the ultimate triumph of the Jews' cause through their God.

The most direct statement of a belief in providence is in Mordecai's words to Esther in 4:14a: "For if you remain silent at this time, relief and deliverance for the Jews will arise from another place."

Many scholars have seen the reference to "place" in 4:14 as an indirect reference to God, starting as early as Josephus (*Antiquities* 11.6.7), the Aramaic Targums of Esther, and an important edition of the Septuagint (the Lucianic recension), and continuing to the present day.[33] In this way, they

---

32. See also David M. Howard, Jr., "Esther, Theology of."
33. John M. Wiebe, "Esther 4:14: 'Will Relief and Deliverance Arise for the Jews from Another Place?'" 411.

have seen in Mordecai's words a guarantee of sorts that God would indeed act.

However, this understanding is problematic for at least two reasons.[34] First, if "place" *is* understood as a substitute word for "God," then "another place" must mean "another god," which would fly in the face of the thrust of the book. It would be absurd to suggest that if Esther did not take action, help would come from "another god." For one thing, no god has been mentioned in the conversation, so for Mordecai to refer to "another" god is a non sequitur. Furthermore, such a reference suggests a polytheistic belief, which no biblical writer would countenance.

A second problem with this understanding of "another place" is that it implies that the proper course of action—i.e., Esther's taking responsibility—is *not* from God. In a sentence in which Mordecai is supposedly referring to salvation coming from God, this explicit reference to salvation not from God makes little sense.

Thus, the reference in 4:14 to "another place" must refer to another human agent, although what agent Mordecai had in mind specifically is not clear.[35] Nevertheless, this text exhibits a strong belief on Mordecai's part in the providential ordering of events on the Jews' behalf. It shows that he believed in the certainty of deliverance for the Jews, a deliverance that ultimately came from God, regardless of the immediate source.

Beyond this important text in 4:14, we certainly can detect God's presence behind the numerous timely and dramatic "coincidences" in the book. These include a Jewish girl's being in the right place at the right time in history to help her people (4:14b), the king's sleeplessness on precisely the night preceding Esther's request for help (6:1–3), and Haman's presence in the king's courts when the king wanted to honor Mordecai (6:4–6). These coincidences fit into an overall pattern of reversal of fortunes in the book.[36] By the end of the book, Mordecai, Esther, and the Jews all have been exalted and delivered from their enemies through dramatic turns of events.

Finally, we can point to the climactic turning point described in 9:1: on the very day when the Jews' enemies had hoped to destroy them, the Jews' fortunes were reversed. In Hebrew, the verb is passive: the NIV translates the clause as "the tables were turned," whereas the NASB has "it was turned to the contrary." The agent responsible for this reversal of actions is

---

34. Fox, "The Structure of the Book of Esther," 298 n. 15; Gordis, "Religion, Wisdom and History in the Book of Esther," 360–61 n. 6; Wiebe, "Esther 4:14," 411.
35. Wiebe, "Esther 4:14," 411–13. Wiebe, it should be noted, advances a third possibility—that the clause in question is itself a question ("Will relief and deliverance arise for the Jews from another place?"), the answer to which is no—thus arguing further for Esther's taking action. This is a very intriguing suggestion, and it makes logical sense. However, it is based upon questionable grammatical assumptions, which weakens its plausibility.
36. Sandra Beth Berg, *The Book of Esther,* 103–13; Fox, "Structure."

not specified, but it clearly is an outside force. The identity of this agent should be obvious: it is God.

It seems clear that the author of Esther deliberately suppressed reference to God. (See below, under "God's Hiddenness.") However, to say this is not to say that he did not believe in God or in God's controlling influence in the world. The book was not written in a vacuum; it was written for and about a people whose God constantly and actively had interceded on their behalf over the centuries. They would have expected to see God's presence in the events around them, even now, however veiled they might have been.

As a final note, the Masoretes, using various methods, identified several acrostics in the book that contain the consonants of God's name, YHWH. These are found in 1:20; 5:4; 5:13; 7:7.[37] Though these are almost universally disregarded today, the one at 5:4—occurring in the phrase "Let the king and Haman come" (*Yābô' Hammelek Wĕ-Hāmān*)—at least bears note. It is the most straightforward acrostic in Hebrew—the letters of God's name occur at the beginning of consecutive words—and it comes at a critical juncture in the story, where the suspense is high concerning Esther's and the Jews' fate. Structurally, it is near the book's exact numerical midpoint (which is at the beginning of 5:7). It is easy to imagine that the author is whispering here, by his very choice of words, that God is indeed present (although silently) at this time of crisis.

GOD'S HIDDENNESS

Esther is one of only two OT books that does not mention God's name, the other being the Song of Songs (although some find it in the latter at 8:9). Not only that, it fails to make mention of the law, the covenant, the Temple, prayer, or other institutions and practices that are at the core of Israel's faith. This is part of the basis for the antagonism of many to the book, and it has led some to speak of God's distancing of Himself from the events and characters in the book. Any discussion of the book's "theology," then, must address this unique state of affairs.

Explanations for the omission are many and varied.[38] Robert Pfeiffer suggested that God's name is omitted because the book is a secular, nationalistic tract.[39] However, that does not account adequately for its acceptance as sacred, canonical literature. L. B. Paton suggested that, since the festival of Purim was one of uninhibited drinking and merrymaking—e.g., The Talmud states that "A man is obligated to drink on Purim until he is unable to

---

37. Paton, *The Book of Esther,* 8.
38. For brief surveys of opinions, see Huey, "Esther," 784–85; Fox, "The Religion of the Book of Esther," 135–38.
39. R. H. Pfeiffer, *Introduction to the Old Testament,* 742–43.

distinguish between 'Blessed be Mordecai' and 'Cursed be Haman'"[40]—God's name was omitted altogether to avoid profaning it when read aloud.[41] However, this theory assumes that the book was written long after the festival was inaugurated and such boisterous practices had arisen or that it was written to be used at an already-existing festival; neither point is supported by the book itself.[42] Others (e.g., Robert Gordis and Shemaryahu Talmon) have linked the book with wisdom literature, which is the most "secular" in outlook of the biblical literature. However, James Crenshaw and others reject this, since it does not otherwise exhibit any of the classical wisdom characteristics.[43]

A fairly radical suggestion is F. B. Huey's that God's hiddenness is intended to show His displeasure with questionable activities of the book's characters, including Esther and Mordecai.[44] These activities would include the following: (1) Esther's hiding her identity, which violates the Pentateuchal injunctions about not lying or deceiving (Lev. 19:11); (2) Esther's apparent willingness to lose her virginity in order to become the queen of an unbelieving Gentile king (cf. Deut. 7:3; Ezra 10); (3) Mordecai's "insufferable" pride that prevented his bowing to Haman, which led to the crisis that threatened the Jews and that resulted in 75,000 Persian deaths in the first place.[45]

For this reason, Huey argues, the author is distancing God from the events in the book, and the book's message is essentially a negative one, showing the problems that God's people will get themselves into (especially the questionable moral and ethical practices found in the book) when He is not relied upon. The author, then, chooses not to mention God in order to emphasize this point.

In some ways, this is an attractive option. It would allow us to dispose of the questionable actions of Esther and Mordecai, for example. However, in the last analysis, it is not fully persuasive. That is because, if it were indeed correct, Esther would be the only book in Scripture where the narrator was reticent to disapprove of people's actions. Huey has not advanced a persuasive reason for the narrator's expressing disapproval in such a roundabout fashion. Furthermore, if the author was indeed attempting to show how badly things would turn out without reference to God, one should ex-

---

40. In *Megillah 7b* (Huey, "Esther," 784).
41. Paton, *The Book of Esther*, 95; see also E. L. Greenstein, "A Jewish Reading of Esther," 225–43.
42. For further refutation, see Fox, "Religion," 138.
43. See Gordis, "Religion, Wisdom and History," 365; S. Talmon, "Wisdom in the Book of Esther," 427; J. L. Crenshaw, "Method in Determining Wisdom Influence," 140–42.
44. Huey, "Esther," 785–88, 793–94; and "Irony as the Key to Understanding the Book of Esther," 36–39.
45. See Huey, "Irony," 37, for this list.

pect the Jews to have been more unsuccessful, rather than so successful. One would expect the author to highlight whatever negative results he could, rather than ending with careful instructions about celebrating Purim and with the glorification of Mordecai.

One logical deduction from God's absence that may be legitimately drawn is that human action is important.[46] Time and again, Esther's and Mordecai's initiatives are what make the difference for the Jews; we do not see them passively waiting for signs from God or for God to perform a dramatic miracle of some type.

The best solution to God's absence from the book, however, would seem to be that the author is being intentionally vague about God's presence in events. Time and again the author seems to come close to mentioning God, only to veer away abruptly. That is true in almost every case of God's providence noted above.

By doing this, the author seems to be affirming, on the one hand, that God indeed is involved with His people (providence) and, on the other hand, that perceiving this involvement is sometimes difficult (God's hiddenness). While the author and his readers know (rationally) that God is always present and in control, the experiences of life show that the specific manifestations of His presence are not always so clear. Thus, we can discern a "carefully crafted indeterminacy" in the book that is an important part of its message. As Fox notes, "The story's indeterminacy conveys the message that the Jews should not lose faith if they, too, are uncertain about where God is in a crisis."[47] (Fox probably goes too far in assuming that the author himself also was uncertain about God [when he says "they too"]; it is more plausible that the author did know about God's whereabouts [witness the many hints of God's presence], but that he was consciously making the point that this presence is often very difficult to discern.)

But this indeterminacy is not a sign of unbelief. "If anything is excluded it is *disbelief*. The author of Esther would have us hold to confidence even when lacking certainty and an understanding of details. . . . When we scrutinize the text of Esther for traces of God's activity, we are doing what the author made us do."[48]

In the end, then, this book is a very realistic commentary upon life, and its author wants to make his readers ponder carefully God's involvement in it. Perhaps readers of Scripture can get inured to God's presence in the lives of its characters by the constant and very obvious references to it on almost every page. The book of Esther, by its radical difference in this

---

46. See D. J. A. Clines, *The Esther Scroll*, 154.
47. Fox, "Religion," 146.
48. Ibid., 146–47; see Fox (*Character and Ideology in the Book of Esther*, 244–47) for further development of this idea of "intentional indeterminacy."

regard, makes the reader sit up and take notice and peer deeply into its pages to detect the presence of God there. And, by extension, the author is telling us that we must also sometimes look for God in our lives in this way.

ROYALTY

A significant motif in the book of Esther is that of royalty.[49] The story unfolds in a royal setting, and Esther, as queen, is obviously a royal figure. She exercises royal power and influence throughout the story, and she is the agent of the Jews' ultimate deliverance.

Less obviously, but also significantly, Mordecai too appears as a royal figure. He is honored with royal robes and a royal procession (6:7–11); he is given the king's signet ring, a symbol of royalty (8:2) and royal robes (8:15); he is invested with royal power and acts like a king in issuing decrees (9:20–23); and he is raised in the end to a position second only to the king's in the kingdom (10:1–3). Mordecai's ancestry is traced in 2:5 to names in the first Israelite king's (Saul's) lineage: Kish and (possibly) Shimei. His enemy in the book is "Haman the Agagite" (3:1), which recalls Saul's enemy Agag in 1 Samuel 15.[50]

The parallels between Saul-Agag and Mordecai-Haman are striking. For example, we see the first pair as the respective ancestors of the second pair (as just noted). In addition, Saul disobeyed God's command, and spared Agag. Mordecai, by contrast, did not spare Haman but killed him. Furthermore, Saul took the best of the booty, also contrary to God's command. Mordecai, on the other hand, did not touch the available booty (Est. 9:10, 15, 16), despite authorization to do so (8:11).

In the context of Esther, the reason for this last action is clear enough: it avoided the Jews' being contaminated by anything Gentile, which reinforces the concept of Jewish superiority over the Gentiles seen in the book.[51] Set against the backdrop of 1 Samuel 15, however, this action takes on added significance. We thus see the Jews, by their actions in Esther 9:10, 15, 16, honoring the obligation ignored by their ancestors.[52] Then the message seems to be—at least in part—that now, finally, the Diaspora community has "gotten it right," in contrast to Saul, who had not.

However, the action in Esther 9 does not parallel Saul's situation exactly, since to do so Mordecai would have had to *destroy* all the booty, not merely avoid touching it.[53] Thus, the message here is also—at least in part—

49. Berg, *The Book of Esther,* 59–72.
50. Ibid., 61–70. On the last point here, see also W. McCane, "A Note on Esther IX and 1 Samuel XV," 260–61.
51. McCane, "A Note," 261.
52. Berg, *Esther,* 67.
53. McCane ("A Note," 260–61) also makes this point.

that Mordecai is not *simply* the "new Saul," who did obey all of God's commands; this might then obviate the need for a Davidic monarchy. Despite the esteem shown him in the book, Mordecai was not to be regarded in the last analysis as a substitute for a *Davidic* descendant; he was, after all, a Benjaminite. His actions do not correspond exactly to the conditions in 1 Samuel 15 that would have resulted in a Benjaminite's house being permanently established. In this way, he is a contrast to David, whose house *was* permanently established.

Nevertheless, his presence as a royal figure serves to remind the Jews that this office still had some validity for them, and his status as a descendant of Saul—a Benjaminite—may be a subtle way of highlighting the inclusiveness of the kingdom that is emphasized in 1 & 2 Chronicles and Ezra-Nehemiah: the concept that "all Israel" still has a place in God's scheme, not just Judah.

COOPERATION WITH FOREIGN POWERS

In the books of Ezra and Nehemiah, we have clear pictures of the benevolent nature of the Persian kings and the advantages that would accrue to the Jews when they cooperated. In Esther, the book's outcome makes somewhat the same point, although the overall message is not nearly as strong as it is in these other two books. The Jews' deliverance is accomplished by Esther's acting quietly, yet forcefully, on their behalf with respect to the king.

Furthermore, the book ends with a notice about both Ahasuerus's and Mordecai's power and stature (10:1–3). The point here is not only that a Jew rose to high position but that he did so at the hand of Ahasuerus and that the two could coexist profitably. So, ultimately, the advantages of the Persian monarchy are seen here in Esther as well, despite the initial threats to the Jews at the edict of the Persian king.[54]

THE FESTIVAL OF PURIM

Purim is the festival inaugurated in the book of Esther, and it is the only biblical festival not mentioned in the Pentateuch. It was ordered by Mordecai to celebrate the events by which the Jews were able to reverse the edict of death that hung over them by killing their enemies instead (9:1–32). It even came to be called "Mordecai's day" by the second century B.C. (2 Macc. 15:36).

The name for this festival comes from a rare Hebrew word, *pûr*, "lot" (pl., *pûrîm*). This word is found only in Esther, the usual word for "lot" in

54. See Clines, *Ezra, Nehemiah, Esther,* 262.

the OT being *gôrāl*.[55] Haman had cast a lot (*pûr*) to determine the best month for his edict of destruction to be enacted (3:7; 9:24); in an ironic reversal, the Jewish festival celebrating its overturning was called "lots" (*pûrîm*: 9:26, 28, 29, 31, 32).

The occasion for the festival was one of great joy for the Jews, and many customs have accrued to it over the years. Stephen Noll describes its modern-day form this way:

> For Jews . . . it is a time to make light of what is essentially a serious theme—the preservation of the Jewish people from persecution. The feast precedes Passover by one month and points to the great events of the exodus. The central act of Purim is the reading of the Megillah or Esther scroll, accompanied by raucous mocking at the name of Haman and his sons and congregational recitation of the verses of redemption (8:15–16; 10:3). Parallel readings from passages about Amalek highlight the long-standing threat to Jews in every generation. The feast is also accompanied by a carnival-like atmosphere—puppet shows and comic plays, drinking contests, the burning of a Haman effigy, and the election of a Purim king.[56]

The entire book of Esther deals with this festival, directly or indirectly. The story behind its origin is told in 1:1–9:19, and careful instructions concerning its observance are given in 9:20–32 (sometimes called the "Purim Appendix"). Indeed, the festival of Purim is but one of many feasts or banquets in the book; as such, the motif of "feasting" is an important one, one that leads throughout the book to this most important of all feasts.[57]

The "Purim Appendix" is significant in blunting certain elements of the book that may seem objectionable to some.[58] First, it establishes the authoritative religious significance of the festival. The word "keep, establish" (Heb. *QWM*) is used at 9:21, 27, 29, 31 (twice), 32,[59] indicating that the festival is thus binding on all successive generations. Second, the appointed time for the festival is set (9:21, 31)—the fourteenth and fifteenth days of the month of Adar (February/March)—establishing it as a regular part of the calendar of festivals. Third, Mordecai's and Esther's letters establish the exact *manner* in which the festival is to be celebrated. Rather than merely being a

---

55. The same word *pur(u)* has been found in an Akkadian inscription, however, on a small cube from the time of Shalmaneser III, king of Assyria (858–824 B.C.). This cube was used for casting lots, just as we see Haman doing. See W. W. Hallo, "The First Purim, 19–29.
56. Stephen F. Noll, "Esther," 327–28.
57. Berg, *The Book of Esther*, 31–57.
58. Brevard S. Childs, *IOTS*, 603–5; on the ethical problem of the "massacre" of 75,000 people, see Walter C. Kaiser, Jr., *Hard Sayings of the Old Testament*, 144–46.
59. NIV translates inconsistently in these verses: it has "celebrate," "establish," "confirm," and "decreed" for Hebrew *QWM*.

vindictive victory celebration, it is to be more generous: the people are to exchange fine gifts and send gifts to the poor (9:22; cf. 9:19). In this way, the "secularity" of the festival is placed into a religious context much more in keeping with the letter and spirit of the law. (This generosity picks up on the motif of gift-giving introduced earlier [see 2:18].) Fourth, the festival was fixed "in writing" (9:26, 27, 32). In this way, the festival acquired an authoritative status akin to that of the law (comparable to the law's status in Ezra and Nehemiah, from a similar time). This forms the basis for the Talmudic elevation of Esther to the level of the Torah, since these are the only two portions of Scripture that establish and give instructions for biblical festivals.

Outline of the Book of Esther

Introduction: Esther and Mordecai in Persia (Esther 1–2)
Introduction to the Court (1:1–22)
The Splendor of the Court (1:1–9)
Queen Vashti's Defiance (1:10–12)
The Consequences of Queen Vashti's Refusal (1:13–22)
The Rise of Esther and Mordecai (2:1–23)
The Search for a New Queen (2:1–4)
Esther and Mordecai Introduced (2:5–11)
Esther's Rise (2:12–18)
Mordecai's Rise (2:19–23)

A Threat to the Jews (Esther 3–5)
Haman's Rise and Mordecai's Affront (3:1–6)
Haman's Plot Against the Jews (3:7–15)
Mordecai's Counter-Measures (4:1–17)
Mourning (4:1–3)
Mordecai's Appeal to Esther (4:4–17)
Esther Sends Garments (4:4)
Esther Asks for Information (4:5–9)
An Action Plan Is Formulated (4:10–17)
Esther's Intervention (5:1–8)
The Zenith of Haman's Fortunes (5:9–14)

Reversals of Fortune (Esther 6:1–9:19)
Mordecai's Reward (6:1–13)
Haman's Downfall (6:14–7:10)
Further Reversals (8:1–17)
Mordecai Replaces Haman (8:1–2)
Haman's Decree Reversed (8:3–17)

BIBLIOGRAPHY

GENERAL RESOURCES

ABD: David Noel Freedman, ed. *Anchor Bible Dictionary.* 6 vols. Garden City, N.Y.: Doubleday, 1992.

ANEH: William W. Hallo and William Kelly Simpson. *The Ancient Near East: A History.* New York: Harcourt Brace Jovanovich, 1971.

ANEP: J. B. Pritchard, ed. *The Ancient Near East in Pictures Relating to the Old Testament.* Princeton, N.J.: Princeton Univ., 1954.

ANET: J. B. Pritchard, ed. *Ancient Near Eastern Texts Relating to the Old Testament.* 3d ed. Princeton, N.J.: Princeton Univ., 1969.

CAH: The Cambridge Ancient History. Cambridge: Cambridge Univ.

> Vol. II.1: *History of the Middle East and the Aegean Region c. 1800–1380 B.C.* 3d ed., edited by I. E. S. Edwards et al. 1973.

> Vol. II.2: *History of the Middle East and the Aegean Region c. 1380–1000 B.C.* 3d ed., edited by I. E. S. Edwards et al. 1975.

> Vol. III.1: *The Prehistory of the Balkans; and the Middle East and the Aegean world, tenth to eighth centuries B.C.* 2d ed., edited by John Boardman et al. 1982.

> Vol. III.2: *The Assyrian and Babylonian Empires and other States of the Near East, from the Eighth to the Sixth Centuries B.C.* 2d ed., edited by John Boardman et al. 1991.

> Vol. IV: *Persia, Greece and the Western Mediterranean c. 525 to 479 B.C.* 2d ed., edited by John Boardman et al. 1988.

DOTT: D. W. Thomas, ed. *Documents from Old Testament Times.* New York: Harper & Row, 1958.

ISBE: G. W. Bromiley, ed. *International Standard Bible Encyclopedia.* Rev. ed. 4 vols. Grand Rapids: Eerdmans, 1979–88.

POTW: A. E. Hoerth et al., eds. *Peoples of the Old Testament World.* Grand Rapids: Baker, 1993.

TANE: J. B. Pritchard, ed. *The Ancient Near East: An Anthology of Texts and Pictures.* Princeton, N.J.: Princeton Univ., 1958.

ZPEB: M. C. Tenney, ed. *Zondervan Pictorial Bible Encyclopedia.* 5 vols. Grand Rapids: Zondervan, 1975.

1. INTRODUCTION TO HISTORICAL NARRATIVE

Abrams, M. H. *A Glossary of Literary Terms.* 6th ed. Fort Worth: Holt, Rinehart & Winston, 1993.

Ahlström, Gösta W. *The History of Ancient Palestine from the Palaeolithic Period to Alexander's Conquest.* Edited by D. Edelman, with a contribution by G. O. Rollefson. JSOTSup 146. Sheffield: JSOT, 1993

Alter, Robert. *The Art of Biblical Narrative.* New York: Basic, 1981.

Alter, Robert, and Frank Kermode, eds. *The Literary Guide to the Bible.* Cambridge, Mass.: Harvard Univ., 1987.

Auerbach, Erich. *Mimesis: The Representaion of Reality in Western Literature.* Princeton, N.J.: Princeton Univ., 1953.

Bar-Efrat, Shimon. *Narrative Art in the Bible.* JSOTSup 70. Sheffield: Almond, 1989.

Barton, John. *Reading the Old Testament: Method in Biblical Study.* Philadelphia: Westminster, 1984.

Bebbington, David W. *Patterns in History: A Christian View.* Downers Grove, Ill.: InterVarsity, 1979, 1992. (Citations here are from the 1979 edition.)

Berlin, Adele. *Poetics and Interpretation of Biblical Narrative.* Sheffield: Almond, 1983.

Booth, Wayne. *The Rhetoric of Fiction.* Chicago: Univ. of Chicago, 1961.

Bright, John. *A History of Israel.* 3d ed. Philadelphia: Westminster, 1981.

Bullock, C. Hassell. *An Introduction to the Old Testament Poetic Books.* Rev. ed. Chicago: Moody, 1988.

————. "An Old Testament Center: A Re-evaluation and Proposition." Paper presented at the Midwest Meetings of the Evangelical Theological Society, St. Paul, Minn., 17 March 1990.

Chatman, Seymour. *Story and Discourse: Narrative Structure in Fiction and Film.* Ithaca, N.Y.: Cornell Univ., 1978.

Clines, D. J. A. "Reading Esther from Left to Right: Contemporary Strategies for Reading a Biblical Text." In *The Bible in Three Dimensions*, edited by D. J. A. Clines, S. E. Fowl, S. E. Porter, 31–52. JSOTSup 87. Sheffield: JSOT, 1990.

Clines, D. J. A., S. E. Fowl, and S. E. Porter, eds. *The Bible in Three Dimensions*. JSOTSup 87. Sheffield: JSOT, 1990.

Craig, W. L. "The Nature of History." M.A. Thesis, Trinity Evangelical Divinity School, Deerfield, Ill., 1976.

Culler, Jonathan. *On Deconstruction: Theory and Criticism After Structuralism*. Ithaca, N.Y.: Cornell Univ., 1982.

Damrosch, David. *The Narrative Covenant: Transformations of Genre in the Growth of Biblical Literature*. San Francisco: Harper & Row, 1987.

Edelman, Diana Vikander, ed. *The Fabric of History*. JSOTSup 127. Sheffield: JSOT, 1991.

Eisenberg, Michael T. *Puzzles of the Past: An Introduction to Thinking About History*. College Station, Tex.: Texas A & M Univ., 1985.

Fee, Gordon D., and Douglas Stuart. *How to Read the Bible for All its Worth*. Grand Rapids: Zondervan, 1981.

Fish, Stanley. *Is There a Text in This Class?* Cambridge, Mass.: Harvard Univ., 1980.

France, R. T. "The Authenticity of the Sayings of Jesus." In *History, Criticism, and Faith*, edited by Colin Brown, 101–43. Downers Grove, Ill.: InterVarsity, 1976.

Frei, Hans W. *The Eclipse of Biblical Narrative*. New Haven, Conn.: Yale Univ., 1974.

Friedman, Richard Elliot, and H. G. M. Williamson, eds. *The Future of Biblical Studies: The Hebrew Scriptures*. Atlanta: Scholars Press, 1987.

Fryde, Edmund B., et al. *Encyclopaedia Britannica: Macropaedia*, vol. 20, s.v. "The Study of History."

Garbini, Giovanni. *History and Ideology in Ancient Israel*, translated by J. Bowden. New York: Crossroad, 1988.

Garraghan, Gilbert J. *A Guide to Historical Method*. New York: Fordham Univ., 1946.

Goldingay, John. "How far do readers make sense? Interpreting biblical narrative." *Themelios* 18.2 (Jan 1993): 5–10.

Good, Edwin. *Irony in the Old Testament*. Sheffield: Almond, 1981.

Gunn, David M. "Reading Right: Reliable and Omniscient Narrator, Omniscient God, and Foolproof Composition in the Hebrew Bible." In *The Bible in Three Dimensions*, edited by D. J. A. Clines, S. E. Fowl, S. E. Porter, 53–64. JSOTSup 87. Sheffield: JSOT, 1990.

Gunn, David M., and Danna Nolan Fewell. "Tipping the Balance: Sternberg's Reader and the Rape of Dinah." *JBL* 110 (1991): 193–211.

Halpern, Baruch. *The First Historians: The Hebrew Bible and History*. San Francisco: Harper & Row, 1988.

Harrison, R. K. *Introduction to the Old Testament.* Grand Rapids: Eerdmans, 1969.

Hasel, Gerhard F. "The Problem of the Center in the OT Debate." *ZAW* 86 (1974): 65–82.

Hayes, John H., and J. Maxwell Miller, eds. *Israelite and Judaean History.* Philadelphia: Westminster, 1977.

Herberg, Will. *Faith Enacted as History: Essays in Biblical Theology.* Philadelphia: Westminster, 1976.

Hirsch, E. D., Jr. *Validity in Interpretation.* New Haven, Conn.: Yale Univ., 1967.

––––––––. "The Politics of Theories of Interpretation." *Critical Inquiry* 9 (1982): 235–47.

––––––––. "Meaning and Significance Reinterpreted." *Critical Inquiry* 11 (1984): 202–25.

Hoffmeier, James K., ed. *Faith, Tradition, and History.* Winona Lake, Ind.: Eisenbrauns, forthcoming.

Holman, C. Hugh. *A Handbook to Literature.* 3d ed. Indianapolis: Bobbs-Merrill, 1972.

Inch, Morris A., and C. Hassell Bullock, eds. *The Literature and Meaning of Scripture.* Grand Rapids: Baker, 1981.

Kahler, M. *The So-Called Historical Jesus.* Philadelphia: Fortress, 1964.

Kaiser, Walter C., Jr. *The Old Testament in Contemporary Preaching.* Grand Rapids: Baker, 1973.

Kennedy, George A. *New Testament Interpretation Through Rhetorical Criticism.* Chapel Hill, N.C.: Univ. of North Carolina, 1984.

Kline, Meredith. *The Structure of Biblical Authority.* Grand Rapids: Eerdmans, 1972.

Krentz, Edgar. *The Historical-Critical Method.* Philadelphia: Fortress, 1975.

Lance, H. Darrell. *The Old Testament and the Archaeologist.* Philadelphia: Fortress, 1981.

Leitch, Vincent B. *Deconstructive Criticism: An Advanced Introduction.* New York: Columbia Univ., 1983.

Licht, Jacob. *Storytelling in the Bible.* Jerusalem: Magnes, 1978.

Liddell, H. D., and R. Scott. *A Greek-English Lexicon.* 9th ed. Oxford: Clarendon, 1940.

Long, V. Philips. *The Art of Biblical History.* Grand Rapids: Zondervan, forthcoming.

Longman, Tremper, III. *Literary Approaches to Biblical Interpretation.* Grand Rapids: Zondervan, 1987.

Matthews, Victor H. *Manners and Customs in the Bible.* Peabody, Mass.: Hendrickson, 1988.

Mendenhall, George E. "Covenant Forms in Israelite Tradition." *BA* 15 (1954): 50–76.

Merrill, Eugene H. *Kingdom of Priests: A History of Old Testament Israel.* Grand Rapids: Baker, 1987.

Miller, J. Maxwell. *The Old Testament and the Historian.* Philadelphia: Westminster, 1986.

Miller, J. Maxwell, and John J. Hayes. *A History of Israel and Judah.* Philadelphia: Westminster, 1986.

Noth, Martin. *The History of Israel.* 2d ed, translated by P. R. Ackroyd. New York: Harper & Row, 1960.

Osborne, Grant. *The Hermeneutical Spiral.* Downers Grove, Ill.: InterVarsity, 1991.

Preminger, Alex, ed. *Princeton Encyclopedia of Poetry and Poetics.* Enlarged ed. Princeton, N.J.: Princeton Univ., 1974.

Renier, Gustaaf Johannes. *History: Its Purpose and Method.* 1950. Reprint. Macon, Ga.: Mercer Univ., 1982.

Ricoeur, Paul. *Time and Narrative.* 3 vols, translated by K. McLaughlin and D. Pellauer. Chicago: Univ. of Chicago, 1984–88.

Richardson, Alan. *History: Sacred and Profane.* Philadelphia: Westminster, 1964.

Rimmon-Kenan, S. *Narrative Fiction.* London: Methuen, 1983.

Ryken, Leland. *The Literature of the Bible.* Grand Rapids: Zondervan, 1987.

_____. *Words of Delight: A Literary Introduction to the Bible.* Grand Rapids: Baker, 1974.

_____. *How to Read the Bible as Literature.* Grand Rapids: Zondervan, 1984.

_____. *Windows to the World.* Grand Rapids: Zondervan, 1985.

Sailhamer, John H. "Exegesis of the Old Testament as a Text." In *A Tribute to Gleason Archer: Essays on the Old Testament,* edited by W. C. Kaiser, Jr. and R. F. Youngblood, 279–96. Chicago: Moody, 1986.

_____. *The Pentateuch as Narrative.* Grand Rapids: Zondervan, 1992.

Scholes, Robert, and Robert Kellogg. *The Nature of Narrative.* New York: Oxford Univ., 1966.

Schubert, Paul. "The Twentieth-Century West and the Ancient Near East." In *The Idea of History in the Ancient Near East*, edited by R. C. Dentan, 311–55. New Haven, Conn.: Yale Univ., 1955.

Shafer, R. J. *A Guide to Historical Method*. Homewood, Ill.: Dorsey, 1974.

Shanks, Hershel, ed. *Ancient Israel*. Englewood Cliffs, N.J.: Prentice-Hall, 1988.

Soggin, J. Alberto. *A History of Ancient Israel*. Philadelphia: Westminster, 1984.

Soulen, Richard N. *Handbook of Biblical Criticism*. 2d ed. Atlanta: John Knox, 1981.

Sternberg, Meir. *The Poetics of Biblical Narrative*. Bloomington, Ind.: Indiana Univ., 1985.

————. "Biblical Poetics and Sexual Politics: From Reading to Counter-Reading." *JBL* 111 (1992): 463–88.

Van Seters, John. *In Search of History*. New Haven, Conn.: Yale Univ., 1983.

Walhout, Clarence, and Leland Ryken, eds. *Contemporary Literary Theory: A Christian Appraisal*. Grand Rapids: Eerdmans, 1991.

Walton, John H. *Ancient Israelite Literature in its Cultural Context*. Grand Rapids: Zondervan, 1989.

Wellek, René, and Austin Warren. *Theory of Literature*. 3d ed. New York: Harcourt Brace Jovanovich, 1977.

Wenham, Gordon. "History and the Old Testament." In *History, Criticism, and Faith*, edited by Colin Brown, 13–75. Downers Grove, Ill.: InterVarsity, 1976.

Wilson, Robert R. *Sociological Approaches to the Old Testament*. Philadelphia: Fortress, 1984.

Wimsatt, W. K., and Monroe C. Beardsley. "The Intentional Fallacy." Reprinted in *On Literary Intention*, edited by D. Newton-Molina, 1–13. Edinburgh: Edinburgh Univ., 1976.

Wright, G. Ernest. *God Who Acts: Biblical Theology as Recital*. London: SCM, 1952.

Younger, K. Lawson, Jr. *Ancient Conquest Accounts: A Study in Ancient Near Eastern and Biblical History Writing*. JSOTSup 98. Sheffield: JSOT, 1990.

2. JOSHUA

Albright, William F. "Archaeology and the Date of the Hebrew Conquest of Palestine." *BASOR* 58 (1935): 10–18.

————. "The Israelite Conquest of Canaan in the Light of Archaeology." *BASOR* 74 (1939): 11–23.

————. "The Amarna Letters From Palestine." *CAH* II.2: 98–116.

————. *Yahweh and the Gods of Canaan.* Garden City, N.Y.: Doubleday/Anchor, 1968.

Aldred, Cyril. "Egypt: The Amarna Period and the End of the Eighteenth Dynasty." *CAH* II.2: 49–63.

Aling, Charles F. *Egypt and Bible History.* Grand Rapids: Baker, 1981.

Allis, Oswald T. *The Five Books of Moses.* Nutley, N.J.: Presby. & Ref., 1949.

Alt, Albrecht. "The Settlement of the Israelites in Palestine." In his collected *Essays on Old Testament History and Religion*, translated by R. A. Wilson. Garden City, N.Y.: Doubleday/Anchor, 1968.

Alter, Robert. *The Art of Biblical Narrative.* New York: Basic, 1981.

Archer, Gleason L., Jr. *A Survey of Old Testament Introduction.* 2d ed. Chicago: Moody, 1974.

————. *Encyclopedia of Bible Difficulties.* Grand Rapids: Zondervan, 1982.

Barnett, R. D. "The Sea Peoples." *CAH* II.2: 359–78.

Bartlett, John R. *Jericho.* In Cities of the Biblical World. Grand Rapids: Eerdmans, 1982.

Beitzel, Barry J. "Review of Norman Gottwald, *The Tribes of Yahweh.*" *Trinity Journal* 1 (1980): 237–43.

Bennett, W. H. *The Book of Joshua: A New English Translation.* Polychrome Bible. New York: Dodd, Mead, 1899.

Bienkowski, Piotr. *Jericho in the Late Bronze Age.* Warminster: Aris & Phillips, 1986.

Bimson, John J. *Redating the Exodus and Conquest.* 2d ed. JSOTSup 5. Sheffield: Almond, 1981.

————. "The origins of Israel in Canaan: an examination of recent theories." *Themelios* 15.1 (Oct 1989): 4–15.

Bimson, John J., and David Livingston. "Saving the Biblical Chronology." *BARev* 13.5 (Sept-Oct 1987): 40–53, 66–68.

Boling, Robert G. *Joshua.* AB 6. Garden City, N.Y.: Doubleday, 1982.

Bright, John. *Ancient Israel in Recent History Writing.* London: SCM, 1956.

————. *A History of Israel.* 3d ed. Philadelphia: Westminster, 1981.

Brueggemann, Walter. *The Land: Place as Gift, Promise, and Challenge in Biblical Faith.* Philadelphia: Fortress, 1977.

————. "Trajectories in Old Testament Literature and the Sociology of Ancient Israel." *JBL* 98 (1979): 161–85.

Butler, Trent C. *Joshua.* WBC 7. Waco, Tex.: Word, 1983.

Callaway, Joseph A. "Ai (et-Tell): Problem Site for Biblical Archaeologists." In *Archaeological and Biblical Interpretation,* edited by L. G. Perdue, L. E. Toombs, G. L. Johnson, 87–99. Atlanta: John Knox, 1987.

Campbell, Edward F., Jr. "The Amarna Letters and the Amarna Period." In *The Biblical Archaeologist Reader* 3, edited by E. F. Campbell, Jr. and D. N. Freedman, 54–75. Garden City, N.Y.: Doubleday/Anchor, 1970.

Cassuto, Umberto. *The Documentary Hypothesis and the Composition of the Pentateuch.* Translated by I. Abrahams. Jerusalem: Magnes, 1961.

Cazelles, H. "The Hebrews." In *Peoples of Old Testament Times,* edited by D. J. Wiseman, 1–28. Oxford: Oxford Univ., 1973.

Chaney, Marvin. "Ancient Palestinian Peasant Movements and the Formation of Premonarchic Israel." In *Palestine in Transition,* edited by D. N. Freedman and D. F. Graf, 39–90. Sheffield: Almond/ASOR, 1983.

Childs, Brevard S. *Introduction to the Old Testament as Scripture.* Philadelphia: Fortress, 1979.

———. "The Etiological Tale Re-examined." *VT* 24 (1974): 385–97.

———. "A Study of the Formula, 'Until This Day.'" *JBL* 82 (1963): 279–92.

Clines, D. J. A. *The Theme of the Pentateuch.* JSOTSup 10. Sheffield: JSOT, 1978.

Coogan, Michael David. *Stories From Ancient Canaan.* Philadelphia: Westminster, 1978.

Coote, Robert B., and Keith W. Whitelam. *The Emergence of Early Israel in Historical Perspective.* Sheffield: Almond, 1987.

Craigie, Peter C. *Ugarit and the Old Testament.* Grand Rapids: Eerdmans, 1983.

Cross, Frank Moore. *Canaanite Myth and Hebrew Epic.* Cambridge, Mass.: Harvard Univ., 1973.

Curtis, Adrian. *Ugarit (Ras Shamra).* In Cities of the Biblical World. Grand Rapids: Eerdmans, 1985.

Desborough, V. R. d'A. "The End of the Mycanaean Civilization and the Dark Age." *CAH* II.2: 658–77.

Driver, G. R. *Canaanite Myths and Legends.* Revised by J. C. L. Gibson. Edinburgh: T & T Clark, 1978.

Driver, S. R. *Introduction to the Literature of the Old Testament.* Rev. ed. New York: Charles Scribner's Sons, 1913.

Drower, Margaret S. "The Amarna Age." *CAH* II.1: 483–93.

———. "Ugarit." *CAH* II.2: 130–60.

Edelman, Diana Vikander, ed. "Toward a Consensus on the Emergence of Israel in Canaan," *Scandinavian Journal of the Old Testament* 2 (1991): 1–116.

Eissfeldt, Otto. *The Old Testament: An Introduction.* Oxford: Basil Blackwell, 1965.

Finkelstein, Israel. *The Archaeology of the Israelite Settlement.* Jerusalem: Israel Exploration Society, 1988.

Flanagan, James. *David's Social Drama: A Hologram of Israel's Early Iron Age.* Sheffield: Almond, 1988.

Fohrer, Georg. *Introduction to the Old Testament.* Translated by D. E. Green. Nashville: Abingdon, 1965.

Freedman, D. N., and E. F. Campbell, Jr. "Chronology of Israel and the Ancient Near East." In *The Bible and the Ancient Near East*, 203–28. Winona Lake, Ind.: Eisenbrauns, 1979.

Frick, Frank S. *The Formation of the State of Ancient Israel.* Sheffield: Almond, 1985.

Fritz, Volkmar. "Conquest or Settlement?" *BA* 50 (1987): 84–100.

Garrett, Duane. *Rethinking Genesis: The Sources and Authorship of the First Book of the Pentateuch.* Grand Rapids: Baker, 1991.

Garstang, John, and J. B. E. Garstang. *The Story of Jericho.* 2d ed. London: Marshall, Morgan, and Scott, 1948.

Gerbrandt, Gerald E. *Kingship According to the Deuteronomistic History.* SBLDS 87. Atlanta: Scholars Press, 1986.

Goetze, A. "The Struggle for the Domination of Syria (1400–1300 B.C.)." *CAH* II.2: 1–20.

Gordon, Cyrus H. "Higher Critics and Forbidden Fruit." *Christianity Today* 4, no. 4 (23 November 1959): 131–34.

———. "Poetic Legends and Myths From Ugarit." *Berytus* 25 (1977): 5–133.

Goslinga, C. J. *Joshua, Judges, Ruth.* Translated by R. Togtman. Bible Student's Commentary. Grand Rapids: Zondervan, 1986.

Gottwald, Norman K. *The Tribes of Yahweh.* Maryknoll, N.Y.: Orbis, 1979.

Gray, John. *The Canaanites.* New York: Praeger, 1964.

———. *The Legacy of Canaan.* 2d ed. SVT 5 (1965).

Green, William Brenton. "The Ethics of the Old Testament." *Princeton Theological Review* 28 (1929): 313–66 [reprinted in W. C. Kaiser, Jr., ed., *Classical Evangelical Essays in Old Testament Interpretation.* Grand Rapids: Baker, 1972, 206–35].

Green, William Henry. *The Higher Criticism of the Pentateuch.* New York: Scribner's, 1896.

————. *The Unity of the Book of Genesis.* New York: Scribner's, 1895.

Greenberg, Moshe. "Hab/piru and Hebrews." In *WHJP* 2, edited by B. Mazar, 188–200. Rutgers, N.J.: Rutgers Univ., 1970.

————. *The Hab/piru.* American Oriental Series 39. New Haven, Conn.: American Oriental Society, 1955.

Grintz, J. M. "Ai which is beside Beth-Aven." *Biblica* 42 (1961): 201–16.

Hallo, W. W., and W. K. Simpson. *The Ancient Near East: A History.* New York: Harcourt Brace Jovanovich, 1971.

Harden, Donald. *The Phoenicians.* 2d ed. New York: Frederick A. Praeger, 1963.

Harrison, R. K. *Introduction to the Old Testament.* Grand Rapids: Eerdmans, 1969.

Hayes, William C. "Egypt: Internal Affairs From Thutmosis I to the Death of Amenophis III." *CAH* II.1: 338–46.

————. "Egypt: From the Death of Ammenemes III to Seqenenre II." *CAH* II.1: 42–76.

Holladay, John S., Jr. "The Day(s) the *Moon* Stood Still." *JBL* 87 (1968): 166–78.

Hopkins, David. *The Highlands of Canaan.* Sheffield: Almond, 1985.

Howard, David M., Jr. "All Israel's Response to Joshua: A Note on the Narrative Framework in Joshua 1." In the David Noel Freedman *Festschrift*, edited by A. Bartelt et al. Winona Lake, Ind.: Eisenbrauns, forthcoming.

————. "The Case for Kingship in Deuteronomy and the Former Prophets." *WTJ* 52 (1990): 101–15.

————. "The Philistines." In *Peoples of the Old Testament World*, edited by A. Hoerth, G. Mattingly, and E. Yamauchi. Grand Rapids: Baker, 1993.

Kaiser, Walter C., Jr. *Toward Old Testament Ethics.* Grand Rapids: Zondervan, 1983.

————. *Hard Sayings of the Old Testament.* Downers Grove, Ill.: InterVarsity, 1988.

————. *More Hard Sayings of the Old Testament.* Downers Grove, Ill.: InterVarsity, 1992.

————, ed. *Classical Evangelical Essays in Old Testament Interpretation.* Grand Rapids: Baker, 1972.

Keil, C. F. *The Book of Joshua.* Grand Rapids: Eerdmans, 1975 reprint.

Kenyon, Kathleen M. *Archaeology in the Holy Land.* 4th ed. London: Ernest Benn, 1979.

―――――. *Digging Up Jericho: The Results of the Jericho Excavations 1952–1956.* New York: Praeger, 1957.

―――――. "Jericho." In *Archaeology and Old Testament Study.* Edited by D. W. Thomas, 264–75. London: Oxford Univ., 1967.

―――――. "Palestine in the Time of the Eighteenth Dynasty." *CAH* II.1: 526–56.

Kikawada, Isaac M., and Arthur Quinn. *Before Abraham Was: A Provocative Challenge to the Documentary Hypothesis.* Nashville: Abingdon, 1985.

Kitchen, Kenneth A. *Ancient Orient and Old Testament.* Chicago: InterVarsity, 1966.

―――――. *The Bible in its World.* Downers Grove, Ill.: InterVarsity, 1977.

―――――. "The Basics of Egyptian Chronology in Relation to the Bronze Age." In *High, Middle or Low?*, edited by P. Åström. Part I (Gothenburg: Paul Åström, 1987), pp. 37–55; Part III (1989), pp. 152–59.

Lapp, Paul W. "The Conquest of Palestine in the Light of Archaeology." *Concordia Theological Monthly* 38 (1967): 283–300.

Livingstone, David. "Location of Biblical Bethel and Ai Reconsidered." *WTJ* 33 (1970): 20–44.

―――――. "Traditional Site of Bethel Questioned." *WTJ* 34 (1971): 39–50.

Long, Burke O. *The Problem of Etiological Narrative in the Old Testament.* BZAW 108. Berlin: Alfred Töpelmann, 1968.

―――――. "The Social World of Ancient Israel." *Interpretation,* 36 (1982): 243–55.

Malamat, Abraham. "Israelite Conduct of War in the Conquest of Canaan." In *Symposia,* edited by F. M. Cross, 35–55. Cambridge, Mass.: ASOR, 1979.

Malina, Bruce. "The Social Sciences and Biblical Interpretation." *Interpretation* 36 (1982): 229–42.

Maunder, E. W. "A Misinterpreted Miracle." *The Expositor* 10 (1910): 359–72.

McKenzie, Steven L. *The Trouble With Kings: The Composition of the Book of Kings in the Deuteronomistic History.* Leiden: E. J. Brill, 1991.

Mendenhall, George E. "The Hebrew Conquest of Palestine." In *Biblical Archaeologist Reader*, edited by E. F. Campbell, Jr. and D. N. Freedman, 3:100–120. Garden City, N.Y.: Doubleday, 1970.

————. "Ancient Israel's Hyphenated History." In *Palestine in Transition,* edited by D. N. Freedman and D. F. Graf, 91–103. Sheffield: Almond/A-SOR, 1983.

————. *The Tenth Generation.* Baltimore: Johns Hopkins Univ., 1973.

Merrill, Eugene H. *Kingdom of Priests: A History of Old Testament Israel.* Grand Rapids: Baker, 1987.

————. "Palestinian Archaeology and the Date of the Conquest: Do Tells Tell Tales?" *Grace Theological Journal* 3 (1982): 107–21.

Miller, J. Maxwell. "The Israelite Occupation of Canaan." In *Israelite and Judaean History,* edited by J. H. Hayes and J. M. Miller, 213–84. Philadelphia: Westminster, 1977.

————. "Is it Possible to Write a History of Israel without Relying on the Hebrew Bible?" In *The Fabric of History*, edited by D. V. Edelman, 93–102. Sheffield: JSOT, 1991.

Miller, Patrick D., Jr. "The Gift of God: The Deuteronomic Theology of the Land." *Interpretation* 23 (1969): 451–65.

Moscati, Sabatino. *The World of the Phoenicians*, translated by A. Hamilton. London: Weidenfeld and Nicholson, 1968.

Niehaus, Jeffrey J. "Joshua and Ancient Near Eastern Warfare." *JETS* 31 (1988): 37–50.

Noth, Martin. *The History of Israel.* 2d ed. Translated by P. R. Ackroyd. New York: Harper & Row, 1960.

————. *The Deuteronomistic History.* JSOTSup 15. 2d ed. Sheffield: JSOT, 1991.

Polzin, Robert. *Moses and the Deuteronomist.* New York: Seabury, 1980.

Radday, Y. T., and H. Shore. *Genesis: An Authorship Study.* Rome: Pontifical Biblical Institute, 1985.

Rainey, Anson F. "Bethel Is Still *Beitîn.*" *WTJ* 33 (1971): 175–88.

Ramm, Bernard. *The Christian View of Science and Scripture.* Grand Rapids: Eerdmans, 1954.

Ramsey, George W. *The Quest for the Historical Israel.* Atlanta: John Knox, 1981.

Rendsburg, Gary. "The Date of the Exodus and the Conquest/Settlement: The Case for the 1100s." *VT* 42 (1992): 510–27.

————. Two Book Reviews. *Journal of the American Oriental Society* 107 (1987): 554–57.

Ringgren, Helmer. *Religions of the Ancient Near East.* Translated by J. Sturdy. Philadelphia: Westminster, 1973.

Rowley, H. H. *From Joseph to Joshua: Biblical Traditions in the Light of Archaeology.* London: Oxford Univ., 1950.

Sandars, N. K. *The Sea Peoples.* London: Thames & Hudson, 1978.

Segal, M. H. *The Pentateuch—Its Composition and Authorship—and Other Biblical Studies.* Jerusalem: Magnes, 1967.

Shanks, Hershel. "The Exodus and the Crossing of the Red Sea, According to Hans Goedicke." *BARev* 7.5 (Sept/Oct 1981): 42–50.

Smedes, Louis B. *Mere Morality.* Grand Rapids: Eerdmans, 1983.

Thiele, Edwin R. *The Mysterious Numbers of the Hebrew Kings.* 3d ed. Grand Rapids: Zondervan, 1983.

Thompson, J. A. *The Bible and Archaeology.* 3d ed. Grand Rapids: Eerdmans, 1982.

Thompson, Thomas L. *Early History of the Israelite People.* Leiden: E. J. Brill, 1992.

von Rad, Gerhard. "The Form-Critical Problem of the Hexateuch." [Originally appeared in 1938.] In *The Problem of the Hexateuch and other essays,* 1–78. Translated by E. W. T. Dicken. New York: McGraw Hill, 1966.

_____. "The Promised Land and Yahweh's Land in the Hexateuch." [Originally appeared in 1943.] In *The Problem of the Hexateuch and other essays,* 79–93. Translated by E. W. T. Dicken. New York: McGraw Hill, 1966.

_____. "There Remains Still a Rest for the People of God: An Investigation of a Biblical Conception." [Originally appeared in 1933.] In *The Problem of the Hexateuch and other essays,* 94–102.

Waltke, Bruce K. "Palestinian Artifactual Evidence Supporting the Early Date for the Exodus." *Bib Sac* 129 (1972): 33–47.

_____. "The Date of the Conquest." *WTJ* 52 (1990): 181–200.

Weippert, Manfred. *The Settlement of the Israelite Tribes in Palestine.* London: SCM, 1971.

_____. "The Israelite 'Conquest' and the Evidence from Transjordan." In *Symposia,* edited by F. M. Cross, 15–34. Cambridge, Mass.: ASOR, 1979.

Wenham, Gordon. "The date of Deuteronomy: linch-pin of Old Testament criticism. Part One." *Themelios* 10.3 (April 1985): 15–20.

_____. "The date of Deuteronomy: linch-pin of Old Testament criticism. Part Two." *Themelios* 11.1 (Sept 1985): 15–18.

Wilson, Robert Dick. "Understanding 'The Sun Stood Still.'" *Princeton Theological Review* 16 (1918): 46–54, [reprinted in W. C. Kaiser, Jr., ed., *Classical Evangelical Essays in Old Testament Interpretation.* Grand Rapids: Baker, 1972, 61–65].

Wilson, Robert R. *Sociological Approaches to the Old Testament.* Philadelphia: Fortress, 1984.

Wolf, Herbert M. *An Introduction to the Old Testament Pentateuch.* Chicago: Moody, 1991.

Wood, Bryant G. "Did the Israelites Conquer Jericho? A New Look at the Archaeological Evidence." *BARev* 16.2 (Mar-Apr 1990): 44–58.

Wood, Leon J. *A Survey of Israel's History.* Rev. ed. Grand Rapids: Zondervan, 1986.

Woudstra, Marten H. *The Book of Joshua.* NICOT. Grand Rapids: Eerdmans, 1981.

Wright, G. Ernest. *Biblical Archaeology.* Rev. ed. Philadelphia: Westminster, 1962.

Yadin, Yigael. *The Art of Warfare in Biblical Lands.* 2 vols. New York: McGraw-Hill, 1963.

3. JUDGES

Aharoni, Yohanan. *The Archaeology of the Land of Israel.* Philadelphia: Westminster, 1982.

Albright, William F. "Syria, the Philistines, and Phoenicia." *CAH* II.2: 507–36.

_____. *The Archaeology of Palestine.* Rev. ed. London: Penguin, 1954.

Alt, Albrecht. "The Origins of Israelite Law." In *Essays on Old Testament History and Religion,* 101–71, translated by R. A. Wilson. Garden City, N.Y.: Doubleday/Anchor, 1968.

Amiran, Ruth. *Ancient Pottery of the Holy Land.* Jerusalem: Massada, 1969.

Bierling, Neal. *Giving Goliath His Due.* Grand Rapids: Baker, 1992.

Bimson, John J. *Redating the Exodus and the Conquest.* 2d ed. JSOTSup 5. Sheffield: Almond, 1981.

Block, Daniel I. "The Period of the Judges: Religious Disintegration under Tribal Rule." In *Israel's Apostasy and Restoration: Essays in Honor of Roland K. Harrison,* edited by A. Gileadi, 39–57. Grand Rapids: Baker, 1988.

Boling, Robert G. *Judges.* AB 6A. Garden City, N.Y.: Doubleday, 1975.

Bright, John. *A History of Israel.* 3d ed. Philadelphia: Westminster, 1981.

Brug, John F. *A Literary and Archaeological Study of the Philistines.* BAR International Series 265. Oxford: B.A.R., 1985.

Cassell, Paulus. "The Book of Judges." In *A Commentary on the Holy Scriptures,* edited by J. P. Lange. New York: Scribner's, 1871.

Chambers, Henry E. "Ancient Amphictyonies, Sic et Non." In *Scripture in Context II: More Essays on the Comparative Method,* edited by W. H. Hallo, J. C. Moyer, L. G. Perdue, 39–59. Winona Lake, Ind.: Eisenbrauns, 1983.

Cundall, Arthur E. *Judges: An Introduction and Commentary.* Downers Grove, Ill.: InterVarsity, 1968.

Day, John. "Asherah in the Hebrew Bible and Northwest Semitic Literature." *JBL* 105 (1986): 385–408.

de Geus, C. H. J. *The Tribes of Israel: An Investigation into Some of the Presuppositions of Martin Noth's Amphictyony Hypothesis.* Assen/Amsterdam: Van Gorcum, 1976.

Dever, William G. "Asherah, Consort of Yahweh? New Evidence from Kuntillet 'Ajrud." *BASOR* 255 (1984): 21–37.

Dothan, Trude. *The Philistines and Their Material Culture.* New Haven, Conn.: Yale Univ., 1982.

Dothan, Trude, and Moshe Dothan. *People of the Sea: The Search for the Philistines.* New York: Macmillan, 1992.

Eichrodt, Walther. *Theology of the Old Testament.* 2 vols. OTL. Philadelphia: Westminster, 1967.

Erickson, Millard. *Christian Theology.* Grand Rapids: Baker, 1986.

Fohrer, Georg. *Introduction to the Old Testament.* Translated by D. E. Green. Nashville: Abingdon, 1965.

Gerbrandt, Gerald E. *Kingship According to the Deuteronomistic History.* SBLDS 87. Atlanta: Scholars Press, 1986.

Gese, Hartmut. "Wisdom, Son of Man, and the Origins of Christology: The Consistent Development of Biblical Theology." *Horizons in Biblical Theology* 3 (1981): 23–57.

Gooding, D. W. "The Composition of the Book of Judges." *Eretz Israel* 16 (1982): 70*–79*.

Goslinga, C. J. *Joshua, Judges, Ruth.* Translated by R. Togtman. Bible Student's Commentary. Grand Rapids: Zondervan, 1986.

Gottwald, Norman K. *The Tribes of Yahweh.* Maryknoll, N.Y.: Orbis, 1979.

Gray, John. *Joshua, Judges, Ruth.* NCBC. Grand Rapids: Eerdmans, 1986.

Halverson, Patricia A. "The Influences Upon and the Motivation for the Making of Jephthah's Vow." Th.M. thesis, Bethel Theological Seminary, St. Paul, Minn., 1990.

Harrison, R. K. *Introduction to the Old Testament.* Grand Rapids: Eerdmans, 1969.

Hauser, Alan J. "The 'Minor Judges'—A Re-Evaluation." *JBL* 94 (1975): 190–200.

Howard, David M., Jr. "The Case for Kingship in Deuteronomy and the Former Prophets." *WTJ* 52 (1990): 101–15.

————. "The Case for Kingship in the Old Testament Narrative Books and the Psalms." *Trinity Journal* 9 (1988): 19–35.

————. "The Philistines." In *Peoples of the Old Testament World*, edited by A. Hoerth, G. Mattingly, and E. Yamauchi. Grand Rapids: Baker, 1993.

Kaiser, Walter C., Jr. *Hard Sayings of the Old Testament.* Downers Grove, Ill.: InterVarsity, 1988.

Kitchen, Kenneth A. *Ancient Orient and Old Testament.* Chicago: InterVarsity, 1966.

Lilley, J. P. U. "A Literary Appreciation of the Book of Judges." *Tyndale Bulletin* 18 (1967): 94–102.

Maier, Walter A., III. *'AŠERAH: Extrabiblical Evidence.* HSM 37. Atlanta: Scholars Press, 1986.

Mayes, A. D. H. *Israel in the Period of the Judges.* SBT 29. Naperville, Ill.: Alec R. Allenson, 1974.

————. "The Period of the Judges and the Rise of the Monarchy." In *Israelite and Judaean History,* edited by J. H. Hayes and J. M. Miller, 299–308. Philadelphia: Westminster, 1977.

Mendenhall, George E. *The Tenth Generation: The Origins of the Biblical Tradition.* Baltimore: Johns Hopkins Univ., 1973.

————. "Social Organization in Early Israel." In *Magnalia Dei: The Mighty Acts of God,* edited by F. M. Cross, W. E. Lemche, P. D. Miller, Jr., 132–51. Garden City, N.Y.: Doubleday, 1976.

Merrill, Eugene H. *Kingdom of Priests: A History of Old Testament Israel.* Grand Rapids: Baker, 1987.

————. "Paul's Use of 'About 450 Years' in Acts 13:20." *Bib Sac* 138 (1981): 246–57.

Meshel, Zeev. "Did Yahweh Have a Consort? The New Religious Inscriptions from Sinai." *BARev* 5.2 (March-April 1979): 24–34.

Mullen, E. Theodore, Jr. "The 'Minor Judges': Some Literary and Historical Considerations." *CBQ* 44 (1982): 185–201.

Negbi, Ora. *Canaanite Gods in Metal.* Tel Aviv: Tel Aviv University Institute of Archaeology, 1976.

Noth, Martin. "Das Amt des 'Richters Israels.'" In *Festschrift Alfred Bertholet*, edited by W. Baumgartner, 404–17. Tübingen: J. C. B. Mohr [Paul Siebeck], 1950.

————. *Das System der zwölf Stämme Israels.* Stuttgart: W. Kohlhammer, 1930.

————. *The History of Israel.* 2d ed. New York: Harper & Row, 1960.

Payne, J. Barton. *The Theology of the Older Testament.* Grand Rapids: Zondervan, 1962.

Roehrs, Walter R. "The Conquest of Canaan According to Joshua and Judges." *Concordia Theological Monthly* 31 (1960): 746–60.

Soggin, J. Alberto. *Judges: A Commentary.* Philadelphia: Westminster, 1981.

Stech-Wheeler, T., et al. "Iron at Taanach and Early Iron Metallurgy in the Eastern Mediterranean." *American Journal of Archaeology* 85 (1981): 245–68.

Thompson, James A. *The Bible and Archaeology.* 3d ed. Grand Rapids: Eerdmans, 1982.

von Rad, Gerhard. *Old Testament Theology.* 2 vols. New York: Harper & Row, 1962.

Warner, Sean M. "The Dating of the Period of the Judges." *VT* 28 (1978): 455–63.

Webb, Barry G. *The Book of Judges: An Integrated Reading.* JSOTSup 46. Sheffield: JSOT, 1987.

Woudstra, Marten H. *The Book of Joshua.* NICOT. Grand Rapids: Eerdmans, 1981.

Wright, G. Ernest. "The Literary and Historical Problem of Joshua 10 and Judges 1." *Journal of Near Eastern Studies* 5 (1946): 105–14.

4. RUTH

Berlin, Adele. *Poetics and Interpretation of Biblical Narrative.* Sheffield: Almond, 1983.

Bertman, Stephen. "Symmetrical Design in the Book of Ruth." *JBL* 84 (1965): 165–68.

Boling, Robert G. *Judges.* AB 6A. Garden City, N.Y.: Doubleday, 1975.

Campbell, Edward F., Jr. *Ruth.* AB 7. Garden City, N.Y.: Doubleday, 1975.

Childs, Brevard S. *Introduction to the Old Testament as Scripture.* Philadelphia: Fortress, 1979.

Feeley-Harnik, Gillian. "Naomi and Ruth: Building Up the House of David." In *Text and Tradition: The Hebrew Bible and Folklore*, edited by S. Niditch, 163–84. Atlanta: Scholars Press, 1990.

Fewell, Danna Nolan, and David Miller Gunn. *Compromising Redemption: Relating Characters in the Book of Ruth.* Louisville: Westminster/John Knox, 1990.

Glueck, Nelson. *Hesed in the Bible.* Cincinnati: Hebrew Union College, 1967.

Gow, Murray F. "The Significance of Literary Structure for the Translation of the Book of Ruth." *Bible Translator* 35 (1984): 309–20.

Green, Barbara. "The Plot of the Biblical Story of Ruth." *JSOT* 23 (1982): 55–68.

Hals, Ronald M. *The Theology of the Book of Ruth.* Facet Books, Biblical Series, 23. Philadelphia: Fortress, 1969.

Howard, David M., Jr. "The Case for Kingship in the Old Testament Narrative Books and the Psalms." *Trinity Journal* 9 (1988): 19–35.

Hubbard, Robert L. *The Book of Ruth.* NICOT. Grand Rapids: Eerdmans, 1988.

Leggett, Donald A. *The Levirate and Goel Institutions in the Old Testament, With Special Attention to the Book of Ruth.* Cherry Hill, N.J.: Mack, 1974.

Loretz, Oswald. "The Theme of the Ruth Story." *CBQ* 22 (1960): 391–99.

Merrill, Eugene H. "The Book of Ruth: Narration and Shared Themes." *Bib Sac* 142 (1985): 130–41.

―――――. *Kingdom of Priests: A History of Old Testament Israel.* Grand Rapids: Baker, 1987.

Morris, Leon. *Ruth: An Introduction and Commentary.* TOTC. Downers Grove, Ill.: InterVarsity, 1968. [1975, American edition]

Rauber, D. F. "Literary Values in the Bible: The Book of Ruth." *JBL* 89 (1970): 27–37.

Sakenfeld, Katherine D. *The Meaning of Hesed in the Hebrew Bible: A New Inquiry.* HSM 17. Missoula, Mont.: Scholars Press, 1978.

Sasson, Jack M. *Ruth: A New Translation with a Philological Commentary and a Formalist-Folklorist Interpretation.* 2d ed. Sheffield: JSOT, 1989.

Trible, Phyllis. *God and the Rhetoric of Sexuality.* Overtures to Biblical Theology, vol. 2. Philadelphia: Fortress, 1978.

Wolfenson, L. B. "Implications of the Place of the Book of Ruth in Editions, Manuscripts, and Canon of the Old Testament." *Hebrew Union College Annual* 1 (1924): 151–78.

5. 1 & 2 SAMUEL

Anderson, A. A. *2 Samuel.* WBC 11. Waco, Tex.: Word, 1989.

Archer, Gleason L., Jr. *Encyclopedia of Bible Difficulties.* Grand Rapids: Zondervan, 1982.

————. *A Survey of Old Testament Introduction.* 2d ed. Chicago: Moody, 1974.

Ariel, Donald T., et al. *Excavations at the City of David 1978–1985.* Vol. 2. *Qedem* 30. Jerusalem: Hebrew Univ., 1990.

Baldwin, Joyce G. *1 & 2 Samuel.* TOTC. Downers Grove, Ill.: InterVarsity, 1988.

Barthélemy, D., et al., eds. *Preliminary and Interim Report on the Hebrew Old Testament Text Project.* 4 vols. New York: United Bible Societies, 1979.

Beitzel, Barry J. *The Moody Atlas of Bible Lands.* Chicago: Moody, 1985.

Bimson, John J. *Redating the Exodus and the Conquest.* 2d ed. JSOTSup 5. Sheffield: Almond, 1981.

Blomberg, Craig A. "The Legitimacy and Limits of Harmonization." In *Canon, Hermeneutics, and Authority*, edited by J. D. Woodbridge and D. A. Carson, 135–74. Grand Rapids: Zondervan, 1986.

Bowman, Richard G. *The Fortune of King David: A Literary Reading of II Samuel.* Bible & Literature Series. Sheffield: Almond, forthcoming.

Černy, J. "Egypt: From the Death of Rameses III to the End of the Twenty-First Dynasty." *CAH* II.2: 606–57.

Childs, Brevard S. *Introduction to the Old Testament as Scripture.* Philadelphia: Fortress, 1979.

Cross, Frank Moore. *Canaanite Myth and Hebrew Epic.* Cambridge, Mass.: Harvard Univ., 1973.

Driver, S. R. *Notes on the Hebrew Text and the Topography of the Books of Samuel.* 2d ed. Oxford: Clarendon, 1913.

Dumbrell, William J. "The Content and Significance of the Books of Samuel: Their Place and Purpose Within the Former Prophets." *JETS* 33 (1990): 49–62.

Dyrness, William. *Themes in Old Testament Theology.* Downers Grove, Ill.: InterVarsity, 1979.

Eichrodt, Walther. *Theology of the Old Testament.* 2 vols. Translated by J. A. Baker. Philadelphia: Westminster, 1967.

Eissfeldt, Otto. *The Old Testament: An Introduction.* Translated by P. R. Ackroyd. New York: Harper & Row, 1965.

Eslinger, Lyle M. *Kingship of God in Crisis: A Close Reading of 1 Samuel 1–12.* Sheffield: JSOT/Almond, 1985.

Fokkelman, J. P. *Narrative Art and Poetry in the Books of Samuel.* Vol. 1: *King David (II Sam. 9–20 & I Kings 1–2).* Assen, The Netherlands: Van Gorcum, 1981.

————. *Narrative Art and Poetry in the Books of Samuel.* Vol. II: *The Crossing Fates (I Sam. 13–31 & II Sam. 1).* Assen, The Netherlands: Van Gorcum, 1986.

————. "Saul and David: Crossed Fates." *Bible Review* 5.3 (June 1989): 20–32.

Gerbrandt, Gerald E. *Kingship According to the Deuteronomistic History.* SBLDS 87. Atlanta: Scholars Press, 1986.

Gordon, Robert P. *I & II Samuel: A Commentary.* Grand Rapids: Zondervan, 1986.

Green, Michael. *I Believe in the Holy Spirit.* Grand Rapids: Eerdmans, 1975.

Gunn, David M. *The Story of King David.* JSOTSup 6. Sheffield: JSOT, 1978.

————. *The Fate of King Saul.* JSOTSup 14. Sheffield: JSOT, 1980.

Gurney, O. R. *The Hittites.* Rev. ed. Baltimore: Penguin, 1954.

Hallo, William H., and William Kelly Simpson. *The Ancient Near East: A History.* New York: Harcourt Brace Jovanovich, 1971.

Harrison, R. K. *Introduction to the Old Testament.* Grand Rapids: Eerdmans, 1969.

Hayes, John H., and Paul R. Hooker. *A New Chronology for the Kings of Israel and Judah.* Atlanta: John Knox, 1988.

Herion, Gary A., and Andrew F. Hill. "Functional Yahwism and Social Control in the Early Israelite Monarchy." *JETS* 29 (1986): 277–84.

Hertzberg, Hans Wilhelm. *I & II Samuel: A Commentary.* Philadelphia: Westminster, 1964.

Hoffner, H. A. "The Hittites and Hurrians." In *Peoples of Old Testament Times,* edited by D. J. Wiseman, 197–228. London: Oxford Univ., 1973.

Howard, David M., Jr. "The Case for Kingship in Deuteronomy and the Former Prophets." *WTJ* 52 (1990): 101–15.

————. "The Transfer of Power from Saul to David in 1 Sam 16:13–14." *JETS* 32 (1989): 473–83.

Kaiser, Walter C., Jr. "The Blessing of David: The Charter of Humanity." In *The Law and the Prophets,* edited by J. H. Skilton, 298–318. Nutley, N.J.: Presby. & Ref., 1974.

————. *Toward an Old Testament Theology.* Grand Rapids: Zondervan, 1978.

————. *Toward Old Testament Ethics.* Grand Rapids: Zondervan, 1983.

————. *Hard Sayings of the Old Testament.* Downers Grove, Ill.: InterVarsity, 1988.

————. *Back Toward the Future: Hints for Interpreting Biblical Prophecy.* Grand Rapids: Baker, 1989.

————. *More Hard Sayings of the Old Testament.* Downers Grove, Ill.: InterVarsity, 1992.

Keil, C. F. *The First Book of Samuel.* Grand Rapids: Eerdmans, 1975. Reprint.

Klein, Ralph W. *1 Samuel.* WBC 10. Waco, Tex.: Word, 1983.

LaSor, William Sanford, David A. Hubbard, and Frederic L. Bush. *Old Testament Survey.* Grand Rapids: Eerdmans, 1982.

Long, V. Philips. *The Reign and Rejection of King Saul: A Case for Literary and Theological Coherence.* SBLDS 118. Atlanta: Scholars Press, 1989.

Malamat, Abraham. "Organs of Statecraft in the Israelite Monarchy." In *Biblical Archaeologist Reader* 3, edited by E. F. Campbell, Jr. and D. N. Freedman, 163–98. Garden City, N.Y.: Doubleday, 1970.

Mare, W. Harold. *The Archaeology of the Jerusalem Area.* Grand Rapids: Baker, 1987.

Martin, John A. "The Structure of 1 and 2 Samuel." *Bib Sac* 141 (1984): 28–42.

————. "The Literary Quality of 1 and 2 Samuel." *Bib Sac* 141 (1984): 131–45.

Mayes, A. D. H. "The Reign of Saul." In *Israelite and Judaean History*, edited by J. M. Miller and J. H. Hayes. Philadelphia: Westminster, 1977.

Mazar, B. "The Era of David and Solomon." In *The Age of the Monarchies: Political History*, edited by A. Malamat, 76–99. WHJP 4.1. Jerusalem: Massada, 1979.

McCarter, P. Kyle. *1 Samuel.* AB 8. Garden City, N.Y.: Doubleday, 1980.

————. *II Samuel.* AB 9. Garden City, N.Y.: Doubleday, 1984.

McCarthy, Dennis J. "II Samuel 7 and the Structure of the Deuteronomistic History." *JBL* 85 (1965): 131–38.

Mendenhall, George E. "The Monarchy." *Interpretation* 29 (1975): 155–70.

Merrill, Eugene H. *Kingdom of Priests: A History of Old Testament Israel.* Grand Rapids: Baker, 1987.

Montague, George T. *The Holy Spirit: Growth of a Biblical Tradition.* New York: Paulus, 1976.

Neve, Lloyd. *The Spirit of God in the Old Testament.* Tokyo: Seibushna, 1972.

Payne, J. Barton. *The Theology of the Older Testament.* Grand Rapids: Zondervan, 1962.

Polzin, Robert. *Samuel and the Deuteronomist.* San Francisco: Harper & Row, 1989.

Rasmussen, Carl G. *NIV Atlas of the Bible.* Grand Rapids: Zondervan, 1989.

Reviv, H. "The Structure of Society." In *The Age of the Monarchies: Culture and Society,* edited by A. Malamat, 125–46. *WHJP* 4.2. Jerusalem: Massada, 1979.

Shanks, Hershel. *The City of David.* 2d ed. Washington, D.C.: Biblical Archaeology Society, 1975.

Shiloh, Yigal. *Excavations at the City of David, I (1978–1982).* Qedem 19. Jerusalem: Hebrew Univ., 1984.

————. "The City of David After Five Years of Digging." *BARev* 11.6 (Nov.-Dec. 1985): 22–38.

Soggin, J. Alberto. "Compulsory Labor under David and Solomon." In *Studies in the Period of David and Solomon and Other Essays,* edited by T. Ishida, 259–67. Winona Lake, Ind.: Eisenbrauns, 1982.

Tadmor, Hayim. "Traditional Institutions and the Monarchy: Social and Political Tensions in the Time of David and Solomon." In *Studies in the Period of David and Solomon and Other Essays,* edited by T. Ishida, 239–57. Winona Lake, Ind.: Eisenbrauns, 1982.

Thiele, Edwin R. *The Mysterious Numbers of the Hebrew Kings.* 3d ed. Grand Rapids: Zondervan, 1983.

Tsevat, M. "The Emergence of the Israelite Monarchy: Eli, Samuel, and Saul." In *The Age of the Monarchies: Political History,* edited by A. Malamat, 61–75. *WHJP* 4.1. Jerusalem: Massada, 1979.

Ulrich, Eugene C., Jr. *The Qumran Text of Samuel and Josephus.* HSM 19. Missoula, Mont.: Scholars Press, 1978.

Vannoy, J. Robert. *Covenant Renewal at Gilgal: A Study of I Samuel 11:14–12:25.* Cherry Hill, N.J.: Mack, 1978.

Weinfeld, Moshe. "The Covenant of Grant in the Old Testament and in the Ancient Near East." *JAOS* 90 (1970): 184–203.

Wellhausen, Julius. *Der Text der Bücher Samuelis untersucht.* Göttingen: Vandenhoeck und Ruprecht, 1871.

————. *Prolegomena to the History of Ancient Israel.* New York: Meridian, 1957 reprint (1878 original).

Wiseman, D. J. "Assyria and Babylonia c. 1200–1000 B.C." *CAH* II.2: 443–81.

Wood, Leon J. *Distressing Days of the Judges.* Grand Rapids: Zondervan, 1975.

————. *The Holy Spirit in the Old Testament.* Grand Rapids: Zondervan, 1976.

————. *Israel's United Monarchy.* Grand Rapids: Baker, 1979.

Yeivin, S. "Administration." In *The Age of the Monarchies: Culture and Society,* edited by A. Malamat, 147–71. *WHJP* 4.2. Jerusalem: Massada, 1979.

6. 1 & 2 KINGS

Armerding, Carl E., and W. Ward Gasque, eds. *A Guide to Biblical Prophecy.* Peabody, Mass.: Hendrickson, 1989.

Barnes, William Hamilton. *Studies in the Chronology of the Divided Monarchy of Israel.* HSM 48. Atlanta: Scholars Press, 1991.

Brueggemann, Walter. "The Kerygma of the Deuteronomistic Historian." *Interpretation* 22 (1968): 387–402.

Bullock, C. Hassell. *An Introduction to the Old Testament Prophetic Books.* Chicago: Moody, 1986.

Campbell, Anthony F. *Prophets and Kings: A Late Ninth-Century Document (1 Samuel 1–2 Kings 10).* CBQ Monograph Series 17. Washington: Catholic Biblical Association of America, 1986.

Carlson, R. A. *David, the chosen King.* Stockholm: Almqvist & Wiksell, 1964.

Childs, Brevard S. *Introduction to the Old Testament as Scripture.* Philadelphia: Fortress, 1979.

Cogan, M., and H. Tadmor. *II Kings.* AB 11. Garden City, N.Y.: Doubleday, 1988.

Cross, Frank Moore. *Canaanite Myth and Hebrew Epic.* Cambridge, Mass.: Harvard Univ., 1973.

DeVries, Simon J. *1 Kings.* WBC 12. Waco, Tex.: Word, 1985.

Eissfeldt, Otto. *The Old Testament: An Introduction.* Translated by P. R. Ackroyd. New York: Harper & Row, 1965.

Fohrer, Georg. *Introduction to the Old Testament.* Translated by D. E. Green. Nashville: Abingdon, 1965.

Gerbrandt, Gerald E. *Kingship According to the Deuteronomistic History.* SBLDS 87. Atlanta: Scholars Press, 1986.

Gooding, D. W. "Review of J. D. Shenkel, *Chronology and Recensional Development.*" *Journal of Theological Studies* 21 (1970): 118–31.

Gray, John. *I and II Kings.* 2d ed. OTL. Philadelphia: Westminster, 1970.

Grayson, A. K. *Assyrian and Babylonian Chronicles.* Locust Valley, N.Y.: Augustin, 1975.

Harrison, R. K. *Introduction to the Old Testament.* Grand Rapids: Eerdmans, 1969.

Hauser, Alan J., and Russell Gregory. *From Carmel to Horeb: Elijah in Crisis.* JSOTSup 85. Sheffield: Almond, 1990.

Hayes, John H., and Paul K. Hooker. *A New Chronology for the Kings of Israel and Judah.* Atlanta: John Knox, 1988.

Hobbs, T. R. *2 Kings.* WBC 13. Waco, Tex.: Word, 1985.

Howard, David M., Jr. "The Case for Kingship in Deuteronomy and the Former Prophets." *WTJ* 52 (1990): 101–15.

Hubbard, Robert L. *First and Second Kings.* Chicago: Moody, 1991.

Jepsen, Alfred. *Die Quellen des Königsbuches.* 2d ed. Halle: Max Niemayer, 1956.

Jones, G. H. *1 and 2 Kings.* NCBC. Grand Rapids: Eerdmans, 1984.

Kaiser, Walter C., Jr. *Back Toward the Future.* Grand Rapids: Baker, 1989.

_____. *Hard Sayings of the Old Testament.* Downers Grove, Ill.: InterVarsity, 1988.

_____. *Toward an Old Testament Theology.* Grand Rapids: Zondervan, 1978.

Keil, C. F. *The First Book of Samuel.* Grand Rapids: Eerdmans, 1975 reprint.

_____. *The First Book of Kings.* Reprint. Grand Rapids: Eerdmans, 1975.

Levenson, Jon D. "The Last Four Verses in Kings." *JBL* 103 (1984): 353–61.

Long, Burke O. *1 Kings, 2 Kings.* 2 vols. FOTL 9–10. Grand Rapids: Eerdmans, 1984, 1991.

McConville, J. G. "Narrative and Meaning in the Books of Kings." *Biblica* 70 (1989): 31–49.

_____. "1 Kings VIII 46–53 and the Deuteronomic Hope." *VT* 42 (1992): 67–79.

_____. *Grace in the End: A Study in Deuteronomic Theology.* Grand Rapids: Zondervan, 1993.

McFall, Leslie. "A Translation Guide to the Chronological Data in Kings and Chronicles." *Bib Sac* 148 (1991): 3–45.

_____. "Did Thiele Overlook Hezekiah's Coregency?" *Bib Sac* 146 (1989): 393–404.

McKenzie, Steven L. *The Trouble With Kings: The Composition of the Book of Kings in the Deuteronomistic History.* Leiden: E. J. Brill, 1991.

Merrill, Eugene H. *Kingdom of Priests: A History of Old Testament Israel.* Grand Rapids: Baker, 1987.

Moore, Rick Dale. *God Saves: Lessons from the Elisha Stories.* JSOTSup 95. Sheffield: JSOT, 1990.

Nelson, Richard D. *The Double Redaction of the Deuteronomistic History.* JSOTSup 18. Sheffield: JSOT, 1981.

Noth, Martin. *The Deuteronomistic History.* 2d ed. JSOTSup 15. Sheffield: JSOT Press, 1991. [German original: 1943.]

O'Brien, Mark A. *The Deuteronomistic History Hypothesis: A Reassessment.* Göttingen: Vandenhoeck und Ruprecht, 1989.

Oswalt, John N. *The Book of Isaiah: Chapters 1–39.* NICOT. Grand Rapids: Eerdmans, 1986.

Payne, J. Barton. *Encyclopedia of Biblical Prophecy.* Grand Rapids: Baker, 1973.

Petersen, David L. *The Roles of Israel's Prophets.* JSOTSup 17. Sheffield: JSOT, 1981.

Provan, Iain W. *Hezekiah and the Books of Kings: A Contribution to the Debate About the Composition of the Deuteronomistic History.* BZAW 172. New York: de Gruyter, 1988.

Savran, George. "1 and 2 Kings." In *The Literary Guide to the Bible,* edited by R. Alter and F. Kermode, 148–64. Cambridge, Mass.: Harvard Univ., 1987.

Sawyer, John F. A. *Prophecy and the Prophets of the Old Testament.* Oxford: Oxford Univ., 1987.

Shenkel, J. D. *Chronology and Recensional Development in the Greek Text of Kings.* HSM 1. Cambridge, Mass.: Harvard Univ., 1968.

Tadmor, Hayim. "The Chronology of the First Temple Period: A Presentation and Evaluation of the Sources." Appendix 2 of J. A. Soggin, *A History of Ancient Israel.* Philadelphia: Westminster, 1984: 368–83, 408–11.

Thiele, Edwin R. *A Chronology of the Hebrew Kings.* Grand Rapids: Zondervan, 1977.

—————. "Coregencies and Overlapping Reigns Among the Hebrew Kings." *JBL* 93 (1974): 174–200.

—————. *The Mysterious Numbers of the Hebrew Kings.* 3d ed. Grand Rapids: Zondervan, 1983.

VanGemeren, Willem A. *Interpreting the Prophetic Word.* Grand Rapids: Zondervan, 1990.

Van Seters, John. *In Search of History.* New Haven, Conn.: Yale Univ., 1983.

von Rad, Gerhard. *Old Testament Theology.* 2 vols. New York: Harper & Row, 1962.

—————. "The Deuteronomistic Theology of History in the Books of Kings." In *Studies in Deuteronomy,* 74–91. SBT. Chicago: Henry Regnery, 1953.

Wilson, Robert R. *Prophecy and Society in Ancient Israel.* Philadelphia: Fortress, 1980.

Wolf, Herbert. *An Introduction to the Old Testament Pentateuch.* Chicago: Moody, 1991.

Wolff, Hans Walter. "The Kerygma of the Deuteronomic Historical Work." In *The Vitality of Old Testament Traditions,* edited by W. Brueggemann and H. W. Wolff. Atlanta: John Knox, 1975.

Young, Edward J. *My Servants the Prophets.* Grand Rapids: Eerdmans, 1955.

7. HISTORICAL AND CULTURAL CONTEXT FOR 1 & 2 KINGS

Albright, W. F. "King Joiachin in Exile." *BA* 5 (1942): 49–55.

Archer, Gleason L., Jr. "Daniel." *Expositor's Bible Commentary* 7:1–157. Grand Rapids: Eerdmans, 1985.

Ariel, Donald T., et al. *Excavations at the City of David 1978–1985.* Vol. 2. *Qedem* 30. Jerusalem: Hebrew Univ., 1990.

Arnold, Bill T. "The Babylonians." In *Peoples of the Old Testament World,* edited by A. Hoerth, G. Mattingly, and E. Yamauchi. Grand Rapids: Baker, 1993.

Avigad, Nahman. *Discovering Jerusalem.* Nashville: Abingdon, 1983.

————. "Jerahmeel and Baruch." *BA* 42 (1979): 114–18.

Bartlett, J. R. "The Moabites and Edomites." In *Peoples of Old Testament Times,* edited by D. J. Wiseman, 229–58. Oxford: Oxford Univ., 1973.

Beitzel, Barry J. *The Moody Atlas of Bible Lands.* Chicago: Moody, 1985.

Bonder, Bayla. "Mesha's Rebellion Against Israel." *JANES* 3 (1970–71): 82–88.

Bright, John. *A History of Israel.* 3d ed. Philadelphia: Westminster, 1981.

Brinkman, J. A., et al., "Assyria and Babylonia." *CAH* III.2: 1–321.

Bullock, C. Hassell. *An Introduction to the Old Testament Prophetic Books.* Chicago: Moody, 1986.

Busink, T. *Der Tempel von Jerusalem.* 2 vols. Leiden: E. J. Brill, 1970–1980.

Cogan, M. and H. Tadmor. *II Kings.* AB 11. Garden City, N.Y.: Doubleday, 1988.

Davies, G. I. *Ancient Hebrew Inscriptions.* Cambridge: Cambridge Univ., 1991.

Dearman, Andrew, ed. *Studies in the Mesha Inscription and Moab.* Atlanta: Scholars Press, 1989.

DeVries, Simon J. *1 Kings.* WBC 12. Waco, Tex.: Word, 1985.

Dumbrell, William J. *The End of the Beginning: Revelation 21–22 and the Old Testament.* Grand Rapids: Baker, 1985.

Emerton, J. A. "New Light on Israelite Religion: The Implications of the Inscriptions from Kuntillet 'Ajrud." *ZAW* 94 (1982): 2–20.

Freedman, David Noel. "Yahweh of Samaria and his Asherah." *BA* 50 (1987): 241–49.

Gibson, John C. L. *Textbook of Syrian Semitic Inscriptions.* 3 vols. Oxford: Clarendon, 1971–82.

Gray, John. *I & II Kings.* OTL. 2d ed. Philadelphia: Westminster, 1970.

Grayson, A. Kirk. "Assyria: Ashue-dan II to Ashur-Nirari V (934–745 B.C.)," *CAH* III.1: 238–81.

Gutmann, J., ed. *The Temple of Solomon.* Missoula, Mont.: Scholars Press, 1976.

Hallo, W. W., and W. K. Simpson. *The Ancient Near East: A History.* New York: Harcourt Brace Jovanovich, 1971.

Halpern, Baruch. "Yaua, Son of Omri, Yet Again." *BASOR* 265 (1987): 81–85.

Harden, Donald. *The Phoenicians.* 2d ed. New York: Frederick A. Praeger, 1963.

Hoffmeier, James K. "The Egyptians." In *Peoples of the Old Testament World*, edited by A. Hoerth, G. Mattingly, and E. Yamauchi. Grand Rapids: Baker, 1993.

Hoglund, Kenneth G. "The Edomites." In *Peoples of the Old Testament World*, edited by A. Hoerth, G. Mattingly, and E. Yamauchi. Grand Rapids: Baker, 1993.

Kitchen, Kenneth A. *Ancient Orient and Old Testament.* Chicago: InterVarsity, 1966.

———. *The Bible in Its World.* Downers Grove, Ill.: InterVarsity, 1978.

Malamat, A. "The Aramaeans." In *Peoples of Old Testament Times*, edited by D. J. Wiseman, 134–55. Oxford: Oxford Univ., 1973.

Mare, W. Harold. *The Archaeology of the Jerusalem Area.* Grand Rapids: Baker, 1987.

Mattingly, Gerald L. "The Moabites." In *Peoples of the Old Testament World*, edited by A. Hoerth, G. Mattingly, and E. Yamauchi. Grand Rapids: Baker, 1993.

Mazar, Benjamin. *The Mountain of the Lord.* Garden City, N.Y.: Doubleday, 1975.

McConville, Gordon. "Jerusalem in the Old Testament." In *Jerusalem Past and Present in the Purposes of God*, edited by P. W. L. Walker, 21–51. Cambridge: Tyndale House, 1992.

Merrill, Eugene H. *Kingdom of Priests: A History of Old Testament Israel.* Grand Rapids: Baker, 1987.

Meshel, Zeev. "Did Yahweh Have a Consort?" *BARev* 5.2 (Mar-Apr 1979): 24–34.

Moscati, Sabatino. *The World of the Phoenicians.* Translated by A. Hamilton. London: Weidenfeld & Nicholson, 1968.

Murray, Margaret A. *The Splendour That Was Egypt.* 2d ed. New York: Hawthorne, 1963.

Newsome, James D. Jr., ed. *A Synoptic Harmony of Samuel, Kings, and Chronicles.* Grand Rapids: Eerdmans, 1986.

Oded, B. "Neighbors on the East." In *The Age of the Monarchies: Political History*, edited by A. Malamat. *WHJP* 4.1 Jerusalem: Massada, 1979.

Ollenburger, Ben C. *Zion: The City of the Great King.* JSOTSup 41. Sheffield: JSOT, 1987.

Oppenheim, A. Leo. *Ancient Mesopotamia.* Rev. ed. Chicago: Univ. of Chicago, 1977.

Parrot, André. *The Temple of Jerusalem.* London: SCM, 1957.

Parunak, H. Van Dyke. "Was Solomon's Temple Aligned to the Sun?" *PEQ* 110 (1978): 29–33.

Patterson, Richard D., and Hermann J. Austel. "1, 2 Kings." *Expositor's Bible Commentary* 4:1–300. Grand Rapids: Zondervan, 1988.

Pitard, Wayne T. "The Arameans." In *Peoples of the Old Testament World*, edited by A. Hoerth, G. Mattingly, and E. Yamauchi. Grand Rapids: Baker, 1993.

Pritchard, J. B., ed. *Solomon and Sheba.* London: Phaidon, 1974.

Rasmussen, Carl G. *NIV Atlas of the Bible.* Grand Rapids: Zondervan, 1989.

Roberts, J. J. M. "Zion in the Theology of the Davidic-Solomonic Empire." In *Studies in the Period of David and Solomon*, edited by T. Ishida. Winona Lake, Ind.: Eisenbrauns, 1982.

Saggs, H. W. F. *The Greatness That Was Babylon.* London: Sidgwick and Jackson, 1964.

————. *The Might That Was Assyria.* London: Sidgwick and Jackson, 1985.

Scott, R. B. Y. "The Pillars Jachin and Boaz." *JBL* 58 (1939): 143–49.

Shanks, Hershel. "The City of David After Five Years of Digging." *BARev* 11.6 (Nov.-Dec. 1985): 22–38

————. *The City of David.* Washington, D.C.: Biblical Archaeology Society, 1973, 1975.

Shea, William H. "Sennacherib's Second Palestine Campaign." *JBL* 104 (1985): 401–18.

Shiloh, Yigal. *Excavations at the City of David, I (1978–1982). Qedem* 19. Jerusalem: Hebrew Univ., 1984.

Tadmor, H. "The Campaigns of Sargon II of Assur." *Journal of Cuneiform Studies,* 12 (1958): 22–40, 77–100.

Unger, Merrill F. *Israel and the Aramaeans of Damascus.* 1957. Reprint. Grand Rapids: Baker, 1980.

Van Zyl, A. H. *The Moabites.* Leiden: E. J. Brill, 1960.

Ward, William A. "The Phoenicians." In *Peoples of the Old Testament World*, edited by A. Hoerth, G. Mattingly, and E. Yamauchi. Grand Rapids: Baker, 1993.

Weinfeld, Moshe. "Zion and Jerusalem as Religious and Political Capital: Ideology and Utopia." In *The Poet and the Historian,* edited by R. E. Friedman, 75–115. HSS 3. Chico, Calif.: Scholars Press, 1983.

Wright, G. Ernest. "Solomon's Temple Resurrected." *BA* 7 (1944): 17–31.

8. 1 & 2 CHRONICLES

Ackroyd, Peter R. "The Chronicler as Exegete." *JSOT* 2 (1977): 2–32.

————. "Chronicles-Ezra-Nehemiah: the Concept of Unity." *BZAW* 100 (1988): 189–201.

————. "The Theology of the Chronicler." *Lexington Theological Quarterly* 8 (1973): 101–116.

Allen, Leslie C. "Kerygmatic Units in 1 & 2 Chronicles." *JSOT* 41 (1988): 21–36.

Anderson, A. A. *2 Samuel.* WBC 11. Dallas: Word, 1989.

Beckwith, Roger. *The Old Testament Canon of the New Testament Church.* Grand Rapids: Eerdmans, 1985.

Boyd, Jonathan. "'Sing an Old Song to the Lord': First Chronicles 16:8–36, the Psalter, and the Chronicler's Historiography." M.A. thesis, Trinity Evangelical Divinity School, Deerfield, Ill., 1991.

Braun, Roddy L. *1 Chronicles.* WBC 14. Waco, Tex.: Word, 1986.

————. "Chronicles, Ezra, and Nehemiah: Theology and Literary History." *SVT* 30 (1979): 52–64.

————. "A Reconsideration of the Chronicler's Attitude Toward the North." *JBL* 96 (1977): 59–62.

————. "Solomon, the Chosen Temple Builder: The Significance of 1 Chronicles 22, 28, and 29 for the Theology of Chronicles." *JBL* 95 (1976): 581–590.

————. "Solomonic Apologetic in Chronicles." *JBL* 92 (1973): 503–16.

Carson, D. A. "Matthew." *Expositor's Bible Commentary* 8:485–86. Grand Rapids: Zondervan, 1984.

Childs, Brevard S. *Introduction to the Old Testament as Scripture.* Philadelphia: Fortress, 1979.

Culver, R. D. "Peculiarities and Problems of Genealogical Method and of Text in the Book of Chronicles." *Bulletin of the Evangelical Theological Society* 5.2 (1962): 1–7.

Curtis, E. L., and A. A. Madsen. *Commentary on the Books of Chronicles.* ICC. Edinburgh: T. &. T. Clark, 1910.

Deboys, David G. "History and Theology in the Chronicler's Portrayal of Abijah." *Biblica* 71 (1990): 48–62.

DeVries, Simon J. *1 and 2 Chronicles.* FOTL 11. Grand Rapids: Eerdmans, 1989.

Dillard, Raymond B. "The Chronicler's Jehoshaphat." *Trinity Journal* 7 (1986): 17–22.

————. "The Chronicler's Solomon." *WTJ* 43 (1981): 289–300.

————. *2 Chronicles.* WBC 15. Waco, Tex.: Word, 1987.

————. "The Reign of Asa (2 Chr 14–16)." *JETS* 23 (1980): 207–18.

————. "Reward and Punishment in Chronicles: The Theology of Immediate Retribution." *WTJ* 46 (1984): 164–72.

Driver, S. R. *Introduction to the Literature of the Old Testament.* Rev. ed. New York: Scribner's, 1913.

Dumbrell, W. J. "The Purpose of the Books of Chronicles." *JETS* 27 (1984): 257–66.

Even-Shoshan, Abraham, ed. *A New Concordance of the Bible.* Jerusalem: Kiryat Sepher, 1981.

Freedman, David Noel. "The Chronicler's Purpose." *CBQ* 23 (1961): 436–42.

Haran, Menahem. "Explaining the Identical Lines at the End of Chronicles and the Beginning of Ezra." *Bible Review* 2.3 (Fall 1986): 18–20.

Harris, R. Laird. "Chronicles and the Canon in New Testament Times." *JETS* 33 (1990): 75–84.

Harrison, R. K. *Introduction to the Old Testament.* Grand Rapids: Eerdmans, 1969.

Howard, D. M., Jr. "The Case for Kingship in the Old Testament Narrative Books and the Psalms." *Trinity Journal* 9 (1988): 19–35.

Japhet, Sara. *The Ideology of the Book of Chronicles and Its Place in Biblical Thought.* Frankfurt am Main: Peter Lang, 1989.

————. "The Supposed Common Authorship of Chronicles and Ezra-Nehemiah Investigated Anew." *VT* 18 (1968): 330–71.

Johnson, M. D. *The Purpose of the Biblical Genealogies.* 2d ed. Cambridge: Cambridge Univ., 1988.

Kaiser, Walter C., Jr. *Hard Sayings of the Old Testament.* Downers Grove, Ill.: InterVarsity, 1988.

————. *Toward an Old Testament Theology.* Grand Rapids: Zondervan, 1978.

————. "The Unfailing Kindnesses Promised to David: Isaiah 55:3." *JSOT* 45 (1989): 91–98.

Keil, C. F. *The Books of the Chronicles.* Grand Rapids: Eerdmans, 1975. Reprint.

————. *The Second Book of Samuel.* Grand Rapids: Eerdmans, 1975. Reprint.

Kitchen, K. A. *Ancient Orient and Old Testament.* Chicago: InterVarsity, 1966.

————. *The Bible in Its World.* Downers Grove, Ill.: InterVarsity, 1977.

Knoppers, Gary N. "Reform and Regression: The Chronicler's Presentation of Jehoshaphat." *Biblica* 72 (1991): 500–24.

Mason, Rex. *Preaching the Tradition: Homily and Hermenuetics after the Exile.* Cambridge: Cambridge Univ., 1990.

McConville, J. G. "Ezra-Nehemiah and the Fulfillment of Prophecy." *VT* 36 (1986): 205–24.

McFall, Leslie. "Was Nehemiah Contemporary With Ezra in 458 BC?" *WTJ* 53 (1991): 263–93.

Myers, Jacob M. *1 Chronicles.* Rev. ed. AB 12. Garden City, N.Y.: Doubleday, 1965.

————. *2 Chronicles.* Rev. ed. AB 13. Garden City, N.Y.: Doubleday, 1965.

Newsome, James D., Jr., ed. *A Synoptic Harmony of Samuel, Kings, and Chronicles.* Grand Rapids: Baker, 1986.

————. "Toward a New Understanding of the Chronicler and His Purposes." *JBL* 94 (1975): 201–17.

North, R. "Theology of the Chronicler." *JBL* 82 (1963): 369–81.

Noth, Martin. *The Chronicler's History.* JSOTSup 50. Sheffield: JSOT, 1987.

Osborne, W. L. *The Genealogies of 1 Chronicles 1–9.* Ph.D. diss., Dropsie Univ., Philadelphia, 1979.

Payne, J. B. "1, 2 Chronicles." *Expositor's Bible Commentary*, 4:301–562. Grand Rapids: Zondervan, 1988.

Saebø, Magne. "Messianism in Chronicles?" *Horizons in Biblical Theology* 2 (1980): 85–109.

Sailhamer, John. *First and Second Chronicles.* Chicago: Moody, 1983.

_____. "1 Chronicles 21:1—A Study in Inter-Biblical Interpretation." *Trinity Journal* 10 (1989): 33–48.

Selman, Martin. "The Kingdom of God in the Old Testament." *Tyndale Bulletin* 40 (1989): 161–83.

Solomon, Anne M. "The Structure of the Chronicler's History: A Key to the Organization of the Pentateuch." *Semeia* 46 (1989): 51–64.

Sugimoto, Tomotoshi. "Chronicles as Independent Literature." *JSOT* 55 (1992): 61–74.

Talshir, David. "A Reinvestigation of the Linguistic Relationship Between Chronicles and Ezra-Nehemiah." *VT* 38 (1988): 165–93.

Torrey, C. C. *The Composition and Historical Value of Ezra-Nehemiah.* Giessen: J. Ricker'sche, 1896.

Welch, Adam C. *The Work of the Chronicler, Its Purpose and Its Date.* London: Oxford Univ., 1939.

Willi, Thomas. *Die Chronik als Auslegung.* Göttingen: Vandenhoeck und Ruprecht, 1972.

Williamson, H. G. M. *1 and 2 Chronicles.* NCBC. Grand Rapids: Eerdmans, 1982.

_____. "The Accession of Solomon in the Books of Chronicles." *VT* 26 (1976): 351–61.

_____. "Did the Author of Chronicles Also Write the Books of Ezra and Nehemiah?" *Bible Review* 3.1 (Spring 1987): 56–59.

_____. "The Dynastic Oracle in the Books of Chronicles." In *Isac Leo Seeligmann Festschrift*, edited by Y. Zakovitch and A. Rofé, 305–18. Jerusalem: E. Rubinstein, 1983.

_____. "Eschatology in Chronicles." *Tyndale Bulletin* 28 (1977): 115–54.

_____. *Israel in the Books of Chronicles.* Cambridge: Cambridge Univ., 1977.

_____. "'The Sure Mercies of David': Subjective or Objective Genitive?" *JSS* 23 (1978): 31–49.

Wilson, Robert R. *Genealogy and History in the Biblical World.* New Haven, Conn.: Yale Univ., 1977.

Wolf, Herbert M. *Introduction to the Old Testament Pentateuch.* Chicago: Moody, 1991.

Wright, John W. "The Legacy of David in Chronicles: The Narrative Function of 1 Chronicles 23–27." *JBL* 110 (1991): 229–42.

9. EZRA-NEHEMIAH

Archer, Gleason L., Jr. *A Survey of Old Testament Introduction.* 2d ed. Chicago: Moody, 1974.

Avigad, N. *Rediscovering Jerusalem.* Nashville: Abingdon, 1983.

Baldwin, Joyce G. *Daniel.* TOTC. Downers Grove, Ill.: InterVarsity, 1973.

Beckwith, Roger. *The Old Testament Canon of the New Testament Church.* Grand Rapids: Eerdmans, 1985.

Cameron, George G. "Ancient Persia." In *The Idea of History in the Ancient Near East*, edited by R. C. Dentan, 77–97. New Haven, Conn.: Yale Univ., 1955.

Charlesworth, James H. *The Old Testament Pseudepigrapha.* 2 vols. Garden City, N.Y.: Doubleday, 1983, 1987.

Clines, D. J. A. *Ezra, Nehemiah, Esther.* NCBC. Grand Rapids: Eerdmans, 1984.

―――――. "Nehemiah 10 as an Example of Early Jewish Biblical Exegesis." *JSOT* 21 (1981): 111–17.

Colless, B. E. "Cyrus the Persian as Darius the Mede in the Book of Daniel." *JSOT* 56 (1992): 113–26.

Dumbrell, William J. "The Theological Intention of Ezra-Nehemiah." *Reformed Theological Review* 45 (1986): 65–72.

Eskenazi, Tamara C. "The Structure of Ezra-Nehemiah and the Integrity of the Book." *JBL* 107 (1988): 641–56.

―――――. "Ezra-Nehemiah: From Text to Actuality." In *Signs and Wonders: Biblical Texts in Literary Focus*, edited by J. C. Exum, 165–97. Atlanta: Scholars Press, 1989.

Fensham, F. Charles. *The Books of Ezra and Nehemiah.* NICOT. Grand Rapids: Eerdmans, 1982.

Garrett, Duane. *Rethinking Genesis: The Sources and Authorship of the First Book of the Pentateuch.* Grand Rapids: Baker, 1991.

Gerbrandt, Gerald E. *Kingship According to the Deuteronomistic History.* SBLDS 87. Atlanta: Scholars Press, 1986.

Harrison, R. K. *Introduction to the Old Testament.* Grand Rapids: Eerdmans, 1969.

Keil, C. F. *The Book of Nehemiah.* Grand Rapids: Eerdmans, 1975. Reprint.

Kaiser, Walter C., Jr. *Toward an Old Testament Theology.* Grand Rapids: Zondervan, 1978.

———. *Hard Sayings of the Old Testament.* Downers Grove, Ill.: Inter-Varsity, 1988.

Kidner, Derek. *Ezra & Nehemiah.* TOTC. Downers Grove, Ill.: InterVarsity, 1979.

Koch, K. "Ezra and the Origins of Judaism." *JSS* 19 (1974): 173–97.

Mason, Rex. *Preaching the Tradition: Homily and Hermenuetics after the Exile.* Cambridge: Cambridge Univ., 1990.

McConville, J. G. "Ezra-Nehemiah and the Fulfillment of Prophecy." *VT* 36 (1986): 205–24.

McFall, Leslie. "Was Nehemiah Contemporary With Ezra in 458 BC?" *WTJ* 53 (1991): 263–93.

Metzger, Bruce M., ed. *The Oxford Annotated Apocrapha.* New York: Oxford Univ., 1977.

Myers, Jacob M. *Ezra-Nehemiah.* AB 14. Garden City, N.Y.: Doubleday, 1965.

Newsome, James D., Jr. "Toward a New Understanding of the Chronicler and His Purposes." *JBL* 94 (1975): 201–17.

Shea, W. H. "Darius the Mede: An Update." *AUSS* 20 (1982): 229–48.

Snell, Daniel C. "Why Is There Aramaic in the Bible?" *JSOT* 18 (1980): 32–51.

Torrey, Charles C. *Ezra Studies.* New York: KTAV, 1970.

Tuland, Carl G. "Ezra-Nehemiah or Nehemiah-Ezra?" *AUSS* 12 (1974): 55–59.

Whitcomb, John C. *Darius the Mede.* Grand Rapids: Eerdmans, 1959.

Williamson, H. G. M. "Nehemiah's Wall Revisited." *PEQ* 116 (1984): 81–88.

———. *Ezra, Nehemiah.* WBC 16. Waco, Tex.: Word, 1985.

Wiseman, D. J. *Notes on Some Problems in the Book of Daniel.* London: Tyndale, 1965.

Yamauchi, Edwin M. "Ezra-Nehemiah." *Expositor's Bible Commentary* 4:563–771. Grand Rapids: Zondervan, 1988.

———. "The Persians." In *Peoples of the Old Testament World*, edited by A. Hoerth, G. Mattingly, and E. Yamauchi. Grand Rapids: Baker, 1993.

———. "The reverse order of Ezra/Nehemiah reconsidered." *Themelios* 5.3 (May 1980): 7–13.

Young, T. C., Jr., et al. "Part I: The Persian Empire." *CAH* IV:1–286.

10. ESTHER

Anderson, Bernhard W. "The Place of the Book of Esther in the Christian Bible." *Journal of Religion* 30 (1950): 32–43.

Baldwin, Joyce G. *Esther.* TOTC. Downers Grove, Ill.: InterVarsity, 1984.

Beckwith, Roger. *The Old Testament Canon of the New Testament Church.* Grand Rapids: Eerdmans, 1985.

Berg, S. B. *The Book of Esther.* SBLDS 44. Missoula, Mont.: Scholars Press, 1979.

Childs, Brevard S. *Introduction to the Old Testament as Scripture.* Philadelphia: Fortress, 1979.

Clines, D. J. A. *The Esther Scroll.* JSOTSup 30. Sheffield: JSOT, 1984.

————. *Ezra, Nehemiah, Esther.* NCBC. Grand Rapids: Eerdmans, 1984.

————. "In Quest of the Historical Mordecai." *VT* 41 (1991): 129–36.

Crenshaw, J. L. "Method in Determining Wisdom Influence." *JBL* 88 (1969): 129–42.

Fox, M. V. "The Structure of the Book of Esther." In *Isac Leo Seeligman Volume*, vol. 3, edited by A. Rofé and Y. Zakovitch, 291–303. Jerusalem: E. Rubinstein, 1983.

————. "The Religion of the Book of Esther." *Judaism* 39 (1990): 135–47.

————. *Character and Ideology in the Book of Esther.* Columbia, S.C.: Univ. of South Carolina, 1991.

Gordis, R. "Religion, Wisdom and History in the Book of Esther—A New Solution to an Old Crux." *JBL* 100 (1981): 359–88.

Greenstein, E. L. "A Jewish Reading of Esther." In *Judaic Perspectives on Ancient Israel*, edited by J. Neusner, B. A. Levine, and E. S. Frerichs, 225–43. Philadelphia: Fortress, 1987.

Hallo, William W. "The First Purim." *BA* 46 (1983): 19–29.

Harrison, R. K. *Introduction to the Old Testament.* Grand Rapids: Eerdmans, 1969.

Horn, S. H. "Mordecai, A Historical Problem." *Biblical Research* 9 (1964): 14–25.

Howard, David M., Jr. "Esther, Theology of." In *New International Dictionary of Old Testament Theology*, edited by W. VanGemeren. Grand Rapids: Zondervan (forthcoming).

Huey, F. B. "Esther." *Expositor's Bible Commentary* 4:773–839. Grand Rapids: Zondervan, 1988.

————. "Irony as the Key to Understanding the Book of Esther." *Southwestern Journal of Theology* 32 (1990): 36–39.

Kaiser, Walter C., Jr. *Hard Sayings of the Old Testament.* Downers Grove, Ill.: InterVarsity, 1988.

Keil, C. F. *The Book of Esther.* 1870. Reprint. Grand Rapids: Eerdmans, 1975.

Loader, J. A. "Esther as a Novel with Different Levels of Meaning." *ZAW* 90 (1978): 417–21.

McCane, W. "A Note on Esther IX and 1 Samuel XV." *Journal of Theological Studies* 12 (1961): 260–61 [reprinted in C. A. Moore, ed., *Studies in the Book of Esther* (New York: KTAV, 1982), pp. 306–7].

Millard, A. R. "The Persian Names in Esther and the Reliability of the Hebrew Text." *JBL* 96 (1977): 481–88.

Miller, C. H. "Esther's Levels of Meaning." *ZAW* 92 (1980): 145–48.

Moore, Carey A. *Esther.* AB 7B. Garden City, N.Y.: Doubleday, 1971.

————. "Eight Questions Most Frequently Asked About Esther." *Bible Review* 3.1 (Spring 1987): 16–31.

————, ed. *Studies in the Book of Esther.* New York: KTAV, 1982.

Noll, Stephen F. "Esther." In *Evangelical Commentary on the Bible,* edited by W. Elwell, 326–33. Grand Rapids: Baker, 1989.

Paton, L. B. *The Book of Esther.* ICC. Edinburgh: T. & T. Clark, 1908.

Pfeiffer, R. H. *Introduction to the Old Testament.* 2d ed. New York: Harper, 1948.

Pierce, Ronald W. "The Politics of Esther and Mordecai: Courage or Compromise?" *Bulletin for Biblical Research* 2 (1992): 75–89.

Shea, William H. "Esther and History." *AUSS* 14 (1976): 227–46.

Talmon, S. H. "Wisdom in the Book of Esther." *VT* 13 (1963): 419–55.

Wiebe, John M. "Esther 4:14: 'Will Relief and Deliverance Arise for the Jews from Another Place?'" *CBQ* 53 (1991): 409–15.

Wright, J. S. "The Historicity of the Book of Esther." In *New Perspectives on the Old Testament,* edited by J. B. Payne, 37–47. Waco, Tex.: Word, 1970.

Yamauchi, Edwin M. "The Archaeological Background of Esther." *Bib Sac* 137 (1980): 99–117.

————. "Mordechai, The Persepolis Tablets, and the Susa Excavations." *VT* 42 (1992): 272–75.

Young, T. C., Jr., et al. "Part I: The Persian Empire," *CAH* IV:1–286.

INDEX OF SUBJECTS AND PERSONS

INDEX OF AUTHORS

INDEX OF SCRIPTURES